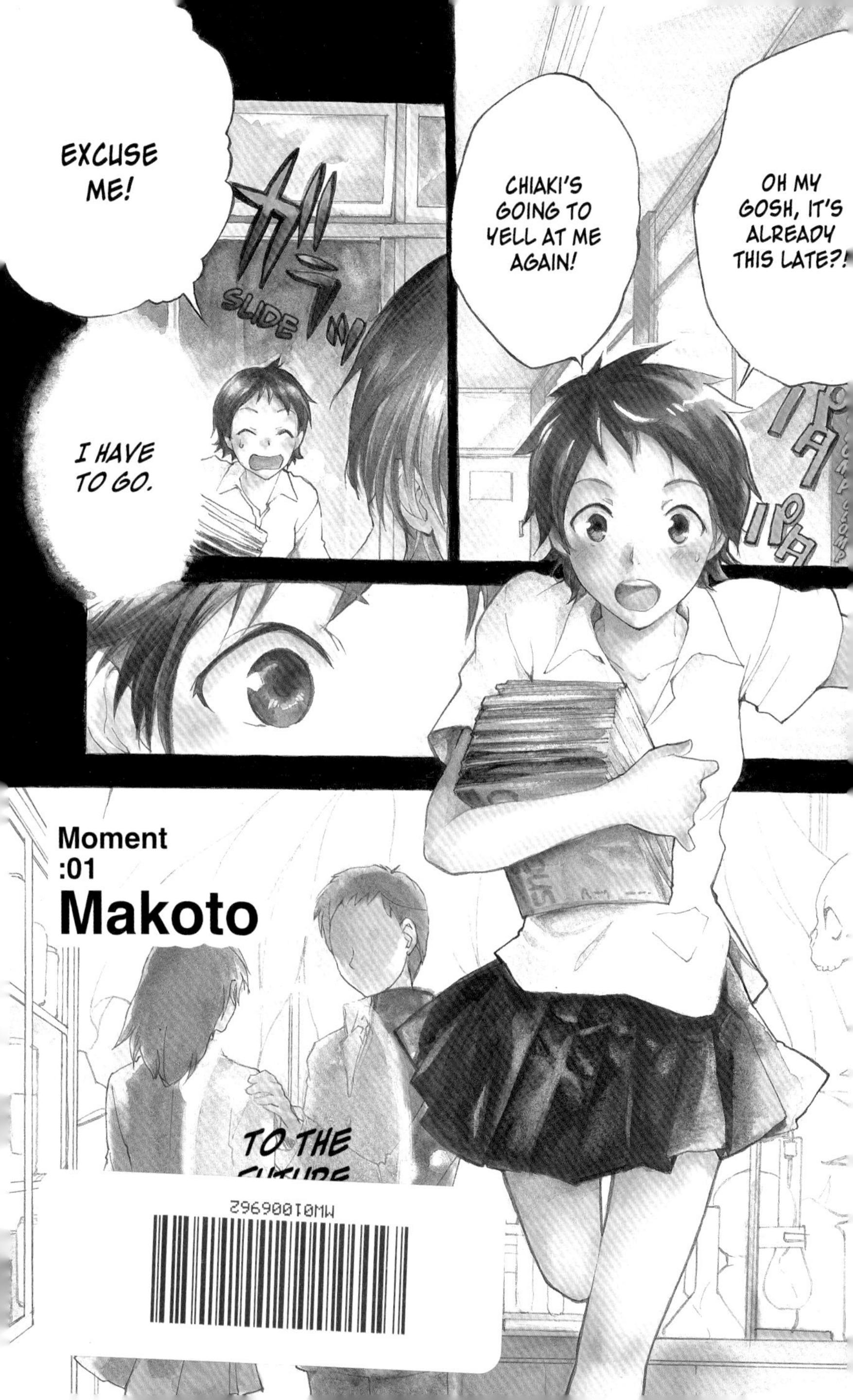
OH MY GOSH, IT'S ALREADY THIS LATE?!
CHIAKI'S GOING TO YELL AT ME AGAIN!
EXCUSE ME!
SLIDE
I HAVE TO GO.
Moment :01
Makoto
TO THE

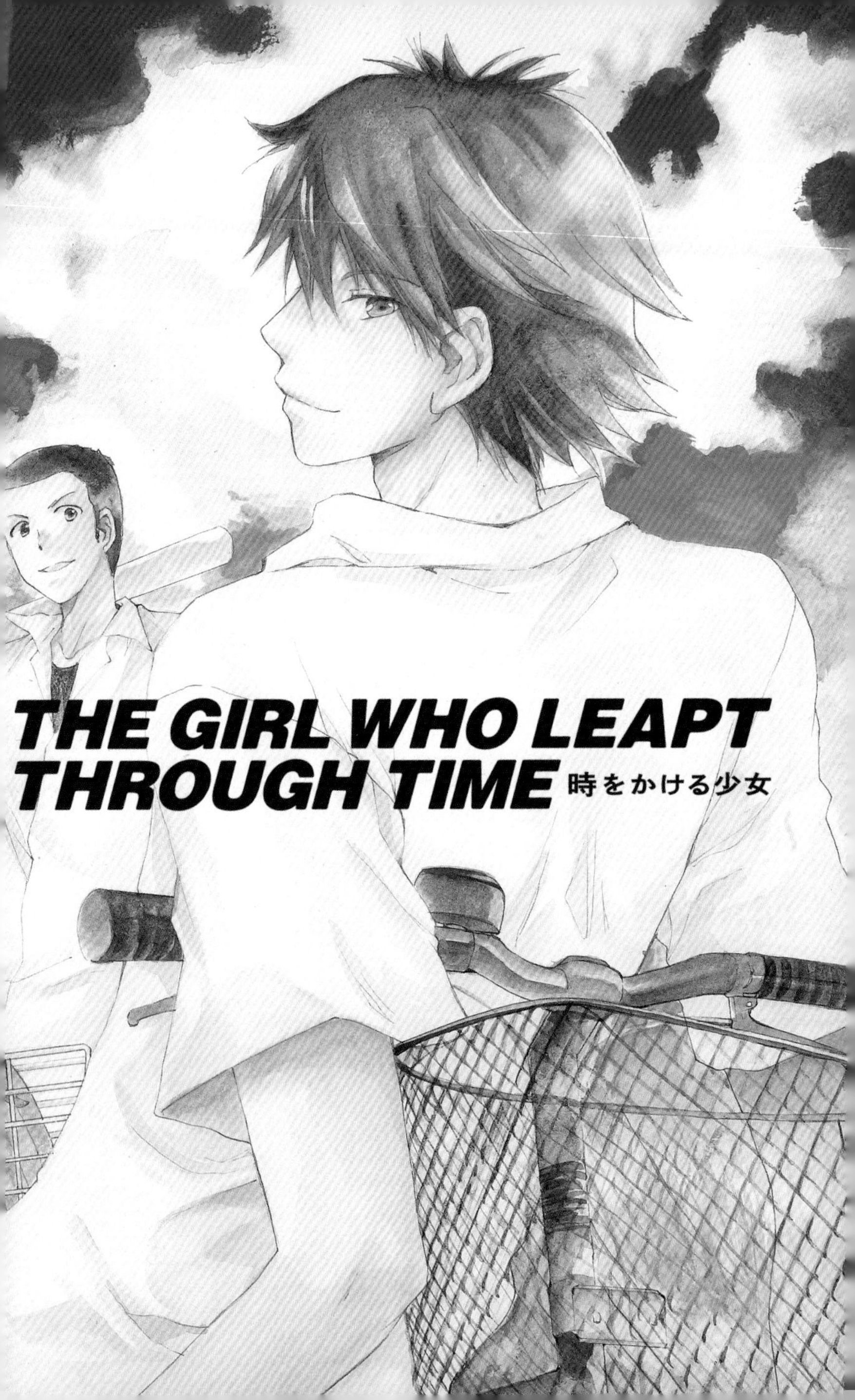
THE GIRL WHO LEAPT
THROUGH TIME
時をかける少女

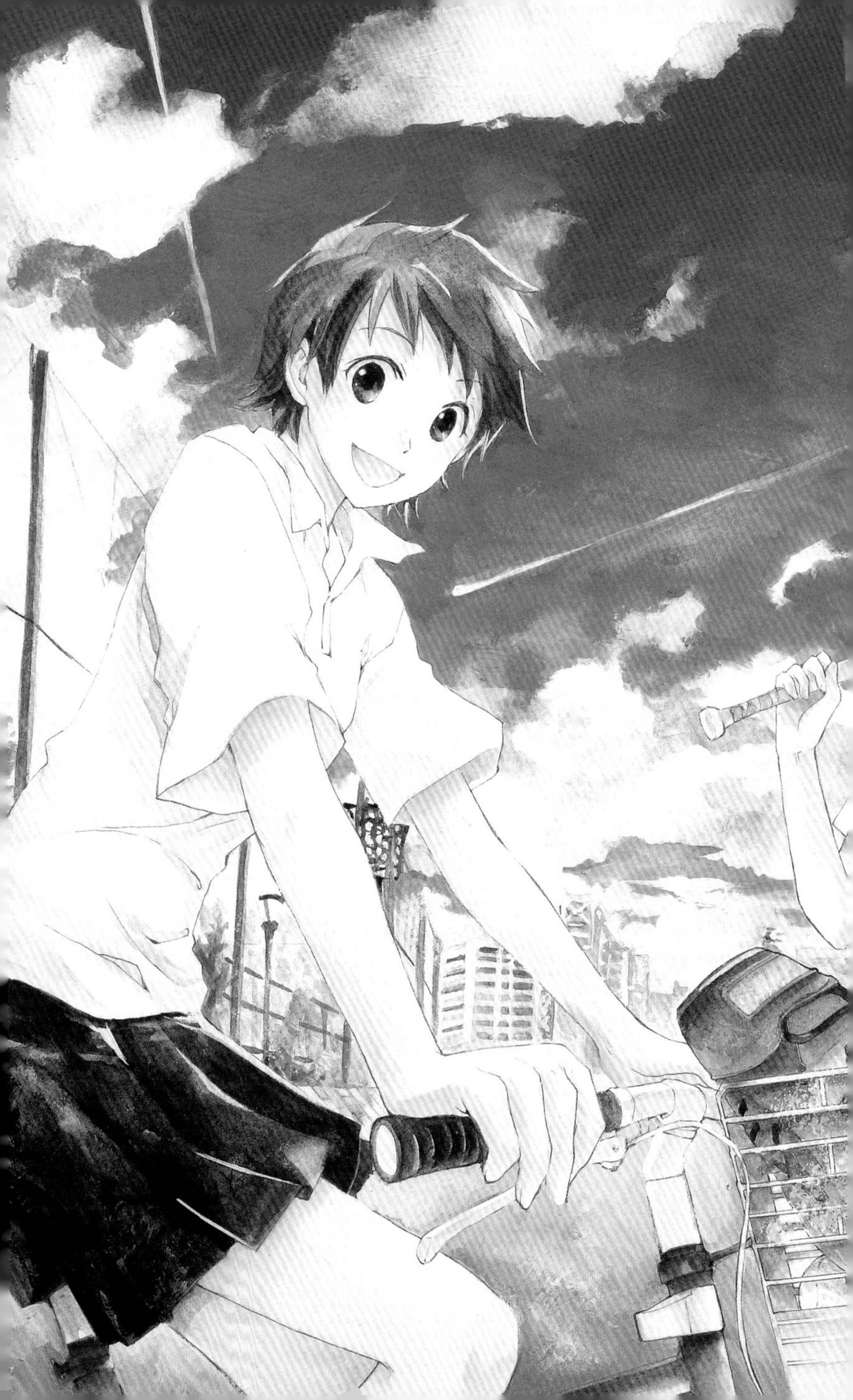

THE GIRL WHO LEAPT THROUGH TIME 時をかける少女

Manga: Kotone Ranmaru
Author: Tsutsui Yasutaka Character Design: Sadamoto Yoshiyuki
Story: "Toki wo kakaeru shoujo" Seisakuiinkai

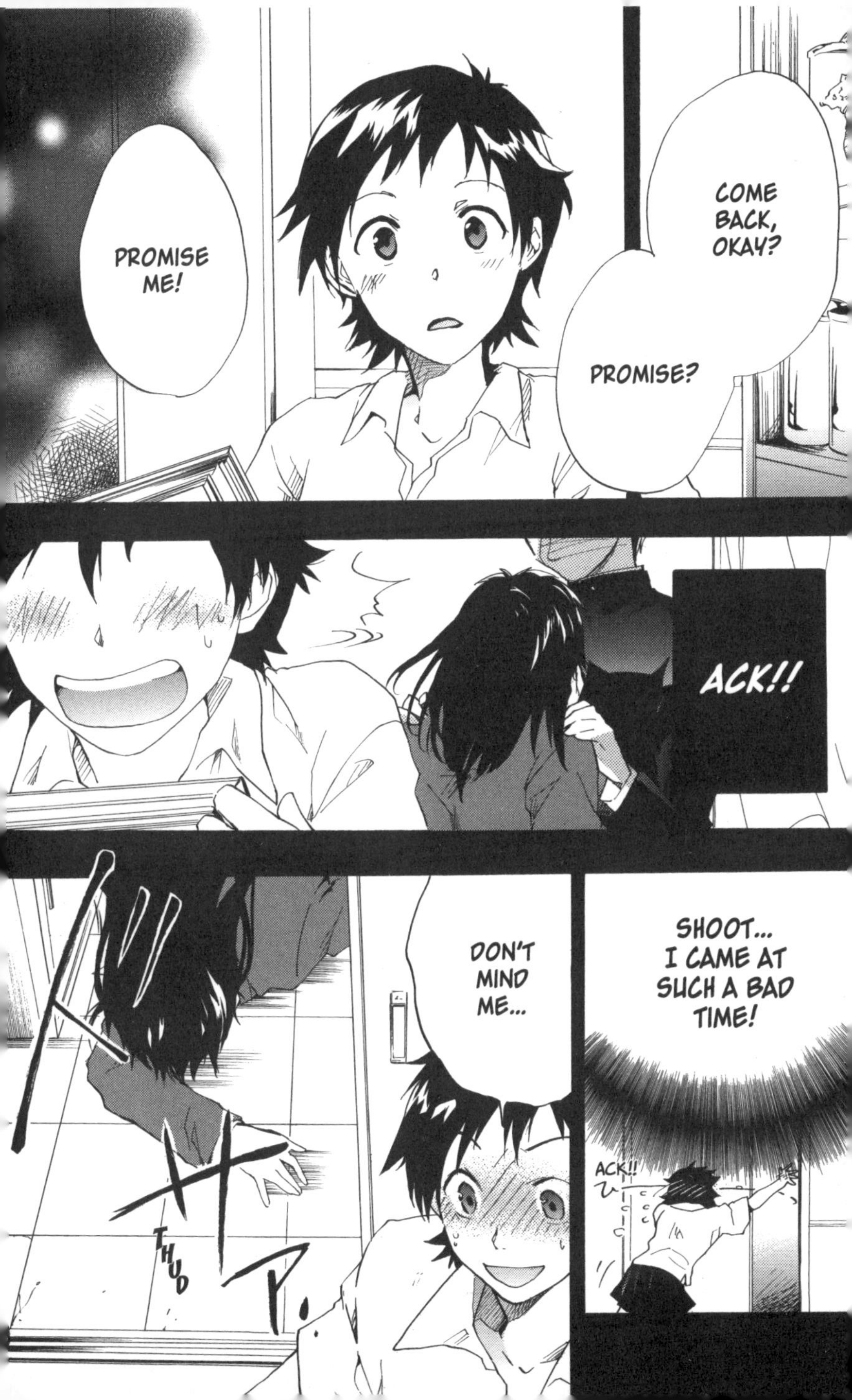
COME BACK, OKAY?
PROMISE?
PROMISE ME!
ACK!!
SHOOT... I CAME AT SUCH A BAD TIME!
ACK!!
DON'T MIND ME...
THUD

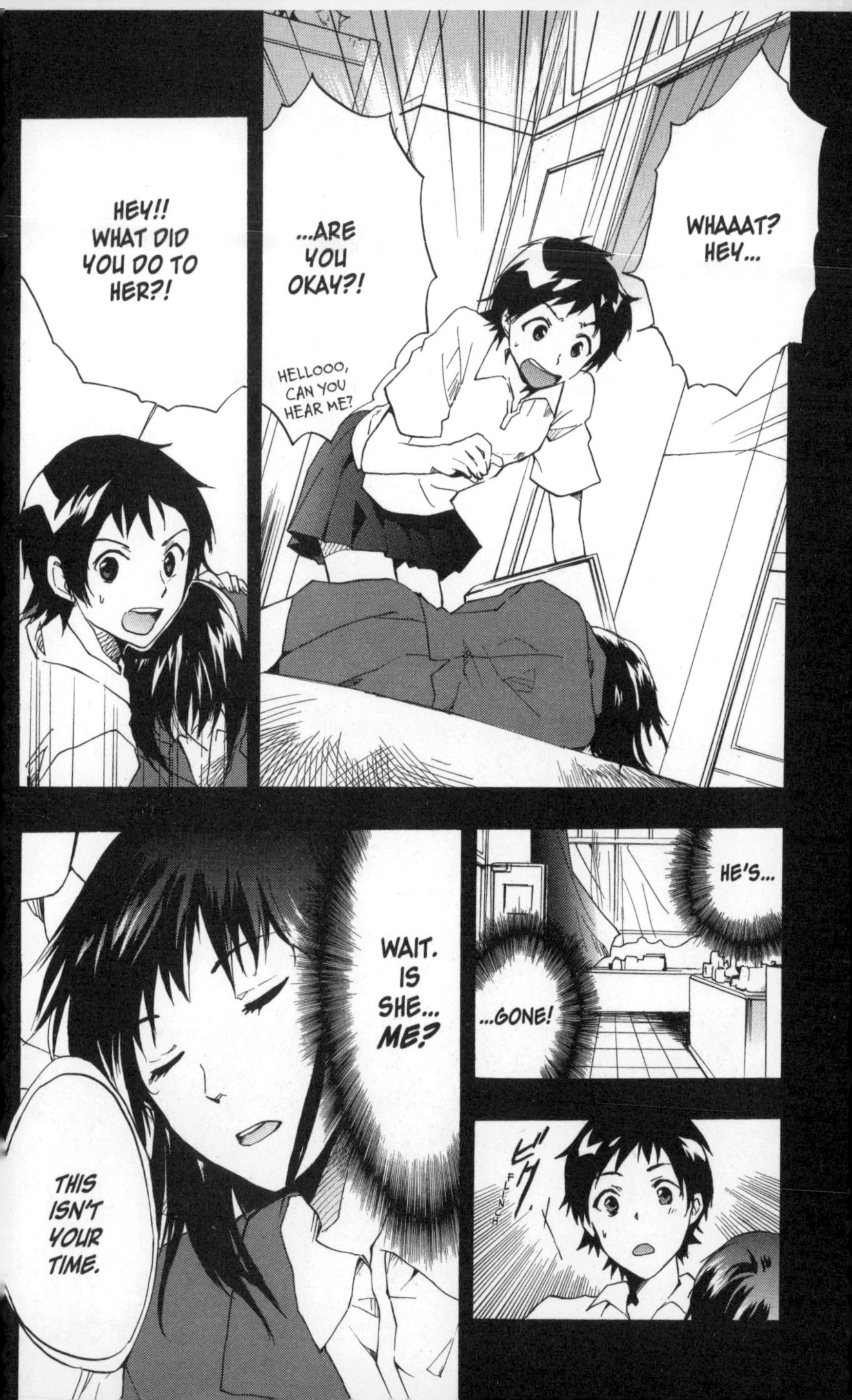
WHAAAT? HEY...
...ARE YOU OKAY?!
HELLOOO, CAN YOU HEAR ME?
HEY!! WHAT DID YOU DO TO HER?!
HE'S...
...GONE!
FLINCH
WAIT. IS SHE... ME?
THIS ISN'T YOUR TIME.

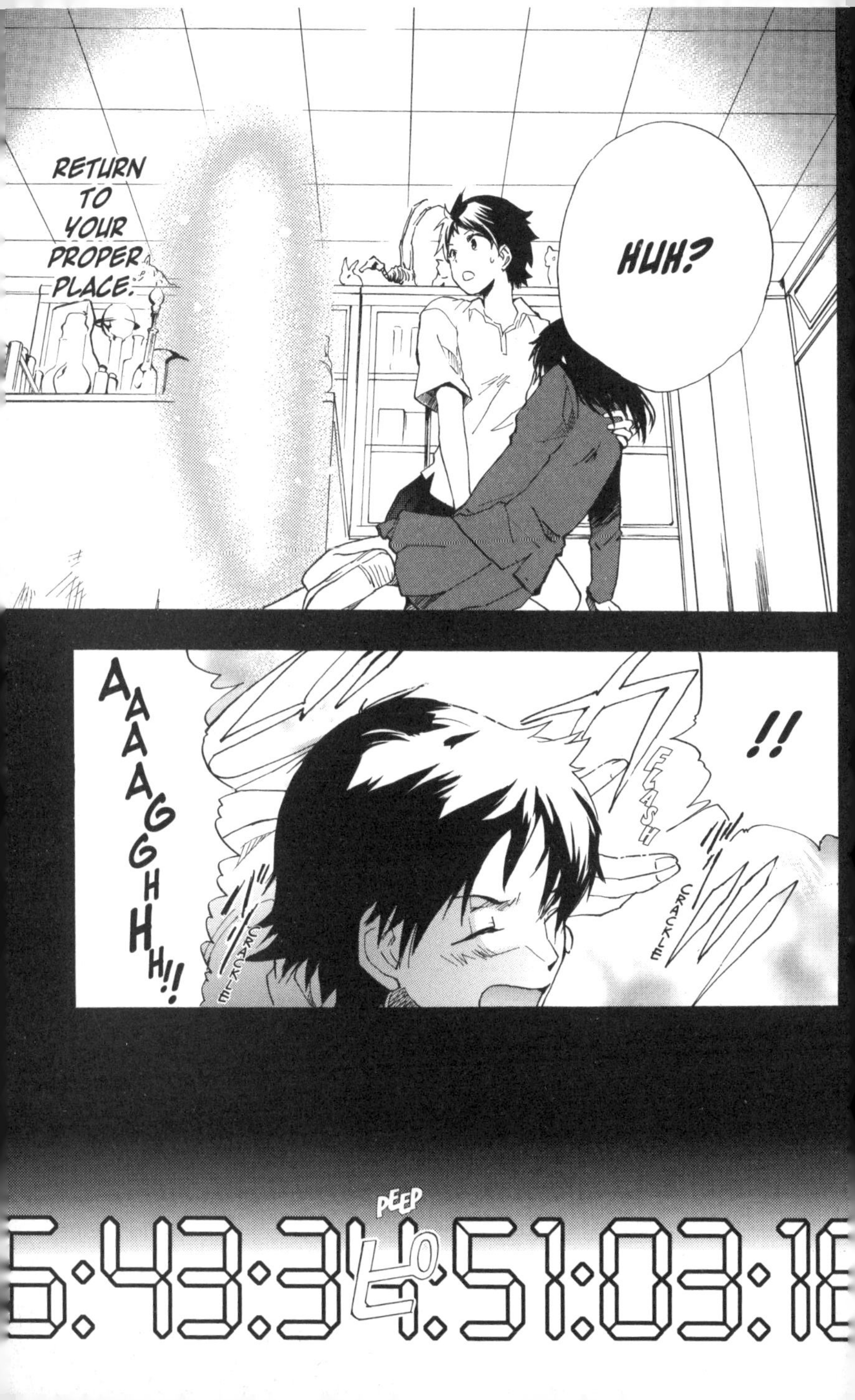
HUH?
RETURN TO YOUR PROPER PLACE.
!!
FLASH
CRACKLE
AAAAGGHHH!!
CRACKLE
PEEP
ピ

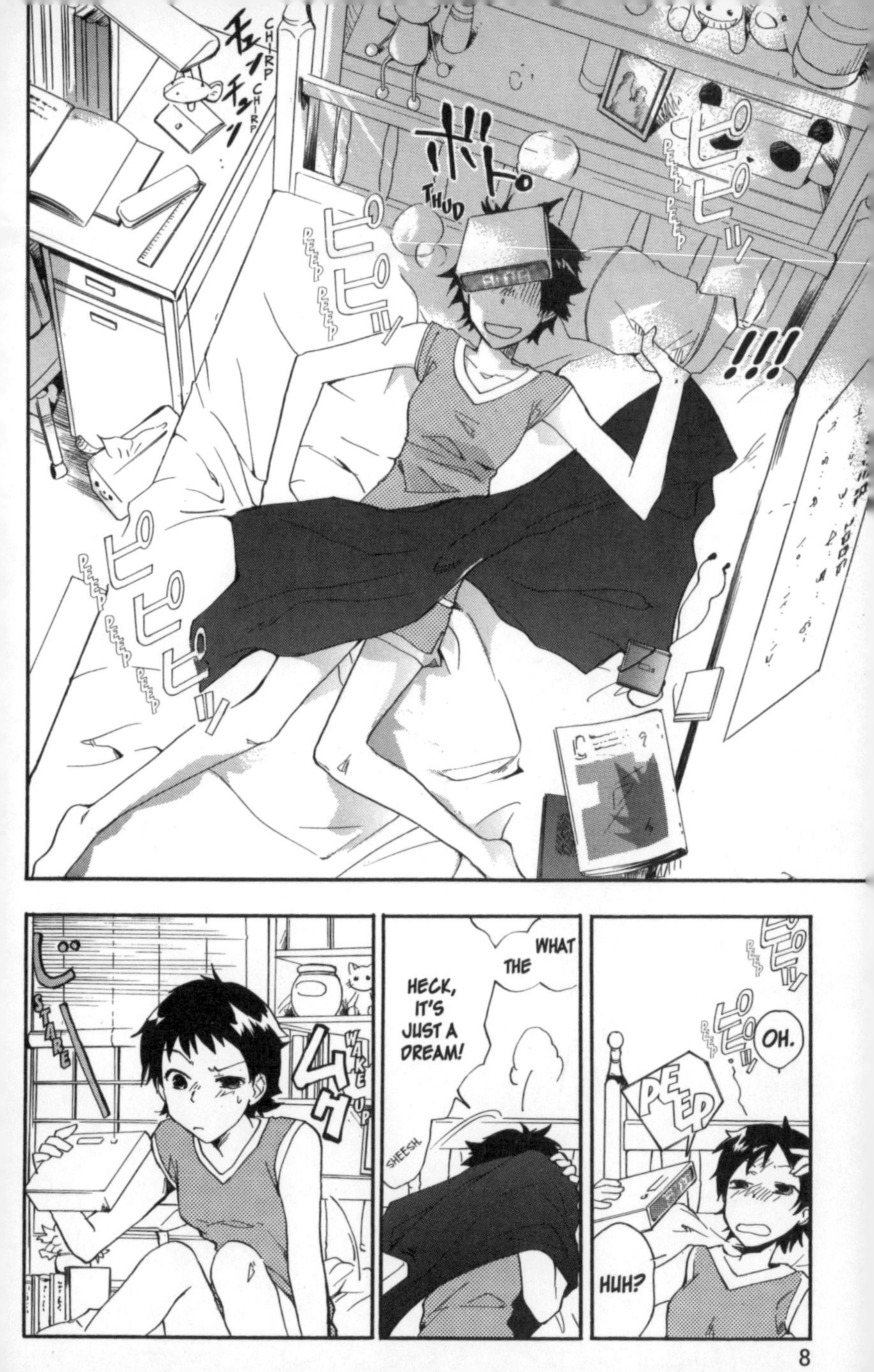

CHIRP CHIRP
THUD
PEEP PEEP
PEEP PEEP
!!!
PEEP PEEP PEEP
PEEP
PEEP PEEP
OH.
HUH?
WHAT THE
HECK, IT'S JUST A DREAM!
SHEESH.
STARE
WAKE UP

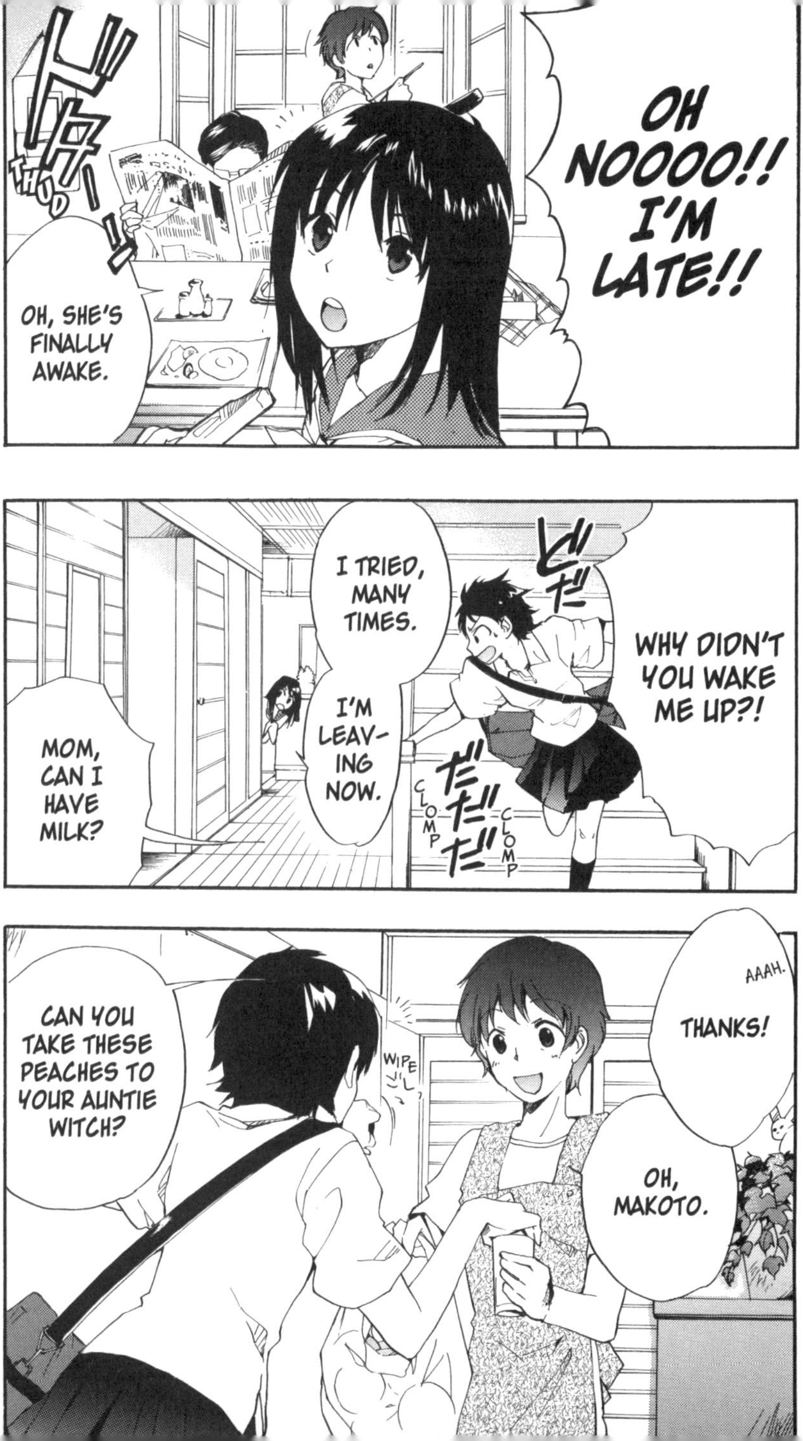
OH NOOOO!! I'M LATE!!
THUD
OH, SHE'S FINALLY AWAKE.
WHY DIDN'T YOU WAKE ME UP?!
I TRIED, MANY TIMES.
CLOMP
CLOMP
I'M LEAVING NOW.
MOM, CAN I HAVE MILK?
AAAH.
THANKS!
OH, MAKOTO.
WIPE
CAN YOU TAKE THESE PEACHES TO YOUR AUNTIE WITCH?

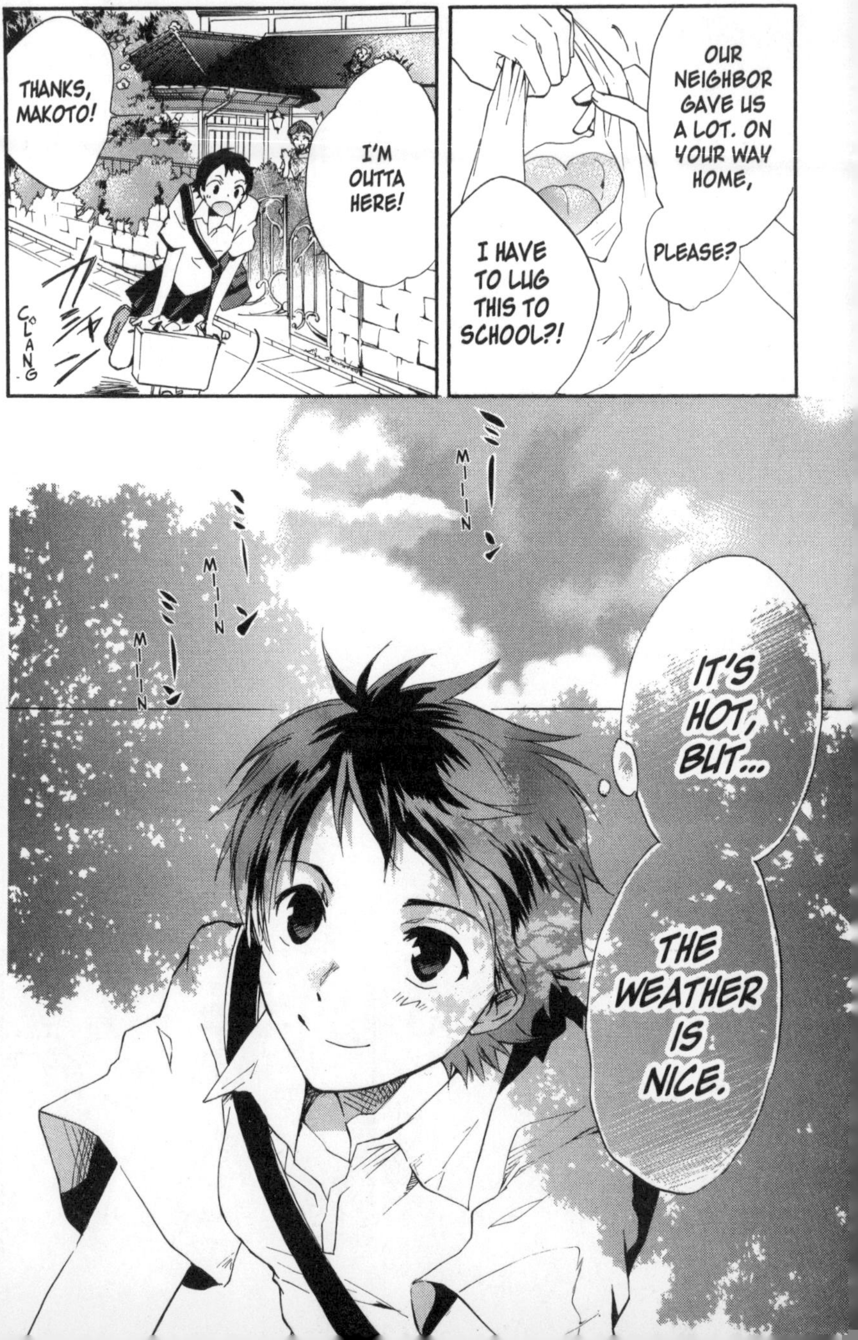
OUR NEIGHBOR GAVE US A LOT. ON YOUR WAY HOME,
PLEASE?
I HAVE TO LUG THIS TO SCHOOL?!
I'M OUTTA HERE!
THANKS, MAKOTO!
CLANG
MIIIN
MIIIN
MIIIN
IT'S HOT, BUT...
THE WEATHER IS NICE.

THE GIRL WHO LEAPT
THROUGH TIME 時をかける少女

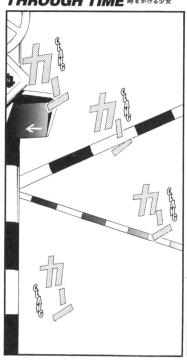

I HAVE A GOOD FEELING ABOUT THIS SUMMER.

IT'S ALMOST SUMMER BREAK.

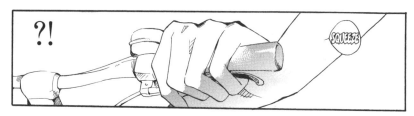

?!

SQUEEZE

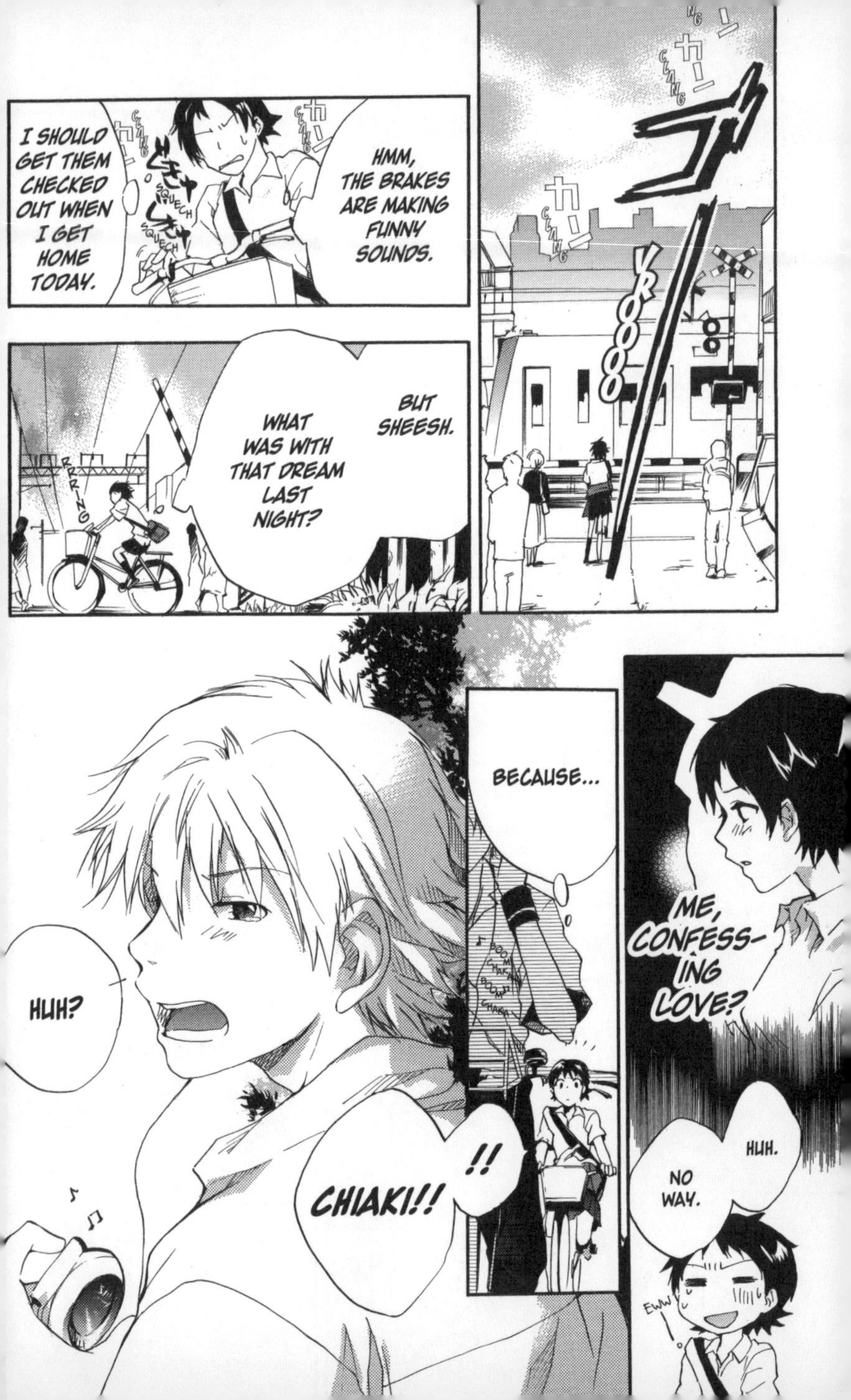
CLANG
CLANG
CLANG
VROOOOO
HMM, THE BRAKES ARE MAKING FUNNY SOUNDS.
CLANG
CLANG
SQUECH SQUECH
I SHOULD GET THEM CHECKED OUT WHEN I GET HOME TODAY.
BUT SHEESH.
WHAT WAS WITH THAT DREAM LAST NIGHT?
RRRING
ME, CONFESSING LOVE?
HUH.
NO WAY.
EWW
BECAUSE...
BOOM CHAKA BOOM CHAKA
!!
CHIAKI!!
HUH?

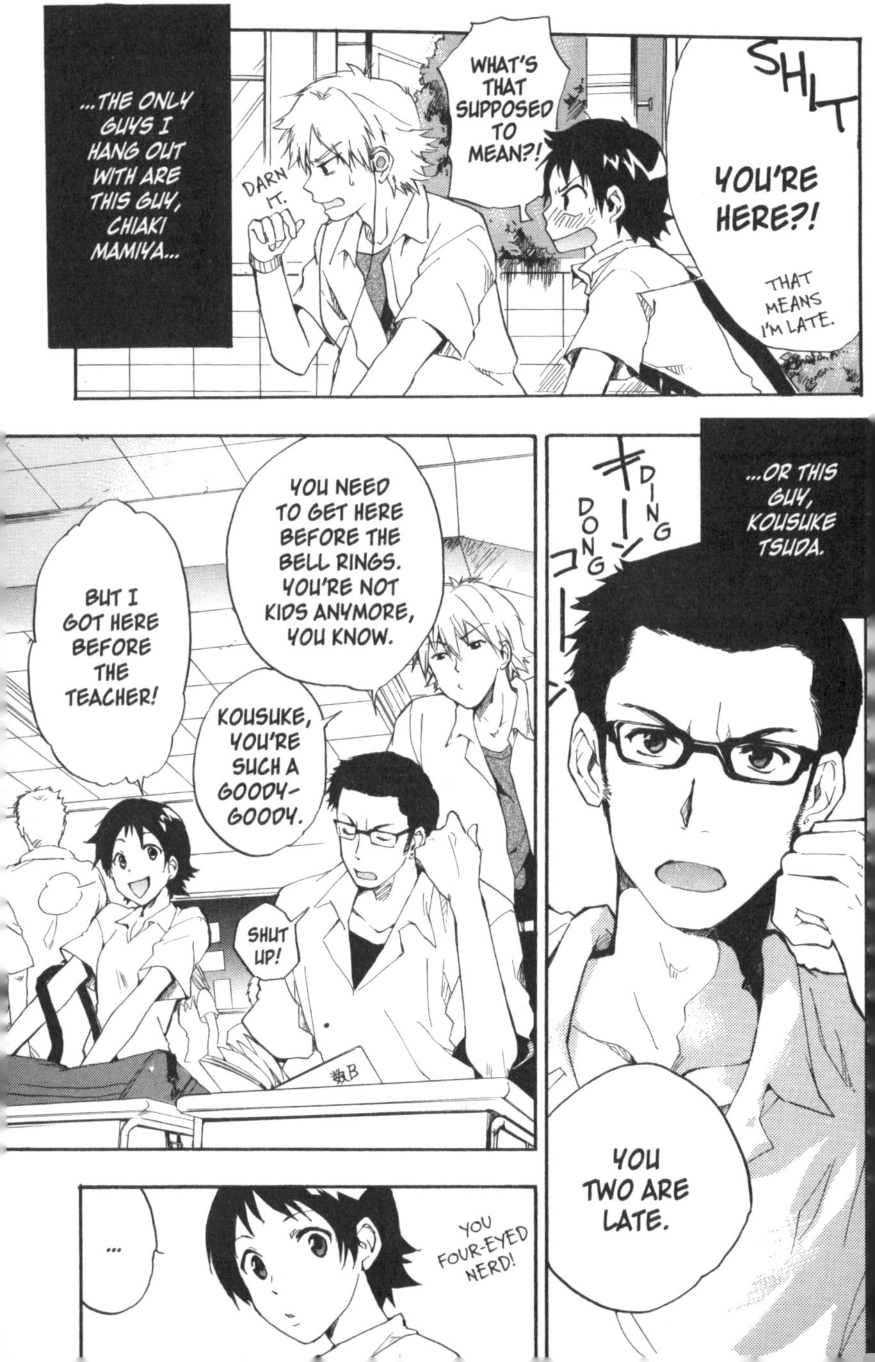
SHIT
YOU'RE HERE?!
THAT MEANS I'M LATE.
WHAT'S THAT SUPPOSED TO MEAN?!
DARN IT.
...THE ONLY GUYS I HANG OUT WITH ARE THIS GUY, CHIAKI MAMIYA...
...OR THIS GUY, KOUSUKE TSUDA.
DING DONG
YOU TWO ARE LATE.
YOU NEED TO GET HERE BEFORE THE BELL RINGS. YOU'RE NOT KIDS ANYMORE, YOU KNOW.
BUT I GOT HERE BEFORE THE TEACHER!
KOUSUKE, YOU'RE SUCH A GOODY-GOODY.
SHUT UP!
数B
YOU FOUR-EYED NERD!
...

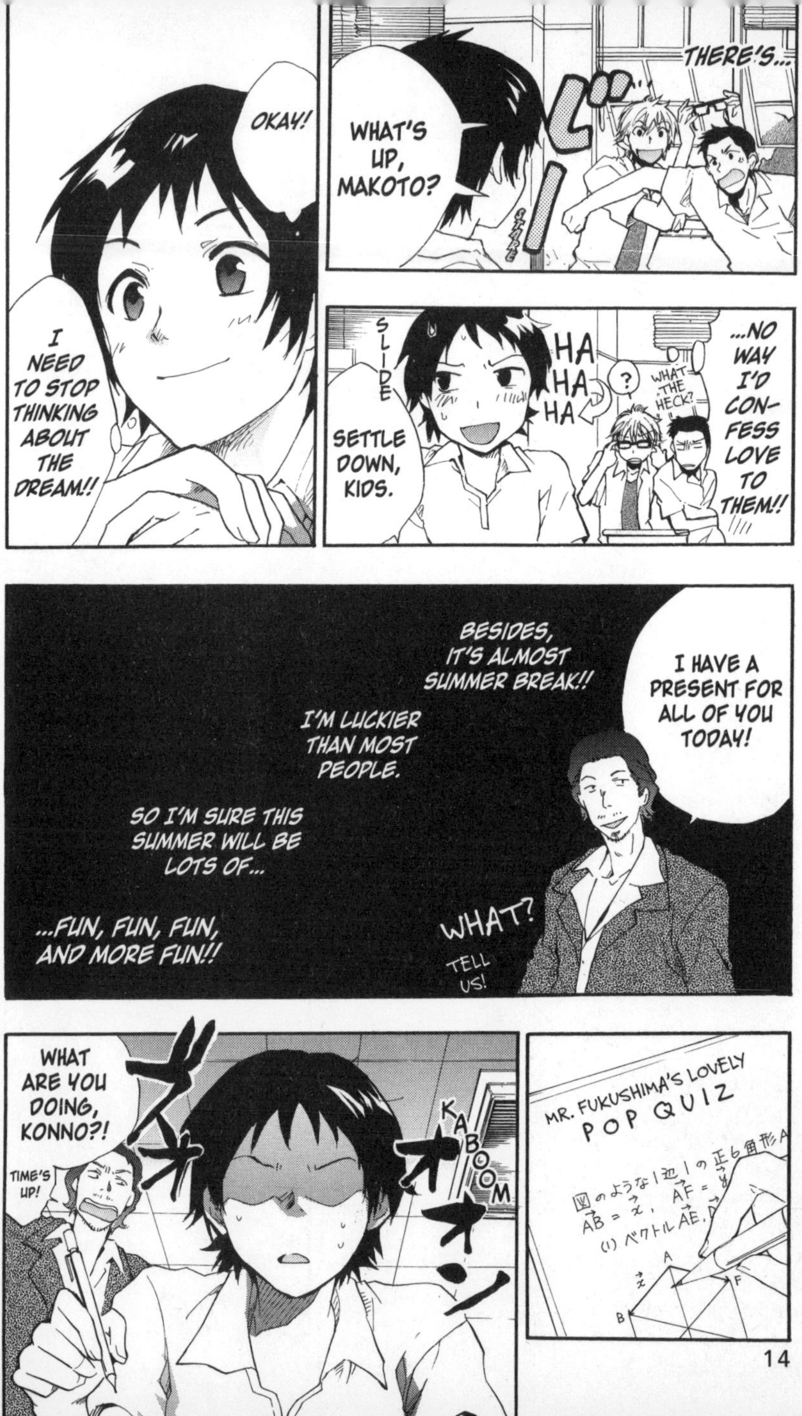
THERE'S...
WHAT'S UP, MAKOTO?
STARE
...NO WAY I'D CONFESS LOVE TO THEM!!
WHAT THE HECK?
?
HA HA HA
SLIDE
SETTLE DOWN, KIDS.
OKAY!
I NEED TO STOP THINKING ABOUT THE DREAM!!
I HAVE A PRESENT FOR ALL OF YOU TODAY!
BESIDES, IT'S ALMOST SUMMER BREAK!!
I'M LUCKIER THAN MOST PEOPLE.
SO I'M SURE THIS SUMMER WILL BE LOTS OF...
WHAT?
TELL US!
...FUN, FUN, FUN, AND MORE FUN!!
MR. FUKUSHIMA'S LOVELY POP QUIZ
KABOOM
WHAT ARE YOU DOING, KONNO?!
TIME'S UP!

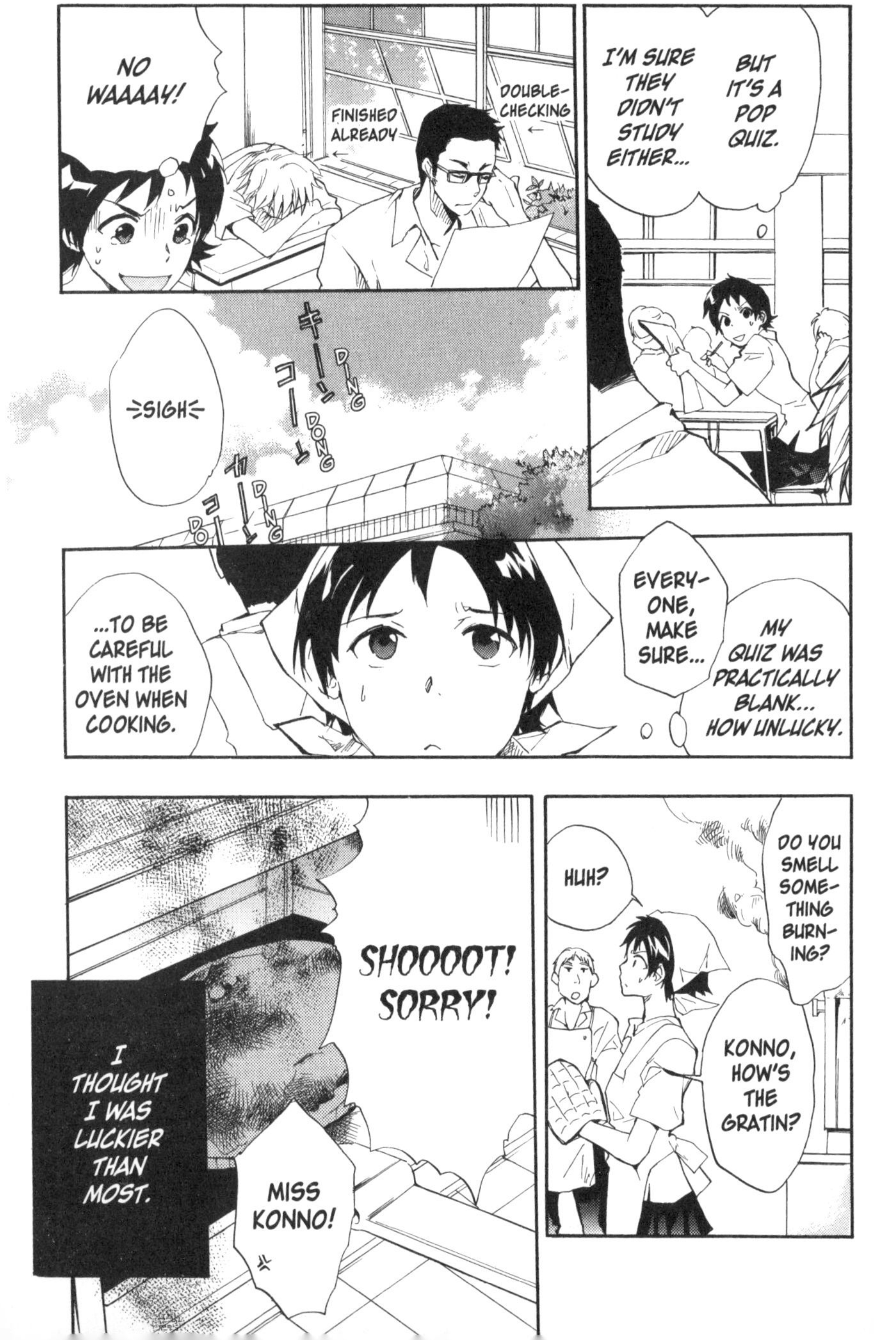
BUT IT'S A POP QUIZ.
I'M SURE THEY DIDN'T STUDY EITHER...
DOUBLE-CHECKING
FINISHED ALREADY
NO WAAAAY!
DING DONG
DING DONG
SIGH
MY QUIZ WAS PRACTICALLY BLANK... HOW UNLUCKY.
EVERY-ONE, MAKE SURE...
...TO BE CAREFUL WITH THE OVEN WHEN COOKING.
DO YOU SMELL SOME-THING BURN-ING?
HUH?
KONNO, HOW'S THE GRATIN?
SHOOOOT! SORRY!
I THOUGHT I WAS LUCKIER THAN MOST.
MISS KONNO!

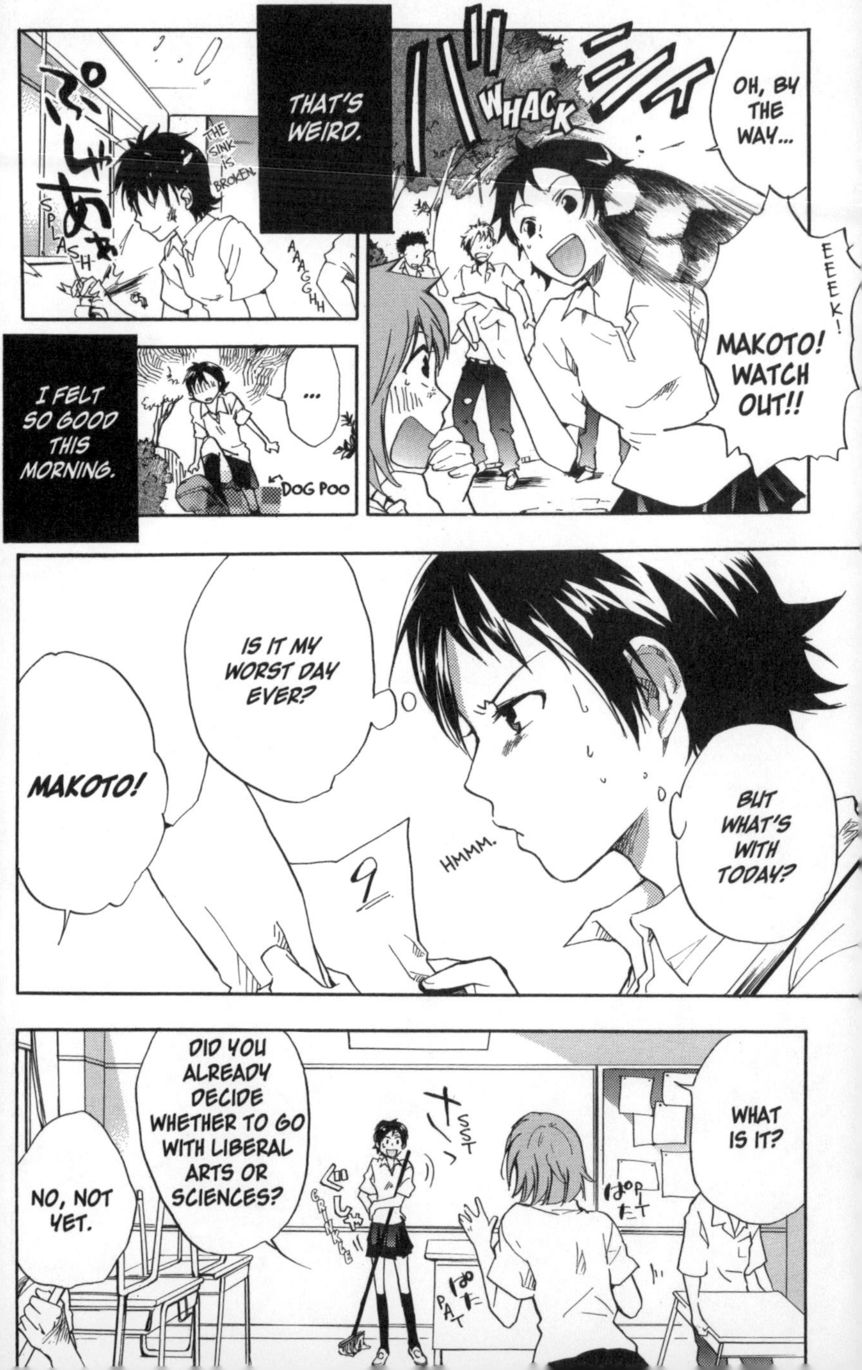

OH, BY THE WAY...
WHACK
EEEK!
MAKOTO! WATCH OUT!!
THAT'S WEIRD.
THE SINK IS BROKEN.
SPLASH
AAAGGHH
I FELT SO GOOD THIS MORNING.
...
DOG POO
BUT WHAT'S WITH TODAY?
IS IT MY WORST DAY EVER?
HMMM.
MAKOTO!
WHAT IS IT?
PAT
SST
CRINKLE
DID YOU ALREADY DECIDE WHETHER TO GO WITH LIBERAL ARTS OR SCIENCES?
NO, NOT YET.

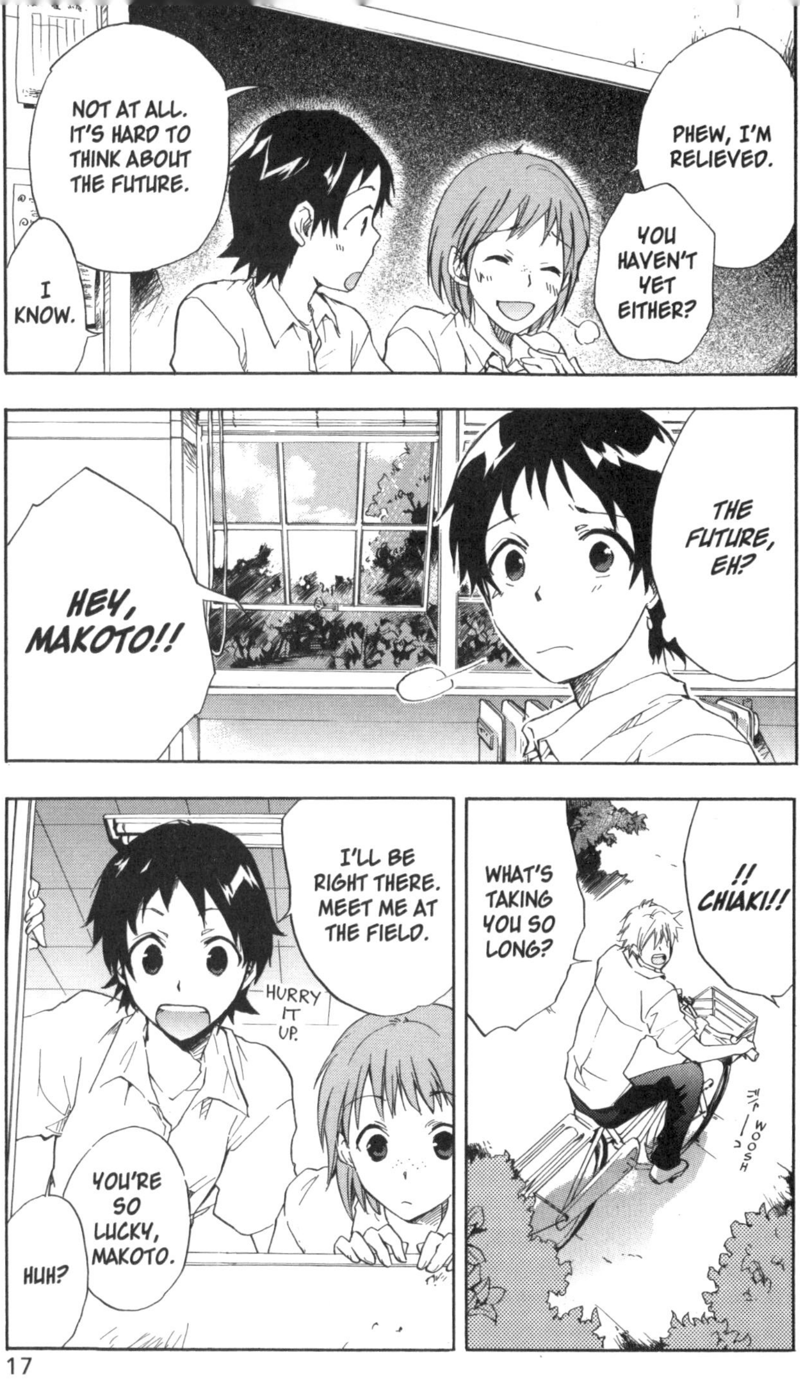
PHEW, I'M RELIEVED.
YOU HAVEN'T YET EITHER?
NOT AT ALL. IT'S HARD TO THINK ABOUT THE FUTURE.
I KNOW.
THE FUTURE, EH?
HEY, MAKOTO!!
!! CHIAKI!!
WHAT'S TAKING YOU SO LONG?
WOOSH
I'LL BE RIGHT THERE. MEET ME AT THE FIELD.
HURRY IT UP.
YOU'RE SO LUCKY, MAKOTO.
HUH?

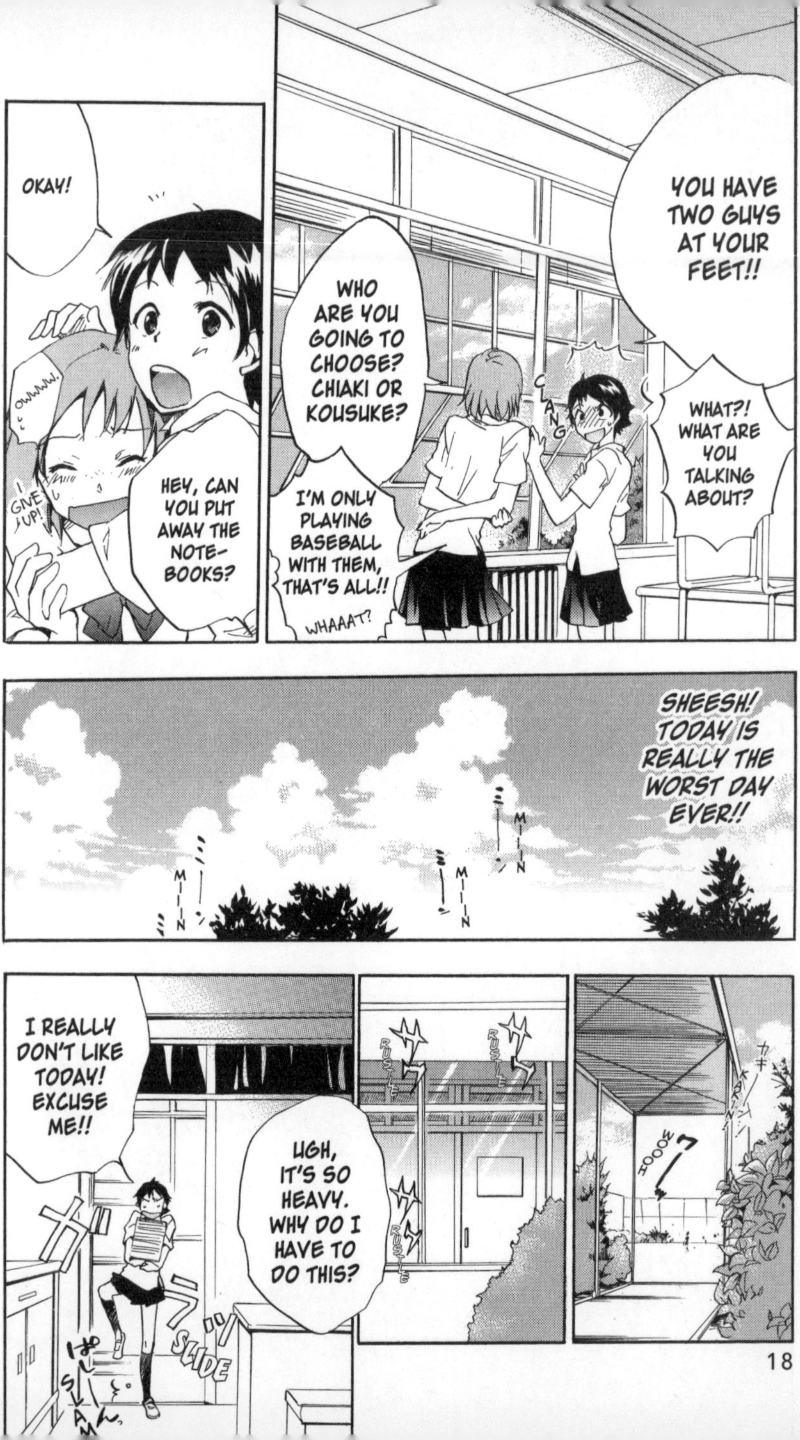
YOU HAVE TWO GUYS AT YOUR FEET!!
CLANG
WHAT?! WHAT ARE YOU TALKING ABOUT?
WHO ARE YOU GOING TO CHOOSE? CHIAKI OR KOUSUKE?
I'M ONLY PLAYING BASEBALL WITH THEM, THAT'S ALL!!
WHAAAT?
OKAY!
HEY, CAN YOU PUT AWAY THE NOTE-BOOKS?
OWWWW.
I GIVE UP!
SHEESH! TODAY IS REALLY THE WORST DAY EVER!!
MI-IN
MI-IN
MI-IN
KARAN
WOOOSH
RUSTLE
RUSTLE
UGH, IT'S SO HEAVY. WHY DO I HAVE TO DO THIS?
RUSTLE
I REALLY DON'T LIKE TODAY! EXCUSE ME!!
SLIDE
SLAM

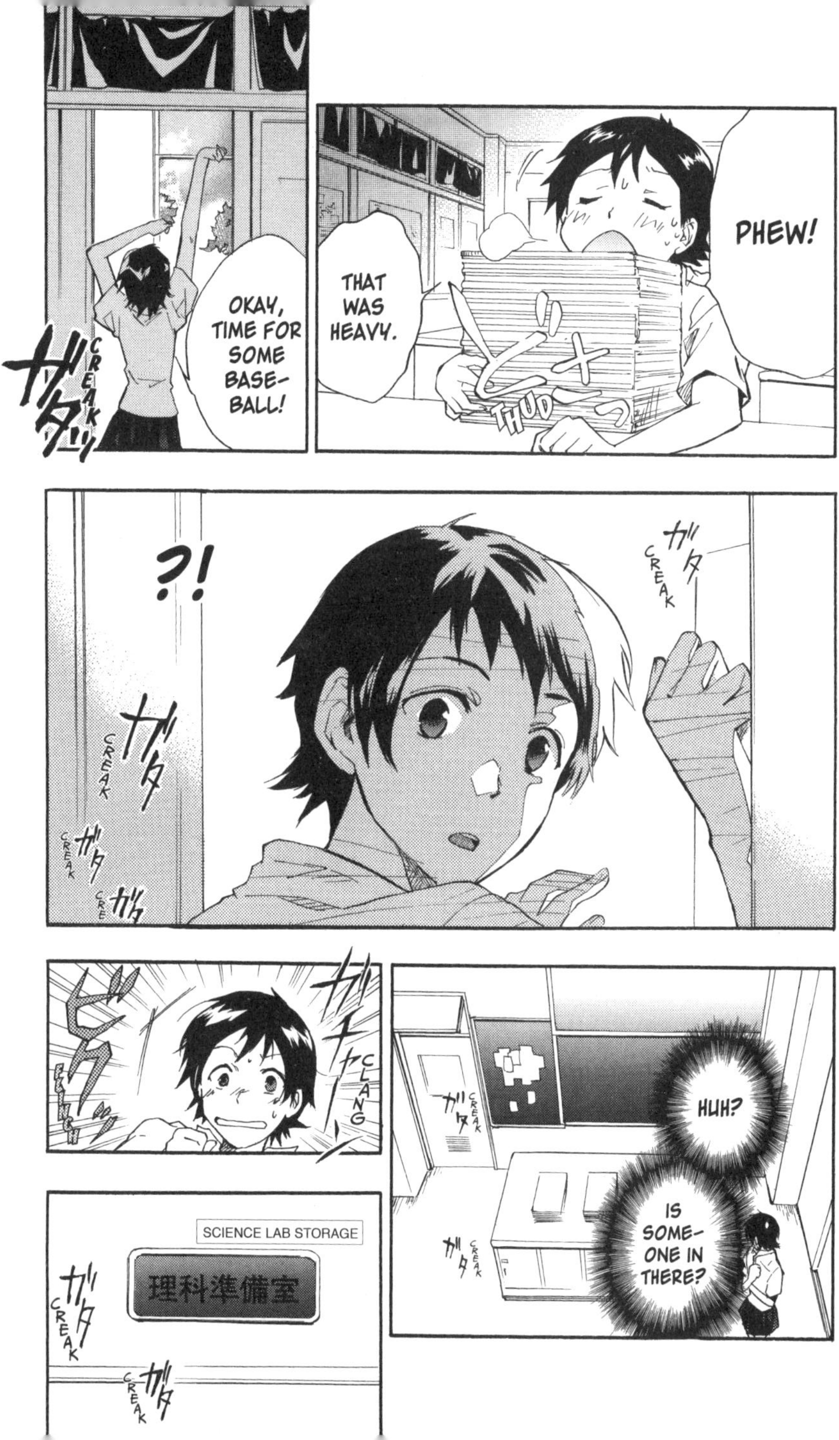
PHEW!
THAT WAS HEAVY.
THUD
OKAY, TIME FOR SOME BASE-BALL!
CREAK
CREAK
?!
CREAK
CREAK
CRE
HUH?
IS SOME-ONE IN THERE?
CREAK
CREAK
CLANG
SCIENCE LAB STORAGE
理科準備室
CREAK
CREAK

SLAAAM

IS...

SOME-
ONE
THERE?!

SILENCE

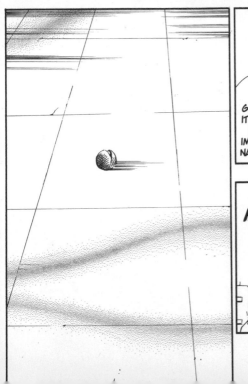

OH. HAHA.

I GUESS IT WAS MY IMAGI-NATION.

HUH?!

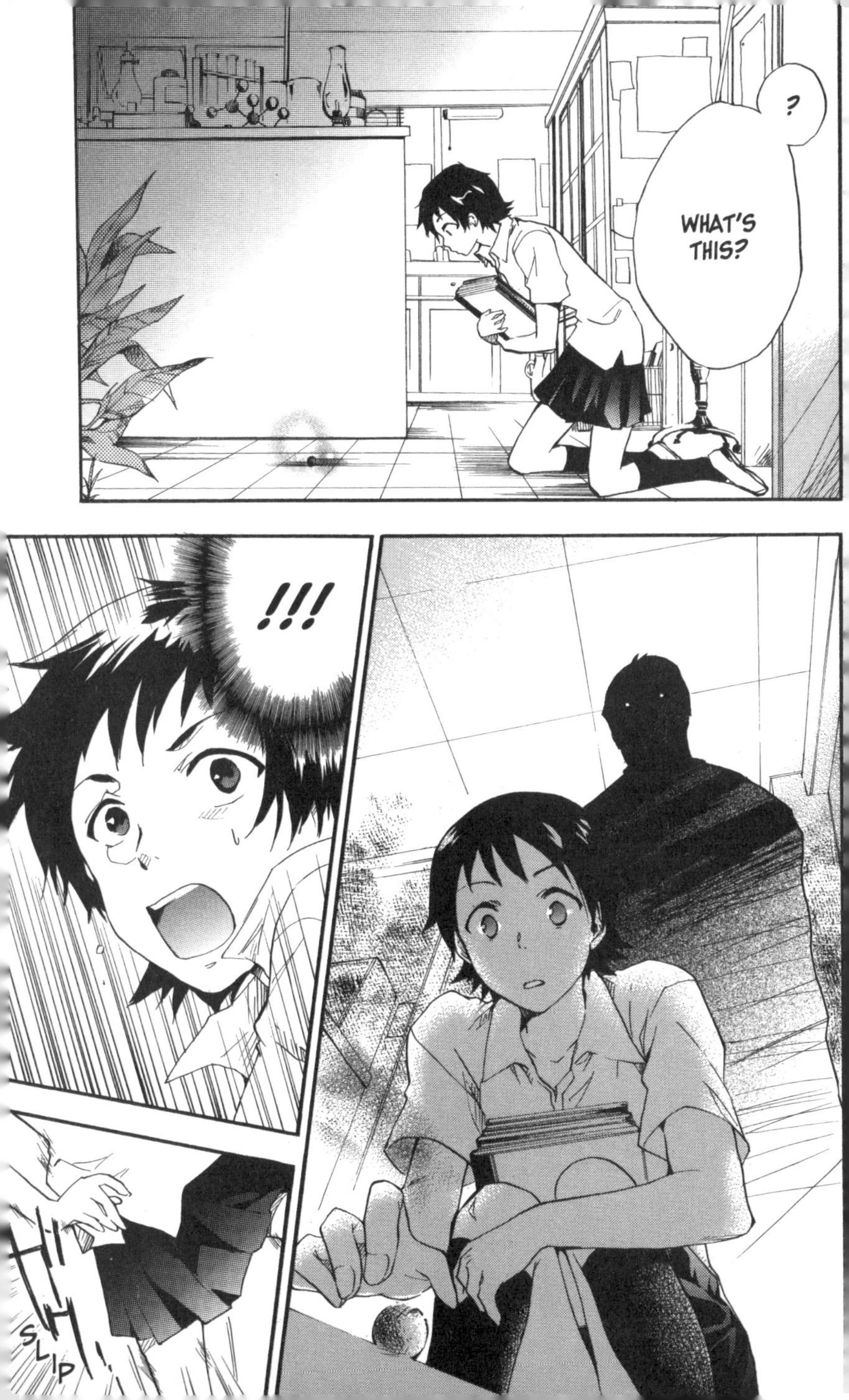
?
WHAT'S THIS?
!!!
SLIP

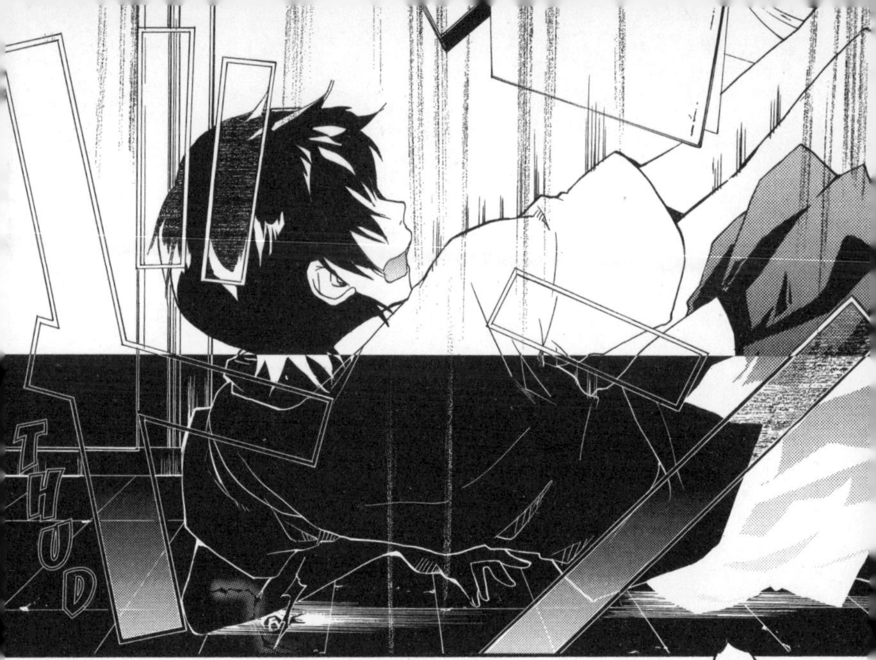
THUD

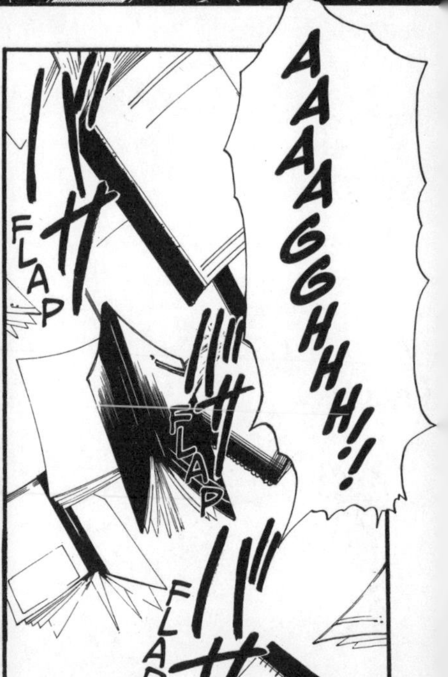
AAAAAGGHHHH!!
FLAP
FLAP
FLAP

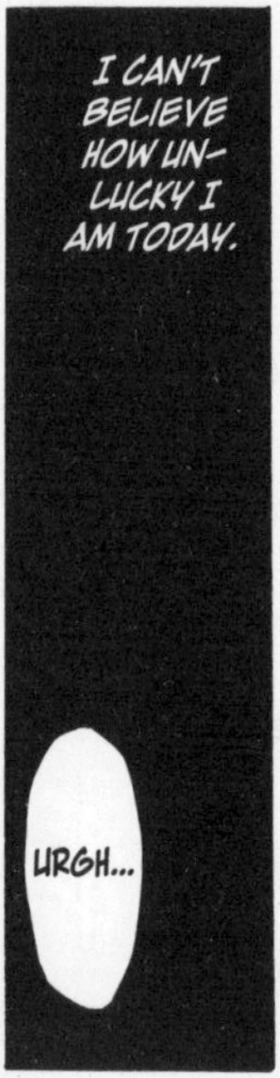
I CAN'T BELIEVE HOW UN-LUCKY I AM TODAY.
URGH...

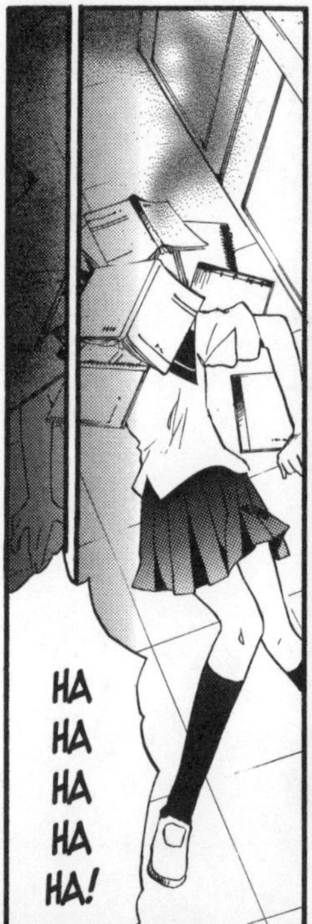
HA HA HA HA HA!

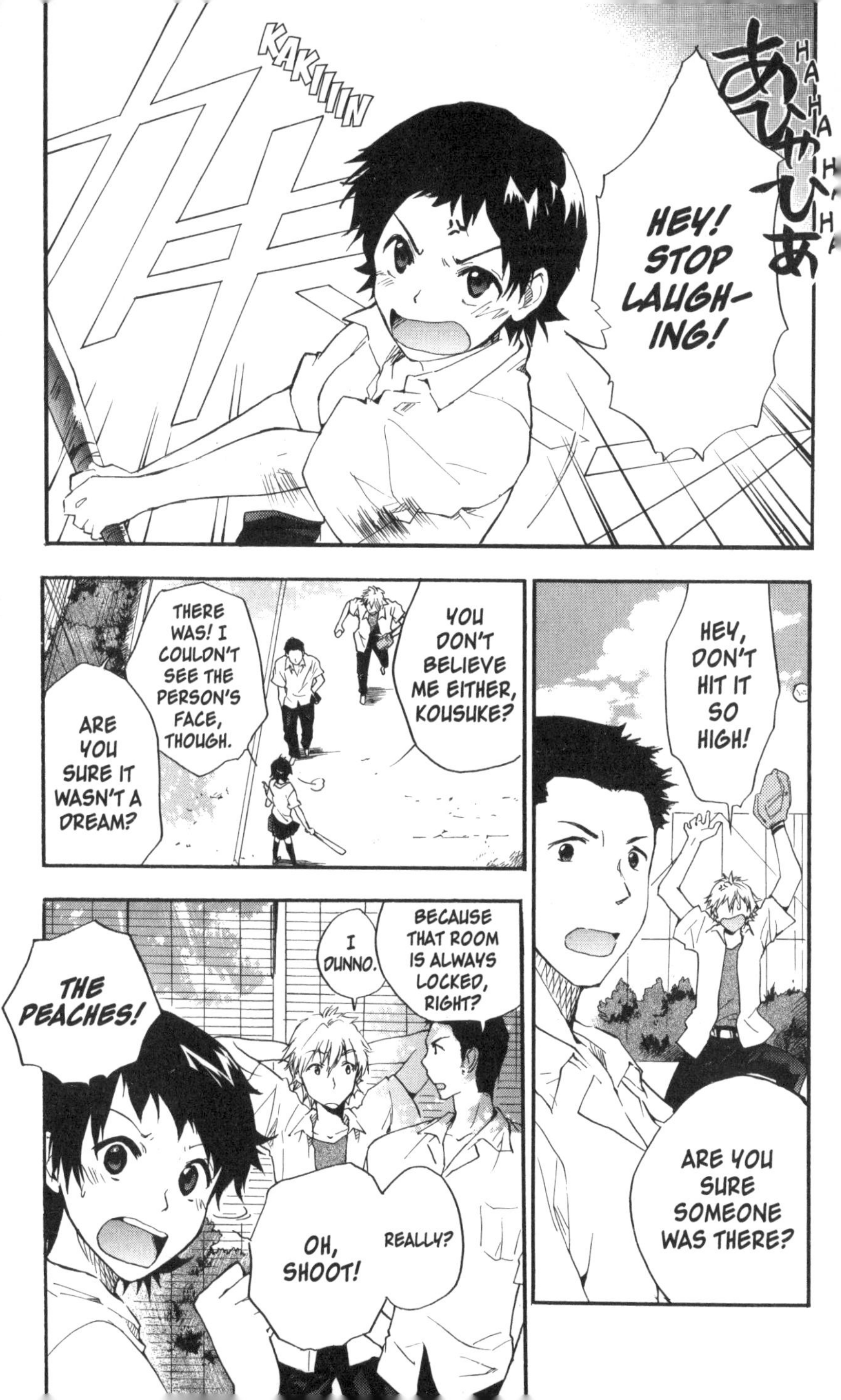

HEY! STOP LAUGHING!
KAKIIIIN
HEY, DON'T HIT IT SO HIGH!
ARE YOU SURE SOMEONE WAS THERE?
YOU DON'T BELIEVE ME EITHER, KOUSUKE?
THERE WAS! I COULDN'T SEE THE PERSON'S FACE, THOUGH.
ARE YOU SURE IT WASN'T A DREAM?
BECAUSE THAT ROOM IS ALWAYS LOCKED, RIGHT?
I DUNNO.
REALLY?
OH, SHOOT!
THE PEACHES!

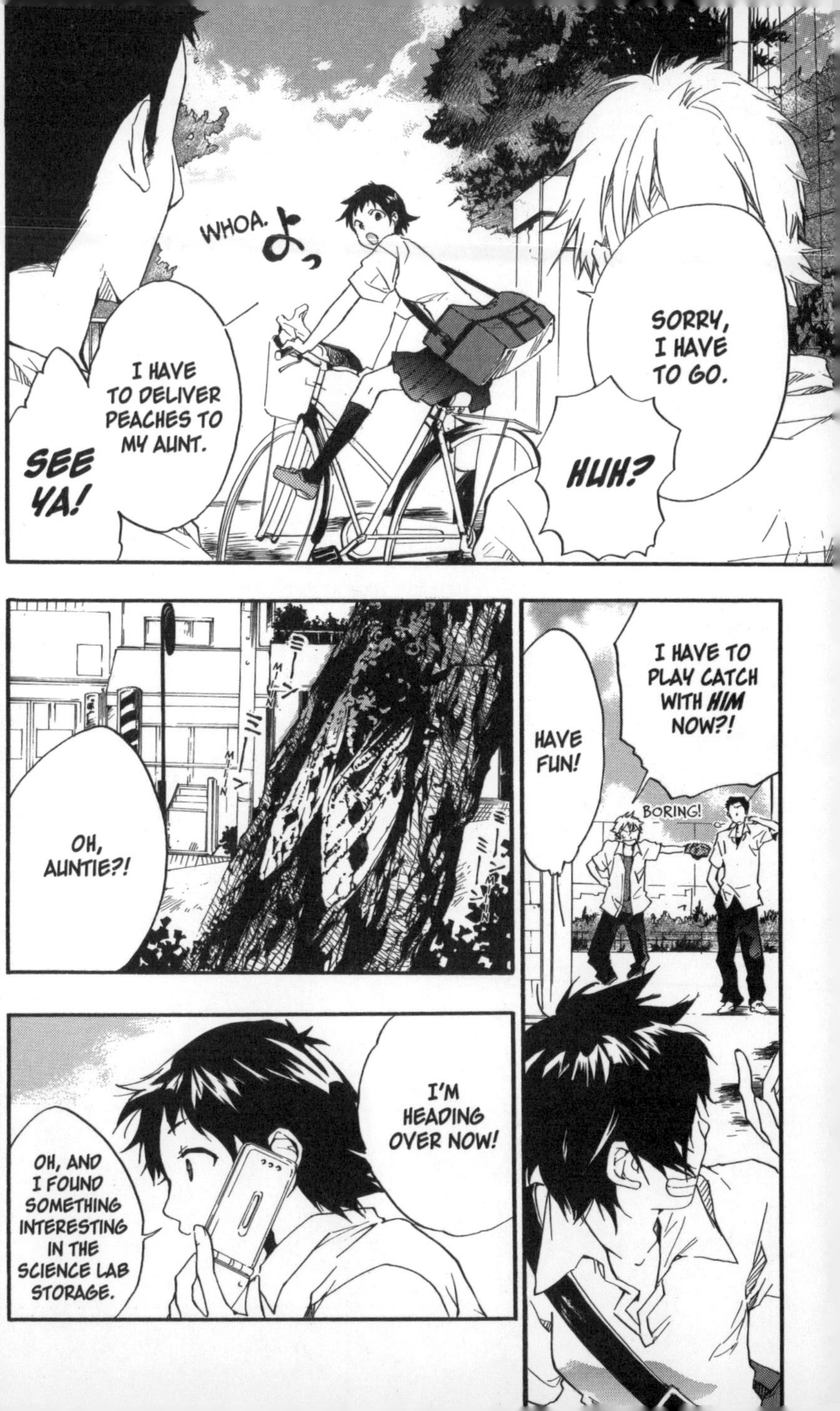
SORRY, I HAVE TO GO.
HUH?
WHOA.
よっ
I HAVE TO DELIVER PEACHES TO MY AUNT.
SEE YA!
I HAVE TO PLAY CATCH WITH HIM NOW?!
BORING!
HAVE FUN!
OH, AUNTIE?!
I'M HEADING OVER NOW!
OH, AND I FOUND SOMETHING INTERESTING IN THE SCIENCE LAB STORAGE.

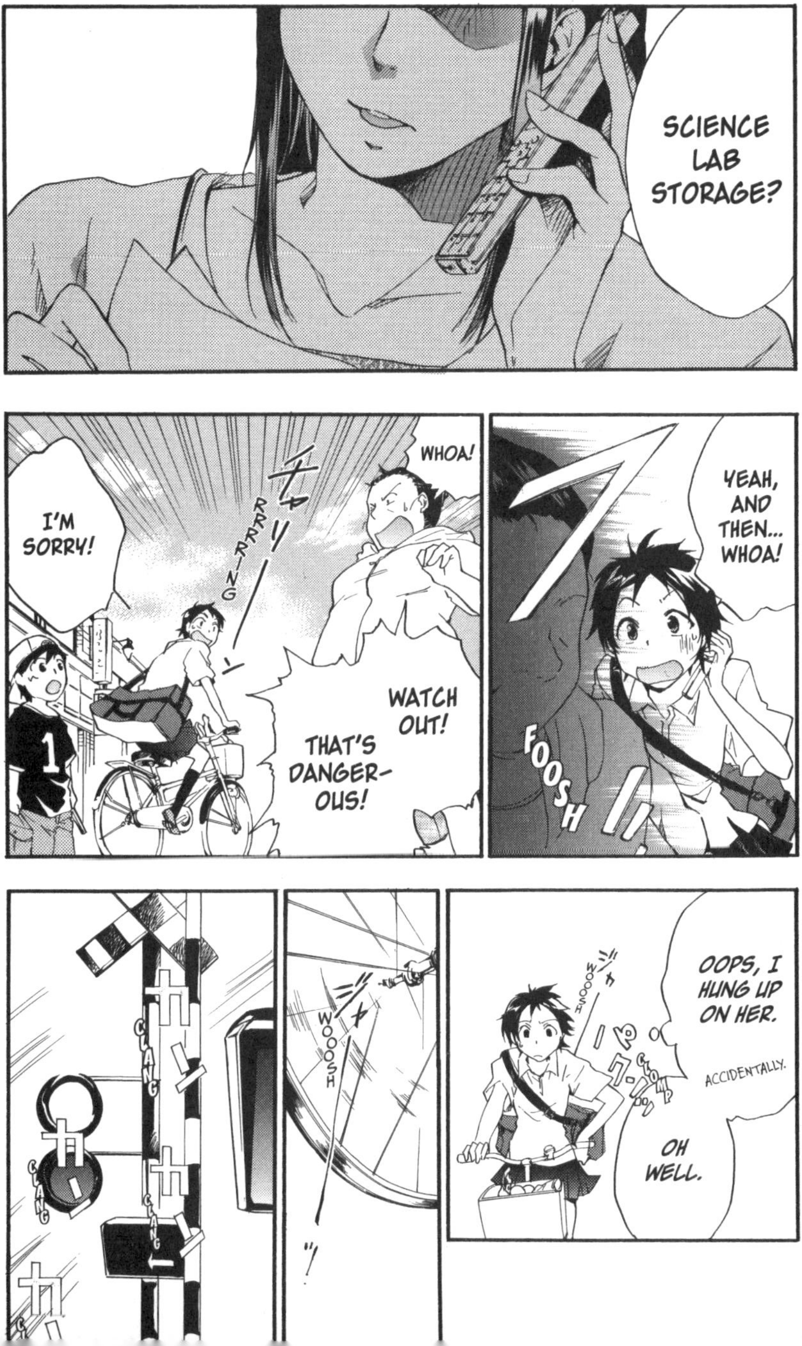
SCIENCE LAB STORAGE?
YEAH, AND THEN... WHOA!
FOOSH
WHOA!
RRRRING
I'M SORRY!
WATCH OUT!
THAT'S DANGER-OUS!
OOPS, I HUNG UP ON HER.
WOOOSH
CLOMP
ACCIDENTALLY.
OH WELL.
WOOOSH
CLANG
CLANG
CLANG

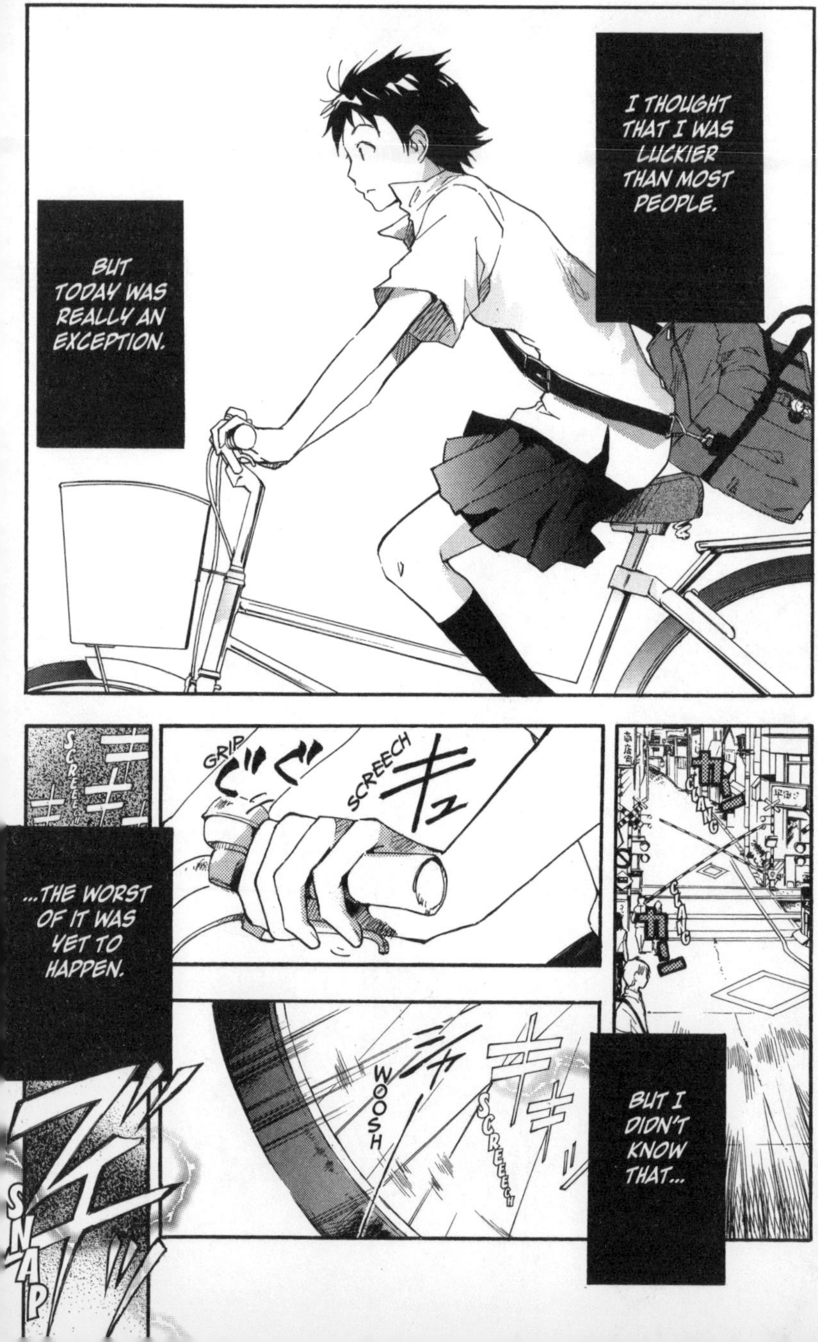
I THOUGHT THAT I WAS LUCKIER THAN MOST PEOPLE.
BUT TODAY WAS REALLY AN EXCEPTION.
CLANG
CLANG
SCREECH
GRIP
BUT I DIDN'T KNOW THAT...
SCREEECH
WOOSH
...THE WORST OF IT WAS YET TO HAPPEN.
SNAP

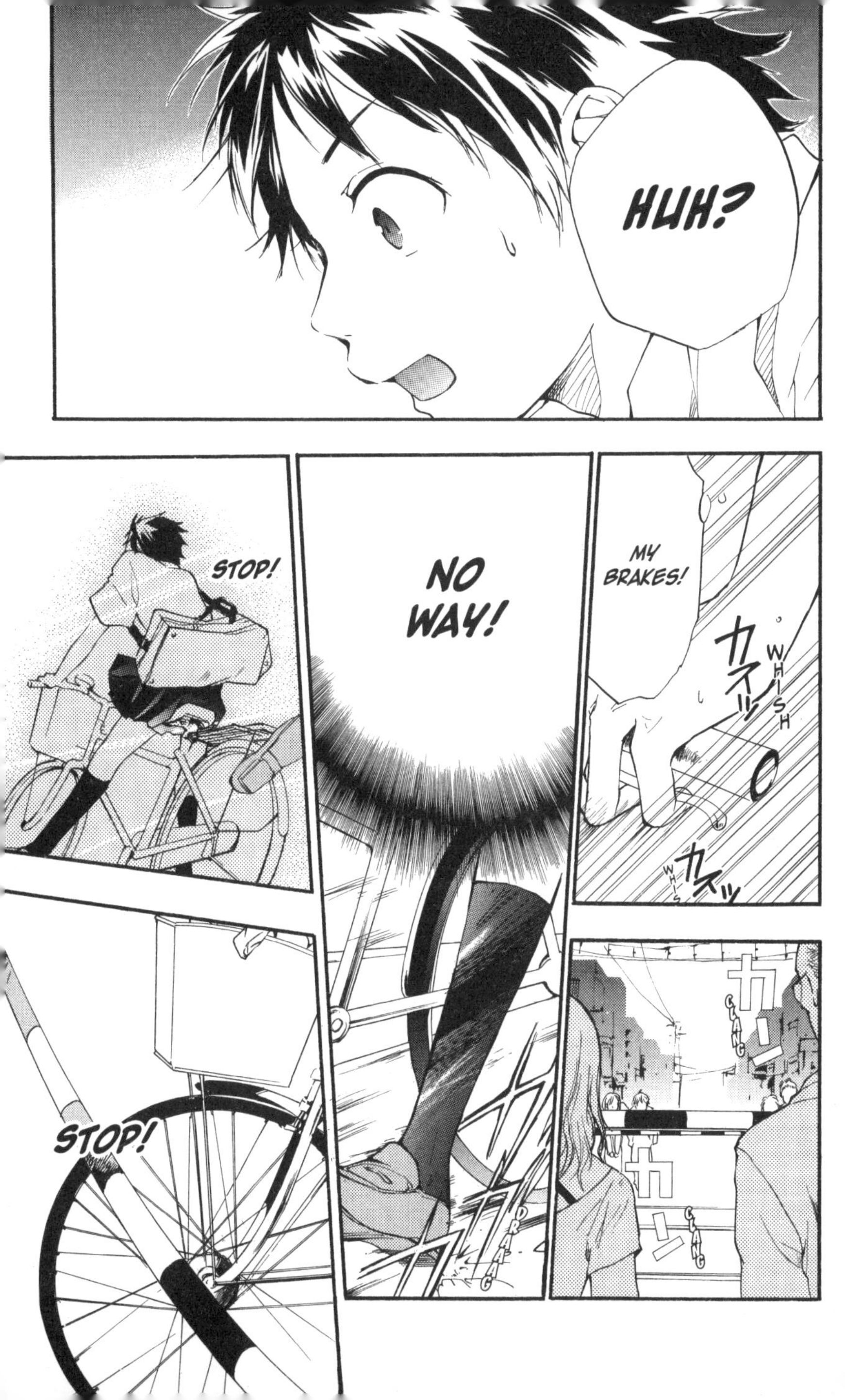
HUH?
MY BRAKES!
カスッ
WHISH
カスッ
WHIS
カーン
CLANG
カーン
CLANG
NO WAY!
DRAAAG
STOP!
STOP!

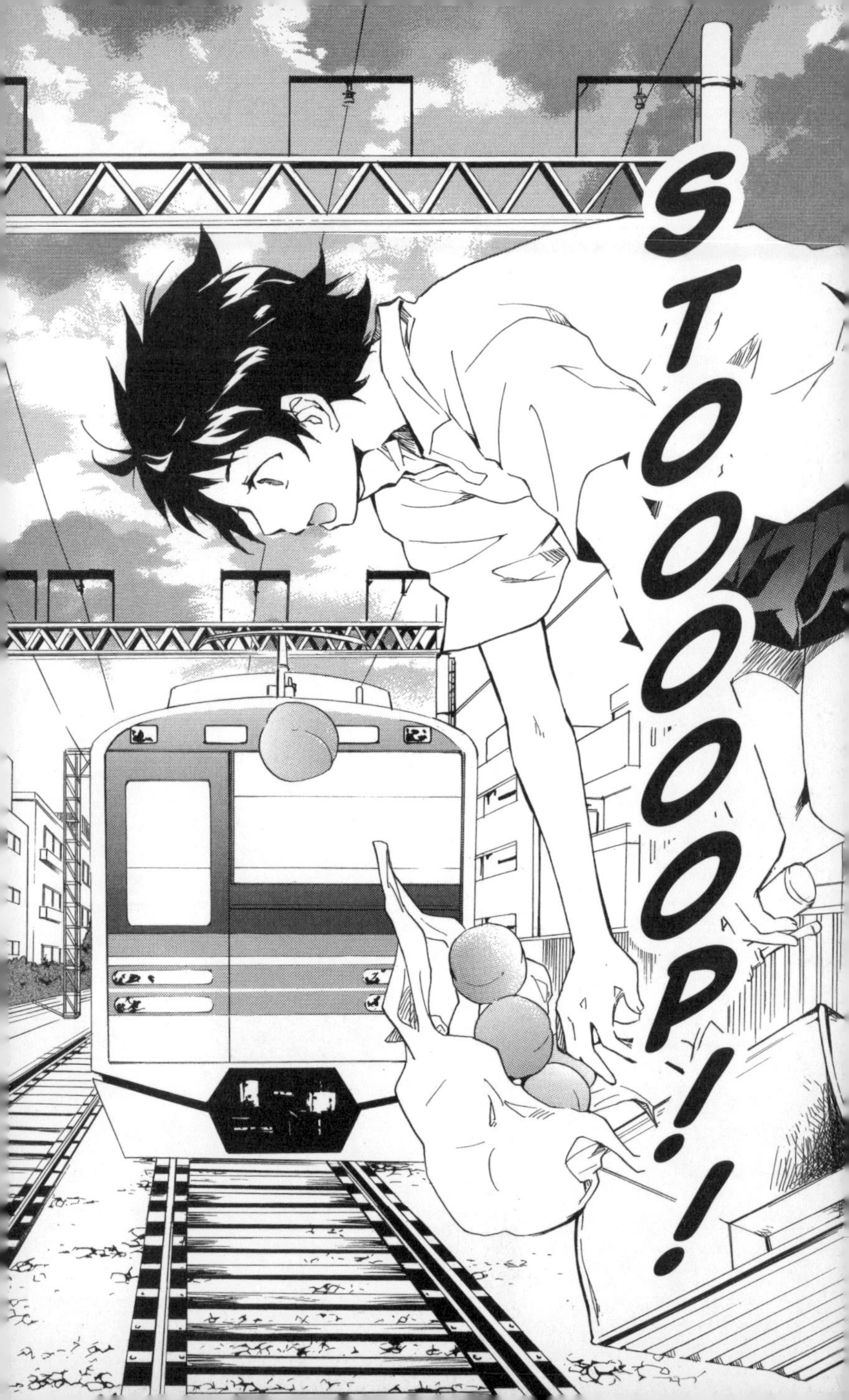
STOOOOOP!!!

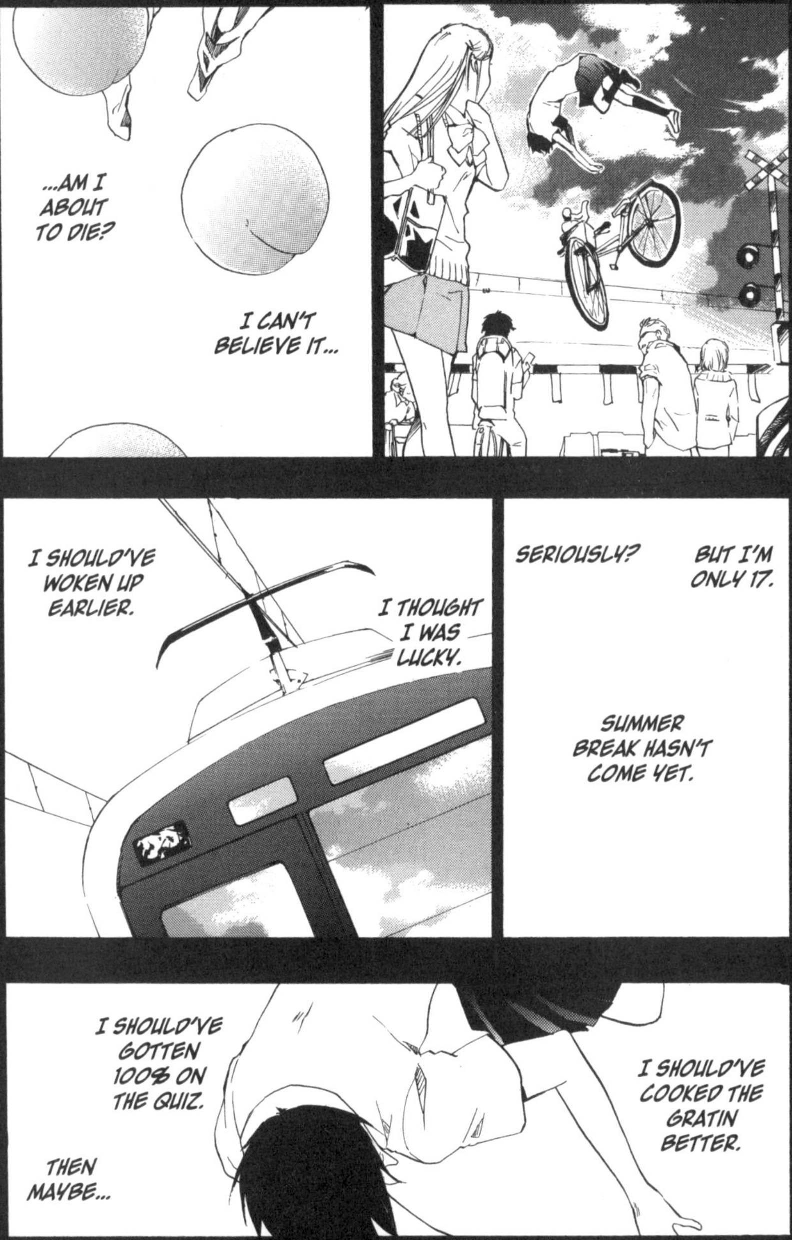
...AM I ABOUT TO DIE?
I CAN'T BELIEVE IT...
BUT I'M ONLY 17.
SERIOUSLY?
SUMMER BREAK HASN'T COME YET.
I THOUGHT I WAS LUCKY.
I SHOULD'VE WOKEN UP EARLIER.
I SHOULD'VE COOKED THE GRATIN BETTER.
I SHOULD'VE GOTTEN 100% ON THE QUIZ.
THEN MAYBE...

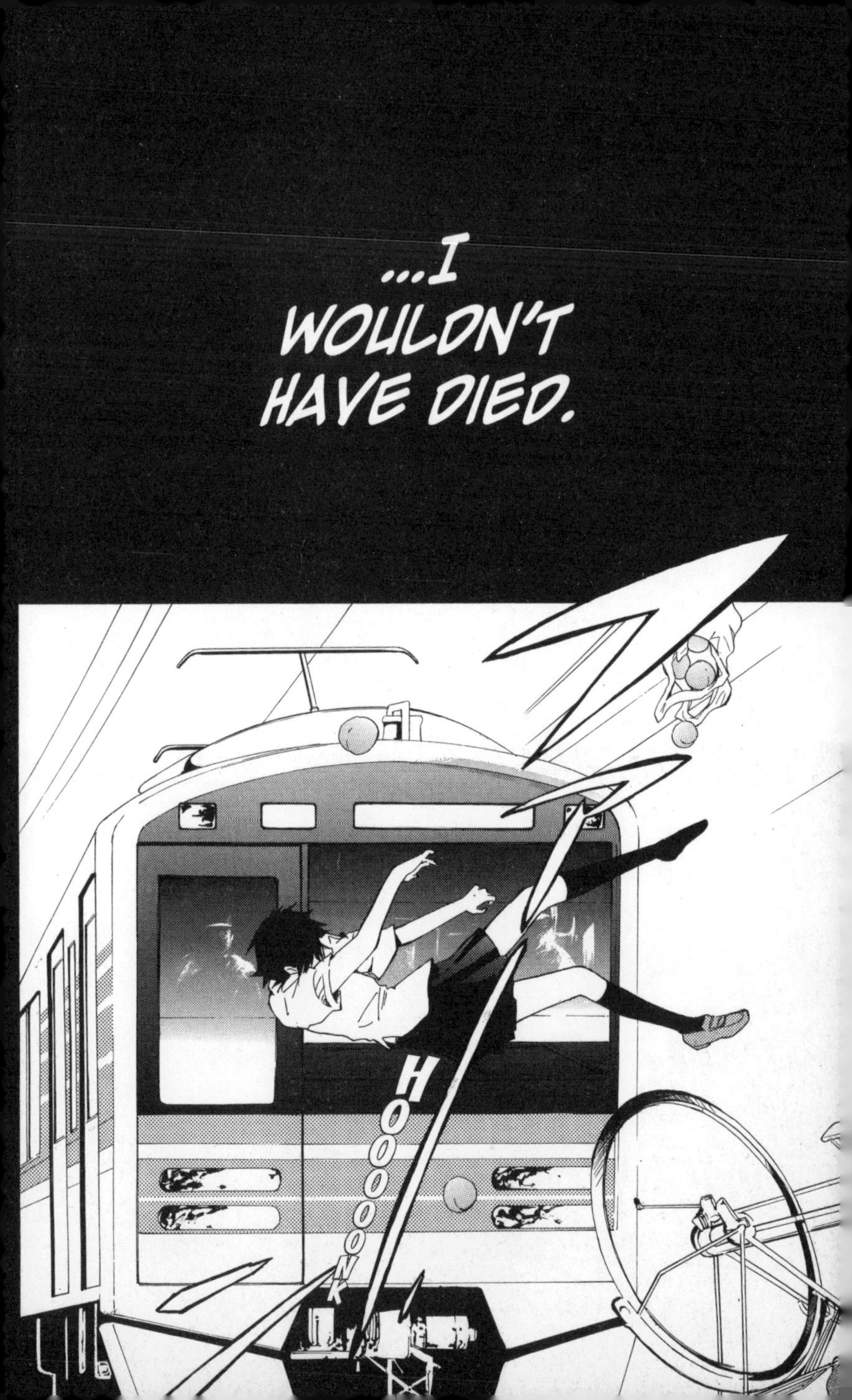
...I WOULDN'T HAVE DIED.
HOOOOONK

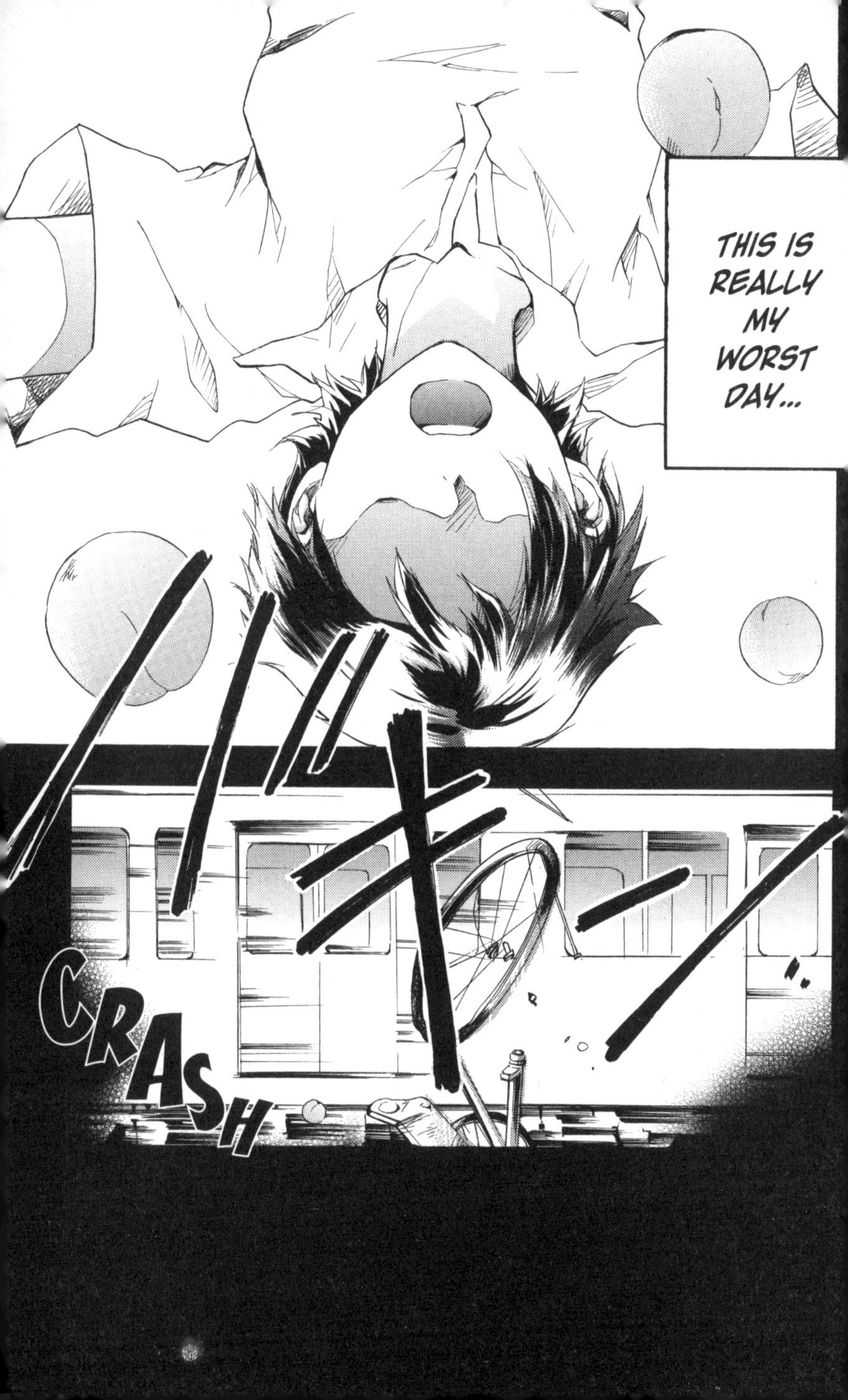
THIS IS REALLY MY WORST DAY...
CRASH

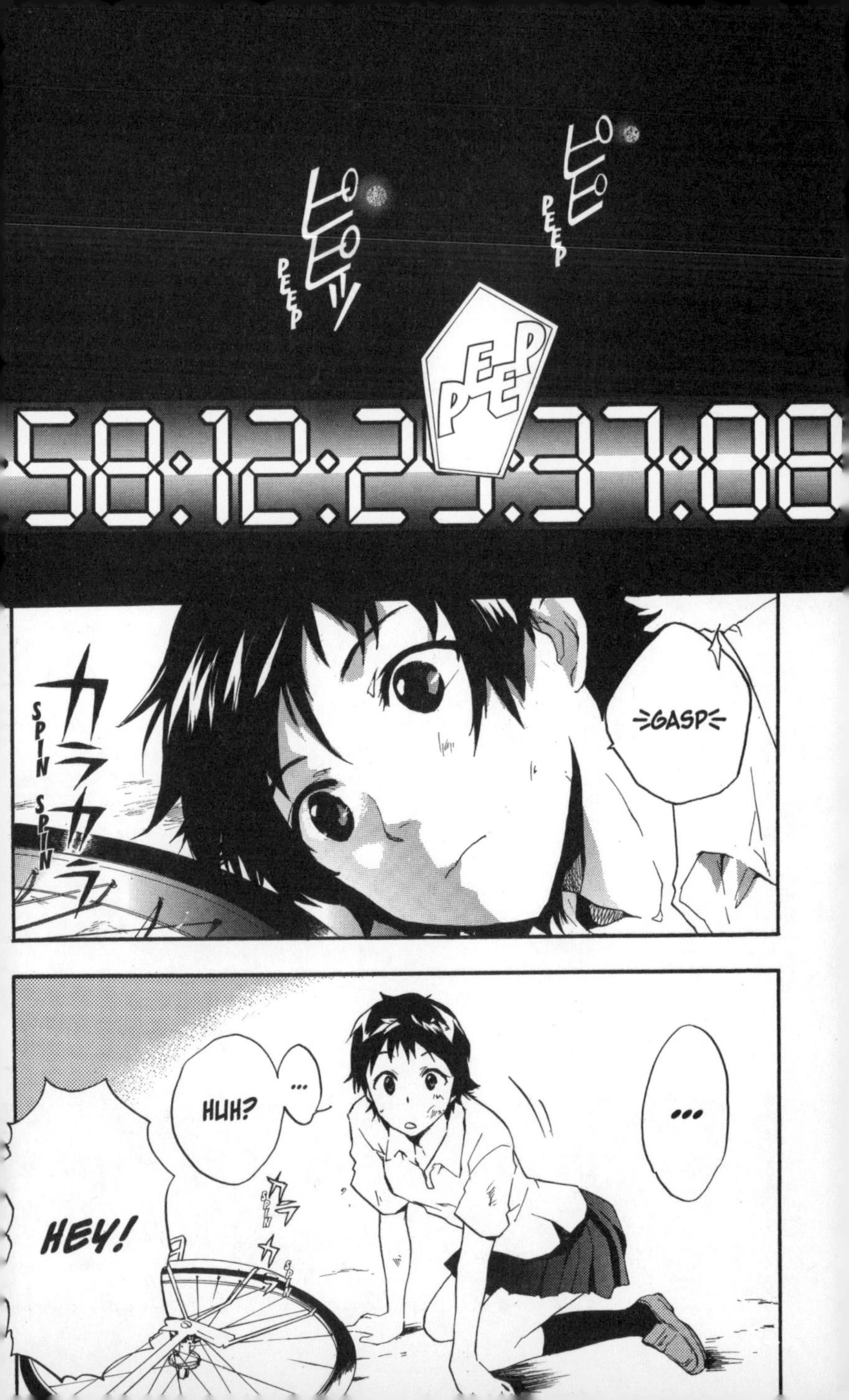

ピピ
PEEP
ピピピッ
PEEP
PEEP
58:12:2
37:08
GASP
カラカラ
SPIN SPIN SPIN
...
... HUH?
カラカラ
SPIN SPIN
HEY!

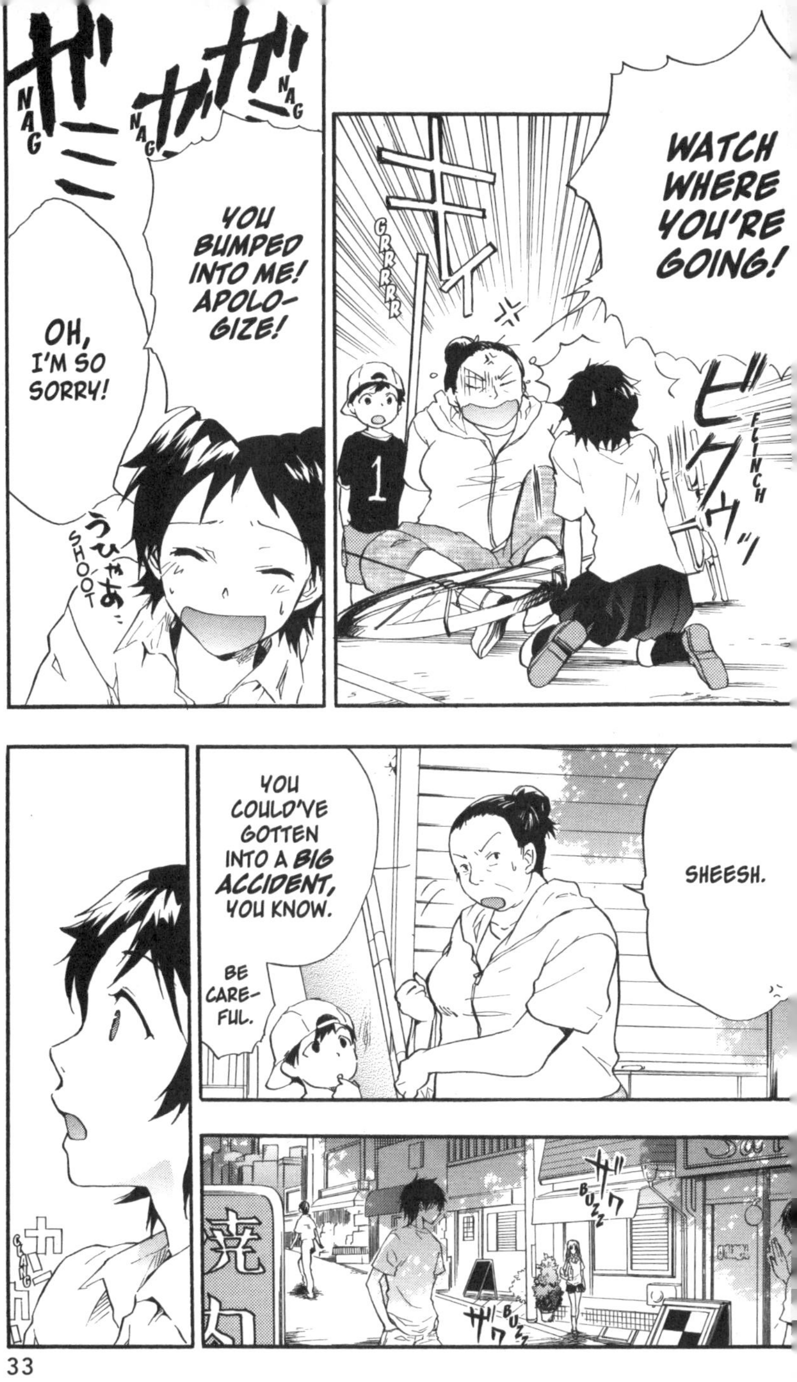
WATCH WHERE YOU'RE GOING!
GRRRR
FLINCH
NAG NAG
NAG NAG
YOU BUMPED INTO ME! APOLO-GIZE!
OH, I'M SO SORRY!
SHOOT
SHEESH.
YOU COULD'VE GOTTEN INTO A *BIG ACCIDENT*, YOU KNOW.
BE CARE-FUL.
BUZZ
BUZZ
CLANG

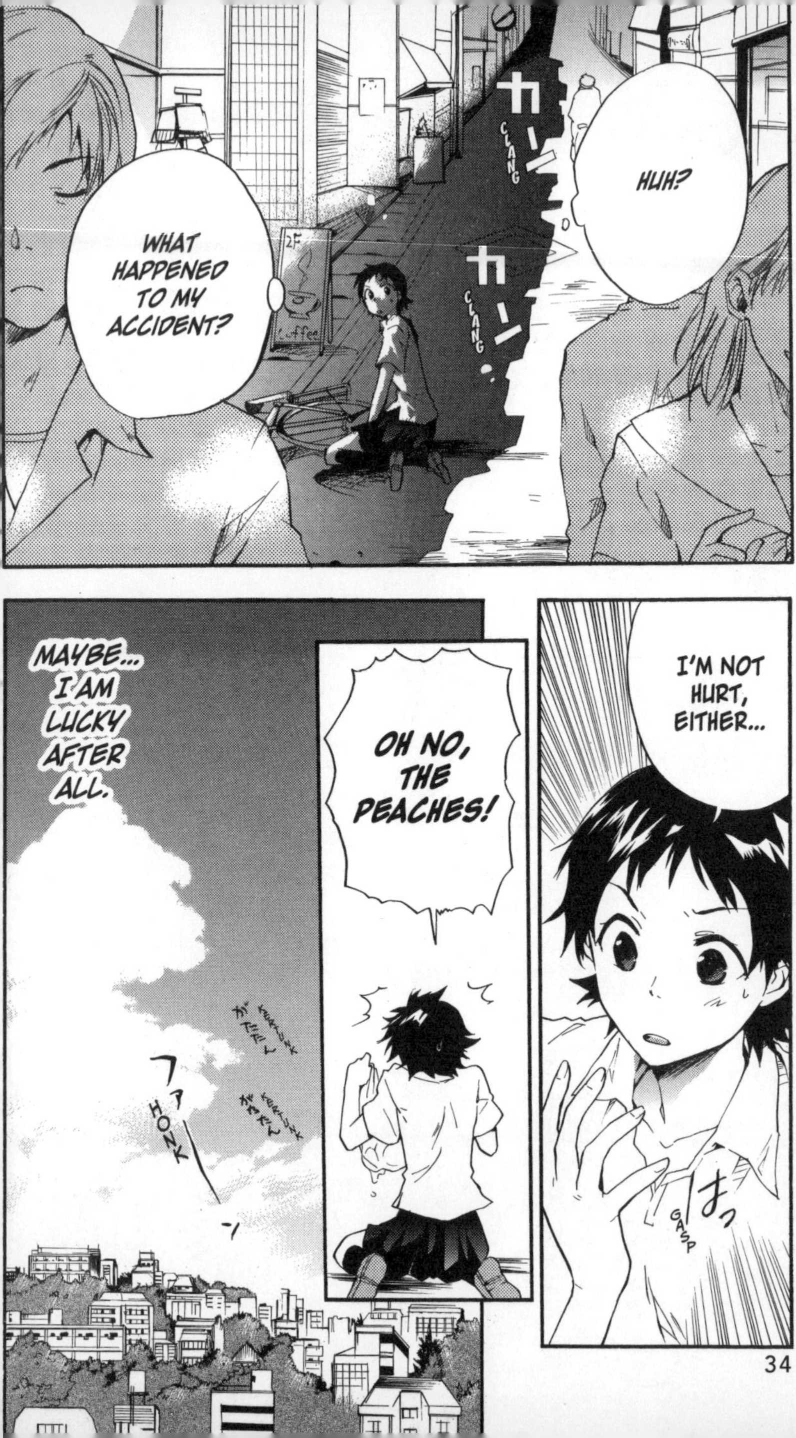
HUH?
CLANG
CLANG
WHAT HAPPENED TO MY ACCIDENT?
I'M NOT HURT, EITHER...
GASP
OH NO, THE PEACHES!
MAYBE... I AM LUCKY AFTER ALL.
KERCLUNK
KERCLUNK
HONK

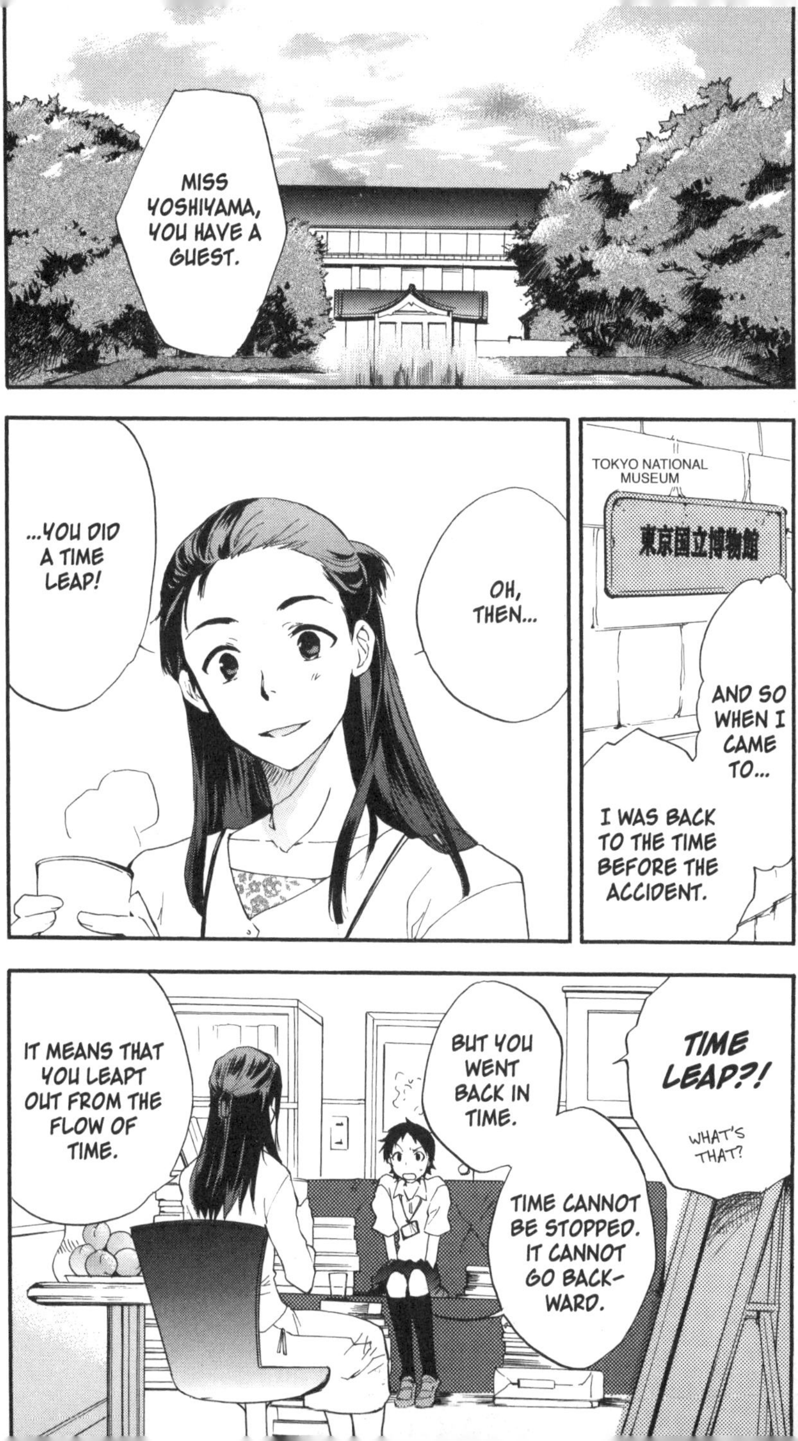
MISS YOSHIYAMA, YOU HAVE A GUEST.
TOKYO NATIONAL MUSEUM
東京国立博物館
AND SO WHEN I CAME TO...
I WAS BACK TO THE TIME BEFORE THE ACCIDENT.
OH, THEN...
...YOU DID A TIME LEAP!
TIME LEAP?!
WHAT'S THAT?
BUT YOU WENT BACK IN TIME.
TIME CANNOT BE STOPPED. IT CANNOT GO BACK-WARD.
IT MEANS THAT YOU LEAPT OUT FROM THE FLOW OF TIME.

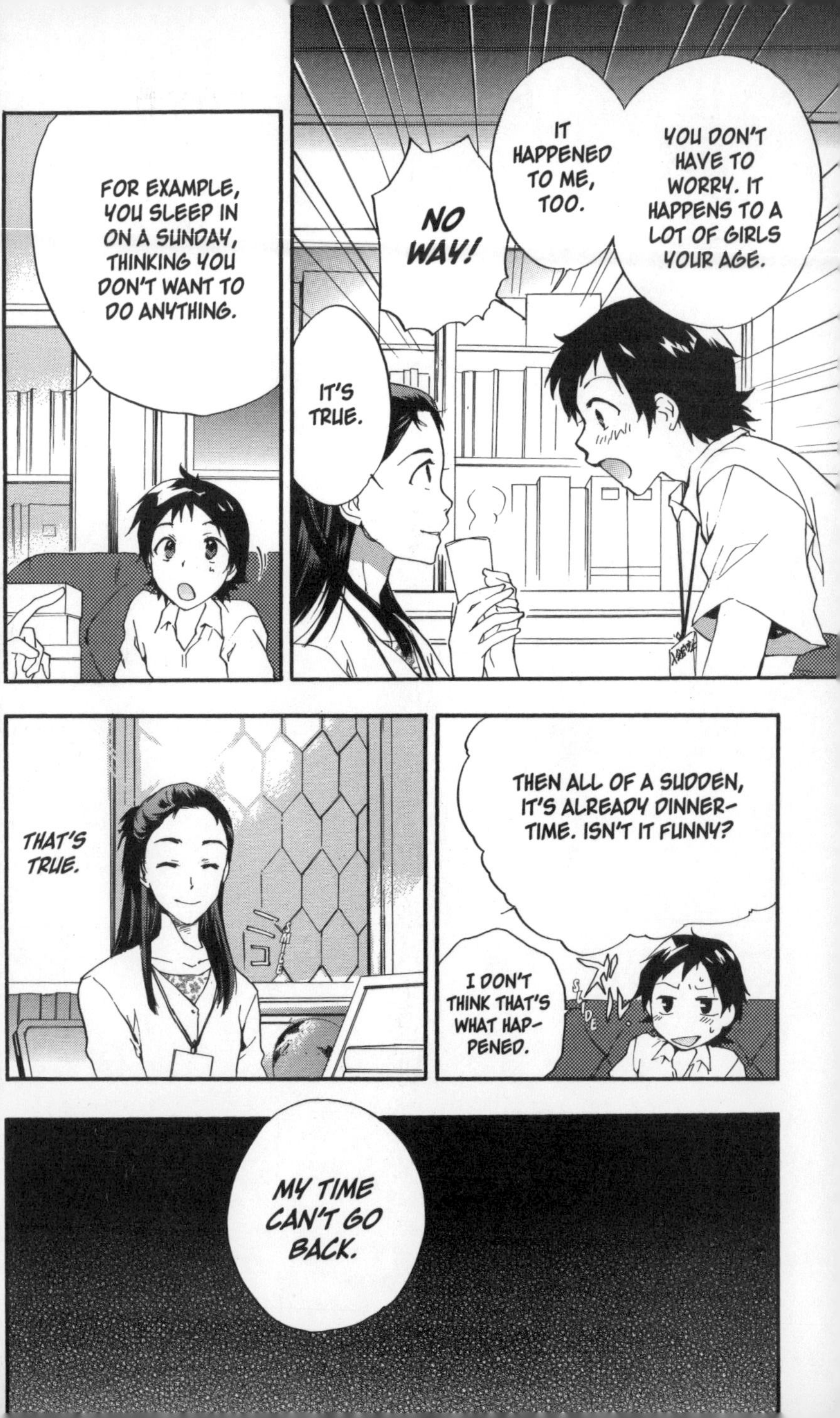
YOU DON'T HAVE TO WORRY. IT HAPPENS TO A LOT OF GIRLS YOUR AGE.
IT HAPPENED TO ME, TOO.
NO WAY!
IT'S TRUE.
FOR EXAMPLE, YOU SLEEP IN ON A SUNDAY, THINKING YOU DON'T WANT TO DO ANYTHING.
THEN ALL OF A SUDDEN, IT'S ALREADY DINNER-TIME. ISN'T IT FUNNY?
SLIDE
I DON'T THINK THAT'S WHAT HAP-PENED.
THAT'S TRUE.
MY TIME CAN'T GO BACK.

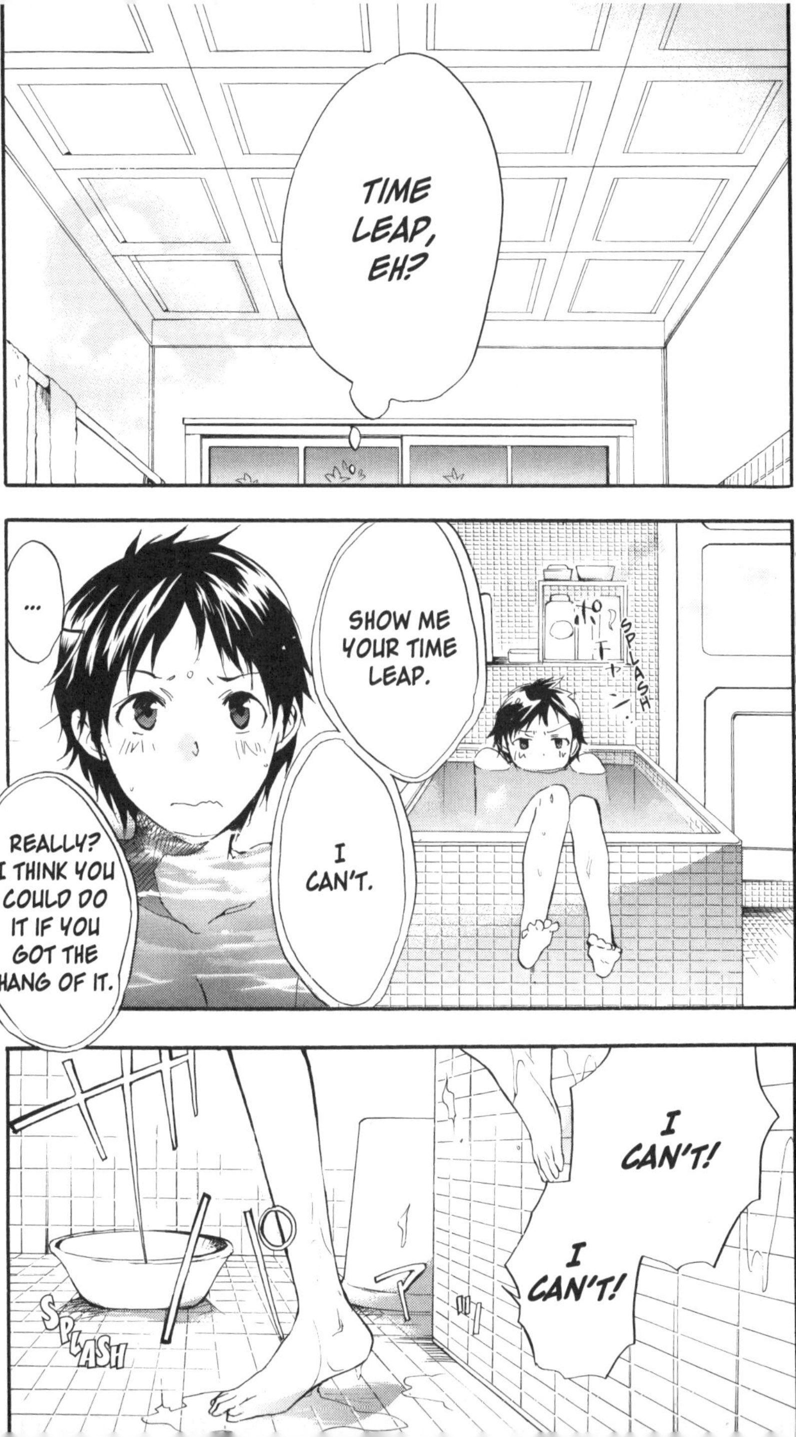
TIME LEAP, EH?
SPLASH
SHOW ME YOUR TIME LEAP.
...
I CAN'T.
REALLY? I THINK YOU COULD DO IT IF YOU GOT THE HANG OF IT.
I CAN'T!
I CAN'T!
SPLASH

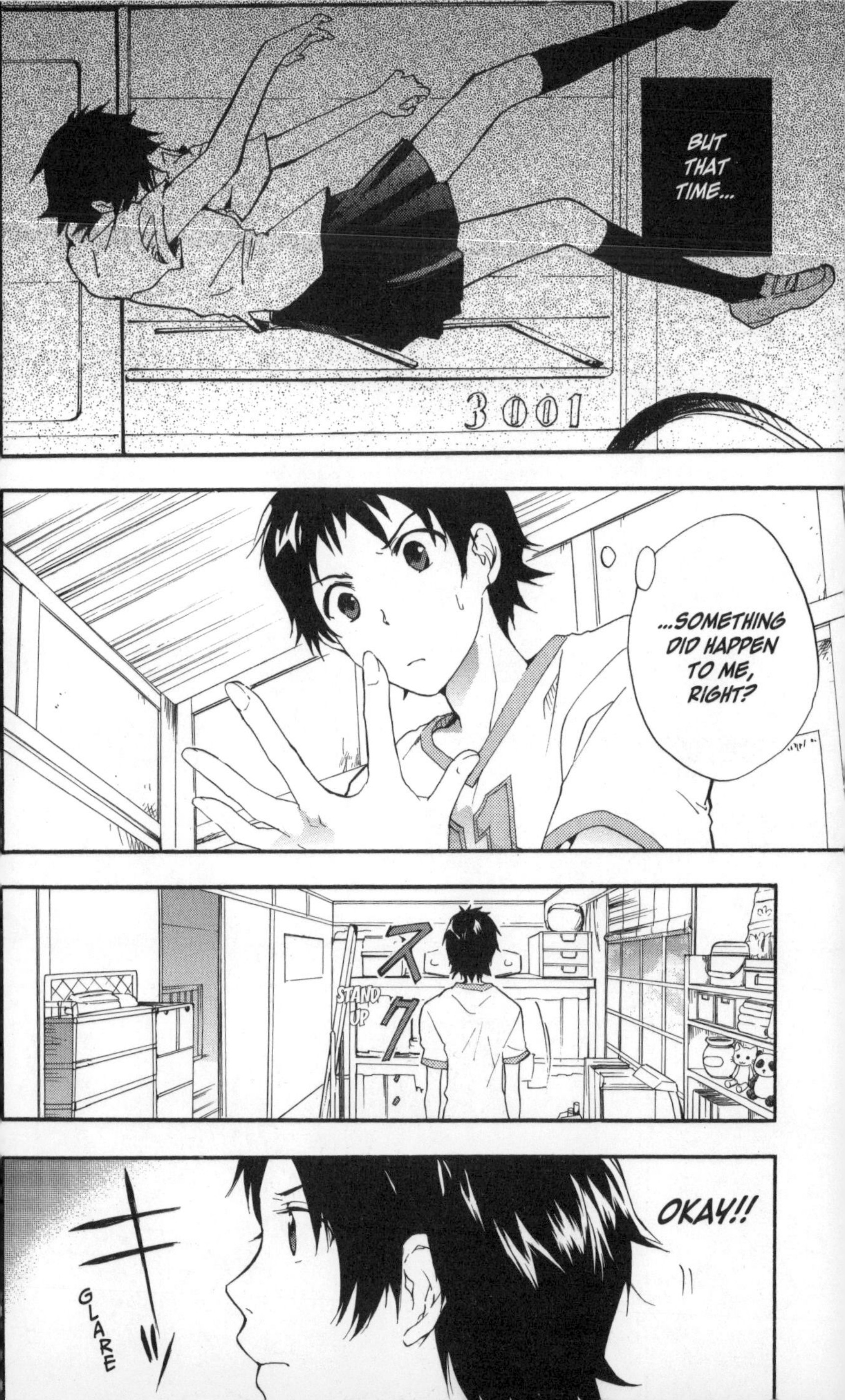
BUT THAT TIME...
...SOMETHING DID HAPPEN TO ME, RIGHT?
ス
ク
STAND UP
OKAY!!
キ
GLARE

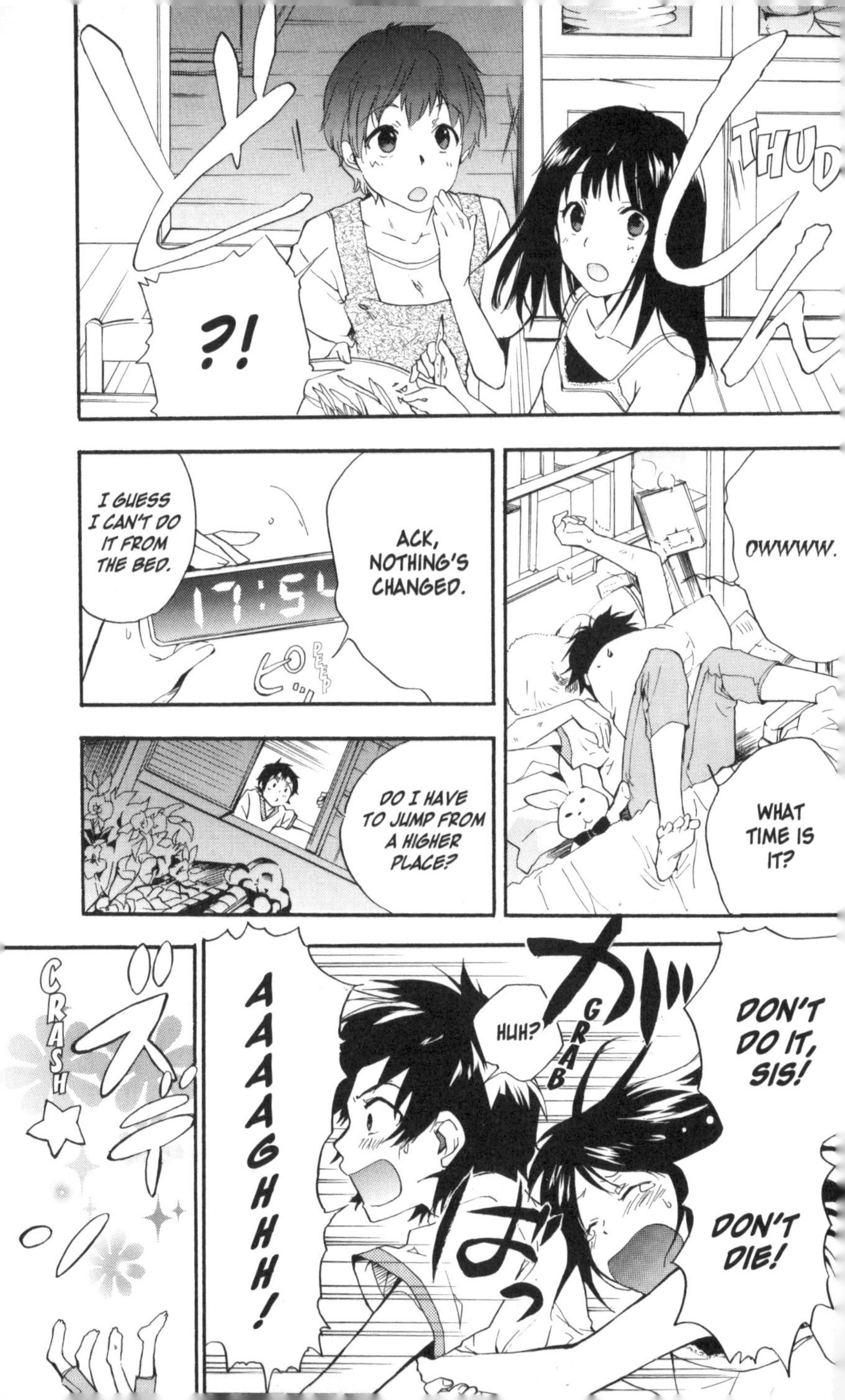
THUD
?!
OWWWW.
WHAT TIME IS IT?
ACK, NOTHING'S CHANGED.
BEEP
I GUESS I CAN'T DO IT FROM THE BED.
DO I HAVE TO JUMP FROM A HIGHER PLACE?
DON'T DO IT, SIS!
GRAB
HUH?
AAAAAGHHHH!
DON'T DIE!
CRASH

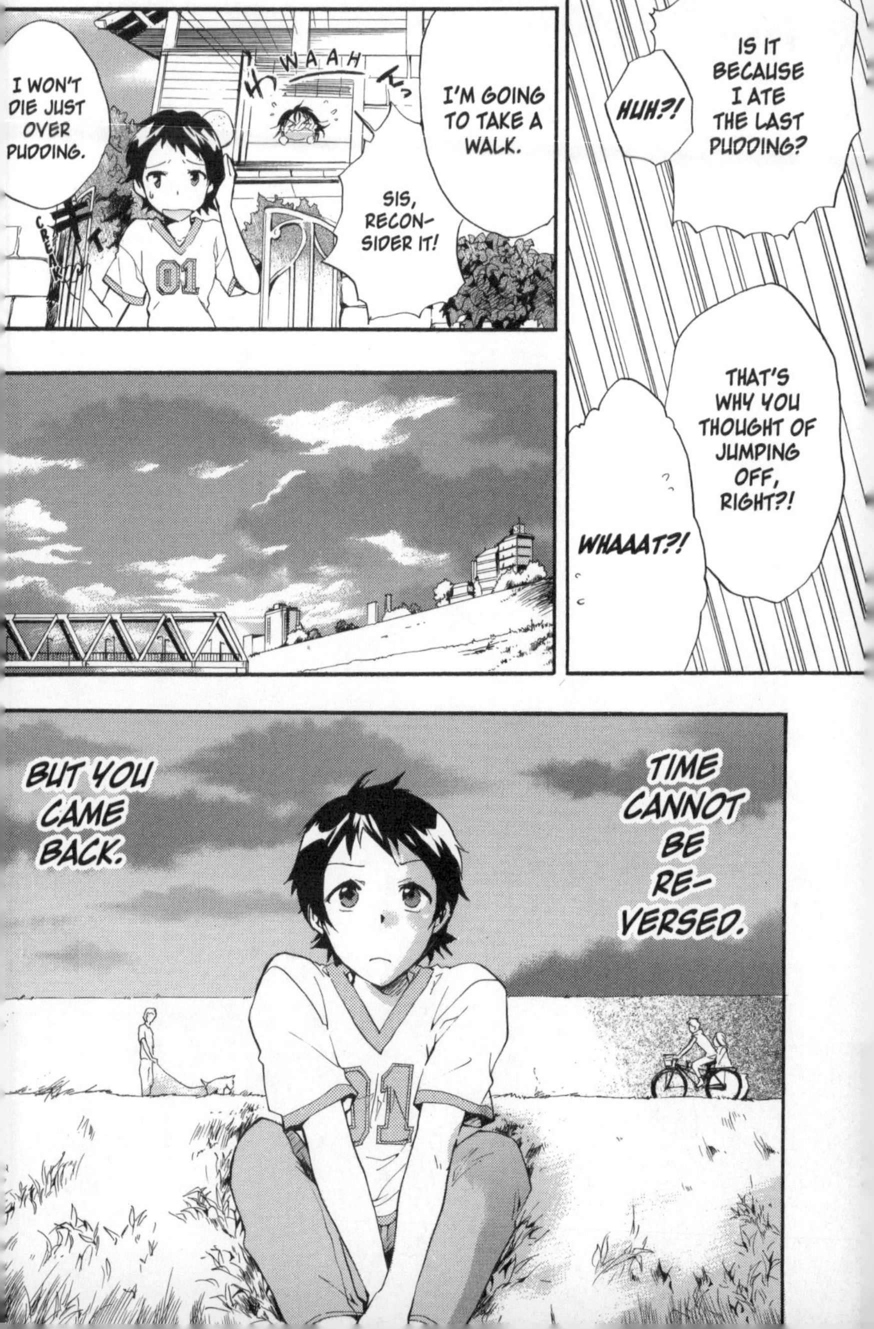
IS IT BECAUSE I ATE THE LAST PUDDING?
HUH?!
THAT'S WHY YOU THOUGHT OF JUMPING OFF, RIGHT?!
WHAAAT?!
I'M GOING TO TAKE A WALK.
WAAAH
SIS, RECON-SIDER IT!
I WON'T DIE JUST OVER PUDDING.
CREAK
TIME CANNOT BE RE-VERSED.
BUT YOU CAME BACK.

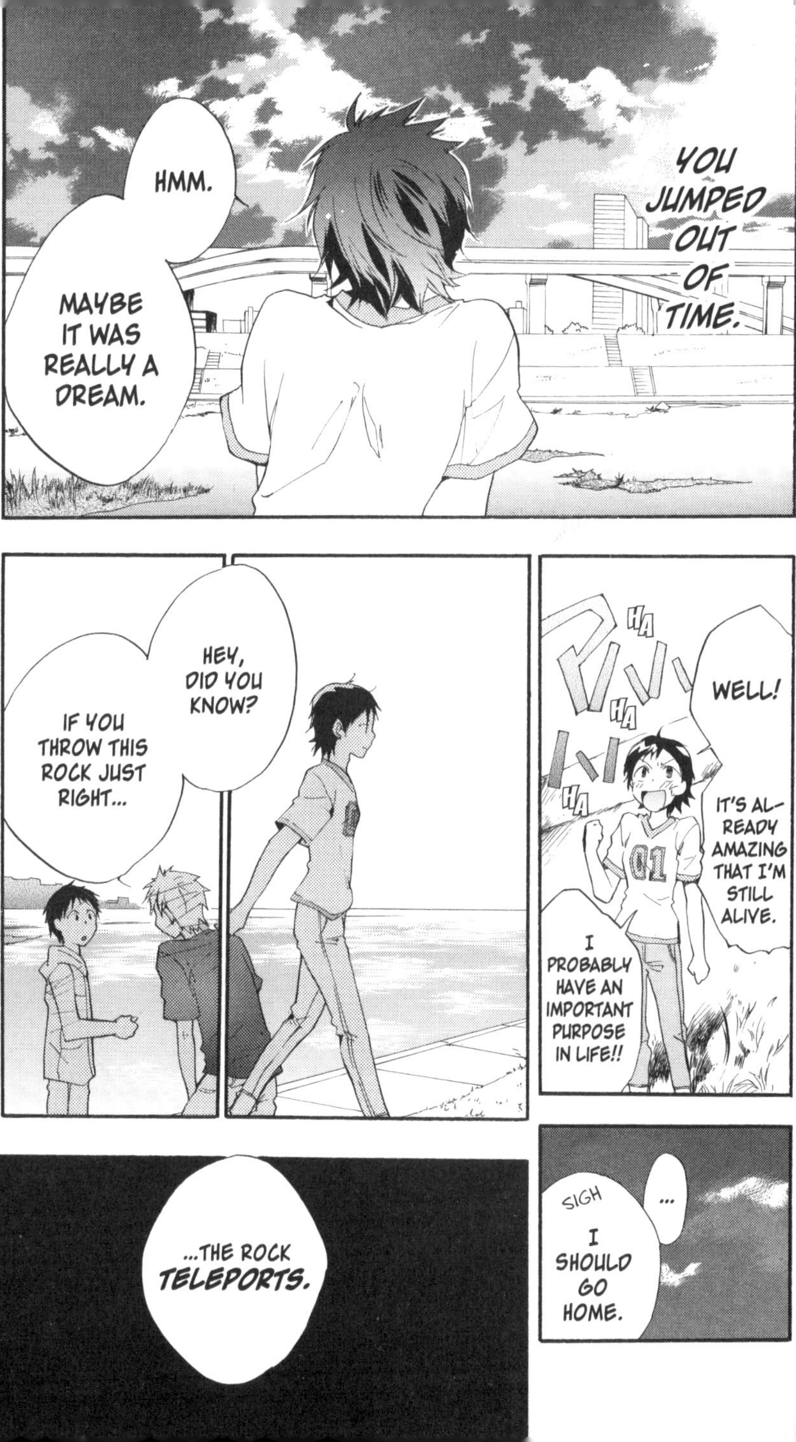
YOU JUMPED OUT OF TIME.
HMM.
MAYBE IT WAS REALLY A DREAM.
HA HA HA HA
WELL!
IT'S AL-READY AMAZING THAT I'M STILL ALIVE.
I PROBABLY HAVE AN IMPORTANT PURPOSE IN LIFE!!
HEY, DID YOU KNOW?
IF YOU THROW THIS ROCK JUST RIGHT...
...
SIGH
I SHOULD GO HOME.
...THE ROCK TELEPORTS.

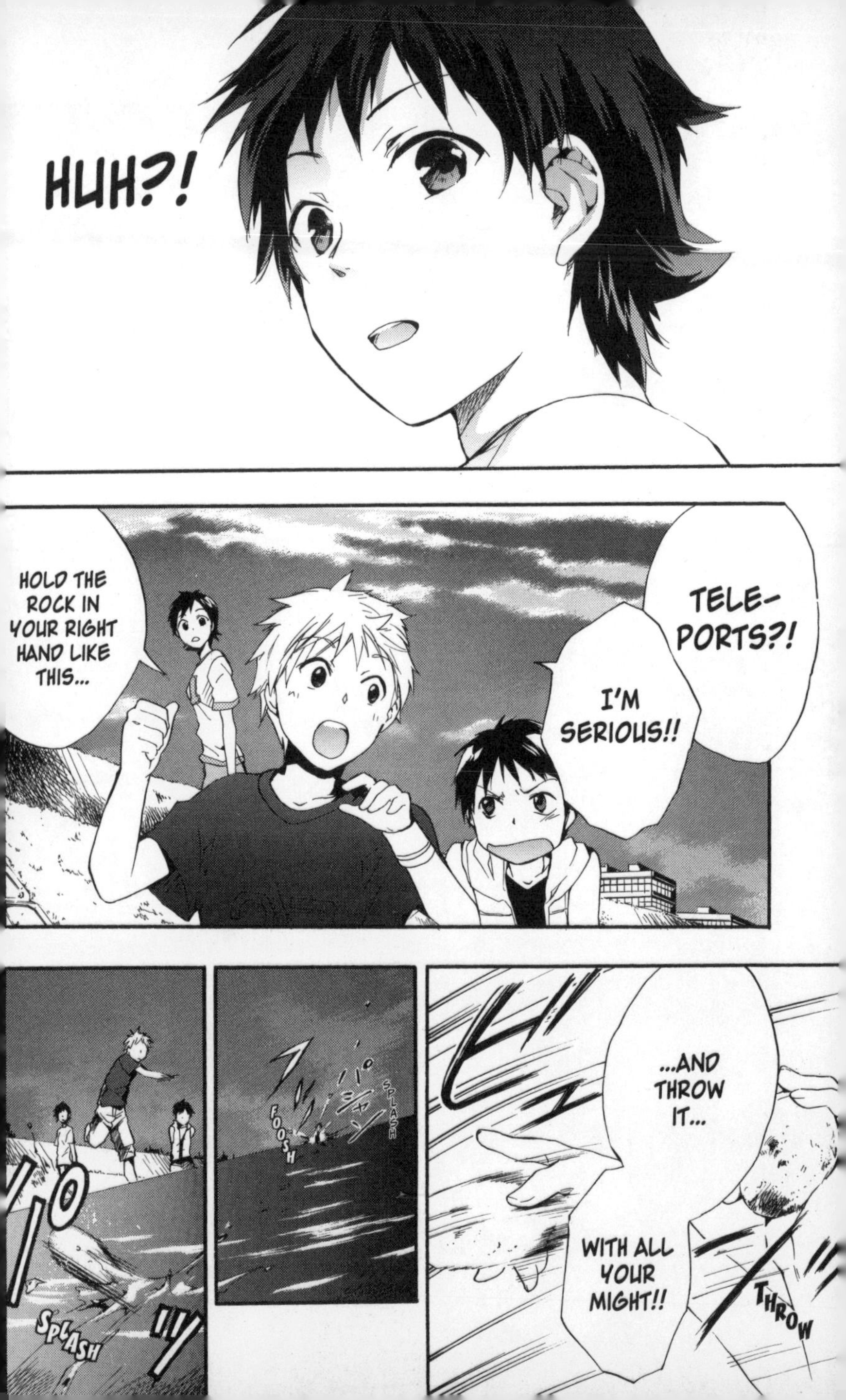

HUH?!
TELE-PORTS?!
I'M SERIOUS!!
HOLD THE ROCK IN YOUR RIGHT HAND LIKE THIS...
...AND THROW IT...
WITH ALL YOUR MIGHT!!
THROW
SPLASH
FOOSH
SPLASH

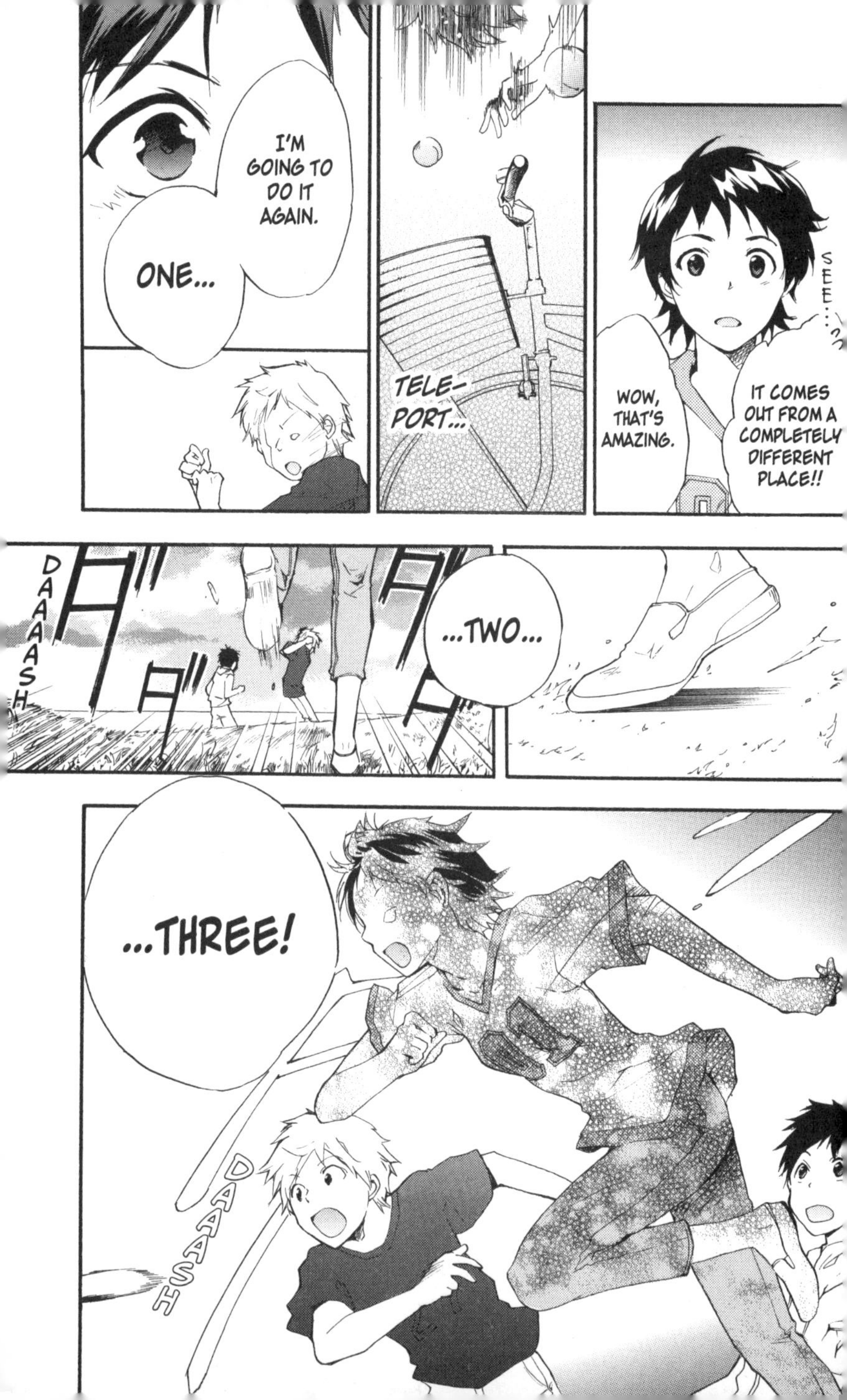
SEE...??
IT COMES OUT FROM A COMPLETELY DIFFERENT PLACE!!
WOW, THAT'S AMAZING.
TELE-PORT...
I'M GOING TO DO IT AGAIN.
ONE...
...TWO...
DAAAAASH
...THREE!
DAAAASH

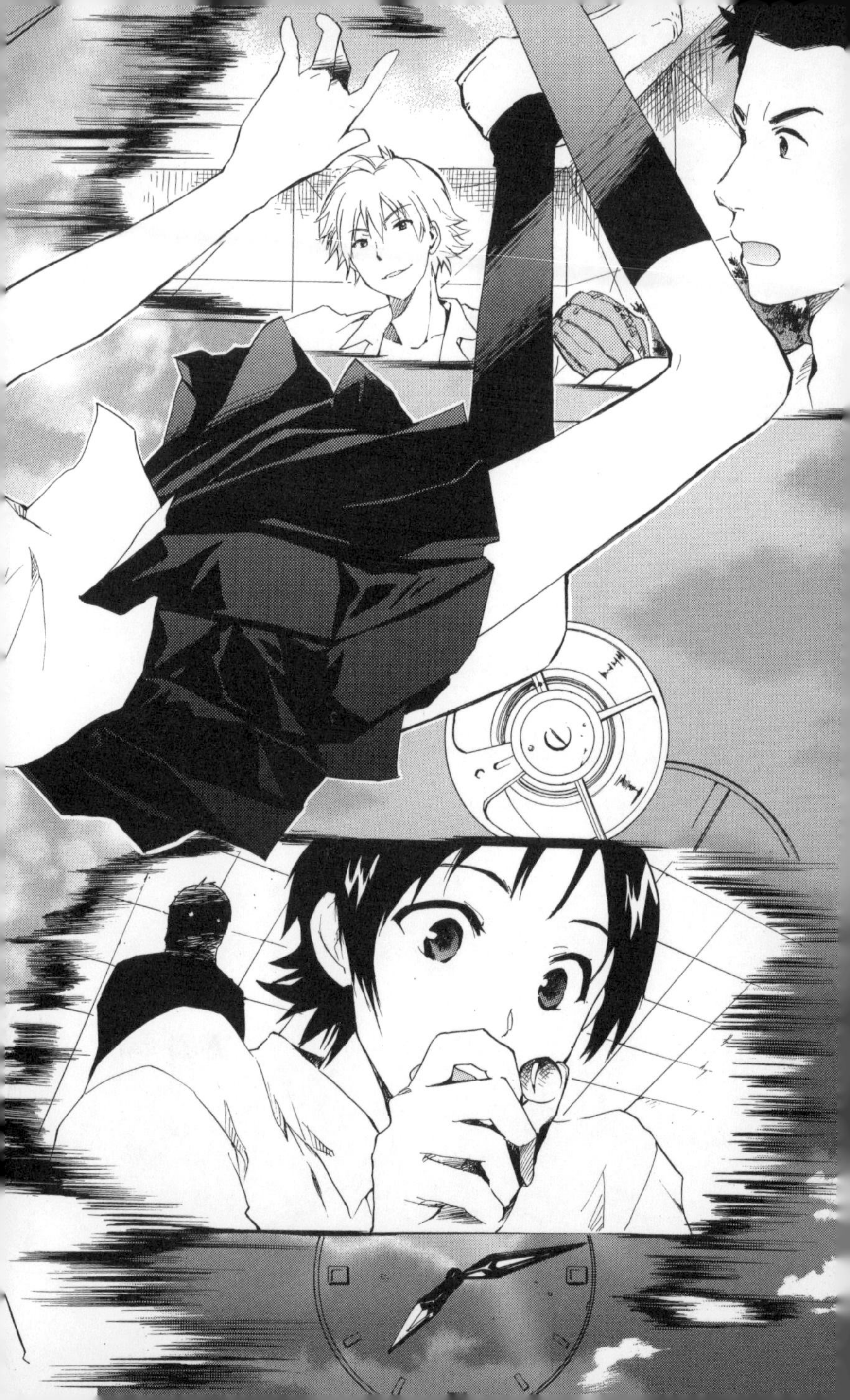

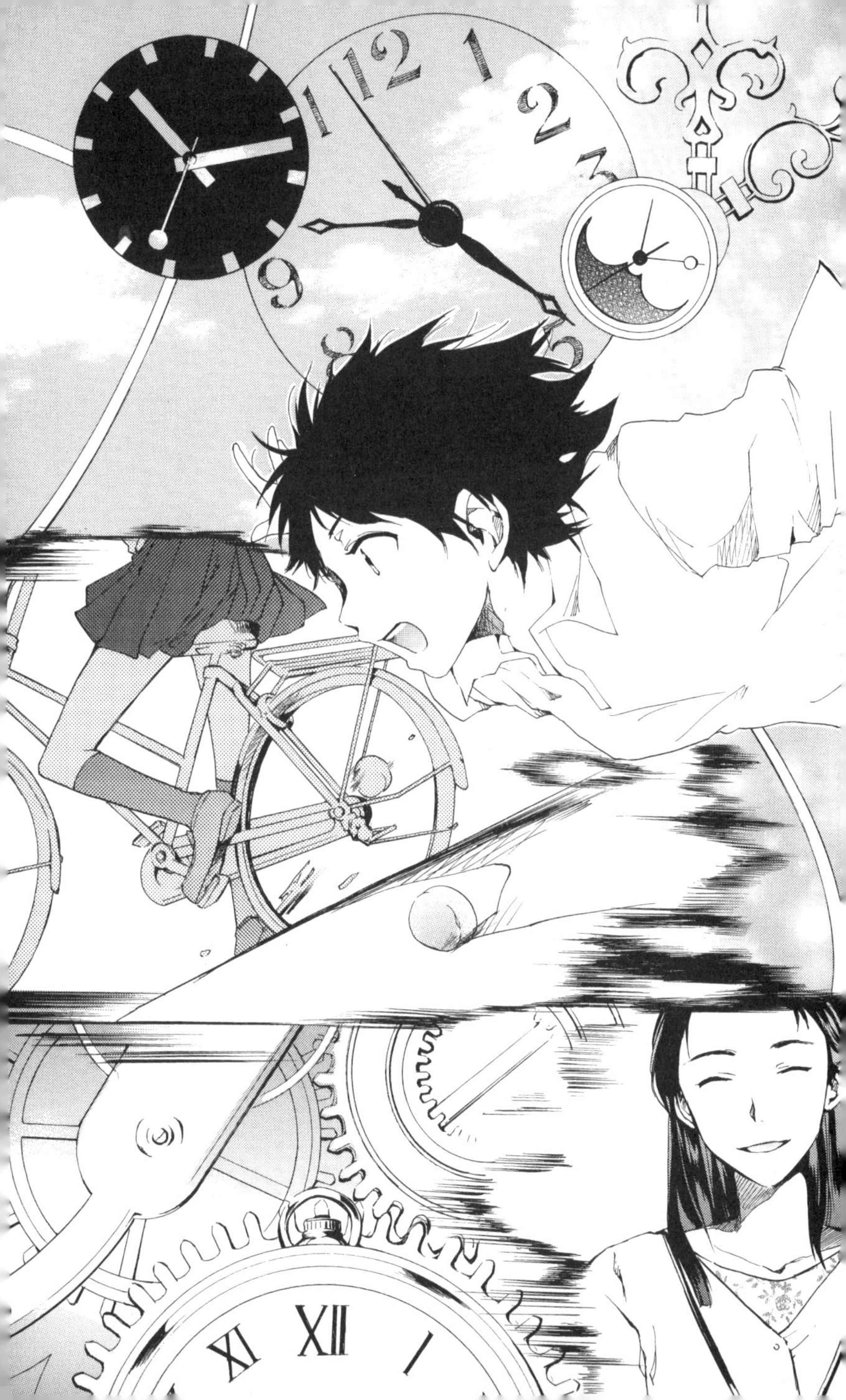

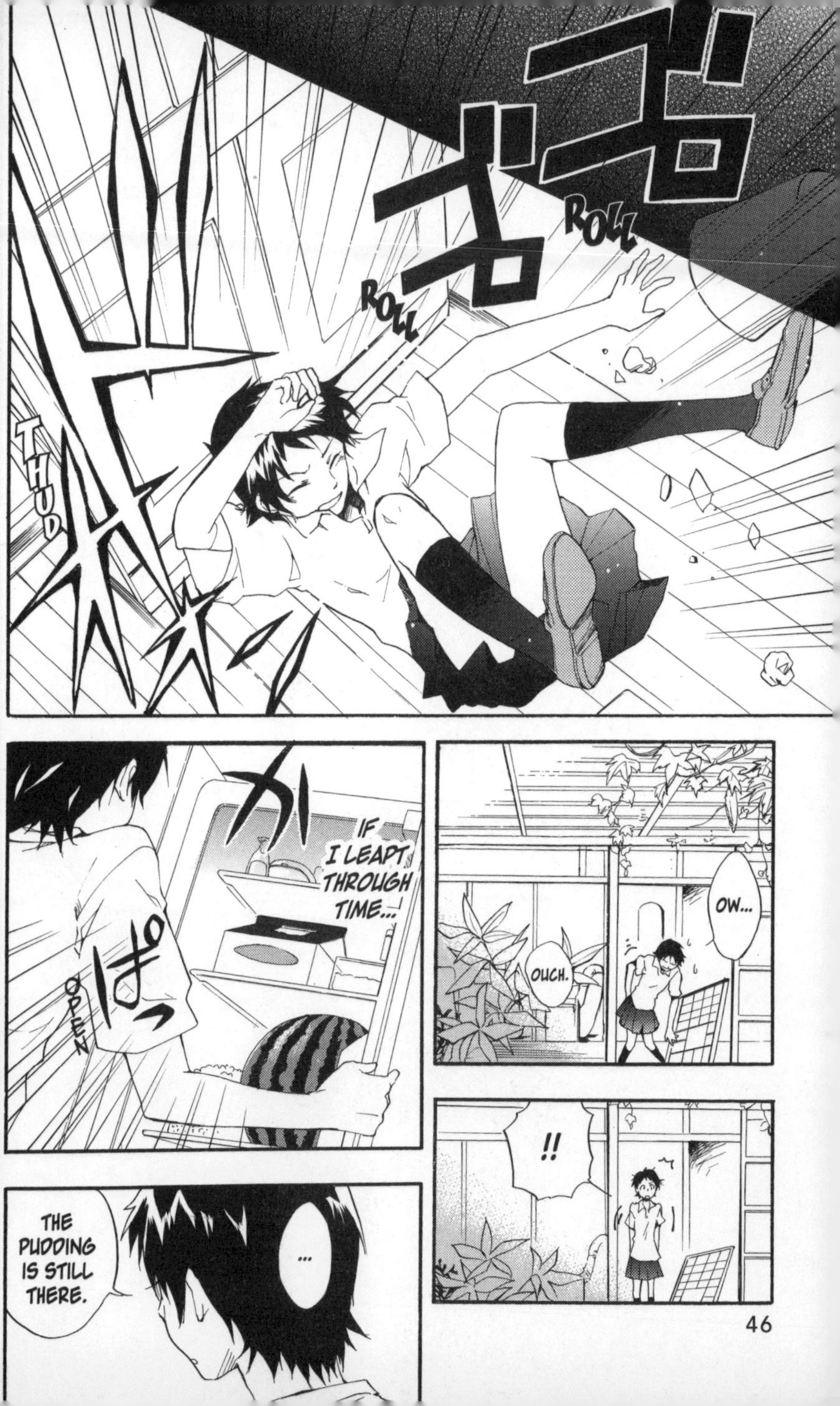
ROLL
ROLL
THUD
OW...
OUCH.
!!
IF I LEAPT THROUGH TIME...
OPEN
...
THE PUDDING IS STILL THERE.

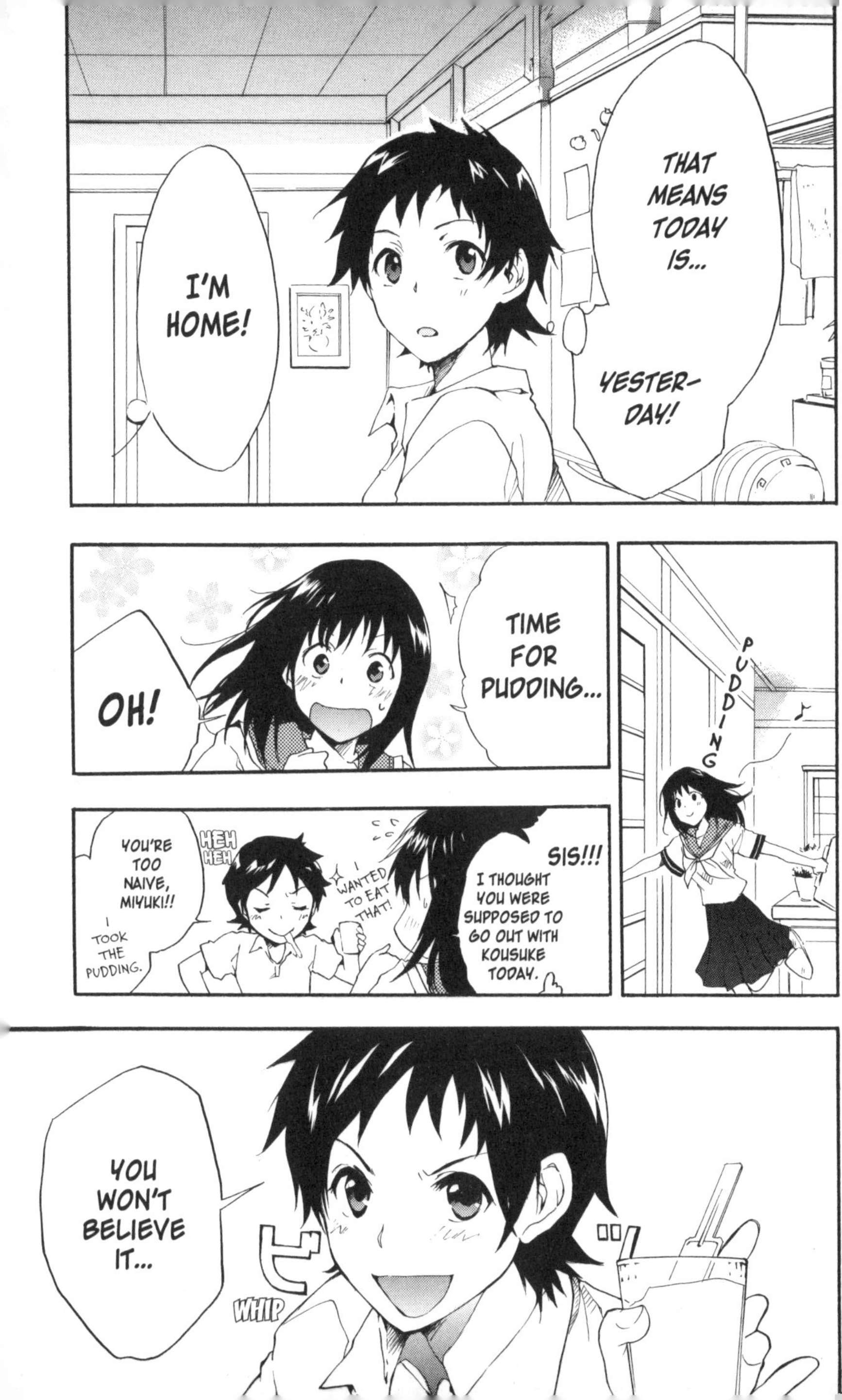
THAT MEANS TODAY IS...
YESTER-DAY!
I'M HOME!
PUDDING
TIME FOR PUDDING...
OH!
SIS!!!
I THOUGHT YOU WERE SUPPOSED TO GO OUT WITH KOUSUKE TODAY.
I WANTED TO EAT THAT!
HEH HEH
YOU'RE TOO NAIVE, MIYUKI!!
I TOOK THE PUDDING.
YOU WON'T BELIEVE IT...
WHIP

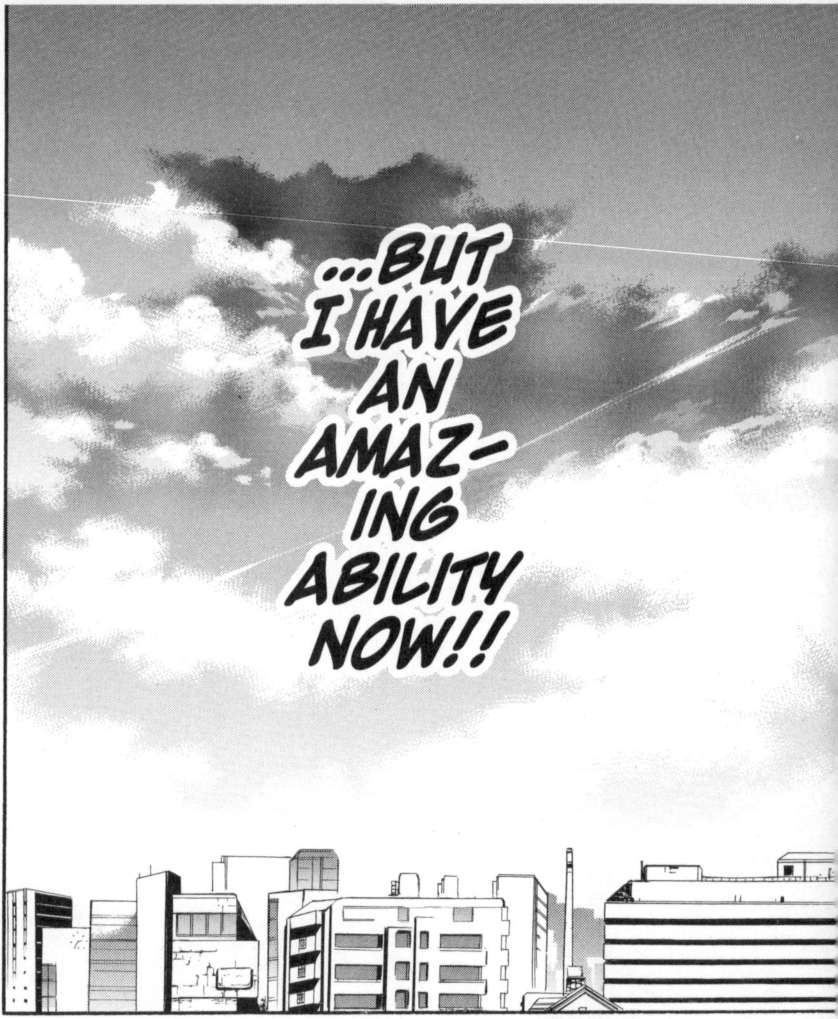
...BUT I HAVE AN AMAZ-ING ABILITY NOW!!

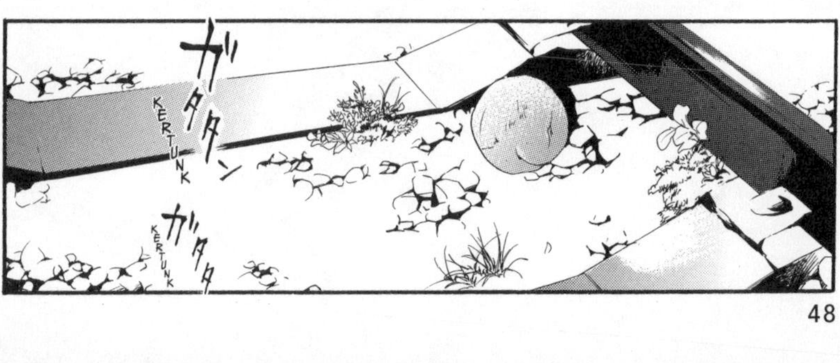
ガタタン
KERTUNK
ガタタ
KERTUNK

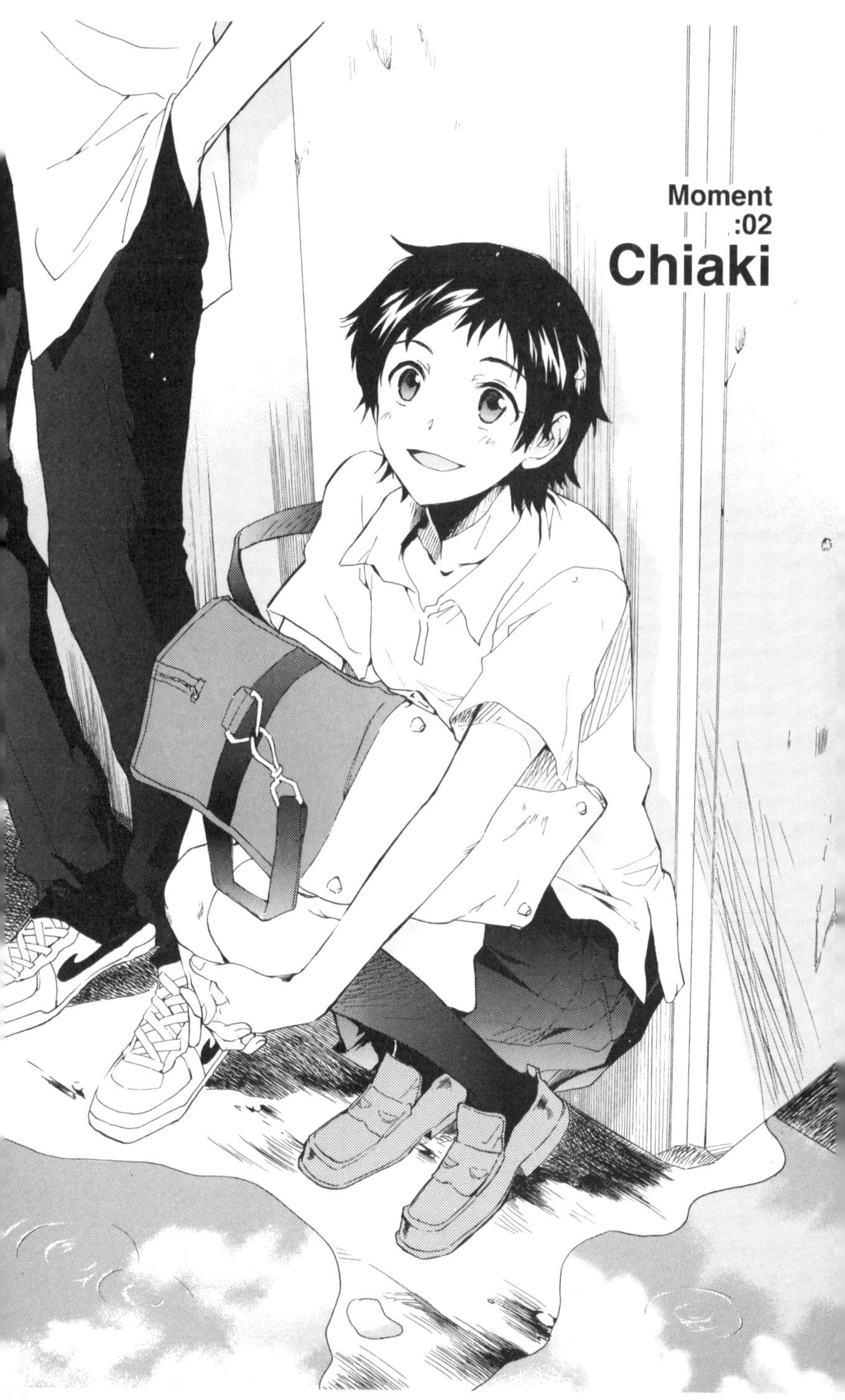
Moment
:02
Chiaki

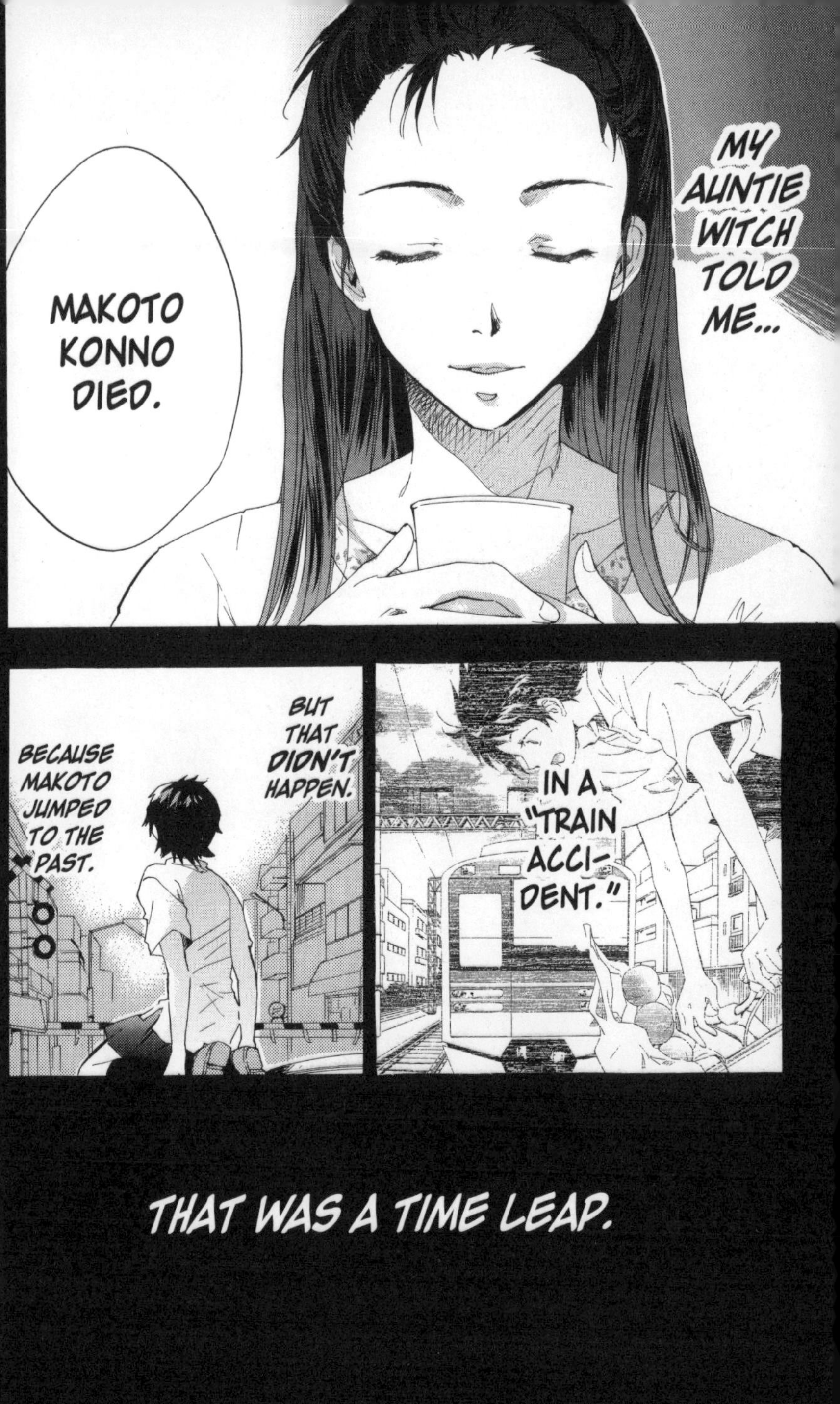
MY AUNTIE WITCH TOLD ME...
MAKOTO KONNO DIED.
IN A "TRAIN ACCI-DENT."
BUT THAT DIDN'T HAPPEN.
BECAUSE MAKOTO JUMPED TO THE PAST.
THAT WAS A TIME LEAP.

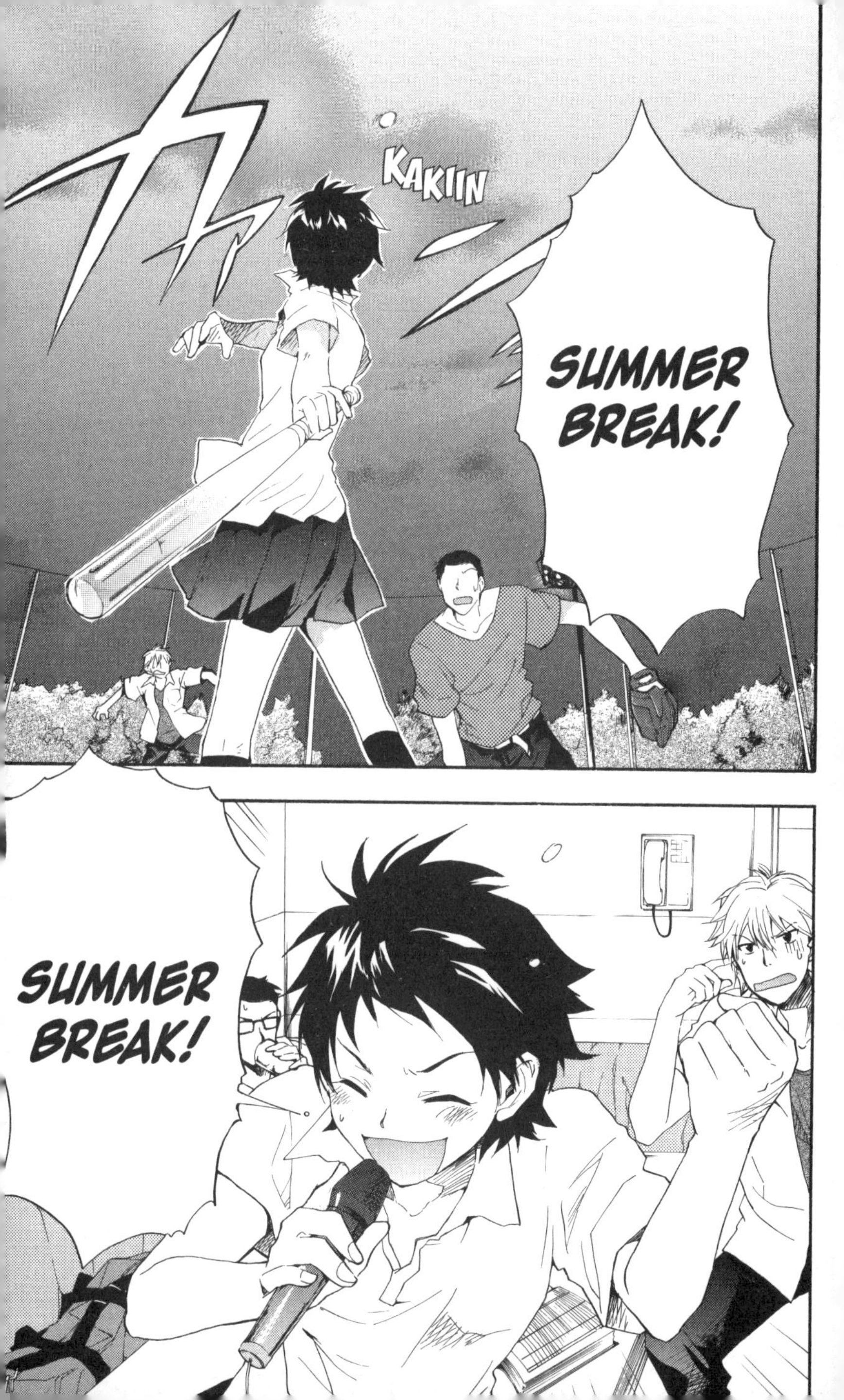
KAKIIN
SUMMER BREAK!
SUMMER BREAK!

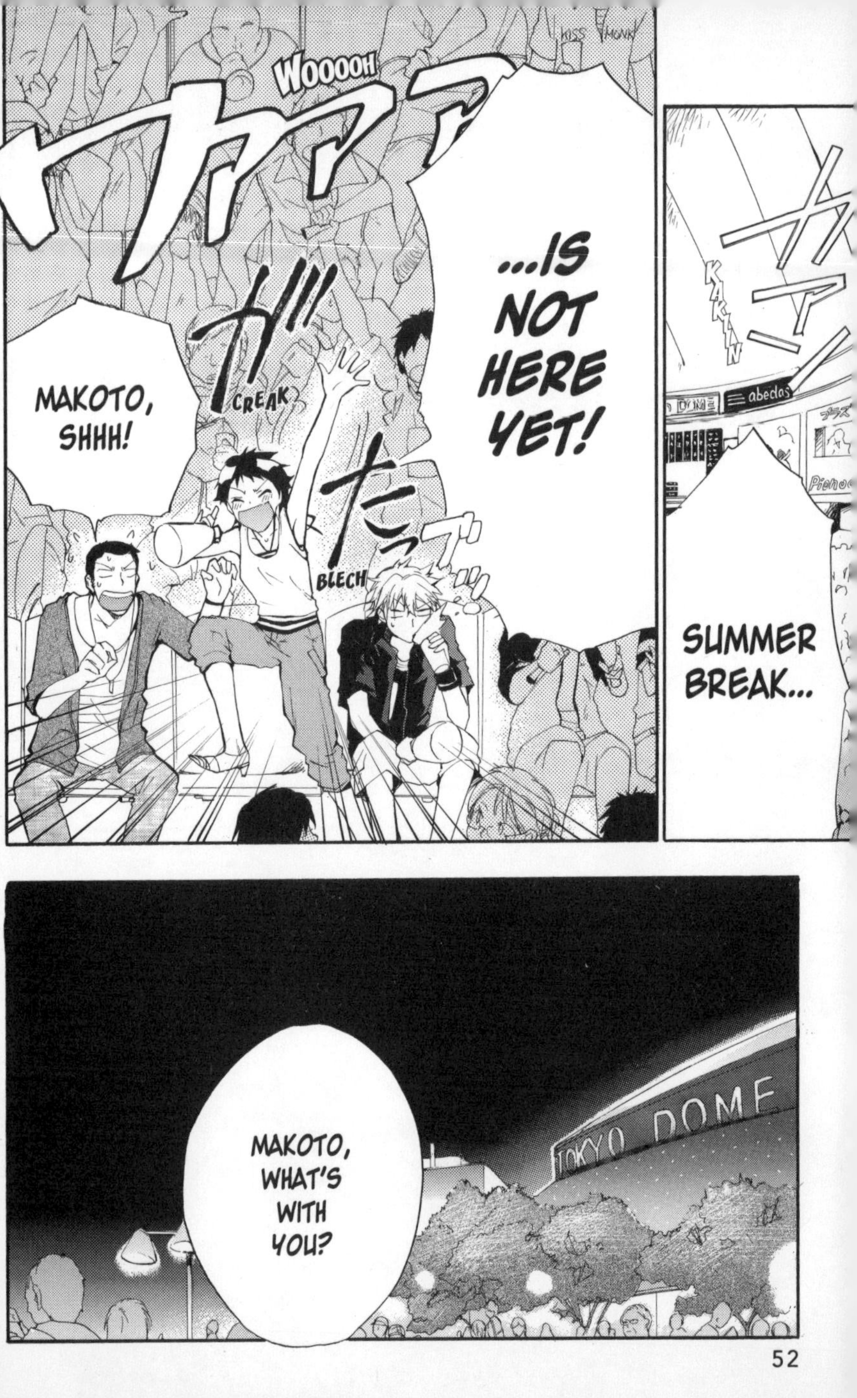
KAKIN
abedas
SUMMER BREAK...
KISS MONK
...IS NOT HERE YET!
WOOOOH
CREAK
MAKOTO, SHHH!
BLECH
TOKYO DOME
MAKOTO, WHAT'S WITH YOU?

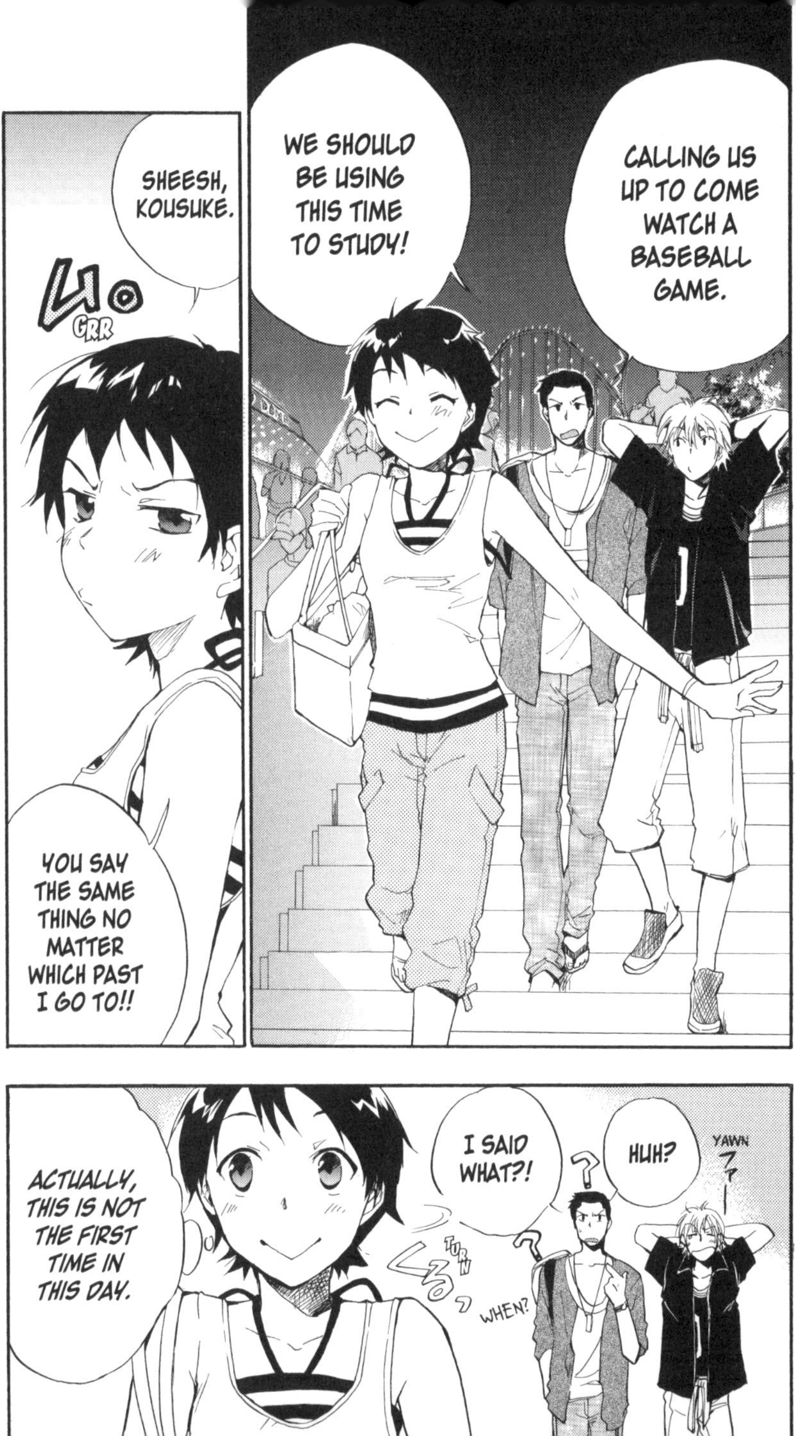
CALLING US UP TO COME WATCH A BASEBALL GAME.
WE SHOULD BE USING THIS TIME TO STUDY!
SHEESH, KOUSUKE.
GRR
YOU SAY THE SAME THING NO MATTER WHICH PAST I GO TO!!
YAWN
HUH?
I SAID WHAT?!
WHEN?
TURN
ACTUALLY, THIS IS NOT THE FIRST TIME IN THIS DAY.

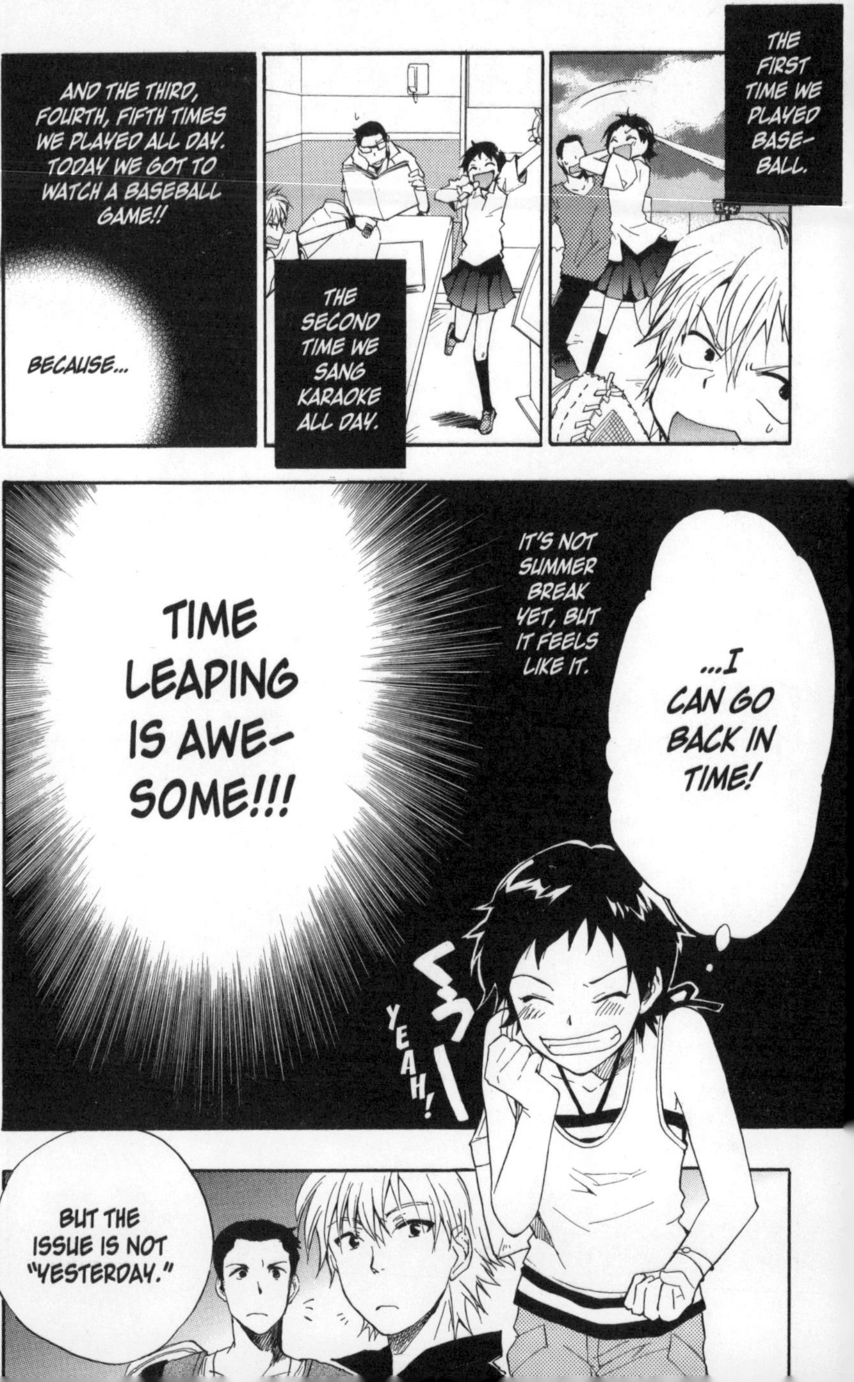
THE FIRST TIME WE PLAYED BASE-BALL.
THE SECOND TIME WE SANG KARAOKE ALL DAY.
AND THE THIRD, FOURTH, FIFTH TIMES WE PLAYED ALL DAY. TODAY WE GOT TO WATCH A BASEBALL GAME!!
BECAUSE...
...I CAN GO BACK IN TIME!
IT'S NOT SUMMER BREAK YET, BUT IT FEELS LIKE IT.
TIME LEAPING IS AWE-SOME!!!
YEAH!
BUT THE ISSUE IS NOT "YESTERDAY."

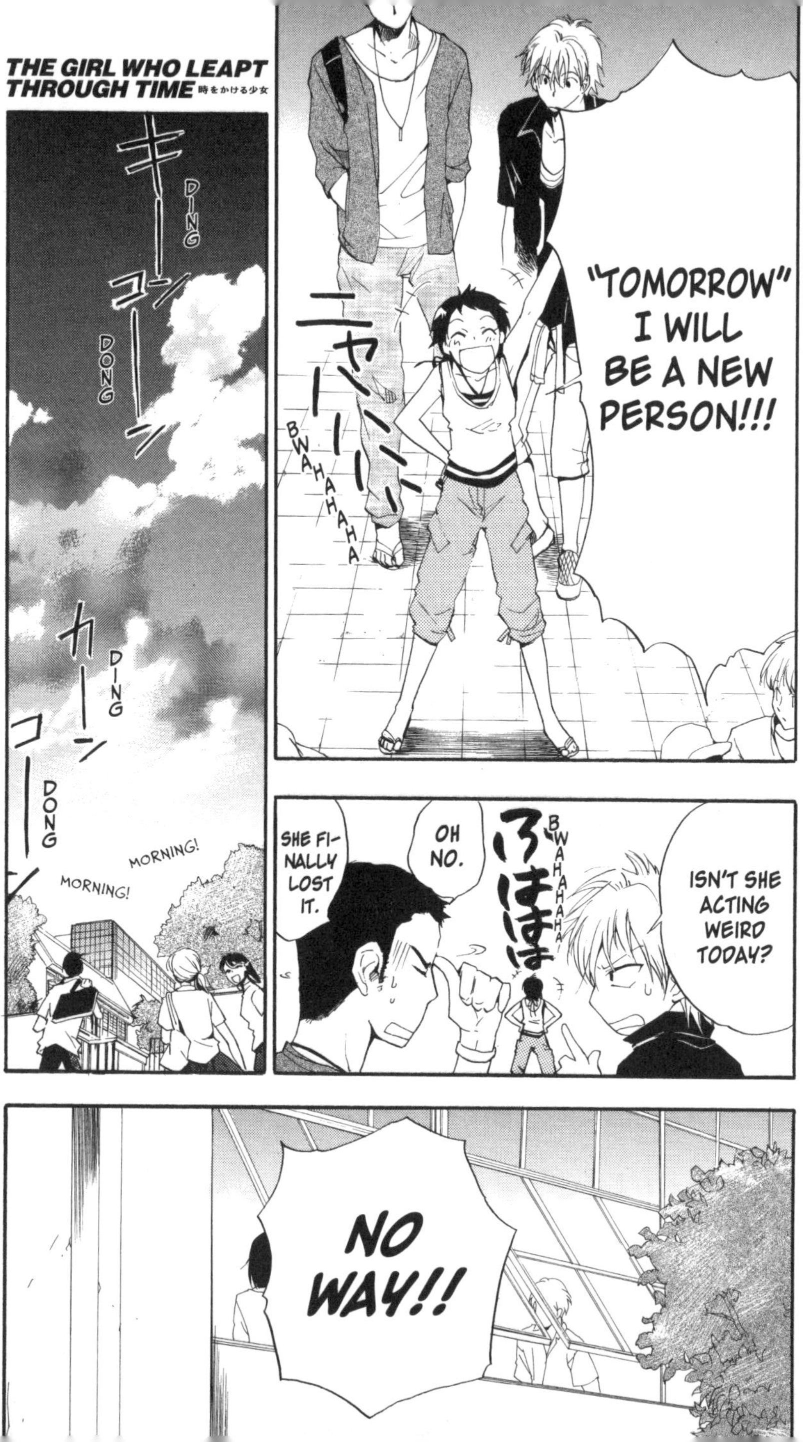
"TOMORROW" I WILL BE A NEW PERSON!!!
BWAHAHAHA
ISN'T SHE ACTING WEIRD TODAY?
BWAHAHAHA
OH NO.
SHE FINALLY LOST IT.
DING
DONG
DING
DONG
MORNING!
MORNING!
NO WAY!!

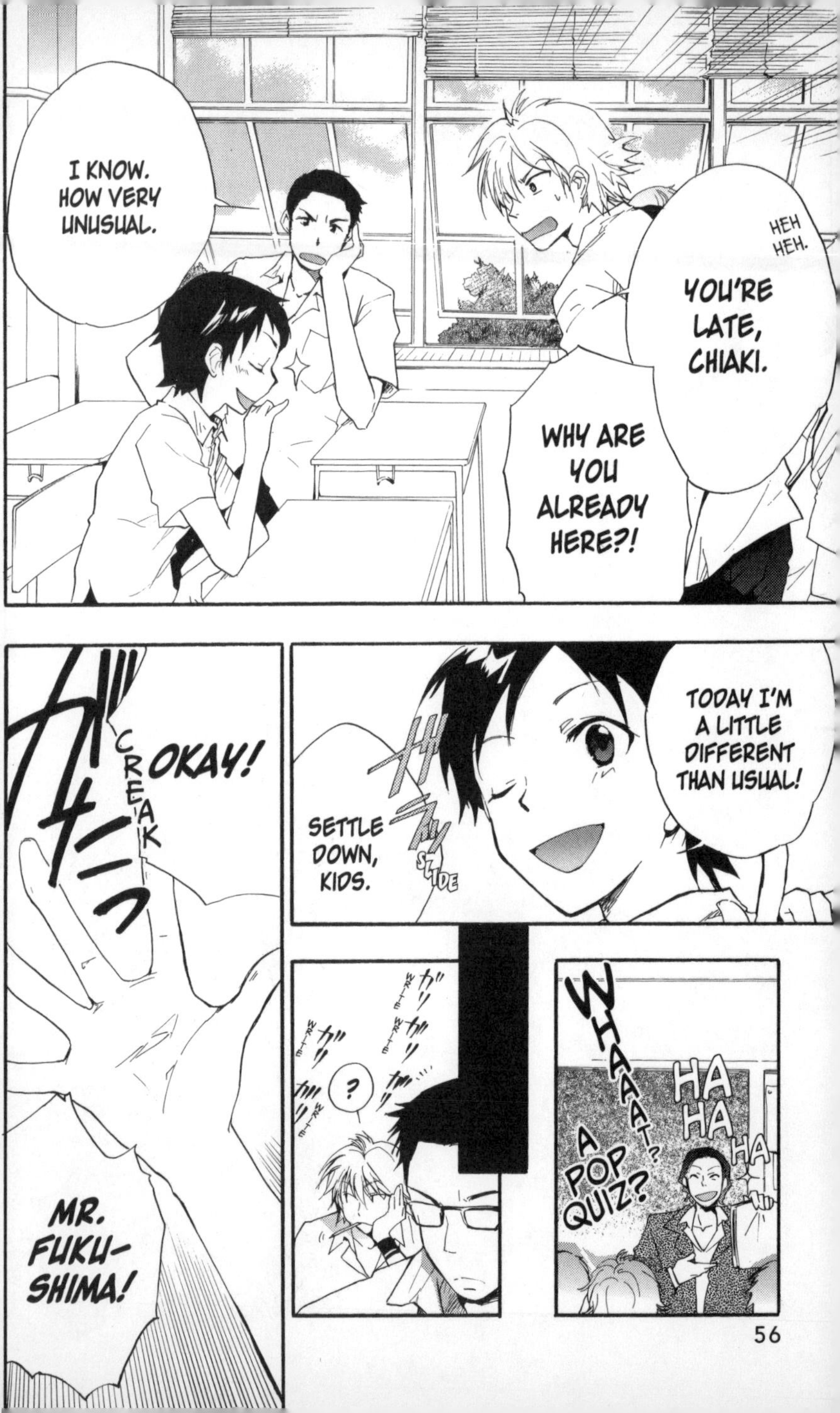
HEH HEH.
YOU'RE LATE, CHIAKI.
WHY ARE YOU ALREADY HERE?!
I KNOW. HOW VERY UNUSUAL.
TODAY I'M A LITTLE DIFFERENT THAN USUAL!
SETTLE DOWN, KIDS.
SLIDE
WHAAAAT?!
A POP QUIZ?
HA HA HA HA
WRITE WRITE
WRITE
WRITE
?
CREAK
OKAY!
MR. FUKU-SHIMA!

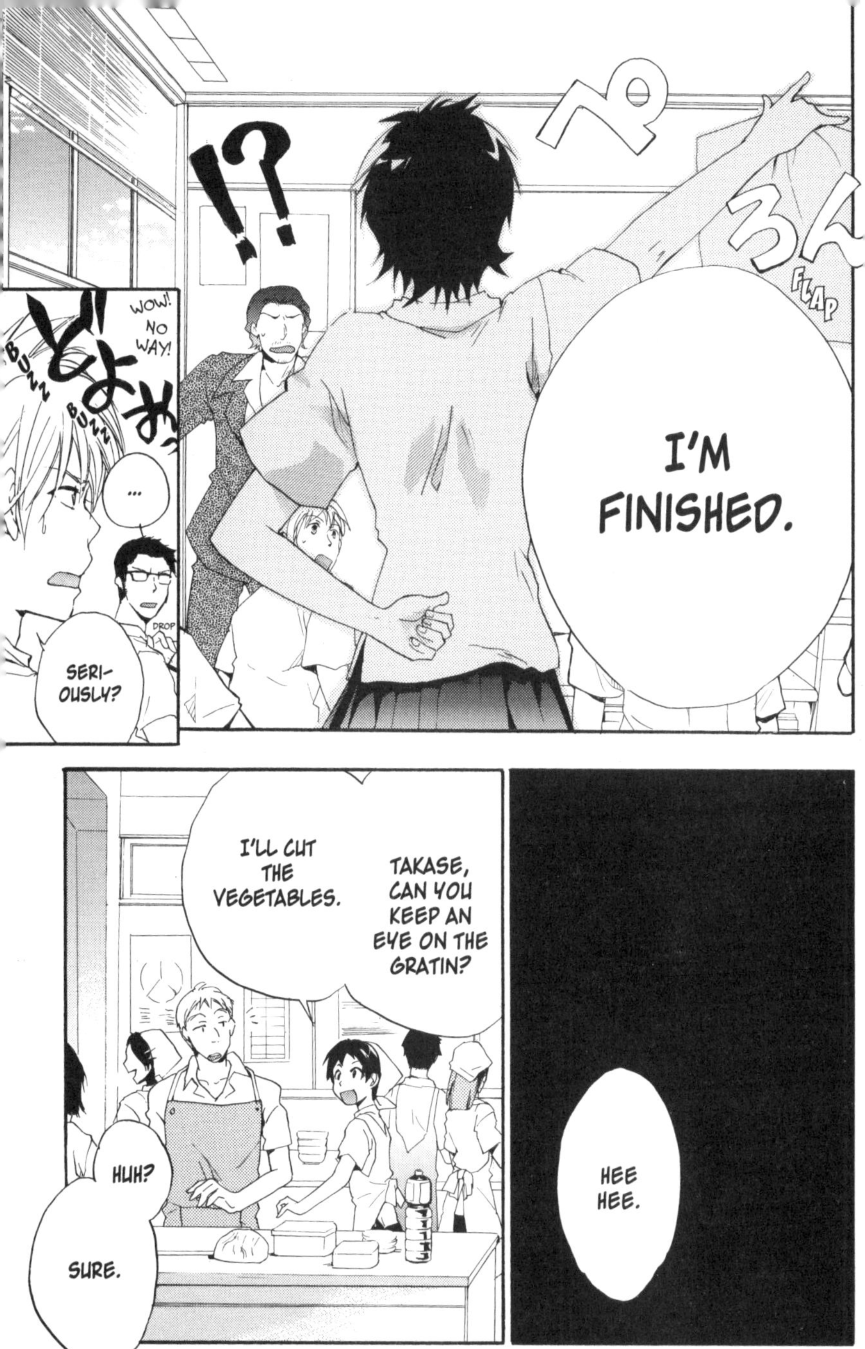
ぺろん
FLAP
!?
I'M FINISHED.
どよめっ
BUZZ BUZZ
WOW! NO WAY!
...
DROP
SERIOUSLY?
HEE HEE.
TAKASE, CAN YOU KEEP AN EYE ON THE GRATIN?
I'LL CUT THE VEGETABLES.
HUH?
SURE.

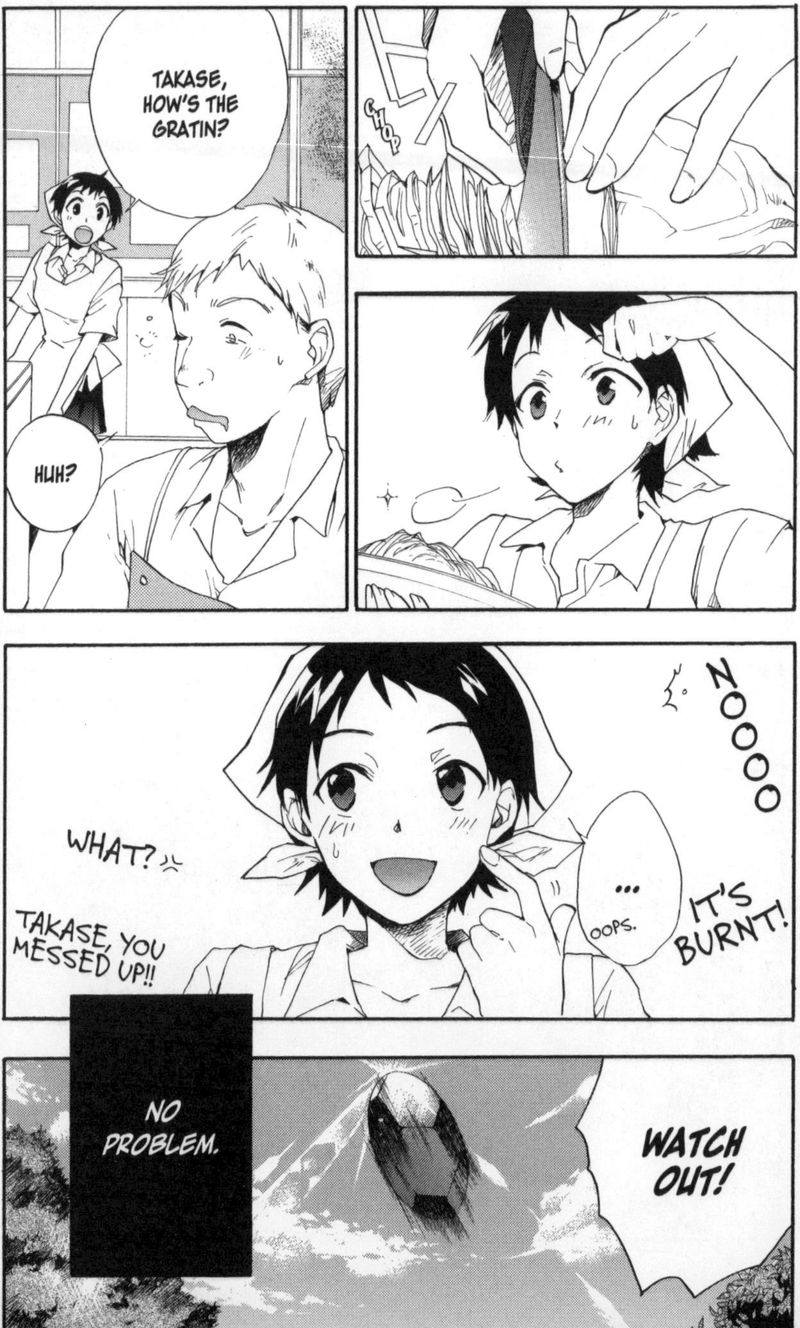
CHOP
TAKASE, HOW'S THE GRATIN?
HUH?
NOOOO
IT'S BURNT!
... OOPS.
WHAT?
TAKASE, YOU MESSED UP!!
WATCH OUT!
NO PROBLEM.

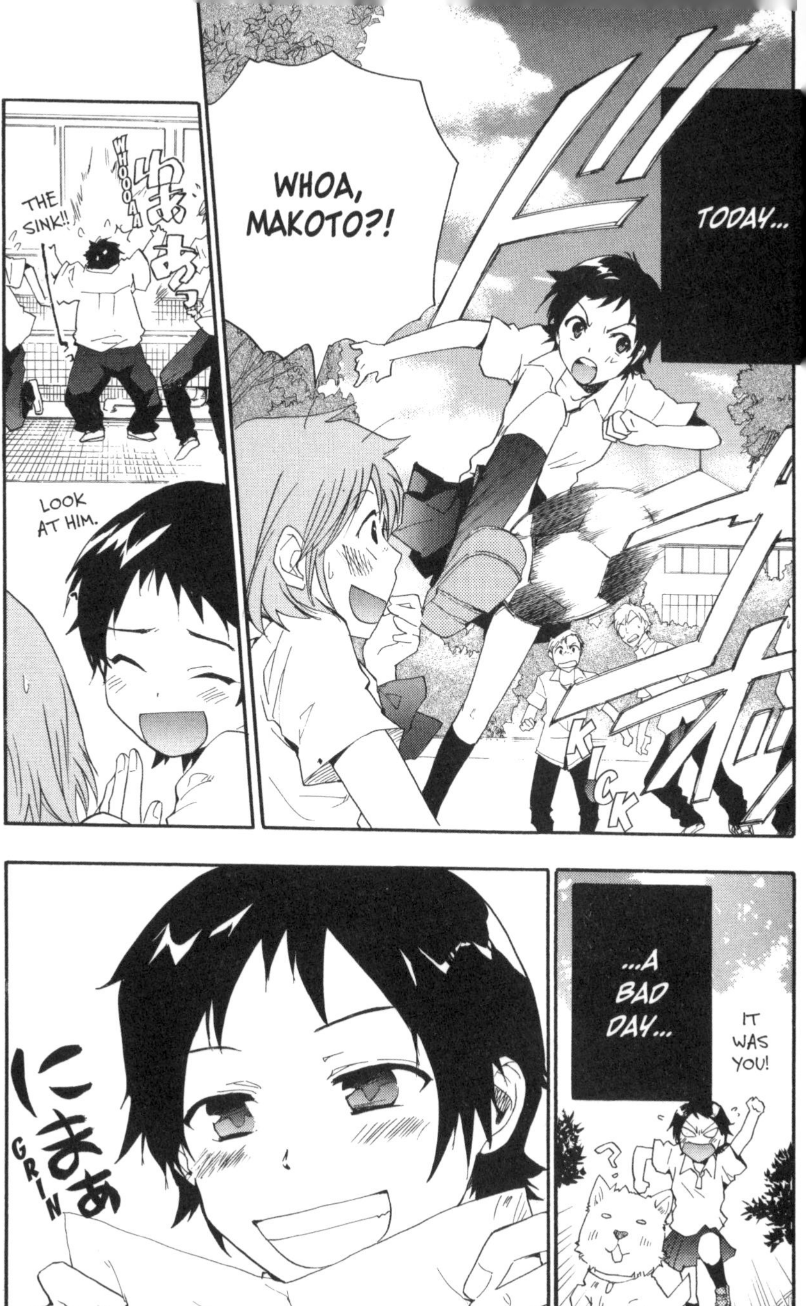
TODAY...
WHOA, MAKOTO?!
KICK
WHOOOAA
THE SINK!!
LOOK AT HIM.
...A BAD DAY...
IT WAS YOU!
にまぁ
GRIN

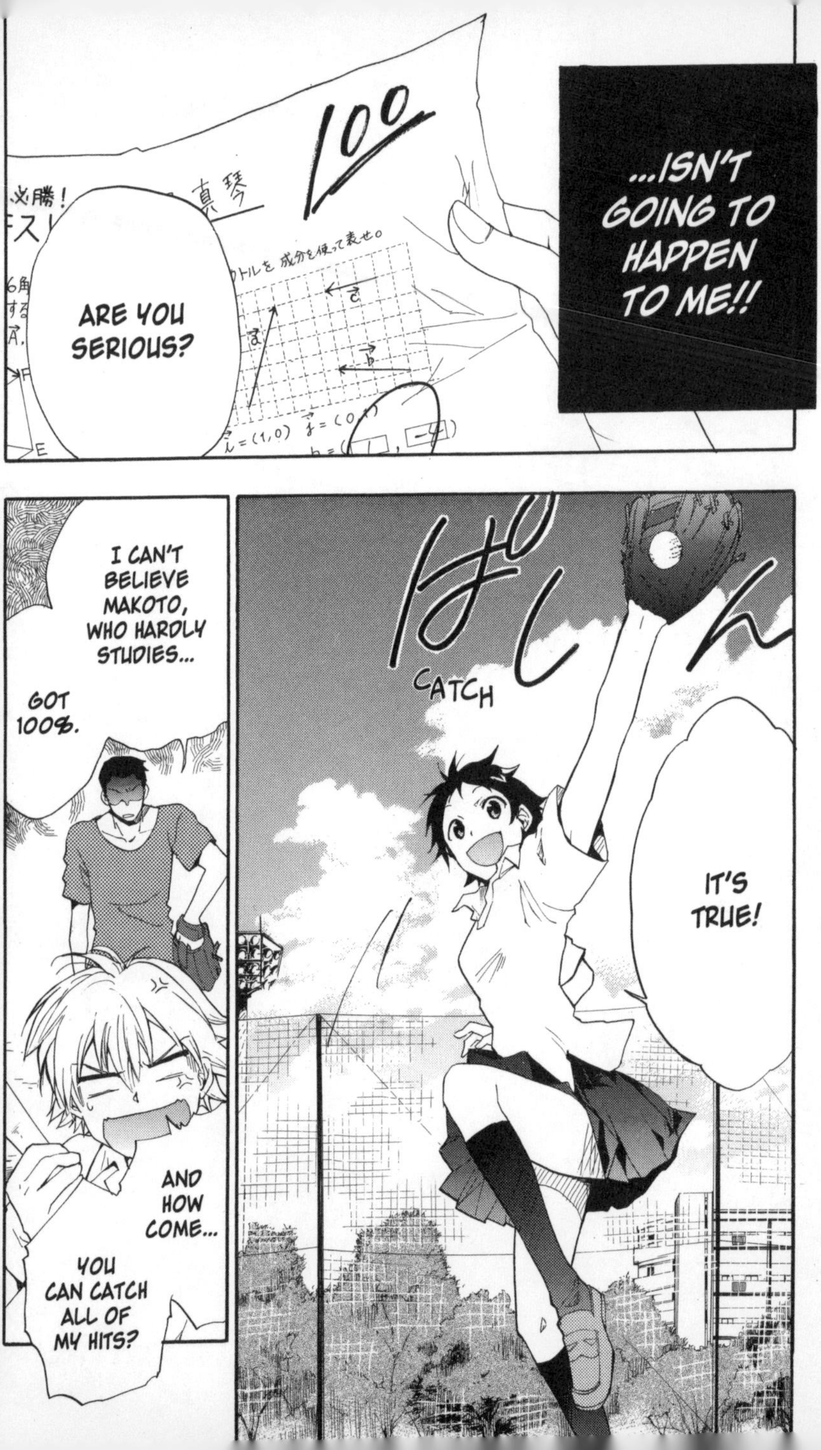

...ISN'T GOING TO HAPPEN TO ME!!
100
ARE YOU SERIOUS?
ぱしん
CATCH
IT'S TRUE!
I CAN'T BELIEVE MAKOTO, WHO HARDLY STUDIES...
GOT 100%.
AND HOW COME...
YOU CAN CATCH ALL OF MY HITS?

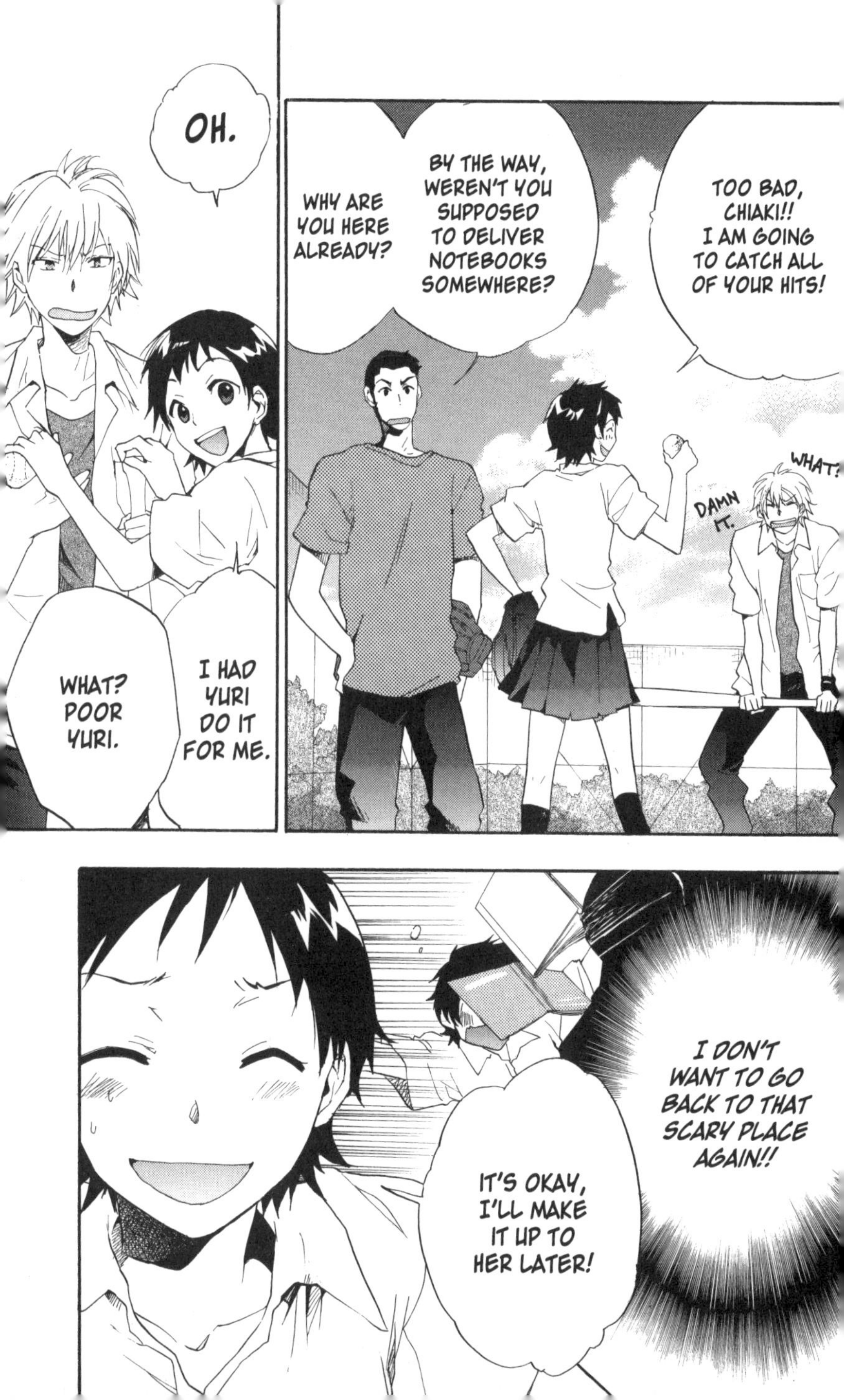
TOO BAD, CHIAKI!! I AM GOING TO CATCH ALL OF YOUR HITS!
WHAT?
DAMN IT.
BY THE WAY, WEREN'T YOU SUPPOSED TO DELIVER NOTEBOOKS SOMEWHERE?
WHY ARE YOU HERE ALREADY?
OH.
I HAD YURI DO IT FOR ME.
WHAT? POOR YURI.
I DON'T WANT TO GO BACK TO THAT SCARY PLACE AGAIN!!
IT'S OKAY, I'LL MAKE IT UP TO HER LATER!

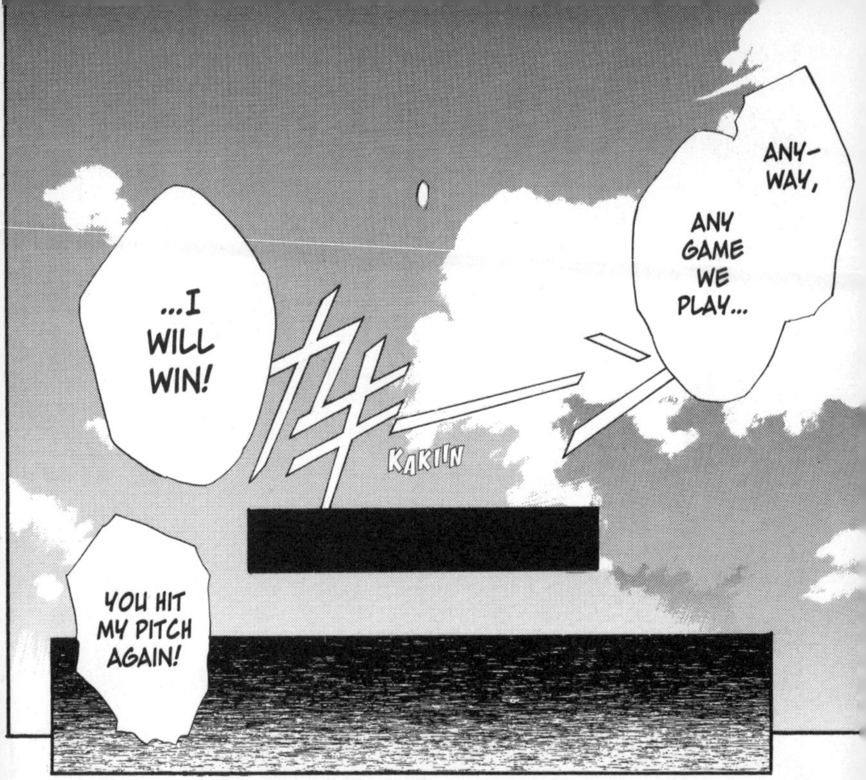
ANY-WAY,
ANY GAME WE PLAY...
...I WILL WIN!
KAKIIN
YOU HIT MY PITCH AGAIN!
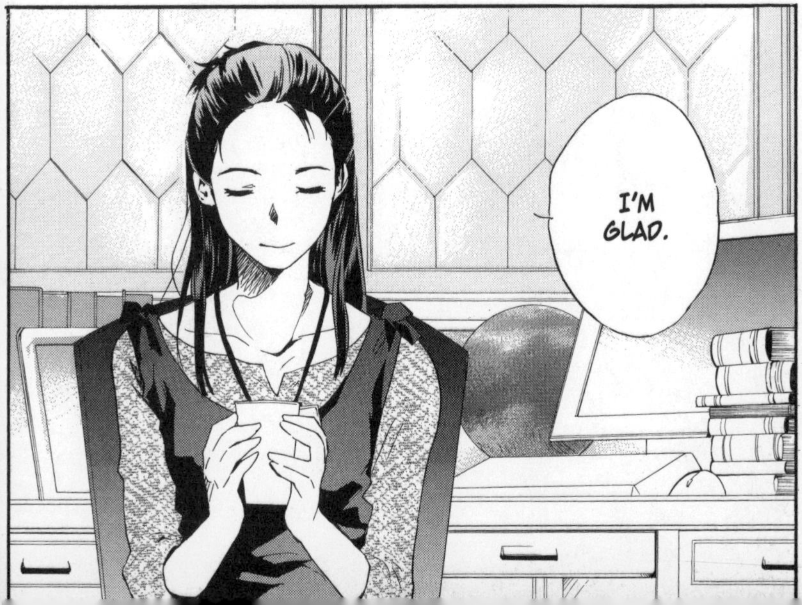
I'M GLAD.

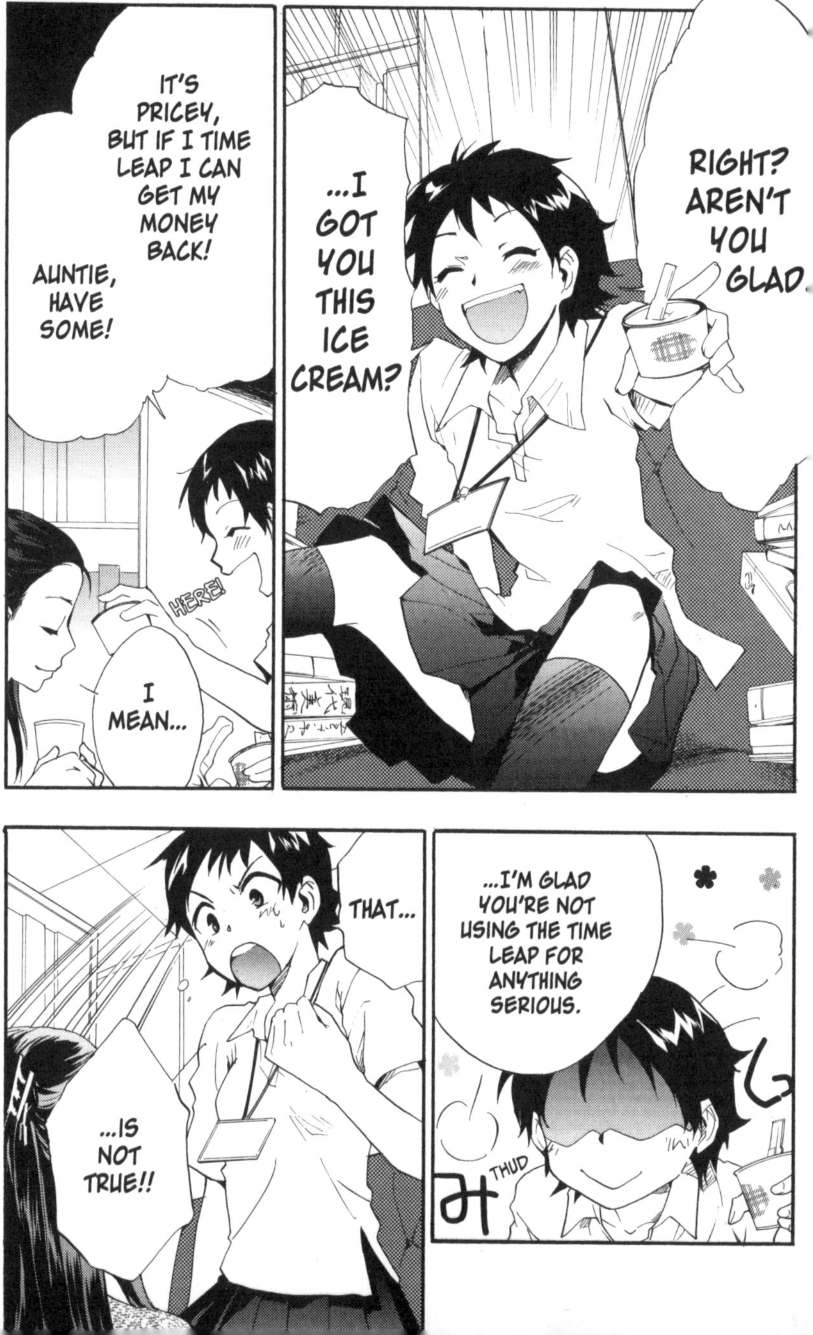
RIGHT? AREN'T YOU GLAD.
...I GOT YOU THIS ICE CREAM?
IT'S PRICEY, BUT IF I TIME LEAP I CAN GET MY MONEY BACK!
AUNTIE, HAVE SOME!
HERE!
I MEAN...
...I'M GLAD YOU'RE NOT USING THE TIME LEAP FOR ANYTHING SERIOUS.
THUD
み
THAT...
...IS NOT TRUE!!

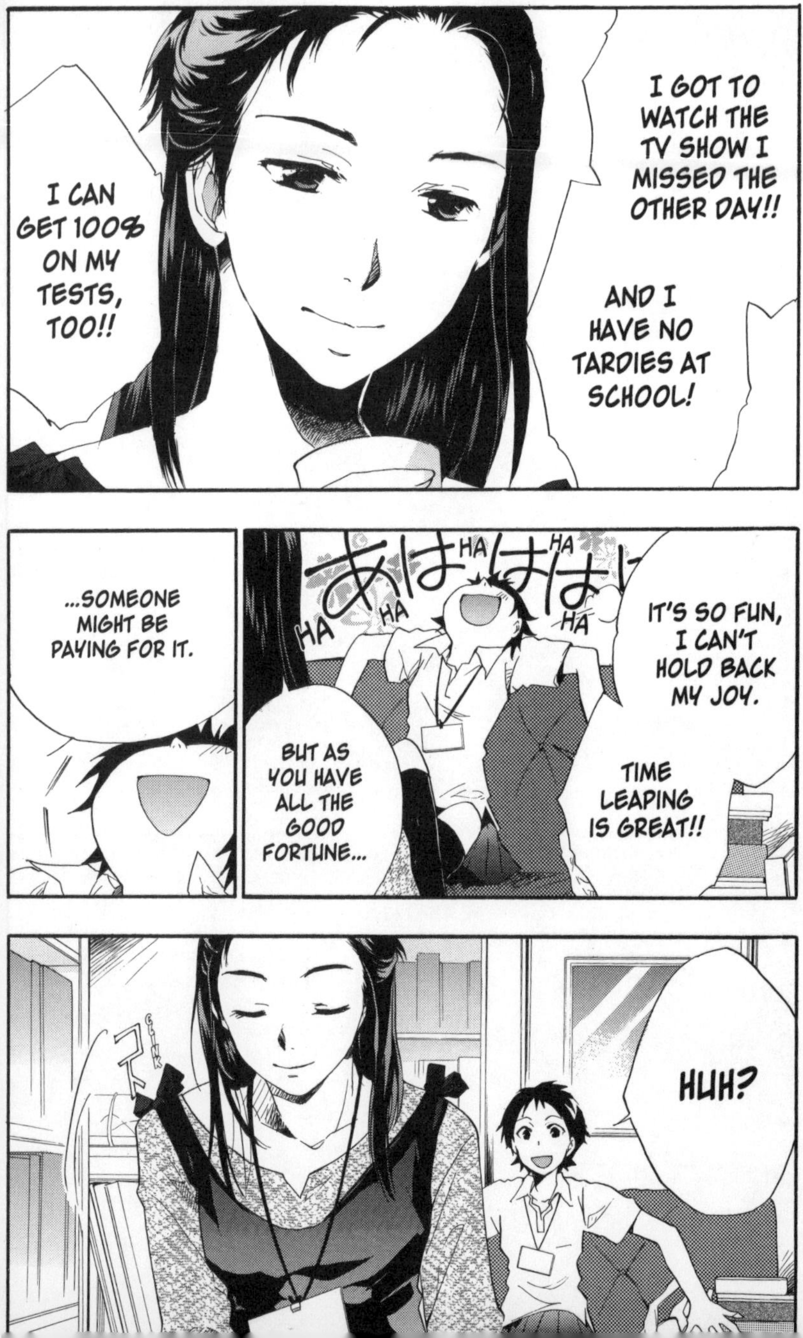
I GOT TO WATCH THE TV SHOW I MISSED THE OTHER DAY!!
AND I HAVE NO TARDIES AT SCHOOL!
I CAN GET 100% ON MY TESTS, TOO!!
あははは
HA HA HA HA HA
IT'S SO FUN, I CAN'T HOLD BACK MY JOY.
TIME LEAPING IS GREAT!!
BUT AS YOU HAVE ALL THE GOOD FORTUNE...
...SOMEONE MIGHT BE PAYING FOR IT.
HUH?
コト
CLINK

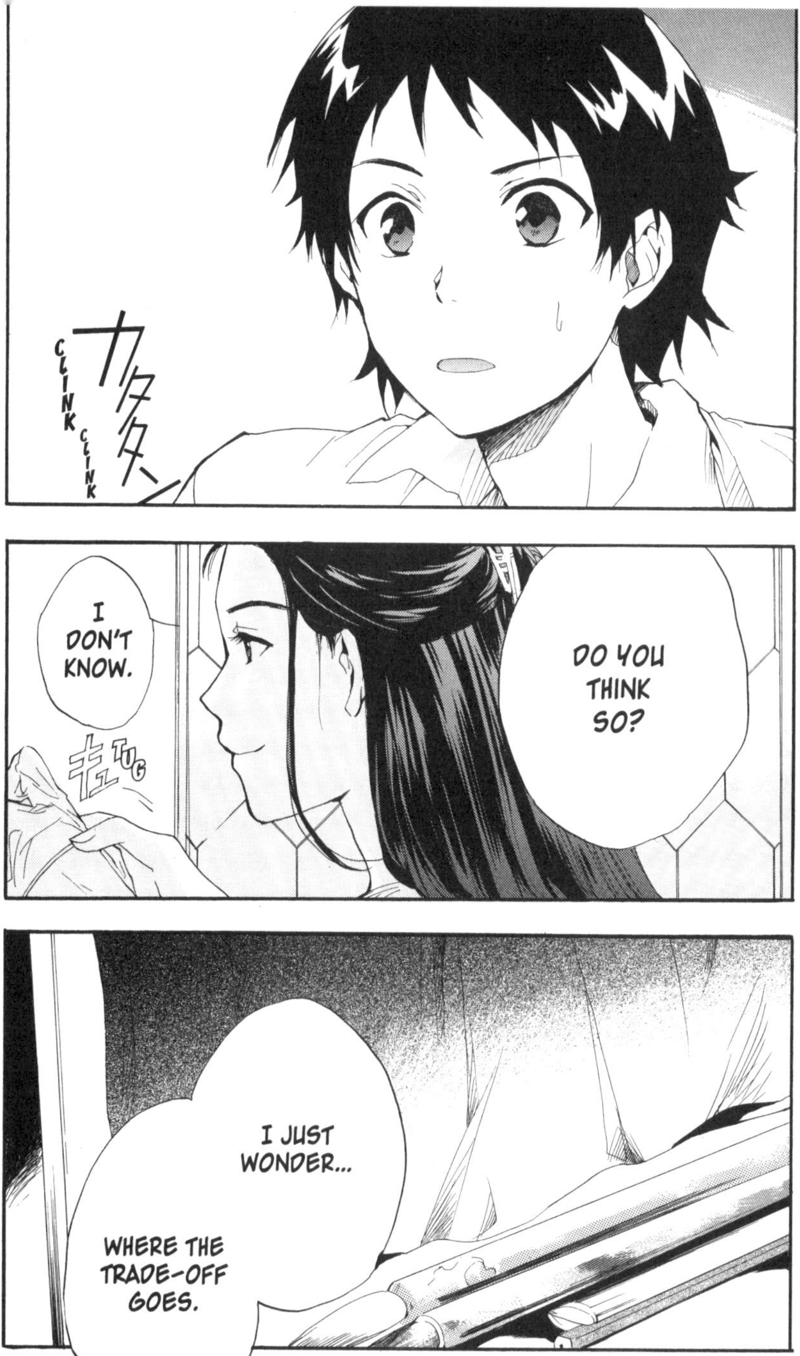

カタタン
CLINK CLINK
DO YOU THINK SO?
I DON'T KNOW.
キュ
TUG
I JUST WONDER...
WHERE THE TRADE-OFF GOES.

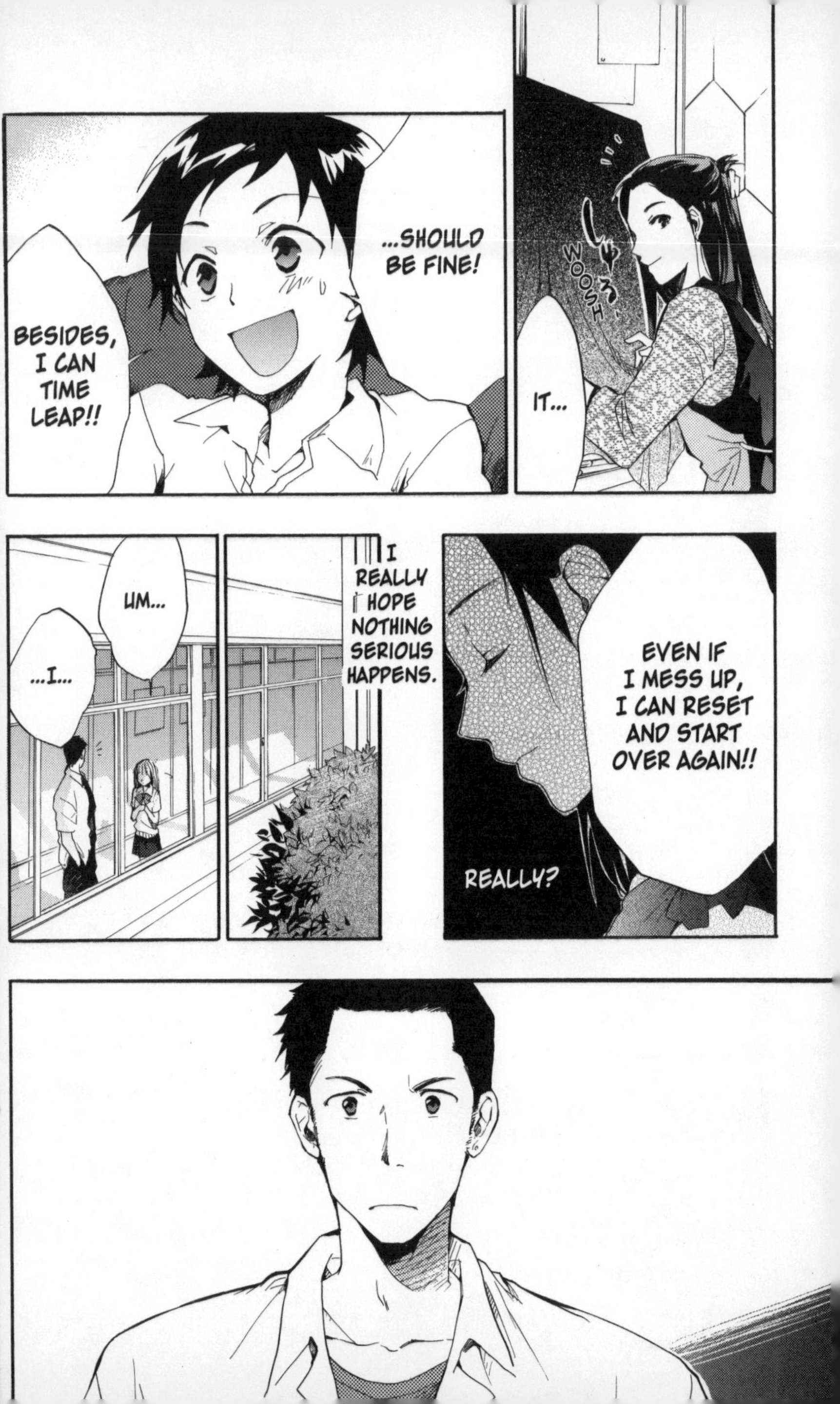
WOOSH
IT...
...SHOULD BE FINE!
BESIDES, I CAN TIME LEAP!!
EVEN IF I MESS UP, I CAN RESET AND START OVER AGAIN!!
REALLY?
I REALLY HOPE NOTHING SERIOUS HAPPENS.
UM...
...I...

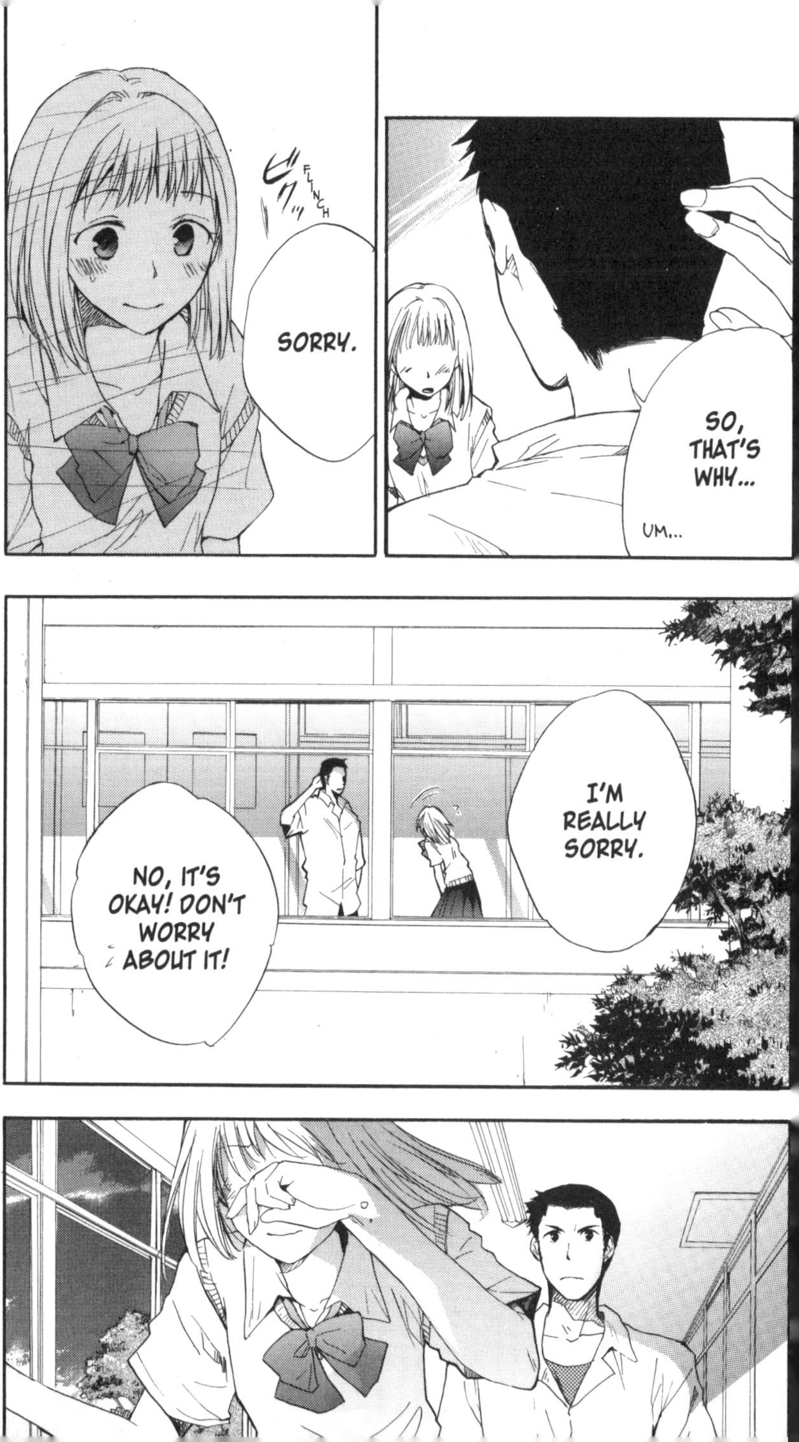
SO, THAT'S WHY...
UM...
FLINCH
SORRY.
I'M REALLY SORRY.
NO, IT'S OKAY! DON'T WORRY ABOUT IT!

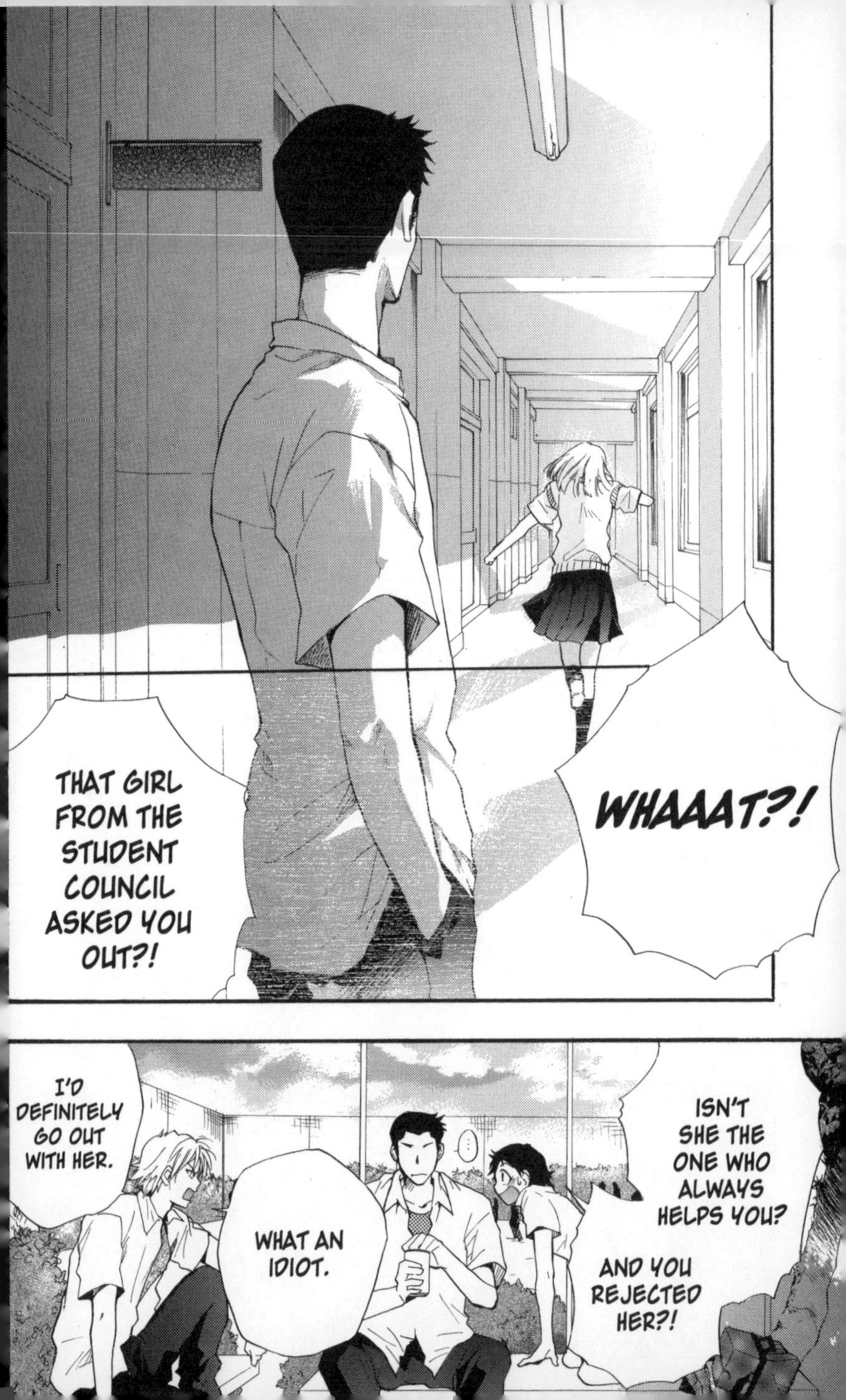
WHAAAT?!
THAT GIRL FROM THE STUDENT COUNCIL ASKED YOU OUT?!
ISN'T SHE THE ONE WHO ALWAYS HELPS YOU?
AND YOU REJECTED HER?!
...
WHAT AN IDIOT.
I'D DEFINITELY GO OUT WITH HER.

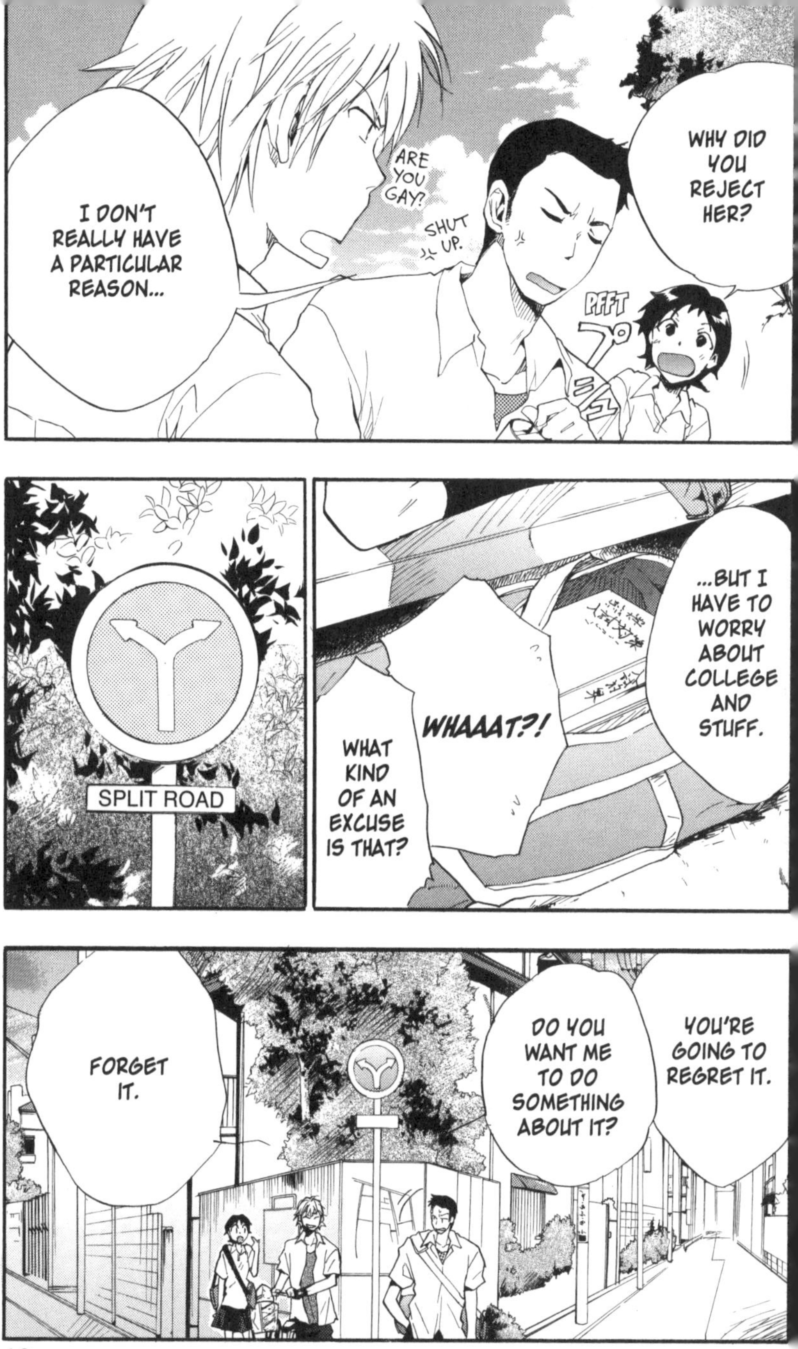

WHY DID YOU REJECT HER?
ARE YOU GAY?
SHUT UP.
PFFT
I DON'T REALLY HAVE A PARTICULAR REASON...
...BUT I HAVE TO WORRY ABOUT COLLEGE AND STUFF.
WHAAAT?!
WHAT KIND OF AN EXCUSE IS THAT?
SPLIT ROAD
YOU'RE GOING TO REGRET IT.
DO YOU WANT ME TO DO SOMETHING ABOUT IT?
FORGET IT.

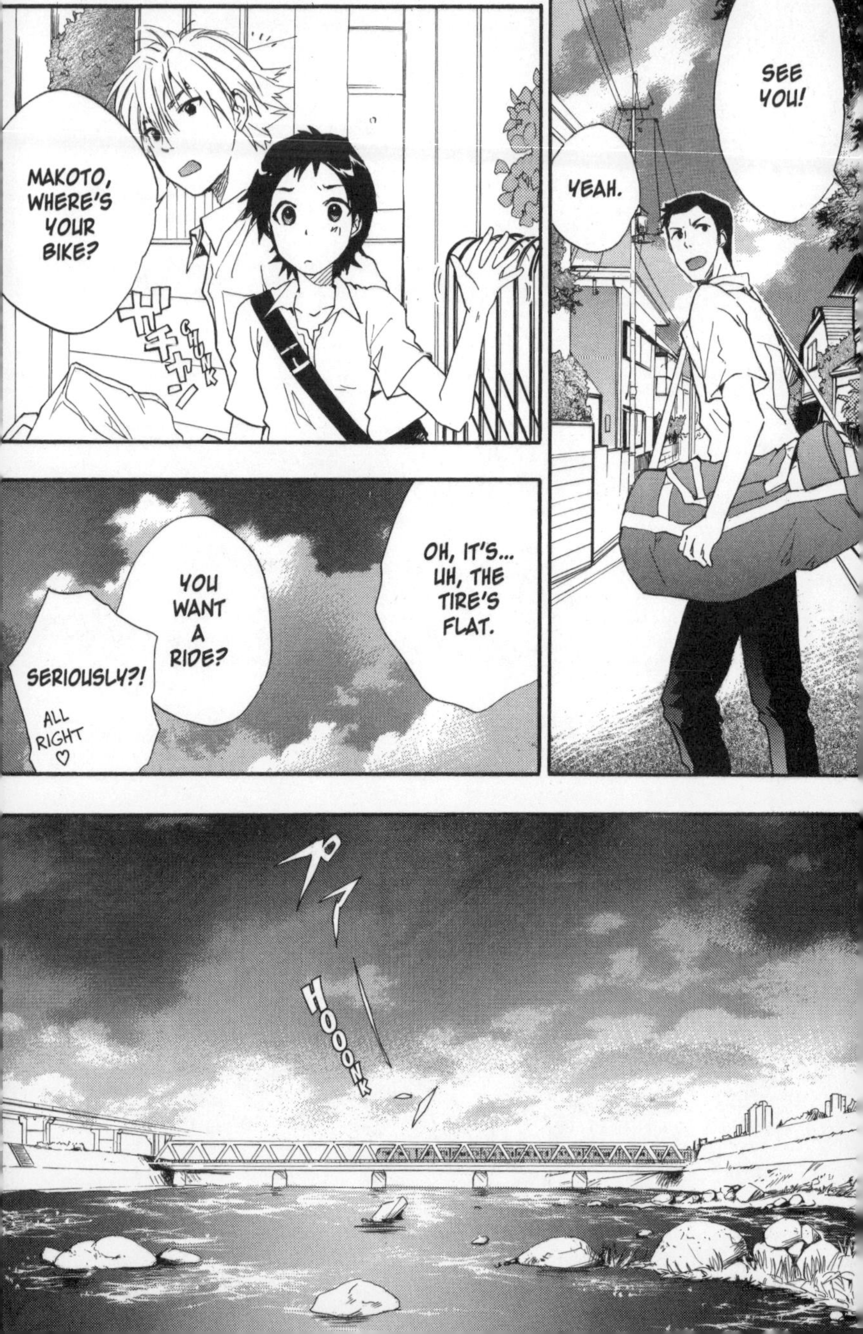
SEE YOU!
YEAH.
MAKOTO, WHERE'S YOUR BIKE?
CHUNK
OH, IT'S... UH, THE TIRE'S FLAT.
YOU WANT A RIDE?
SERIOUSLY?!
ALL RIGHT ♡
HOOONK

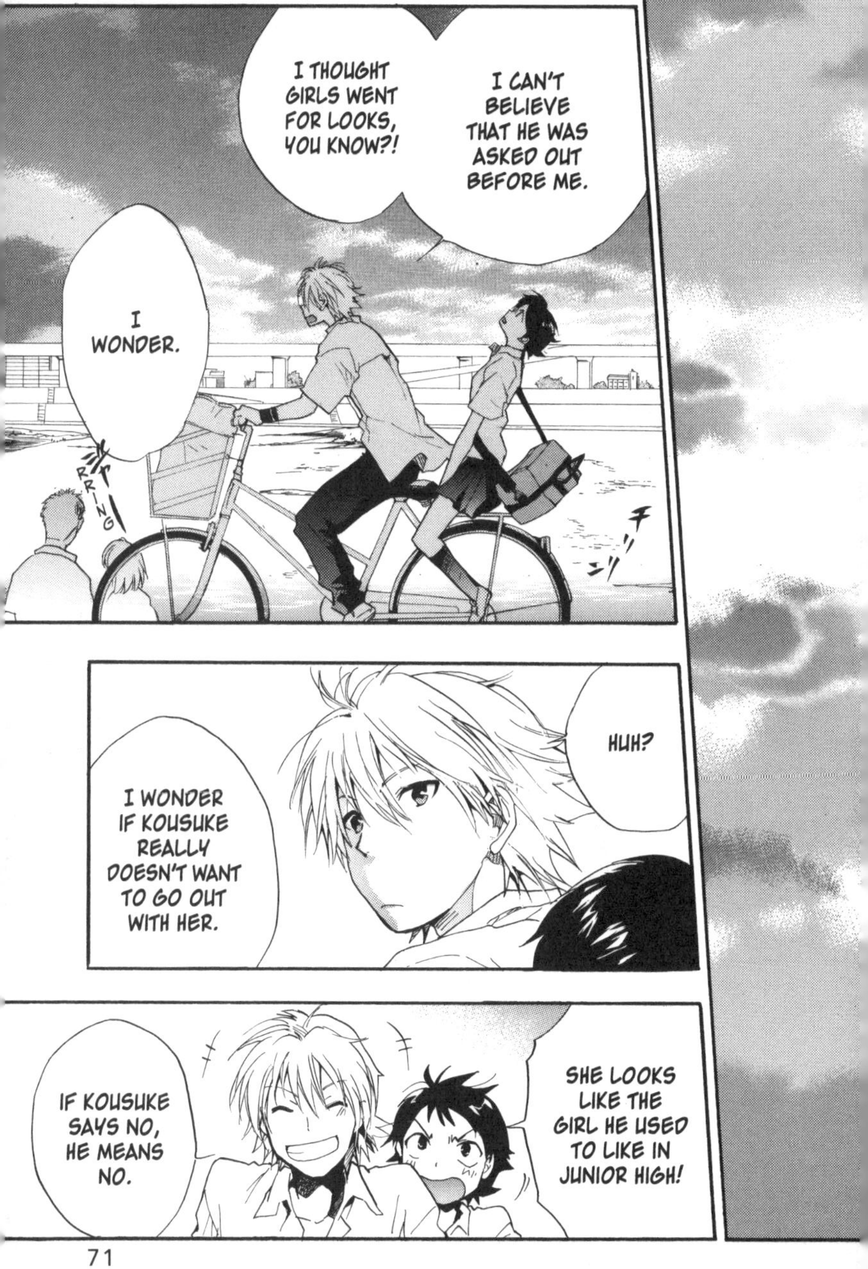
I CAN'T BELIEVE THAT HE WAS ASKED OUT BEFORE ME.
I THOUGHT GIRLS WENT FOR LOOKS, YOU KNOW?!
I WONDER.
RRRING
チリン
HUH?
I WONDER IF KOUSUKE REALLY DOESN'T WANT TO GO OUT WITH HER.
SHE LOOKS LIKE THE GIRL HE USED TO LIKE IN JUNIOR HIGH!
IF KOUSUKE SAYS NO, HE MEANS NO.

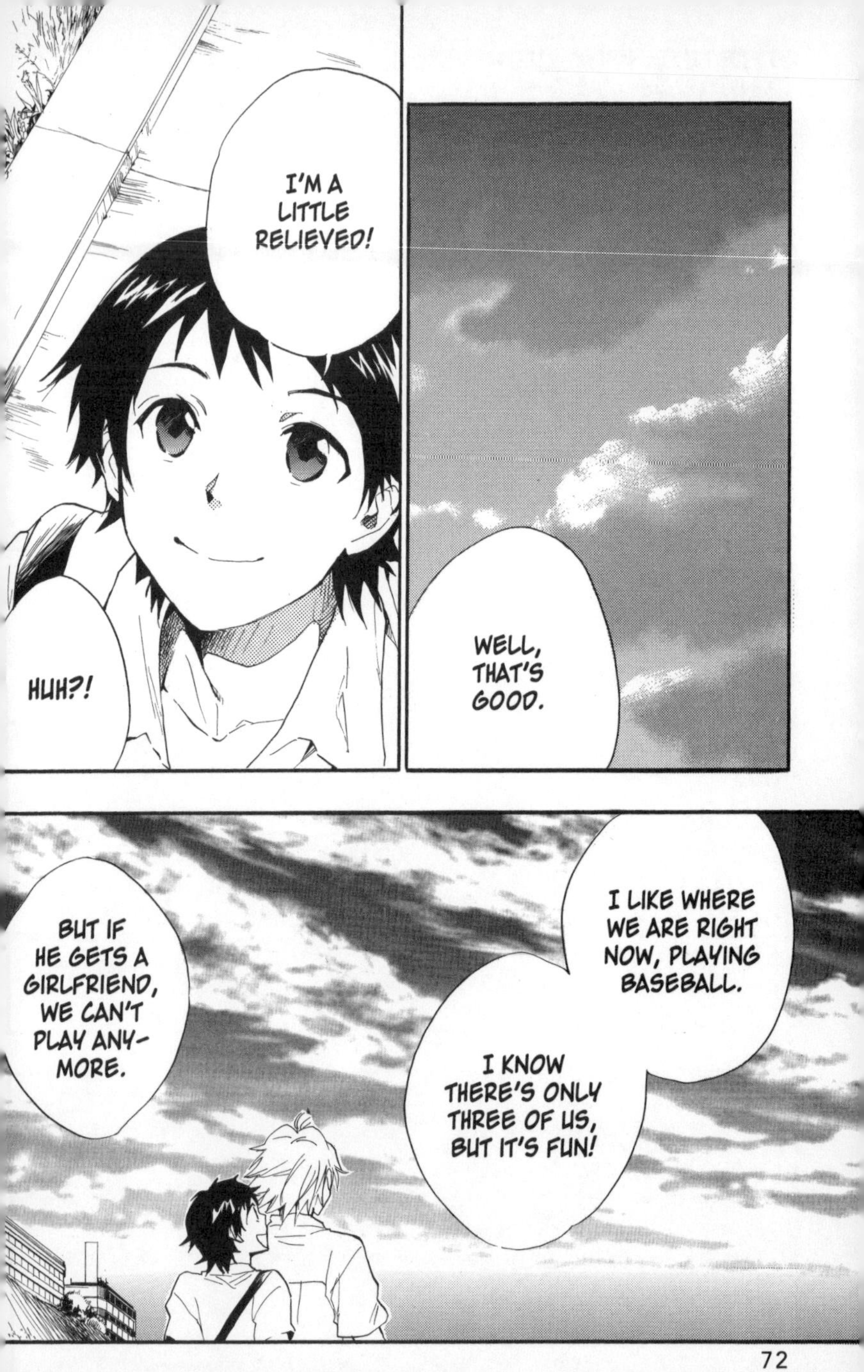
WELL, THAT'S GOOD.
I'M A LITTLE RELIEVED!
HUH?!
I LIKE WHERE WE ARE RIGHT NOW, PLAYING BASEBALL.
I KNOW THERE'S ONLY THREE OF US, BUT IT'S FUN!
BUT IF HE GETS A GIRLFRIEND, WE CAN'T PLAY ANY-MORE.

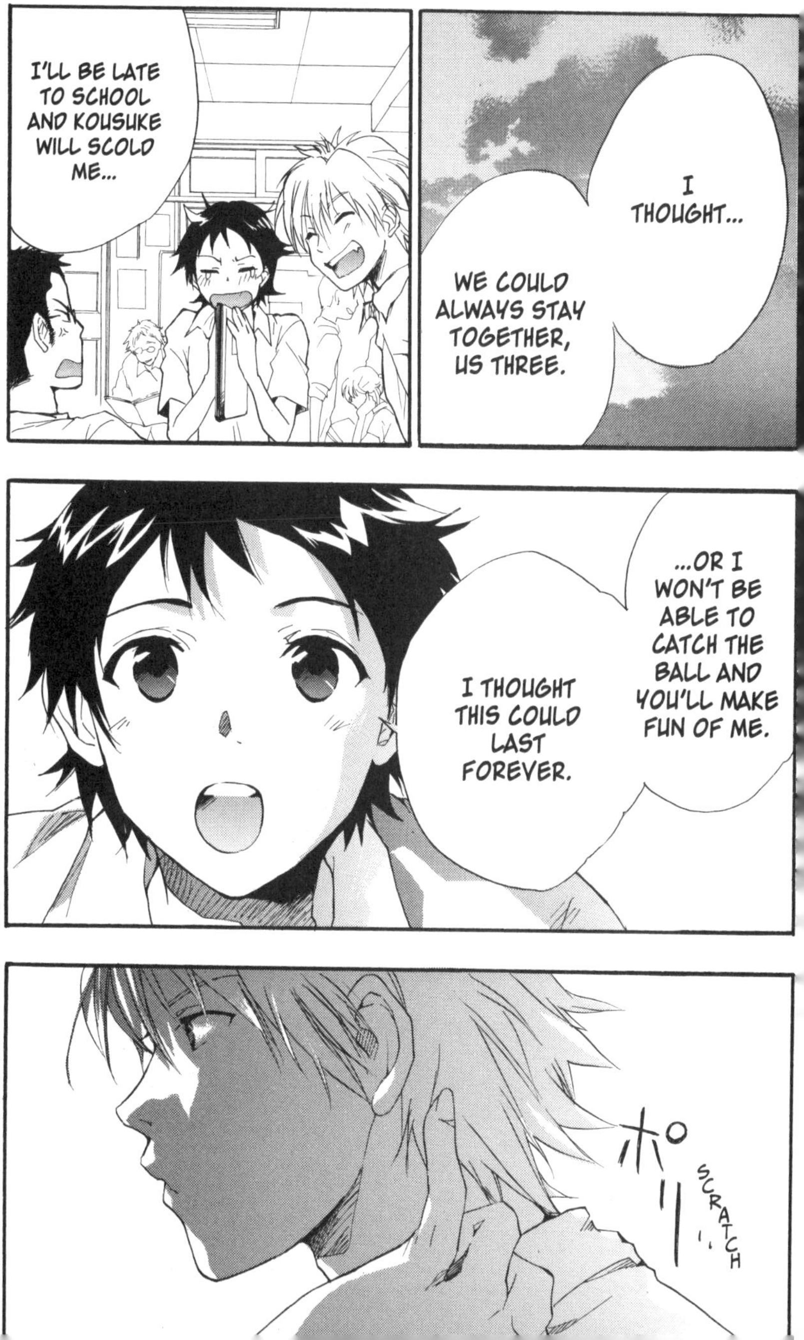
I THOUGHT...
WE COULD ALWAYS STAY TOGETHER, US THREE.
I'LL BE LATE TO SCHOOL AND KOUSUKE WILL SCOLD ME...
...OR I WON'T BE ABLE TO CATCH THE BALL AND YOU'LL MAKE FUN OF ME.
I THOUGHT THIS COULD LAST FOREVER.
ポリ
SCRATCH

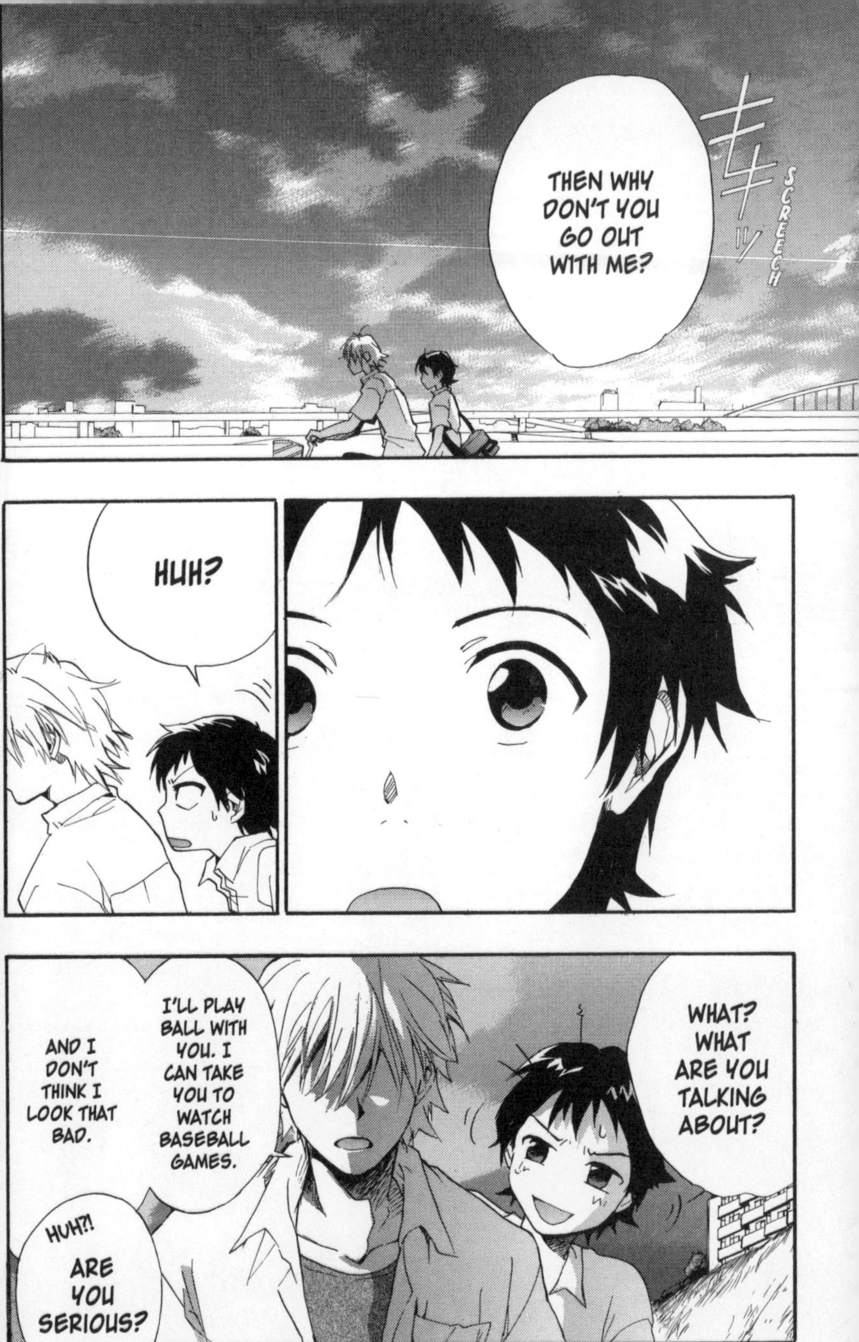

キキッ
SCREECH
THEN WHY DON'T YOU GO OUT WITH ME?
HUH?
WHAT? WHAT ARE YOU TALKING ABOUT?
I'LL PLAY BALL WITH YOU. I CAN TAKE YOU TO WATCH BASEBALL GAMES.
AND I DON'T THINK I LOOK THAT BAD.
HUH?! ARE YOU SERIOUS?

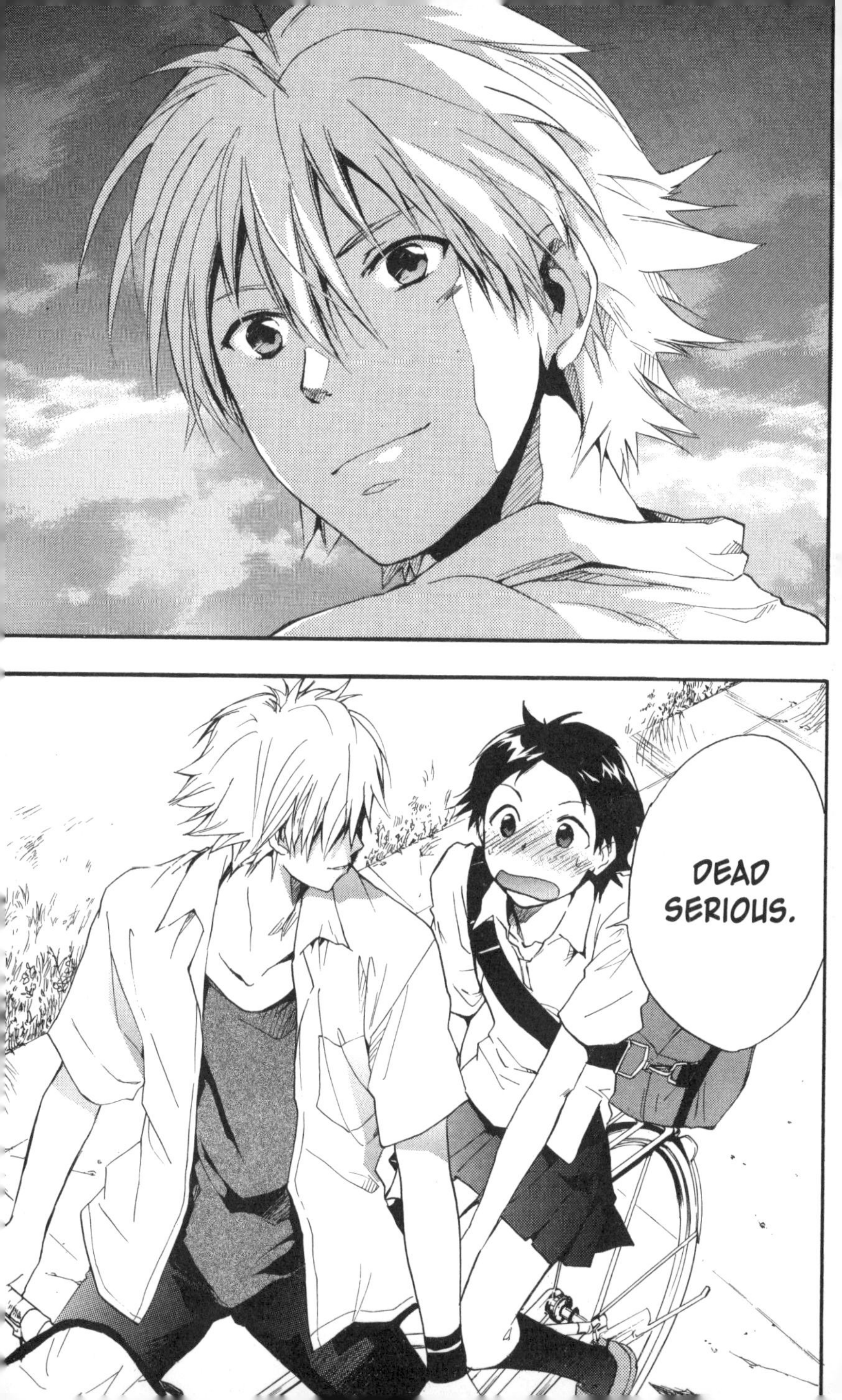
DEAD SERIOUS.

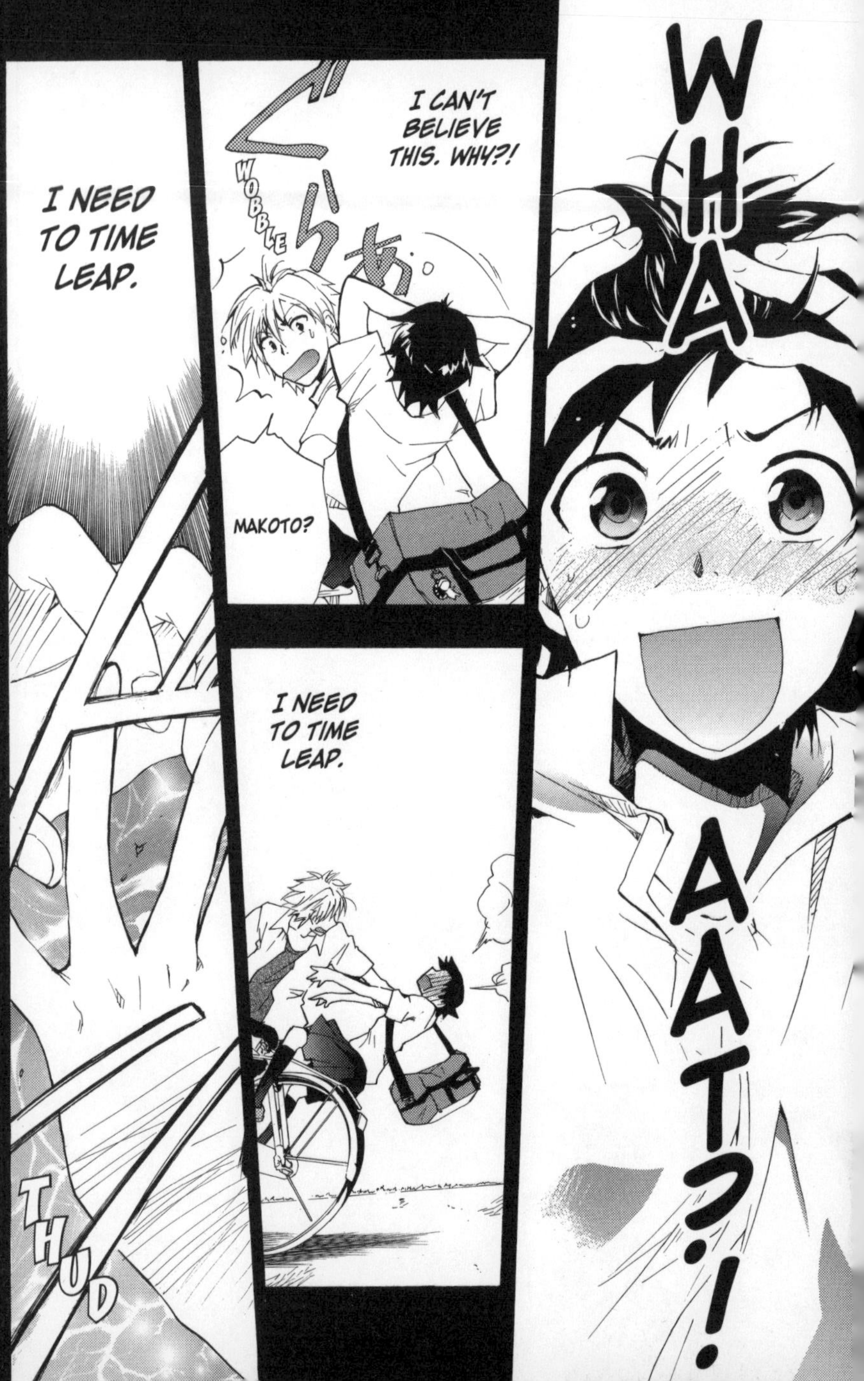
WHAAAT?!
WOBBLE
I CAN'T BELIEVE THIS. WHY?!
MAKOTO?
I NEED TO TIME LEAP.
I NEED TO TIME LEAP.
THUD

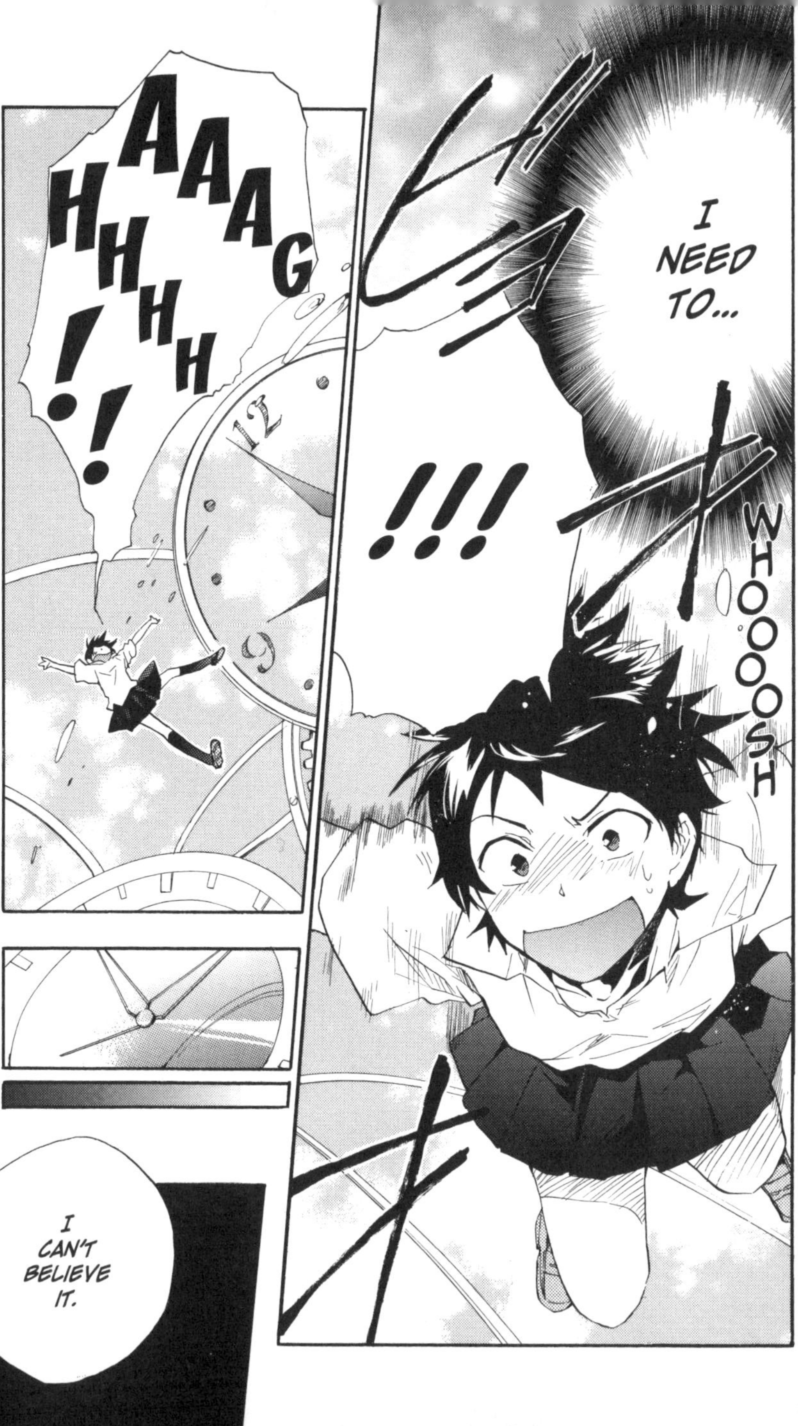
I NEED TO...
!!!
WHOOOOSH
AAAGHHHH!!
I CAN'T BELIEVE IT.

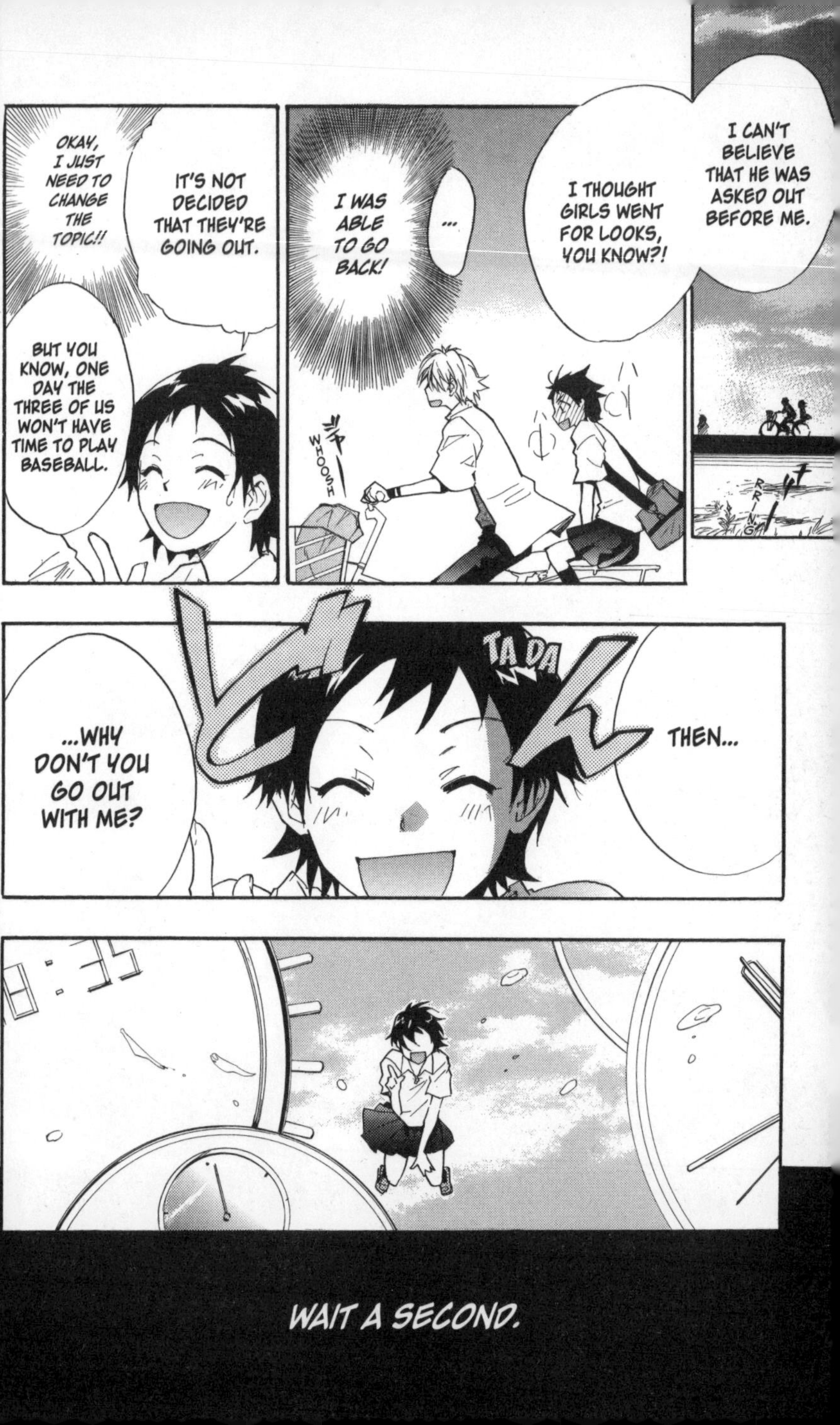
I CAN'T BELIEVE THAT HE WAS ASKED OUT BEFORE ME.
RRING
I THOUGHT GIRLS WENT FOR LOOKS, YOU KNOW?!
...
I WAS ABLE TO GO BACK!
WHOOSH
IT'S NOT DECIDED THAT THEY'RE GOING OUT.
OKAY, I JUST NEED TO CHANGE THE TOPIC!!
BUT YOU KNOW, ONE DAY THE THREE OF US WON'T HAVE TIME TO PLAY BASEBALL.
THEN...
TA DA
...WHY DON'T YOU GO OUT WITH ME?
WAIT A SECOND.

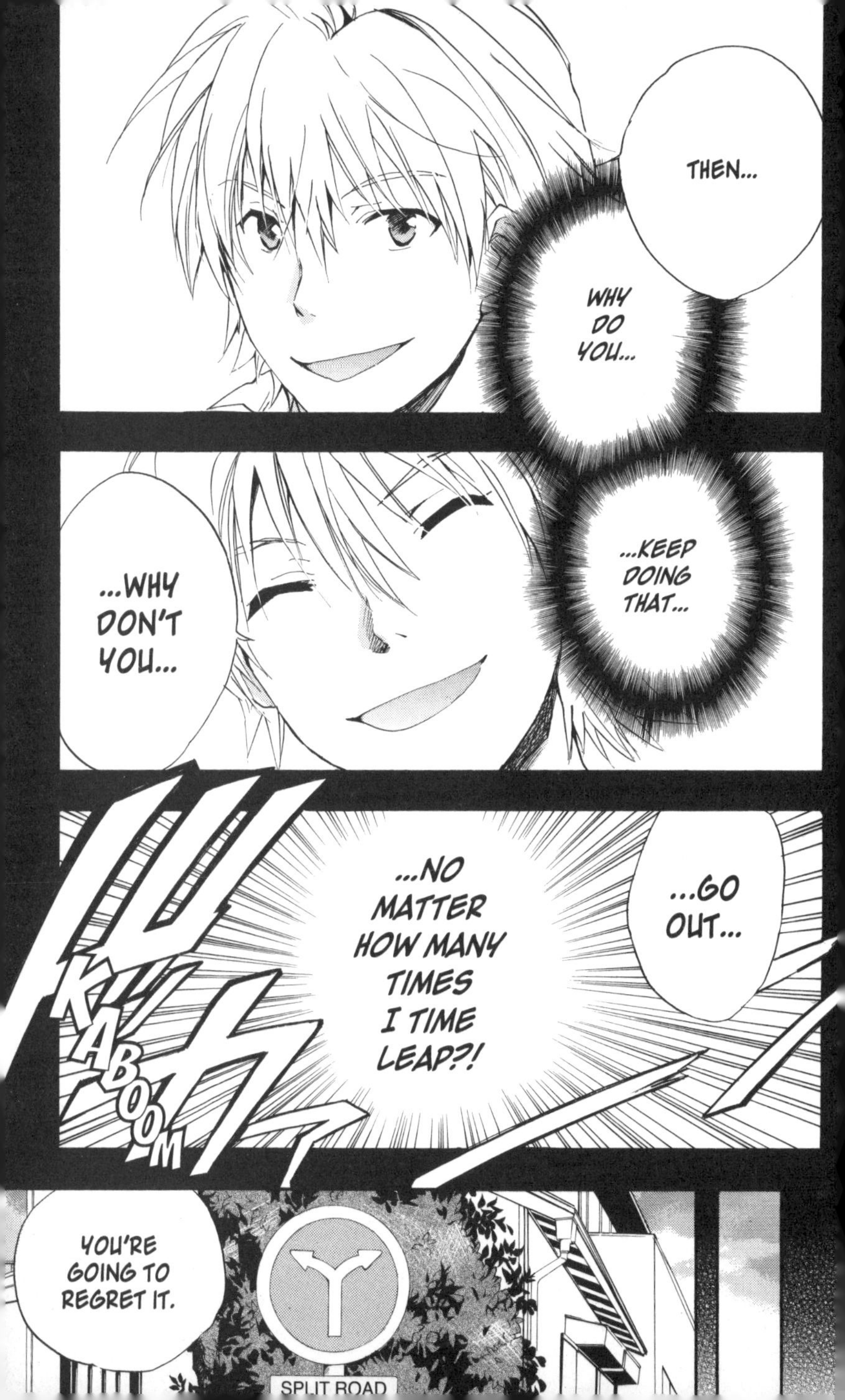
THEN...
WHY DO YOU...
...KEEP DOING THAT...
...WHY DON'T YOU...
...GO OUT...
...NO MATTER HOW MANY TIMES I TIME LEAP?!
KABOOM
YOU'RE GOING TO REGRET IT.
SPLIT ROAD

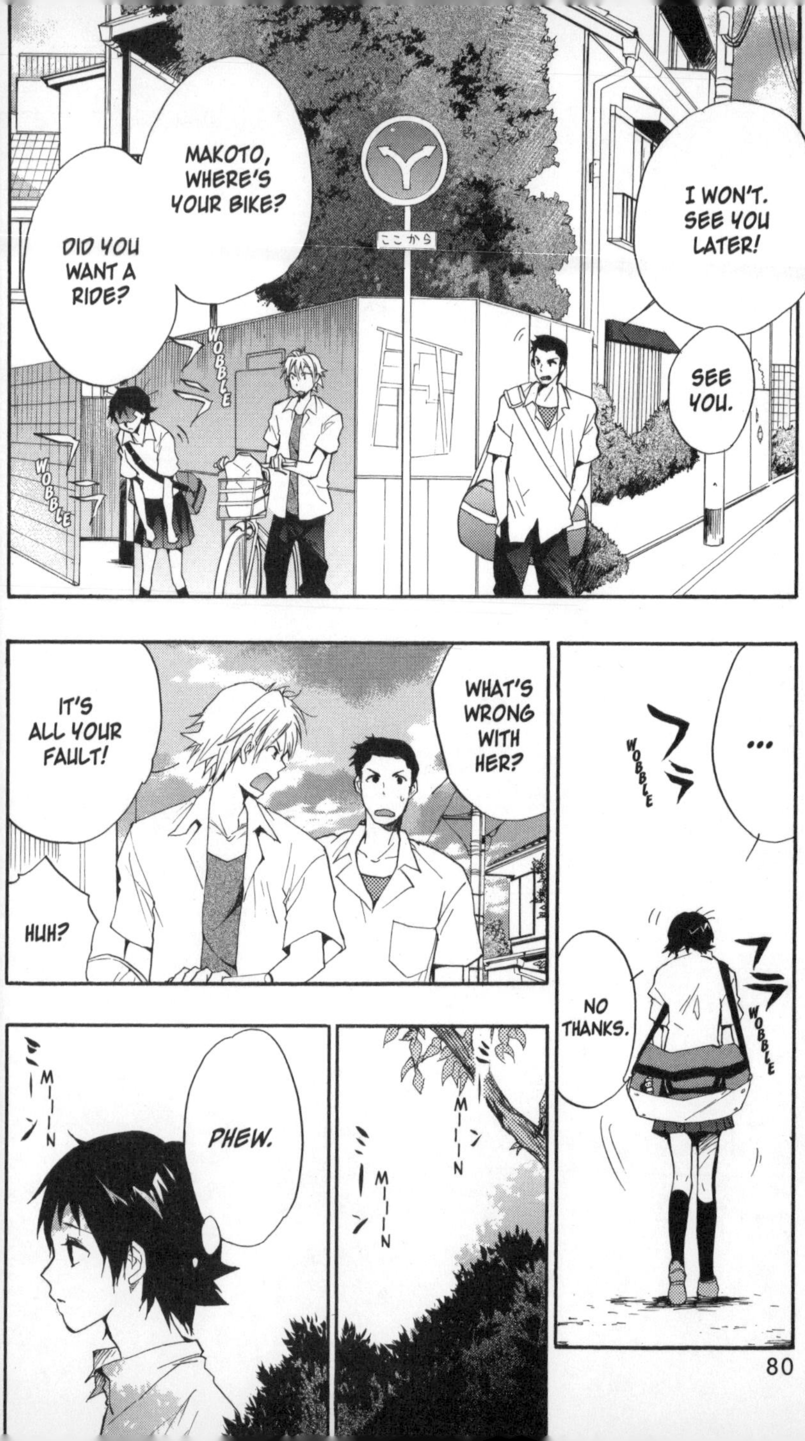
I WON'T. SEE YOU LATER!
SEE YOU.
MAKOTO, WHERE'S YOUR BIKE?
DID YOU WANT A RIDE?
ここから
WOBBLE
WOBBLE
...
WOBBLE
NO THANKS.
WOBBLE
WHAT'S WRONG WITH HER?
IT'S ALL YOUR FAULT!
HUH?
MIIIN
MIIIN
PHEW.
MIIIN

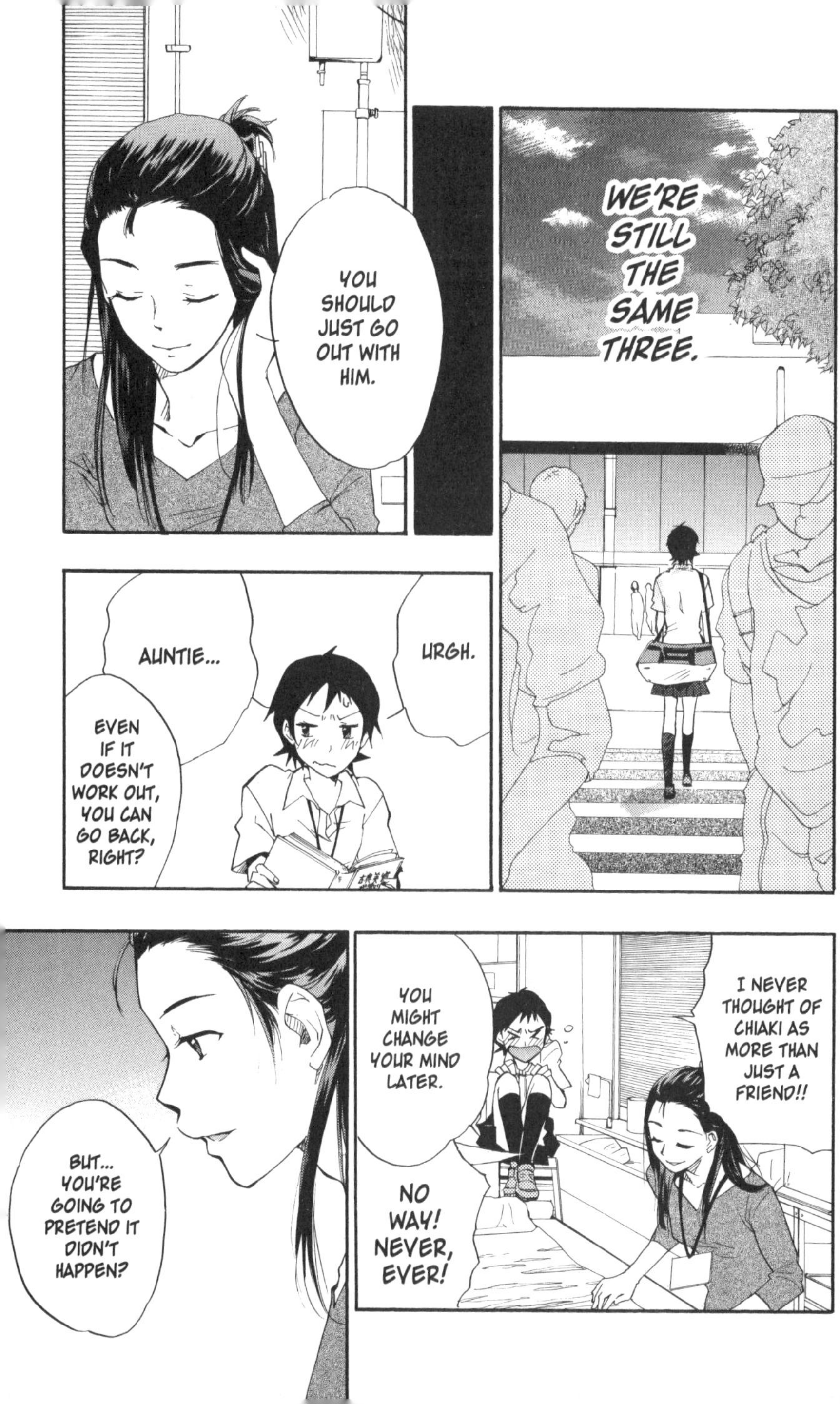
WE'RE STILL THE SAME THREE.
YOU SHOULD JUST GO OUT WITH HIM.
URGH.
AUNTIE...
EVEN IF IT DOESN'T WORK OUT, YOU CAN GO BACK, RIGHT?
I NEVER THOUGHT OF CHIAKI AS MORE THAN JUST A FRIEND!!
YOU MIGHT CHANGE YOUR MIND LATER.
NO WAY! NEVER, EVER!
BUT... YOU'RE GOING TO PRETEND IT DIDN'T HAPPEN?

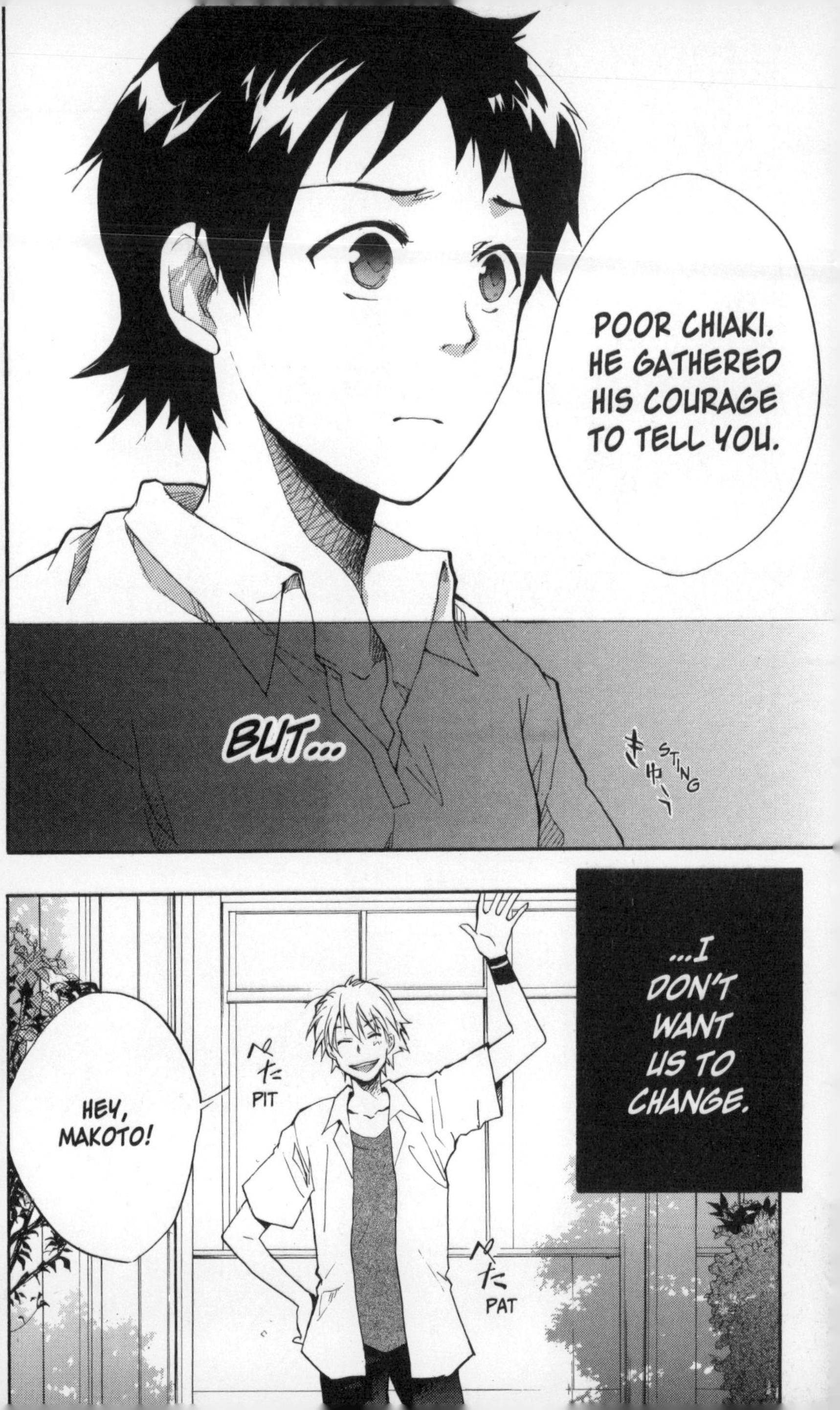
POOR CHIAKI. HE GATHERED HIS COURAGE TO TELL YOU.
BUT...
きゅー
STING
...I DON'T WANT US TO CHANGE.
ぺた
PIT
HEY, MAKOTO!
ぺた
PAT

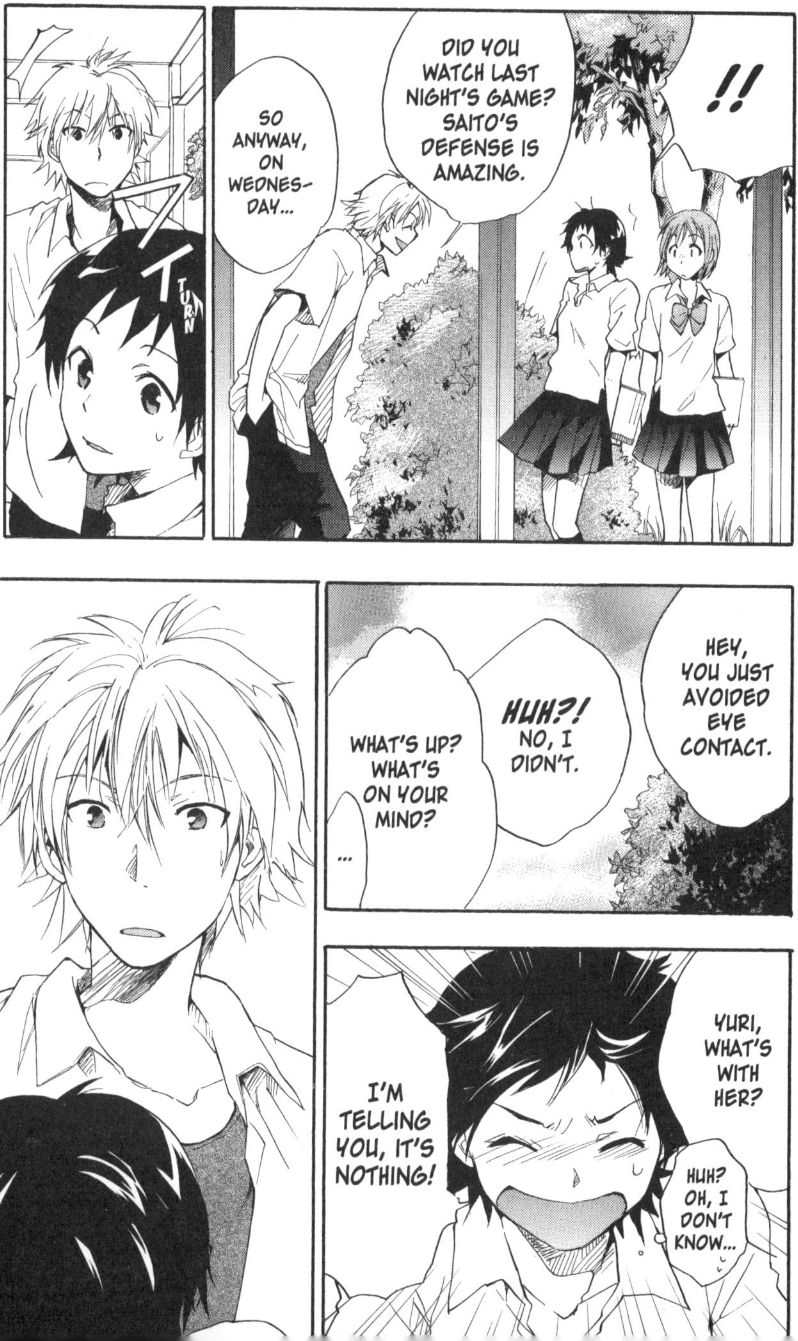
!!
DID YOU WATCH LAST NIGHT'S GAME? SAITO'S DEFENSE IS AMAZING.
SO ANYWAY, ON WEDNES-DAY...
TURN
HEY, YOU JUST AVOIDED EYE CONTACT.
HUH?! NO, I DIDN'T.
WHAT'S UP? WHAT'S ON YOUR MIND?
...
YURI, WHAT'S WITH HER?
HUH? OH, I DON'T KNOW...
I'M TELLING YOU, IT'S NOTHING!

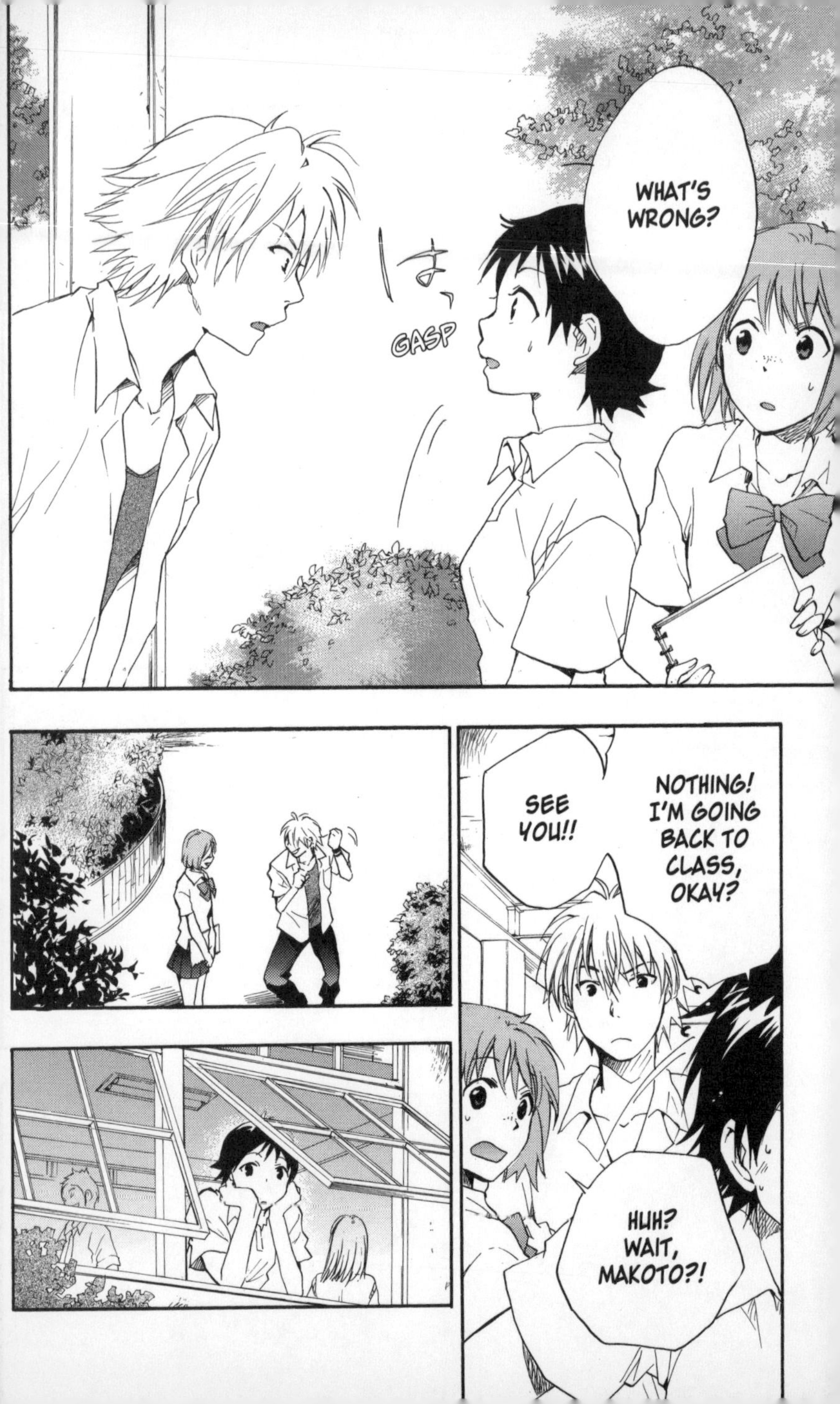
WHAT'S WRONG?
は、
GASP
NOTHING! I'M GOING BACK TO CLASS, OKAY?
SEE YOU!!
HUH? WAIT, MAKOTO?!

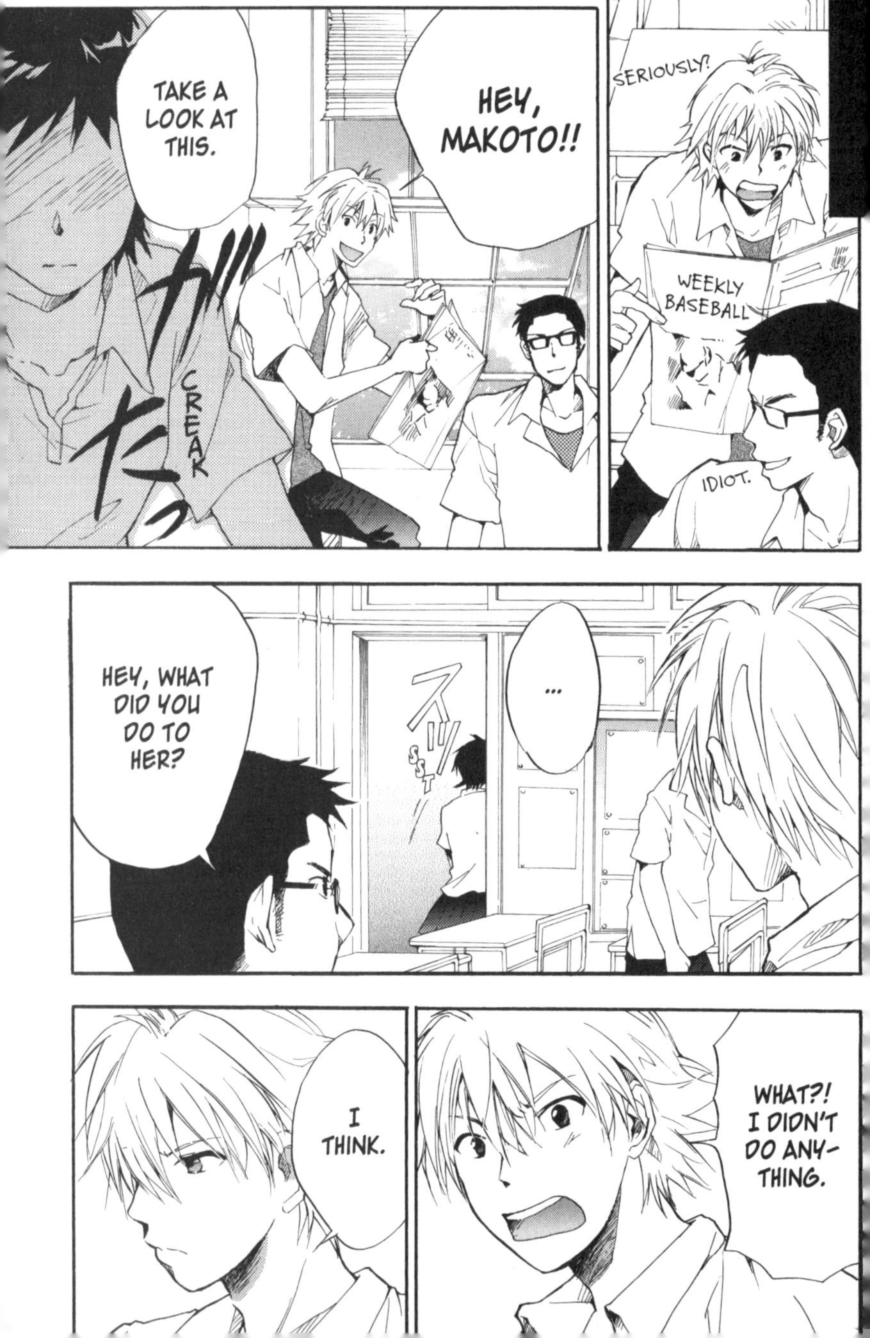
SERIOUSLY?
WEEKLY BASEBALL
IDIOT.
HEY, MAKOTO!!
TAKE A LOOK AT THIS.
CREAK
...
SST
HEY, WHAT DID YOU DO TO HER?
WHAT?! I DIDN'T DO ANY-THING.
I THINK.

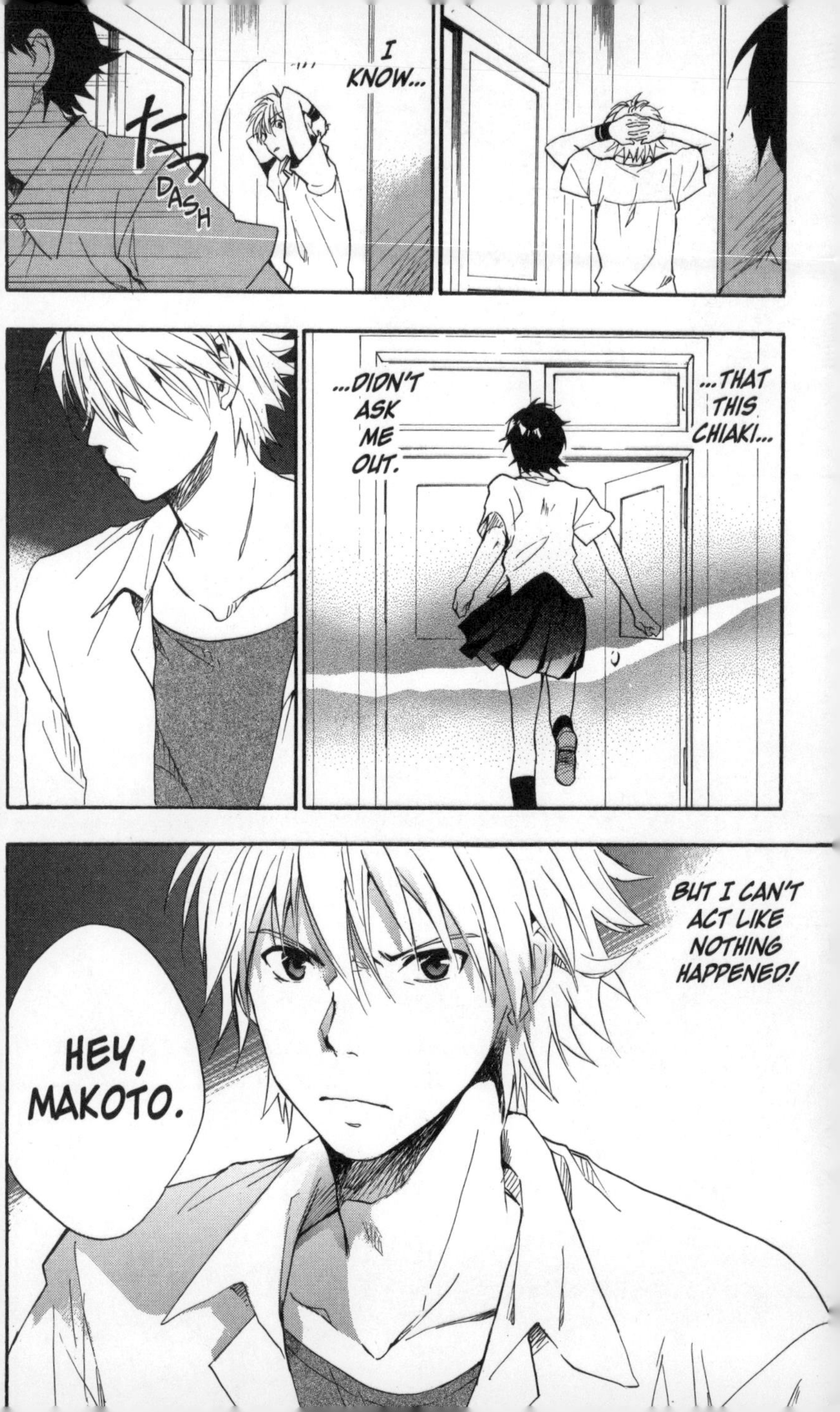

I KNOW...
DASH
...THAT THIS CHIAKI...
...DIDN'T ASK ME OUT.
BUT I CAN'T ACT LIKE NOTHING HAPPENED!
HEY, MAKOTO.

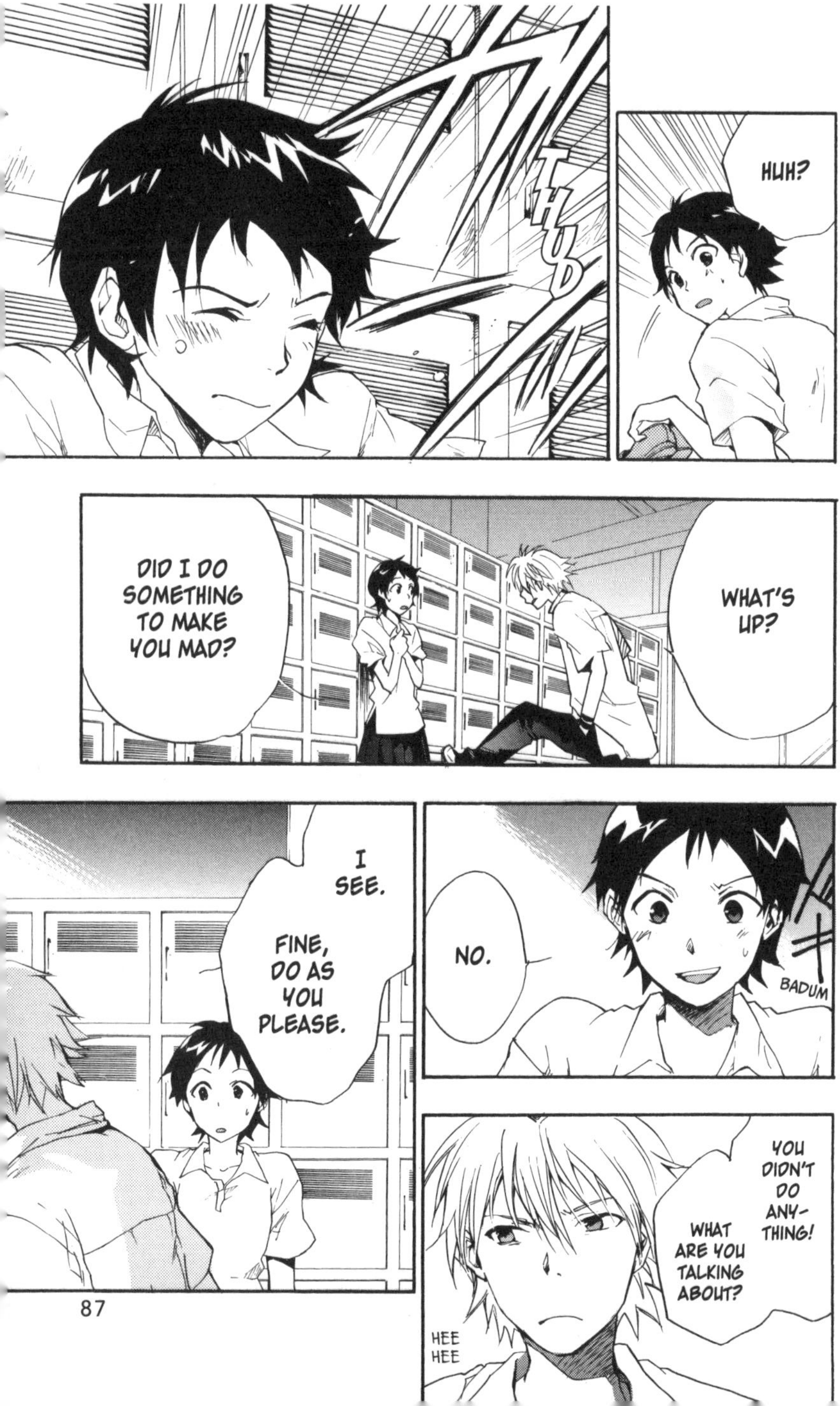
HUH?
THUD
WHAT'S UP?
DID I DO SOMETHING TO MAKE YOU MAD?
NO.
BADUM
YOU DIDN'T DO ANY-THING!
WHAT ARE YOU TALKING ABOUT?
HEE HEE
I SEE.
FINE, DO AS YOU PLEASE.

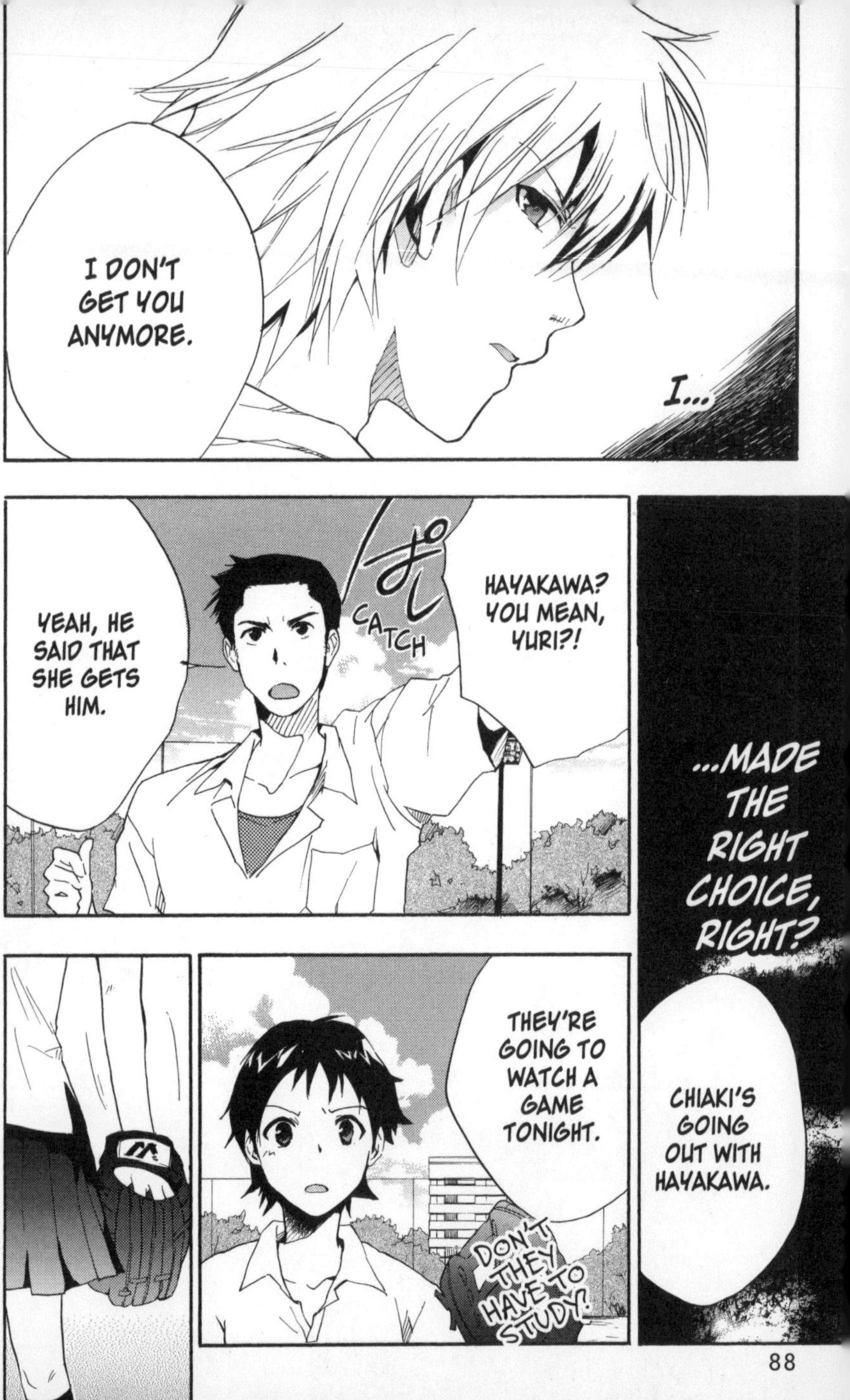
I DON'T GET YOU ANYMORE.
I...
...MADE THE RIGHT CHOICE, RIGHT?
HAYAKAWA? YOU MEAN, YURI?!
CATCH
YEAH, HE SAID THAT SHE GETS HIM.
CHIAKI'S GOING OUT WITH HAYAKAWA.
THEY'RE GOING TO WATCH A GAME TONIGHT.
DON'T THEY HAVE TO STUDY!

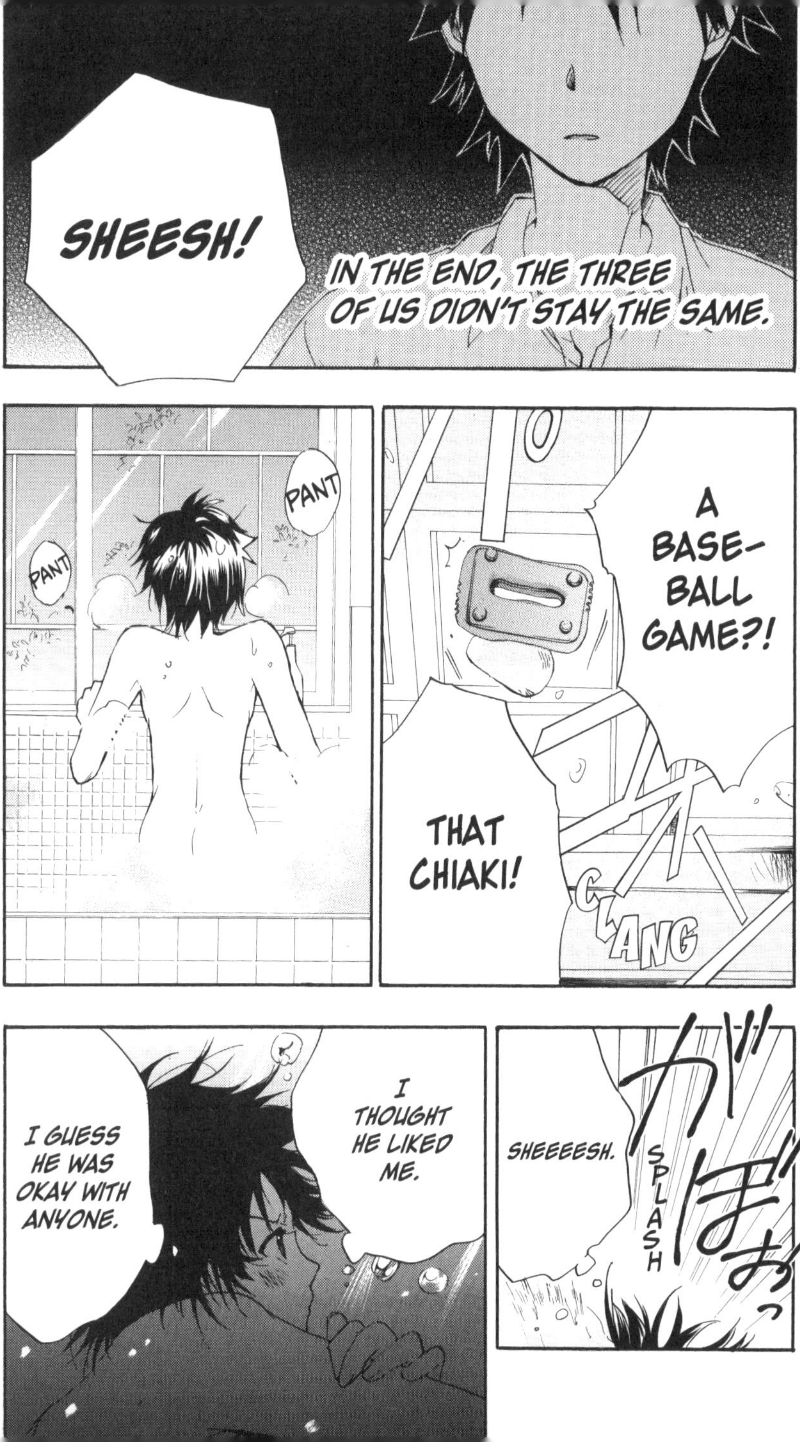
IN THE END, THE THREE OF US DIDN'T STAY THE SAME.
SHEESH!
A BASE-BALL GAME?!
THAT CHIAKI!
CLANG
PANT
PANT
がぼぉっ
SPLASH
SHEEEESH.
I THOUGHT HE LIKED ME.
I GUESS HE WAS OKAY WITH ANYONE.

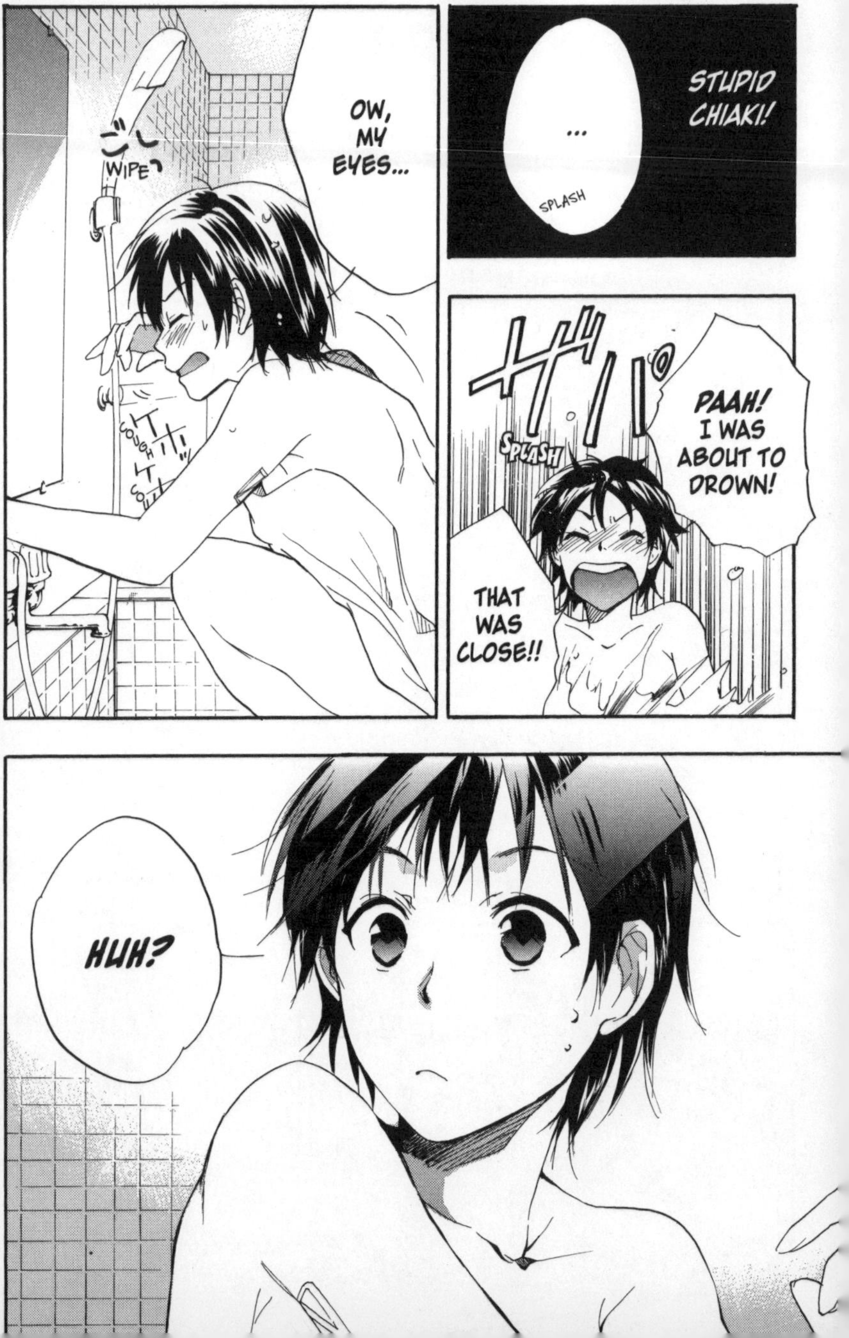

...
SPLASH
STUPID CHIAKI!
SPLASH
PAAH! I WAS ABOUT TO DROWN!
THAT WAS CLOSE!!
OW, MY EYES...
WIPE
COUGH
HUH?

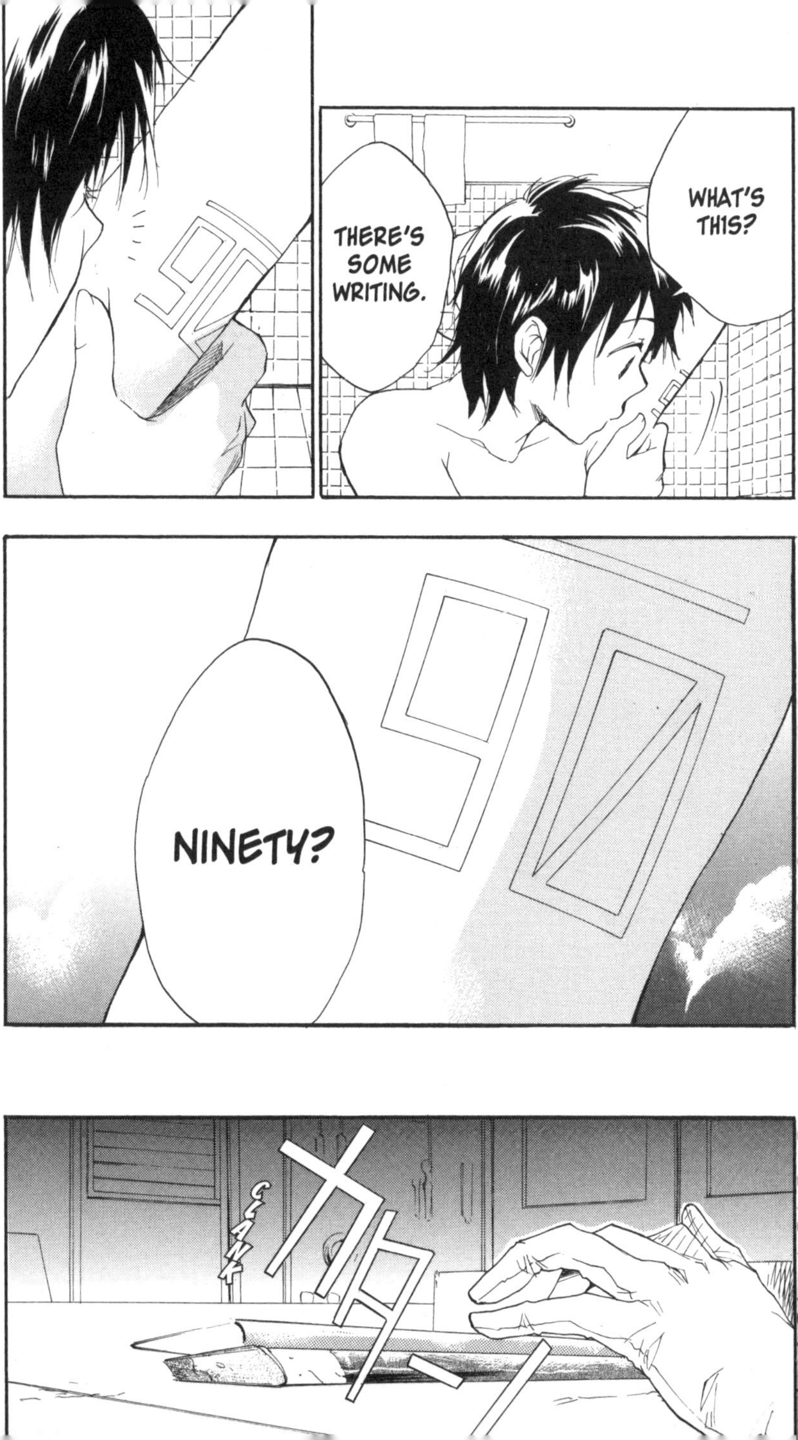
WHAT'S THIS?
THERE'S SOME WRITING.
NINETY?
CLANK

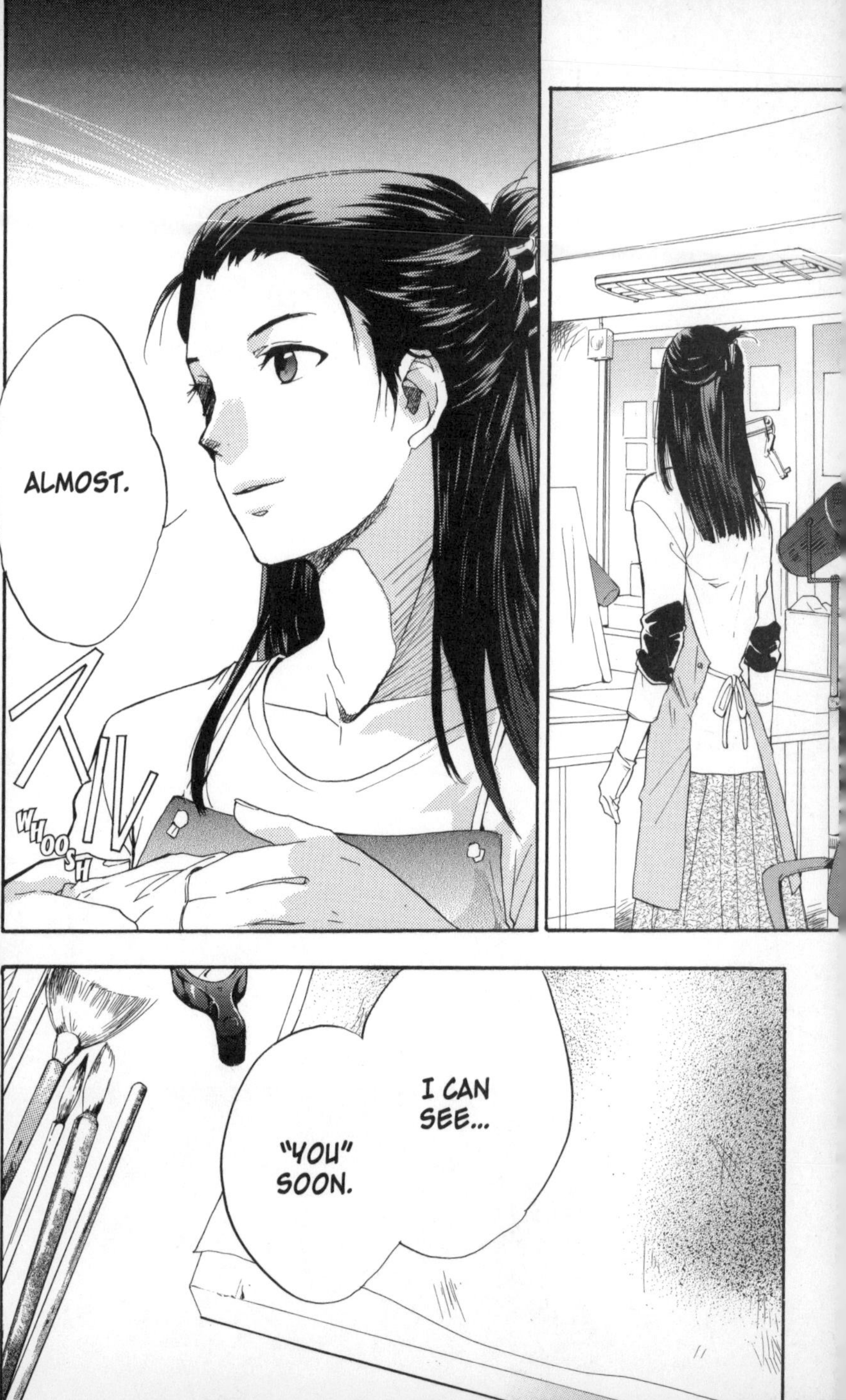
ALMOST.
WHOOSH
I CAN SEE...
"YOU" SOON.

Moment :03 Kousuke

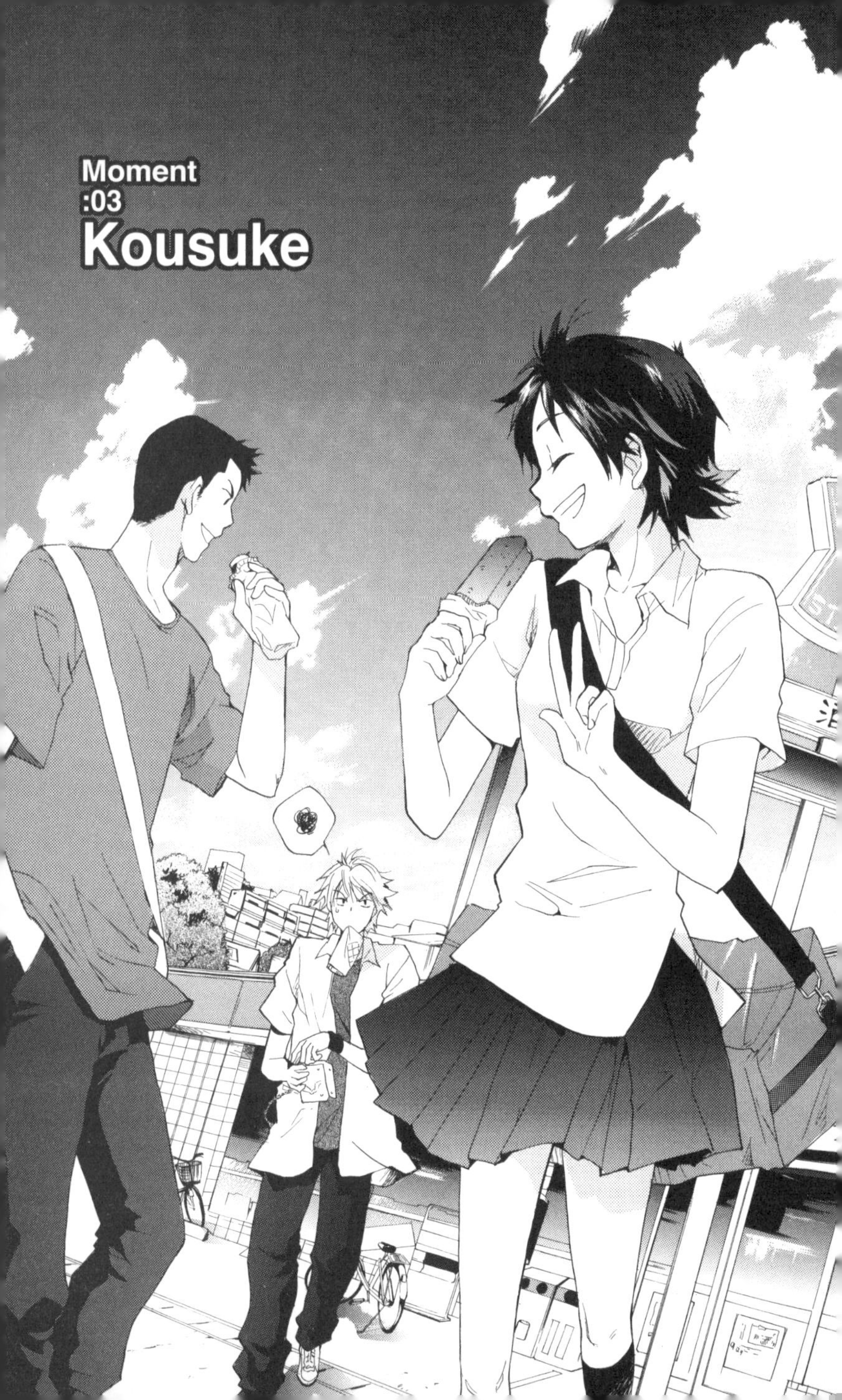

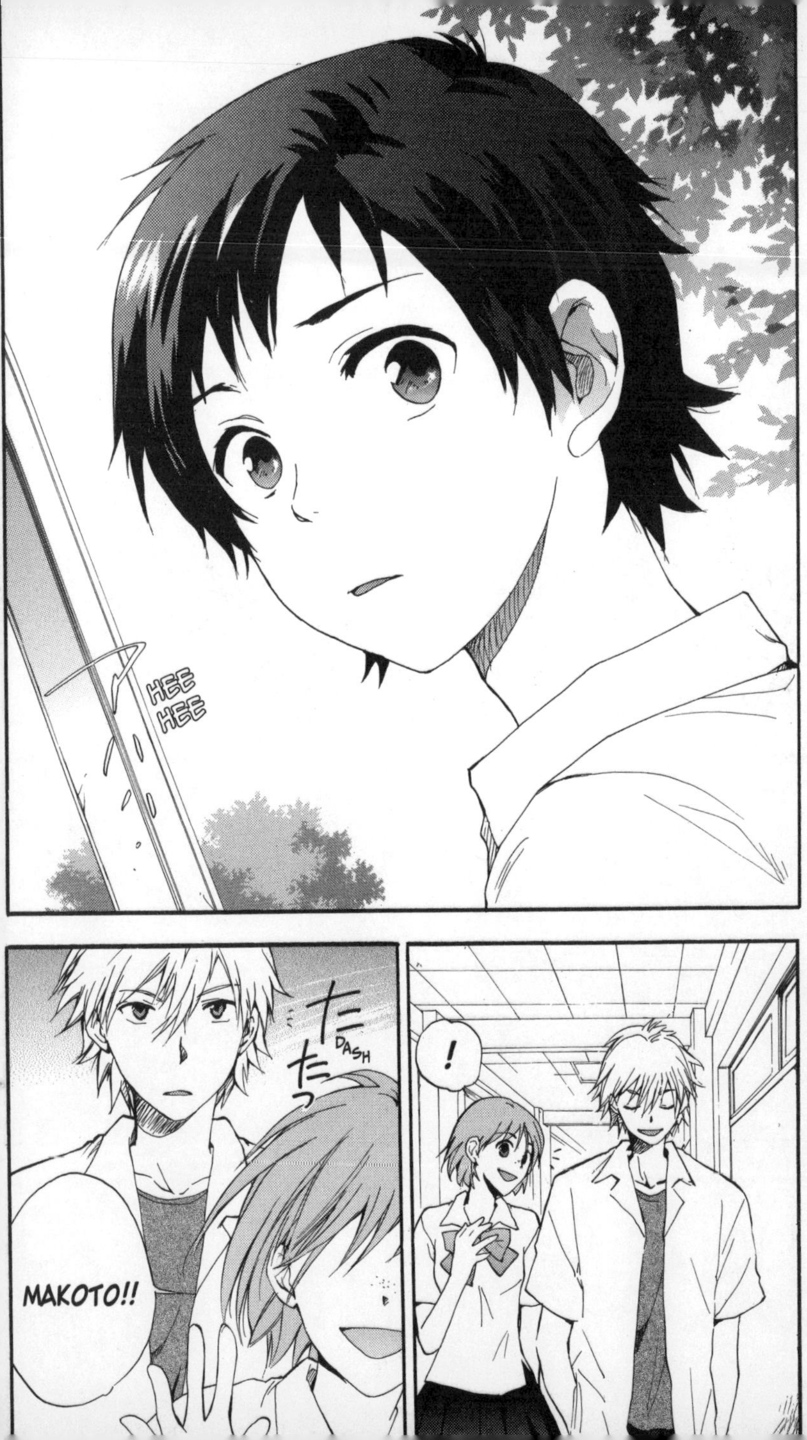
HEE HEE
!
たたっ
DASH
MAKOTO!!

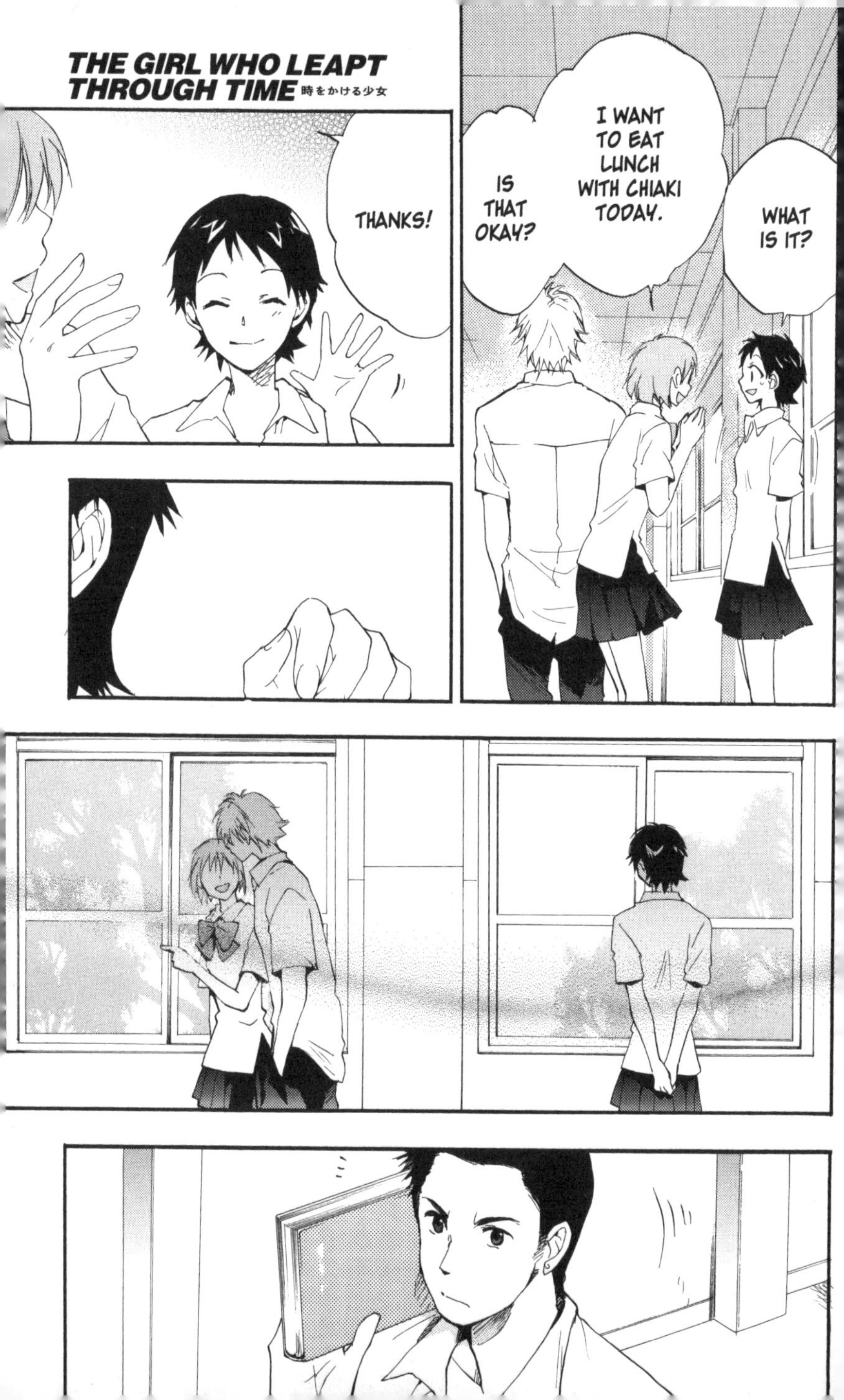
WHAT IS IT?
I WANT TO EAT LUNCH WITH CHIAKI TODAY.
IS THAT OKAY?
THANKS!

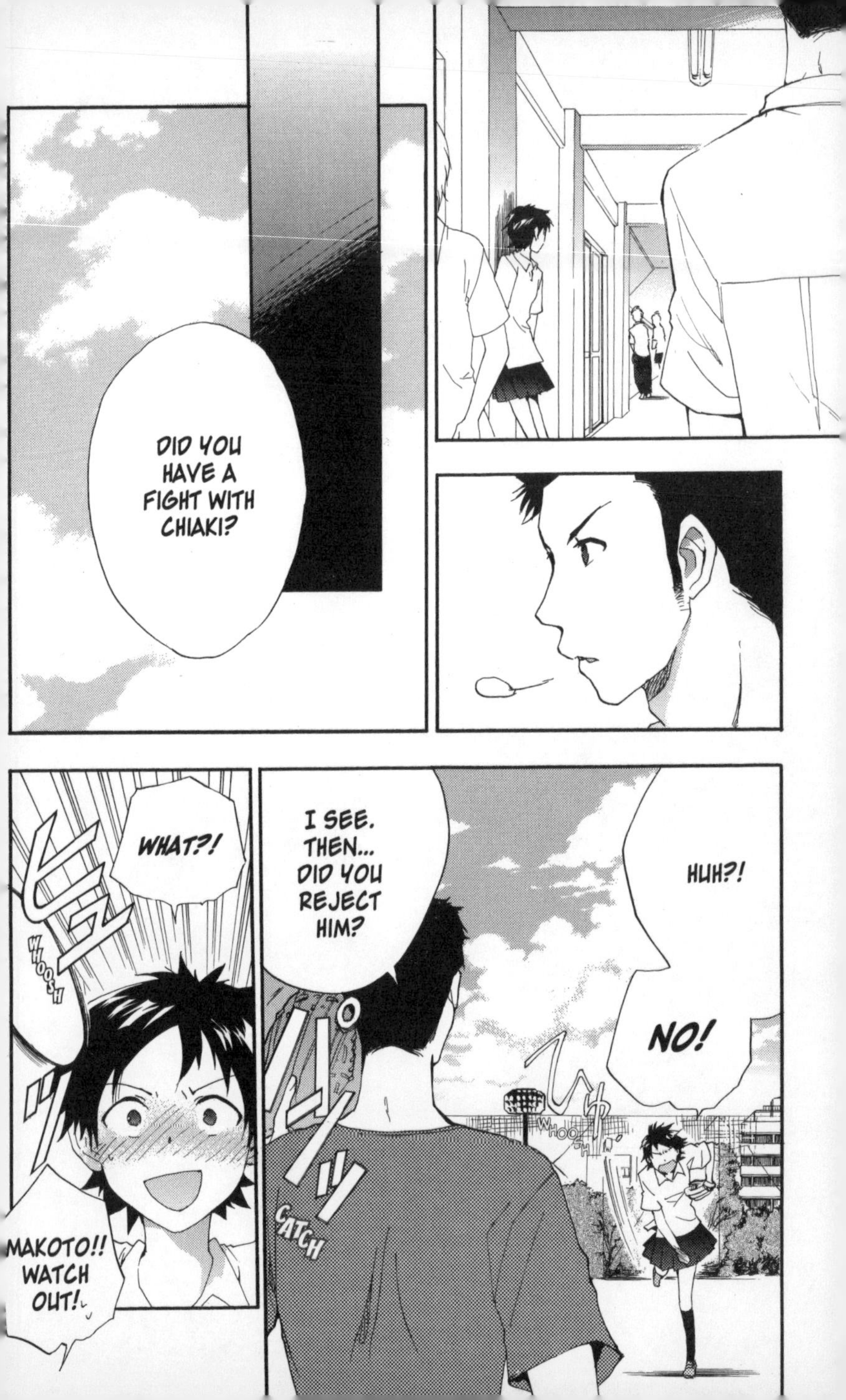
DID YOU HAVE A FIGHT WITH CHIAKI?
HUH?!
I SEE. THEN... DID YOU REJECT HIM?
NO!
WHOOSH
CATCH
WHAT?!
WHOOSH
MAKOTO!! WATCH OUT!

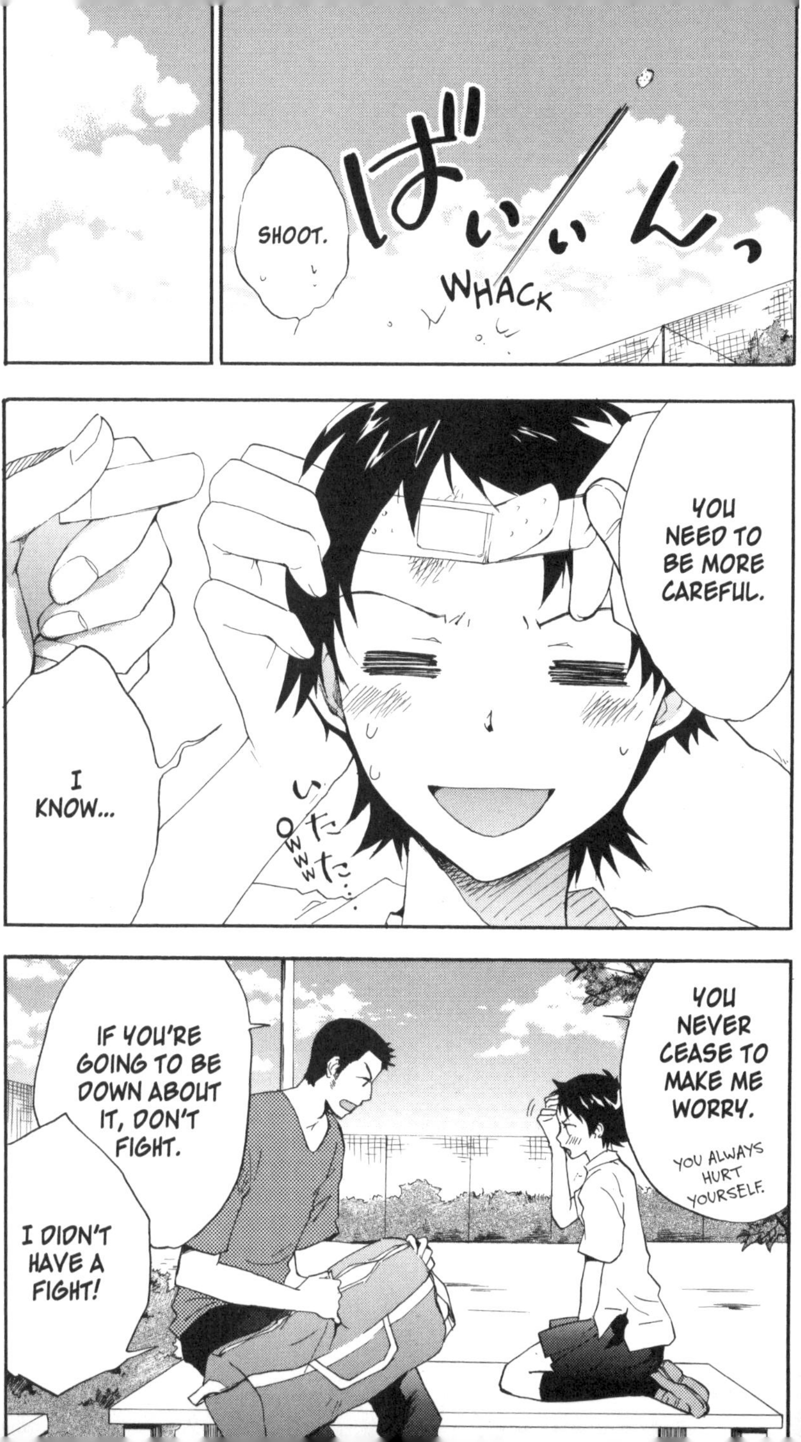
ばいいんっ
WHACK
SHOOT.
YOU NEED TO BE MORE CAREFUL.
いたた…
OWWW
I KNOW...
YOU NEVER CEASE TO MAKE ME WORRY.
YOU ALWAYS HURT YOURSELF.
IF YOU'RE GOING TO BE DOWN ABOUT IT, DON'T FIGHT.
I DIDN'T HAVE A FIGHT!

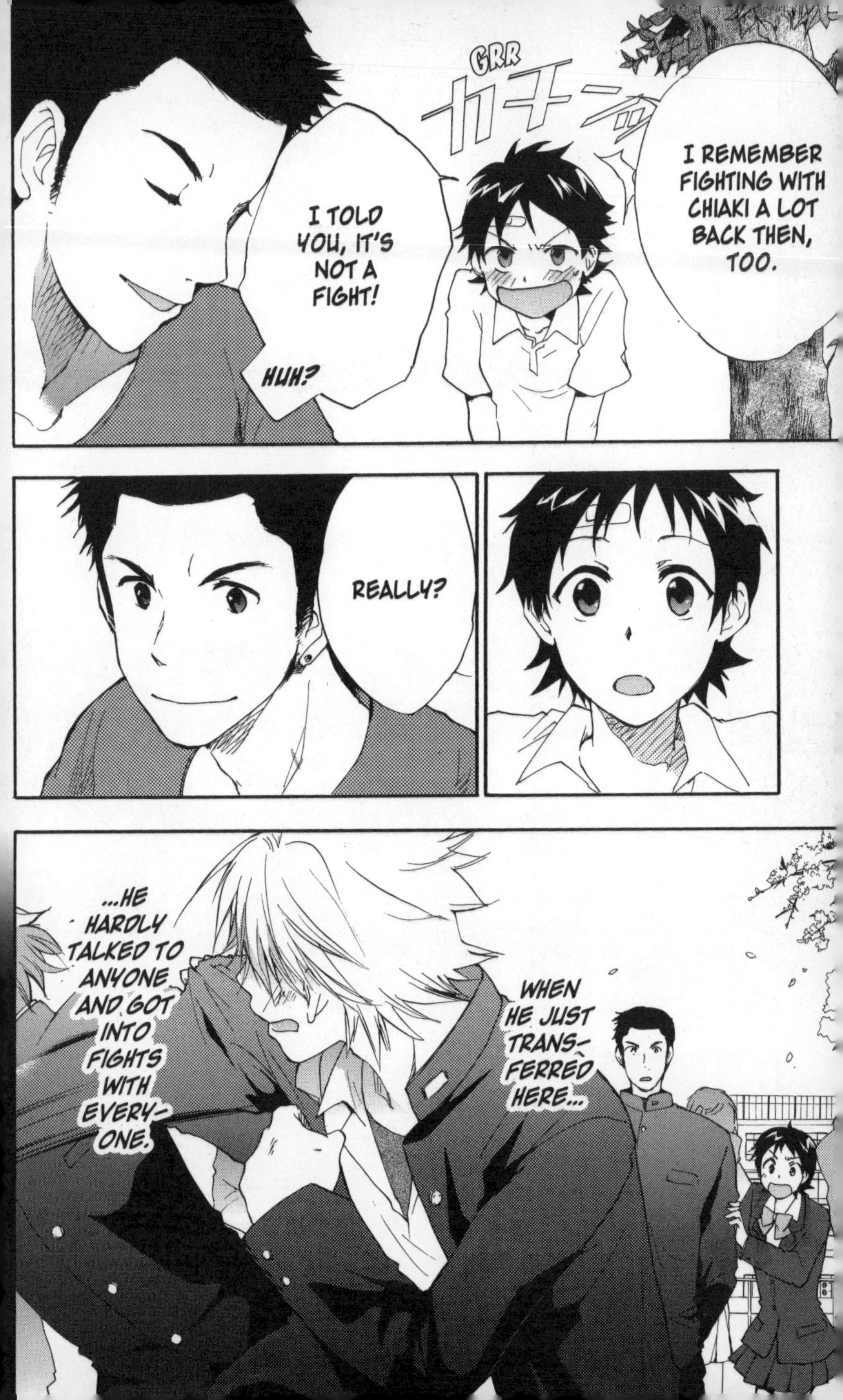
I REMEMBER FIGHTING WITH CHIAKI A LOT BACK THEN, TOO.
GRR
I TOLD YOU, IT'S NOT A FIGHT!
HUH?
REALLY?
WHEN HE JUST TRANS-FERRED HERE...
...HE HARDLY TALKED TO ANYONE AND GOT INTO FIGHTS WITH EVERY-ONE.

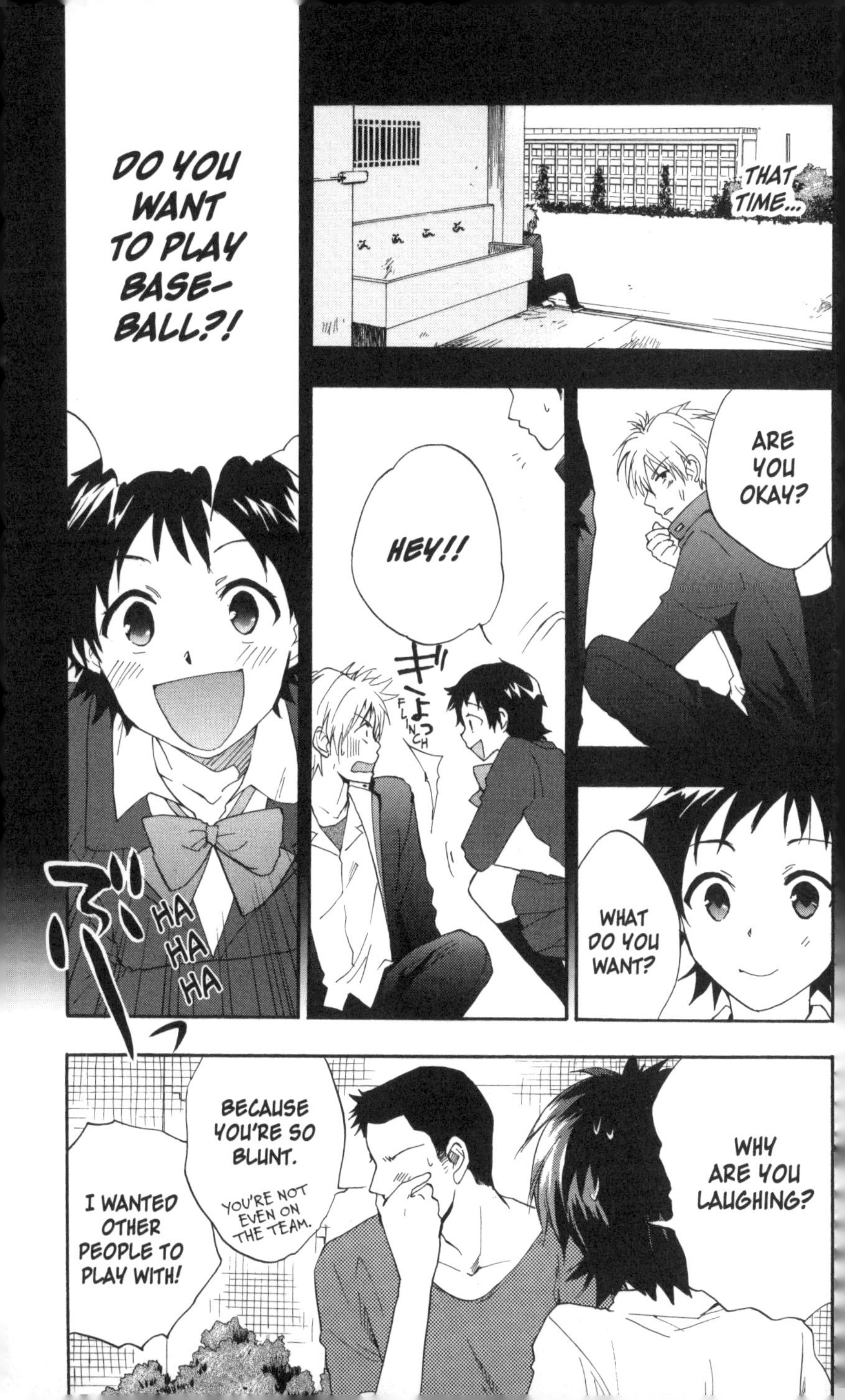
THAT TIME...
ARE YOU OKAY?
HEY!!
FLINCH
WHAT DO YOU WANT?
DO YOU WANT TO PLAY BASE-BALL?!
HA HA HA
WHY ARE YOU LAUGHING?
BECAUSE YOU'RE SO BLUNT.
YOU'RE NOT EVEN ON THE TEAM.
I WANTED OTHER PEOPLE TO PLAY WITH!

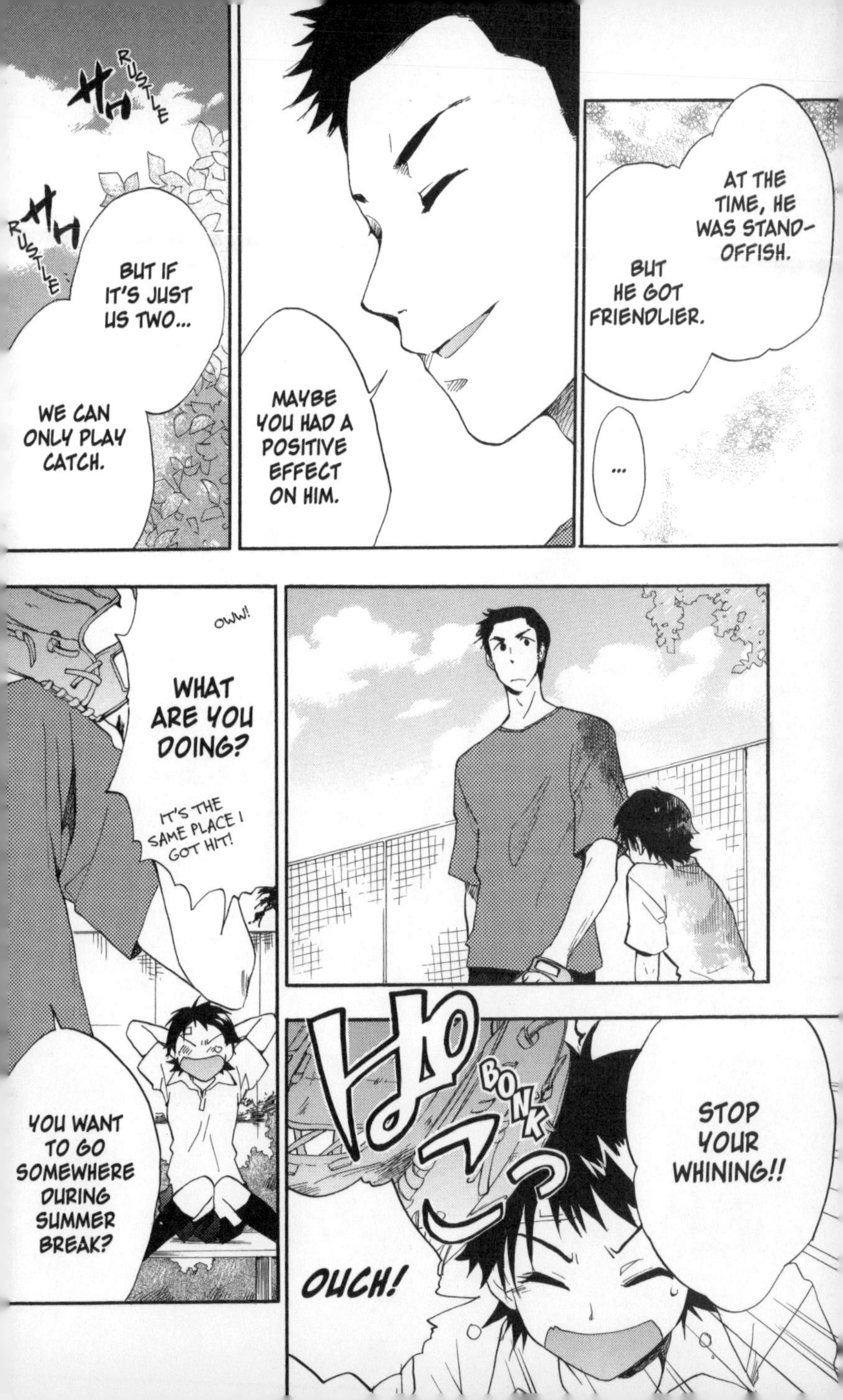
AT THE TIME, HE WAS STAND-OFFISH.
BUT HE GOT FRIENDLIER.
...
MAYBE YOU HAD A POSITIVE EFFECT ON HIM.
RUSTLE
RUSTLE
BUT IF IT'S JUST US TWO...
WE CAN ONLY PLAY CATCH.
STOP YOUR WHINING!!
BONK
OUCH!
OWW!
WHAT ARE YOU DOING?
IT'S THE SAME PLACE I GOT HIT!
YOU WANT TO GO SOMEWHERE DURING SUMMER BREAK?

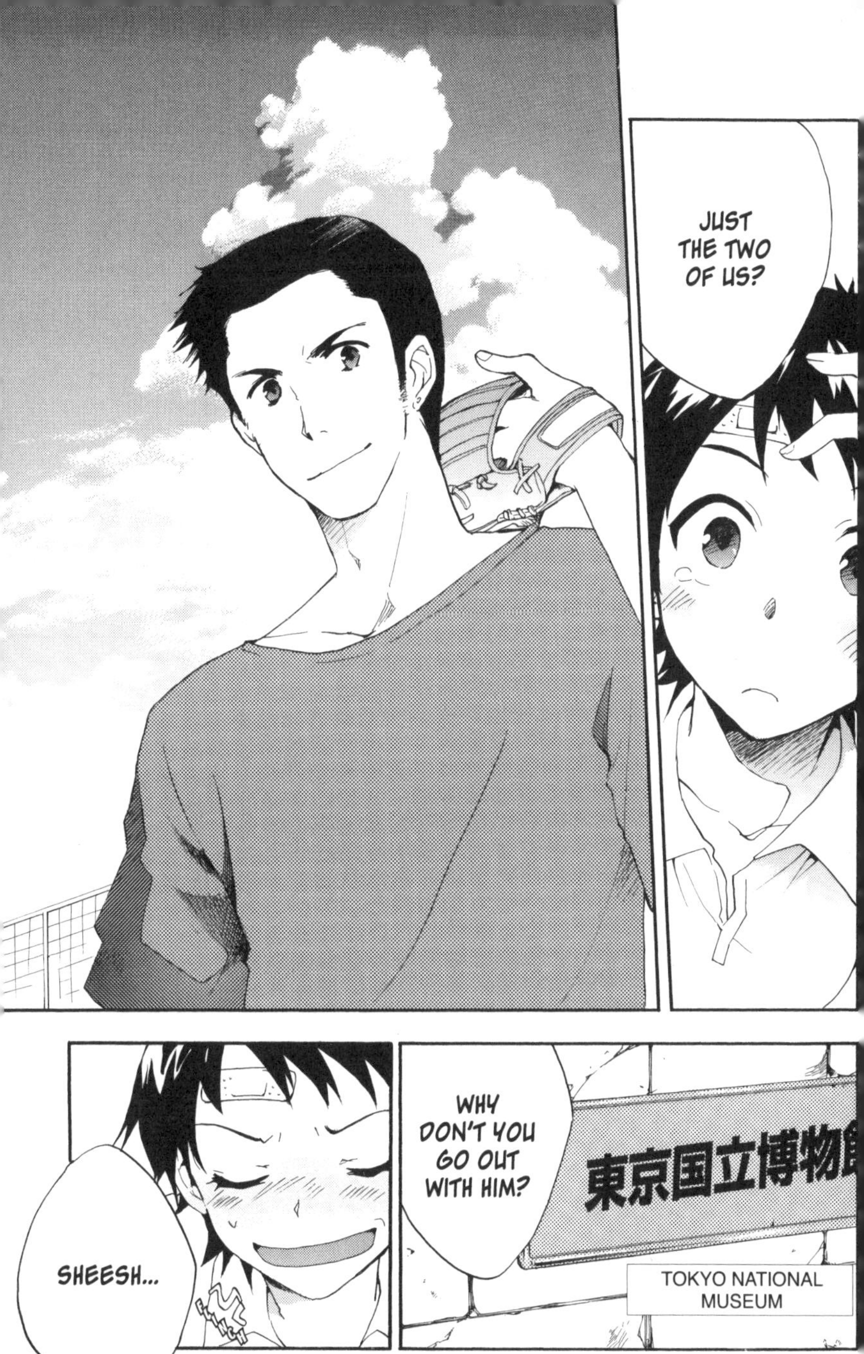
JUST THE TWO OF US?
WHY DON'T YOU GO OUT WITH HIM?
東京国立博物
TOKYO NATIONAL MUSEUM
SHEESH...

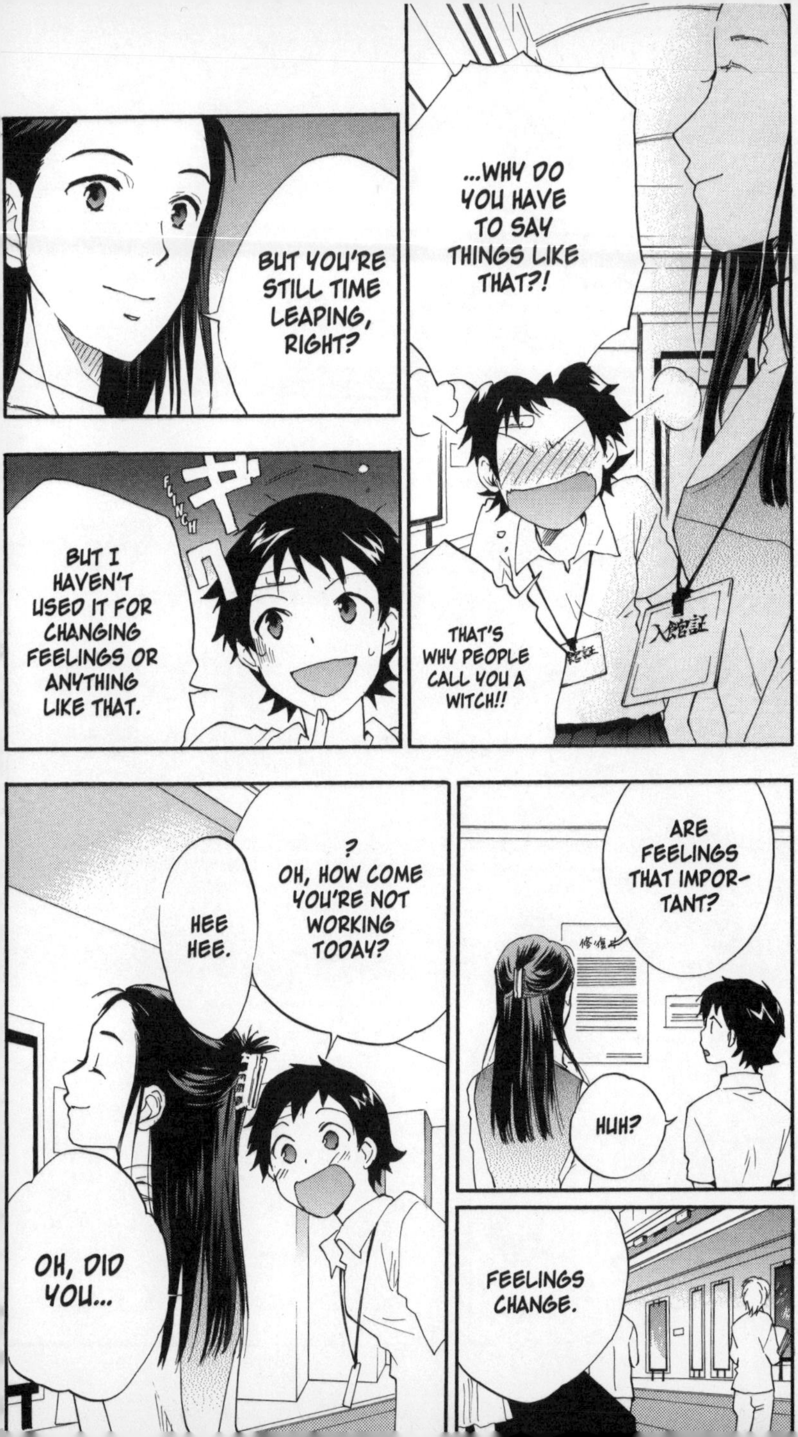
...WHY DO YOU HAVE TO SAY THINGS LIKE THAT?!
THAT'S WHY PEOPLE CALL YOU A WITCH!!
入館証
BUT YOU'RE STILL TIME LEAPING, RIGHT?
ギク
FLINCH
BUT I HAVEN'T USED IT FOR CHANGING FEELINGS OR ANYTHING LIKE THAT.
ARE FEELINGS THAT IMPORTANT?
HUH?
FEELINGS CHANGE.
? OH, HOW COME YOU'RE NOT WORKING TODAY?
HEE HEE.
OH, DID YOU...

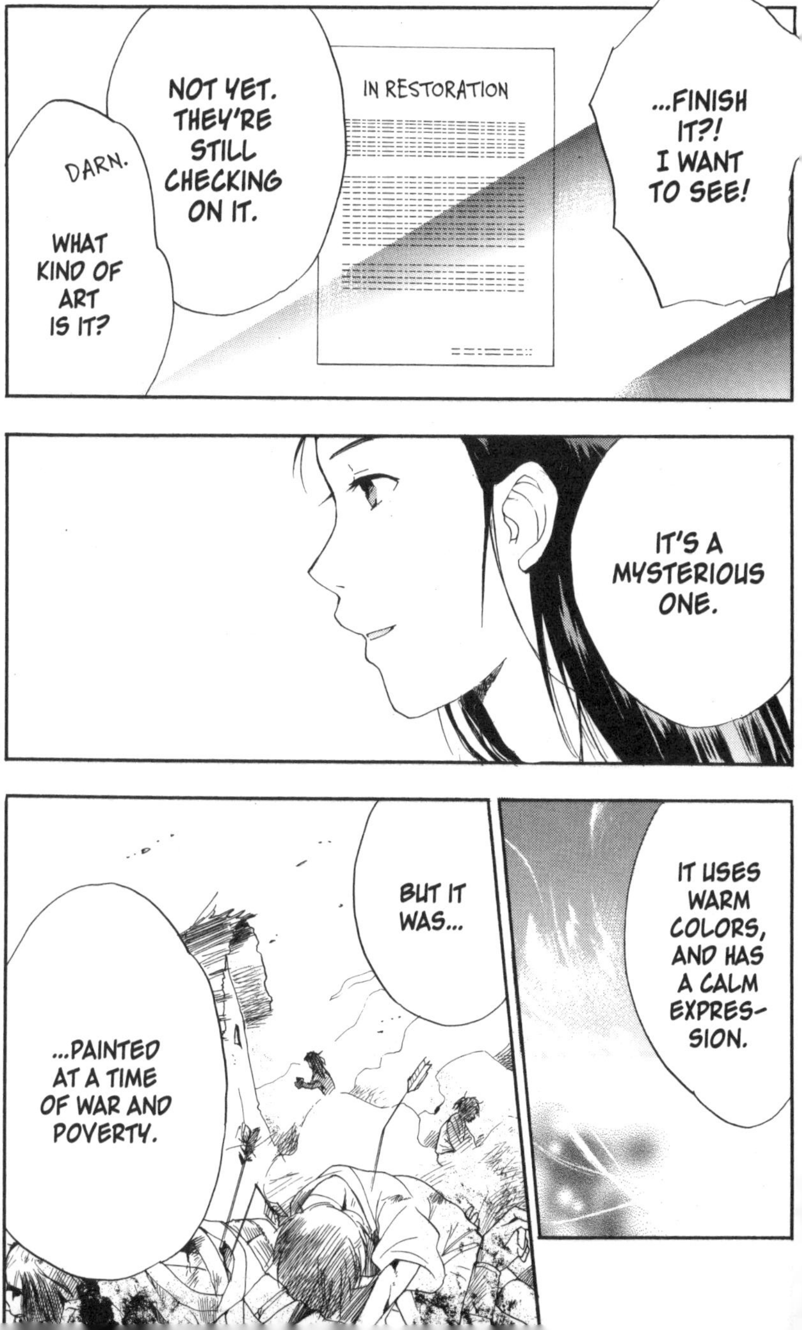
...FINISH IT?! I WANT TO SEE!
IN RESTORATION
NOT YET. THEY'RE STILL CHECKING ON IT.
DARN.
WHAT KIND OF ART IS IT?
IT'S A MYSTERIOUS ONE.
IT USES WARM COLORS, AND HAS A CALM EXPRES-SION.
BUT IT WAS...
...PAINTED AT A TIME OF WAR AND POVERTY.

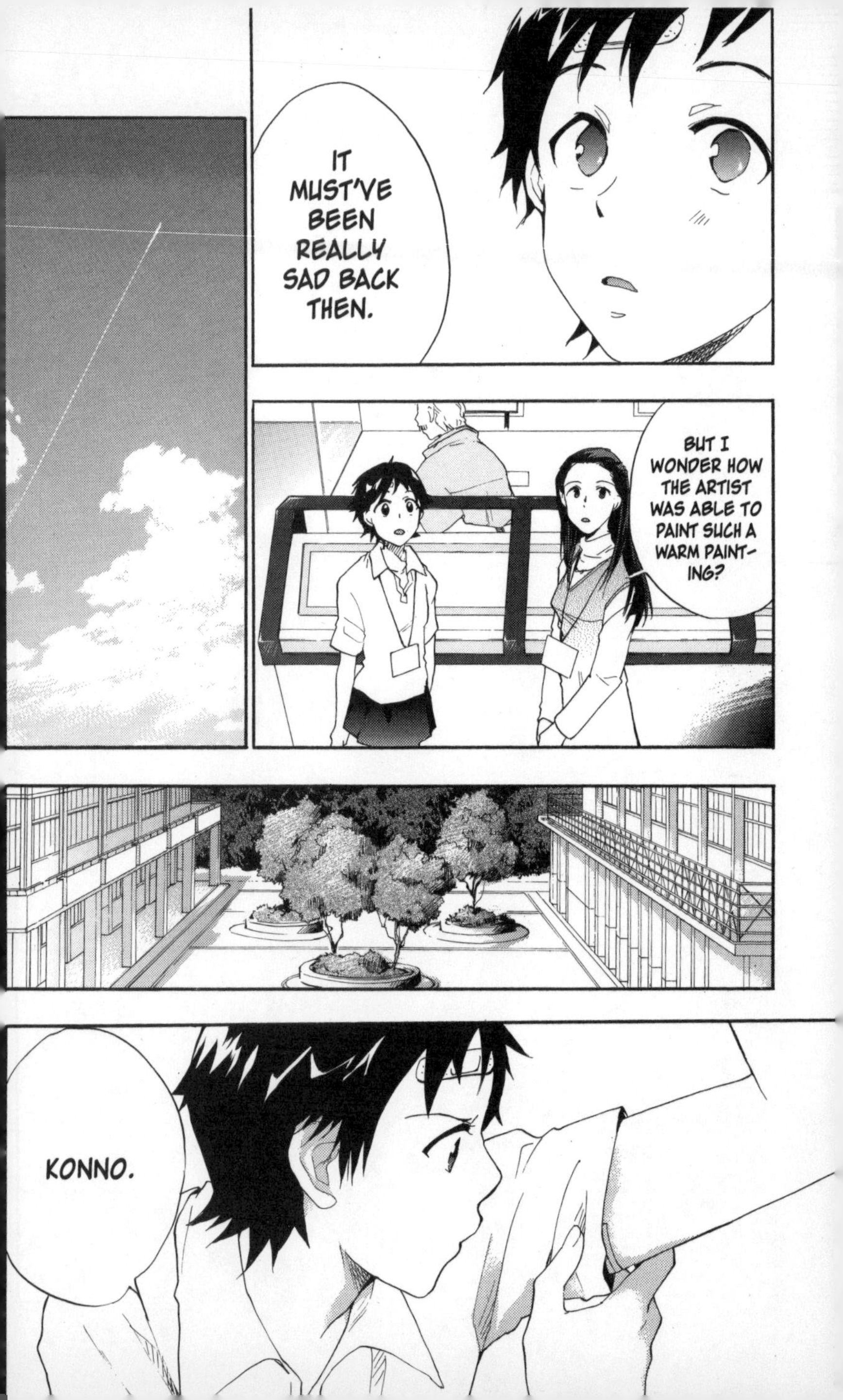
IT MUST'VE BEEN REALLY SAD BACK THEN.
BUT I WONDER HOW THE ARTIST WAS ABLE TO PAINT SUCH A WARM PAINT-ING?
KONNO.

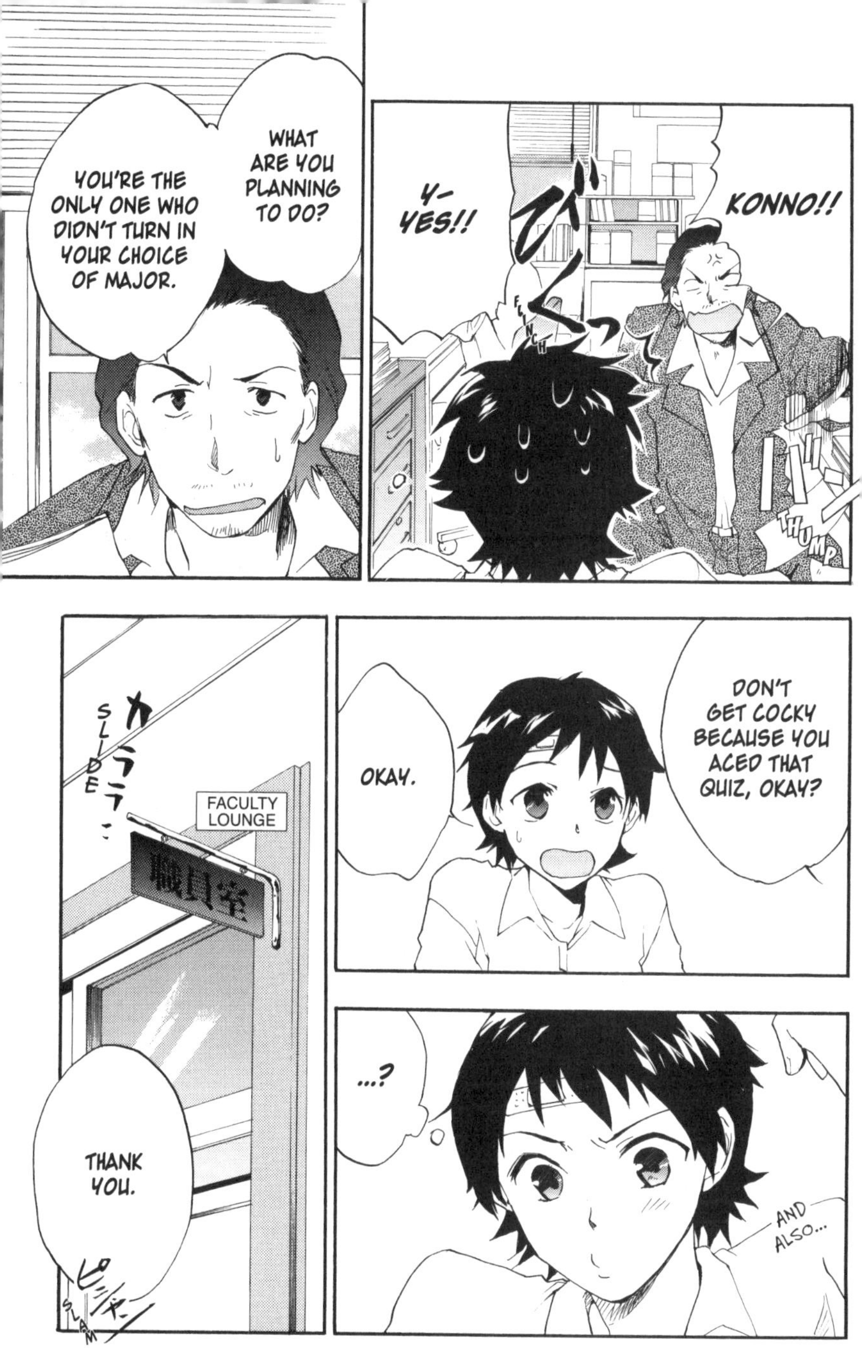
KONNO!!
Y-YES!!
FLINCH
THUMP
WHAT ARE YOU PLANNING TO DO?
YOU'RE THE ONLY ONE WHO DIDN'T TURN IN YOUR CHOICE OF MAJOR.
DON'T GET COCKY BECAUSE YOU ACED THAT QUIZ, OKAY?
OKAY.
AND ALSO...
...?
SLIDE
FACULTY LOUNGE
職員室
THANK YOU.
SLAM

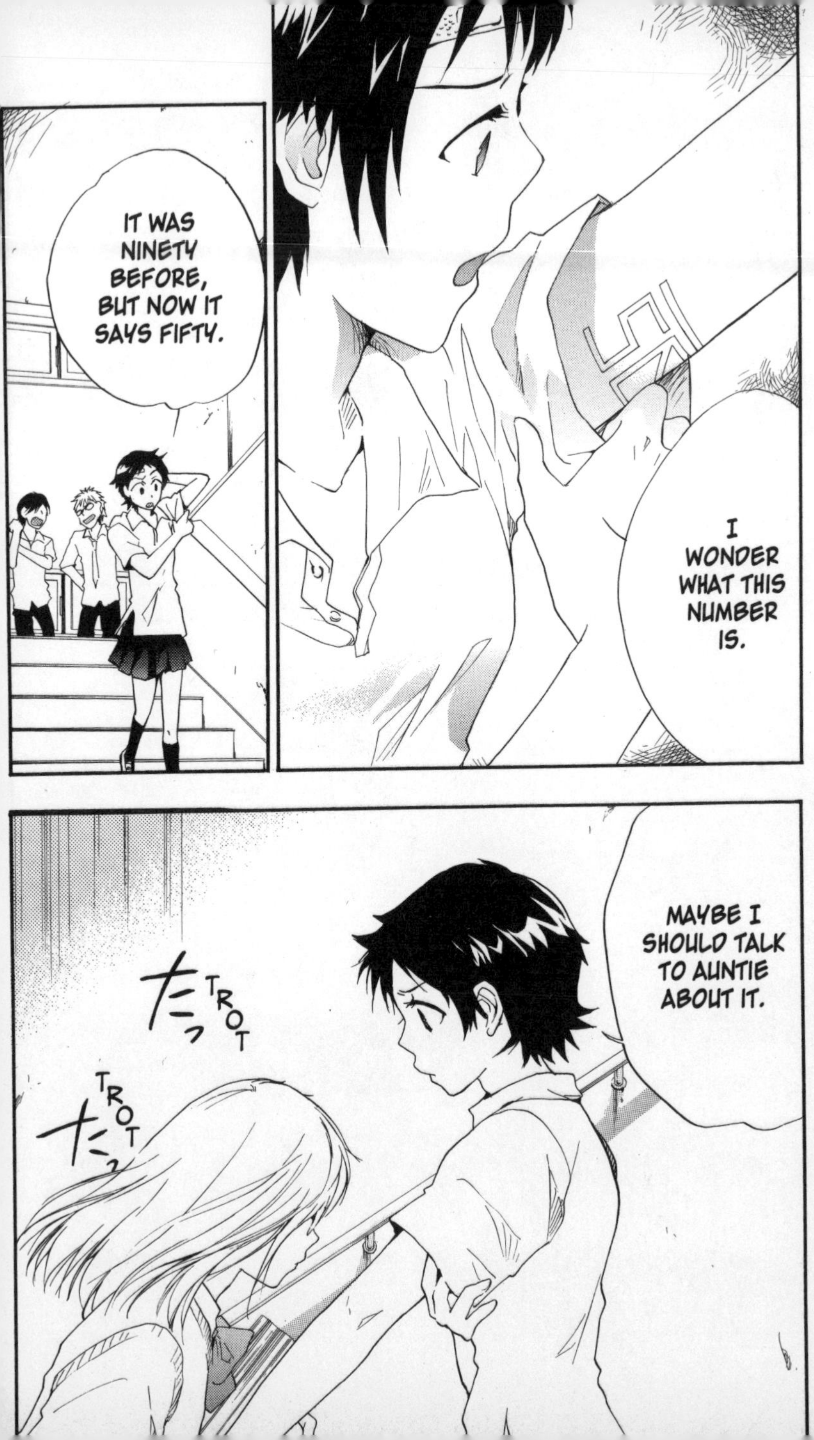
I WONDER WHAT THIS NUMBER IS.
IT WAS NINETY BEFORE, BUT NOW IT SAYS FIFTY.
MAYBE I SHOULD TALK TO AUNTIE ABOUT IT.
TROT
TROT

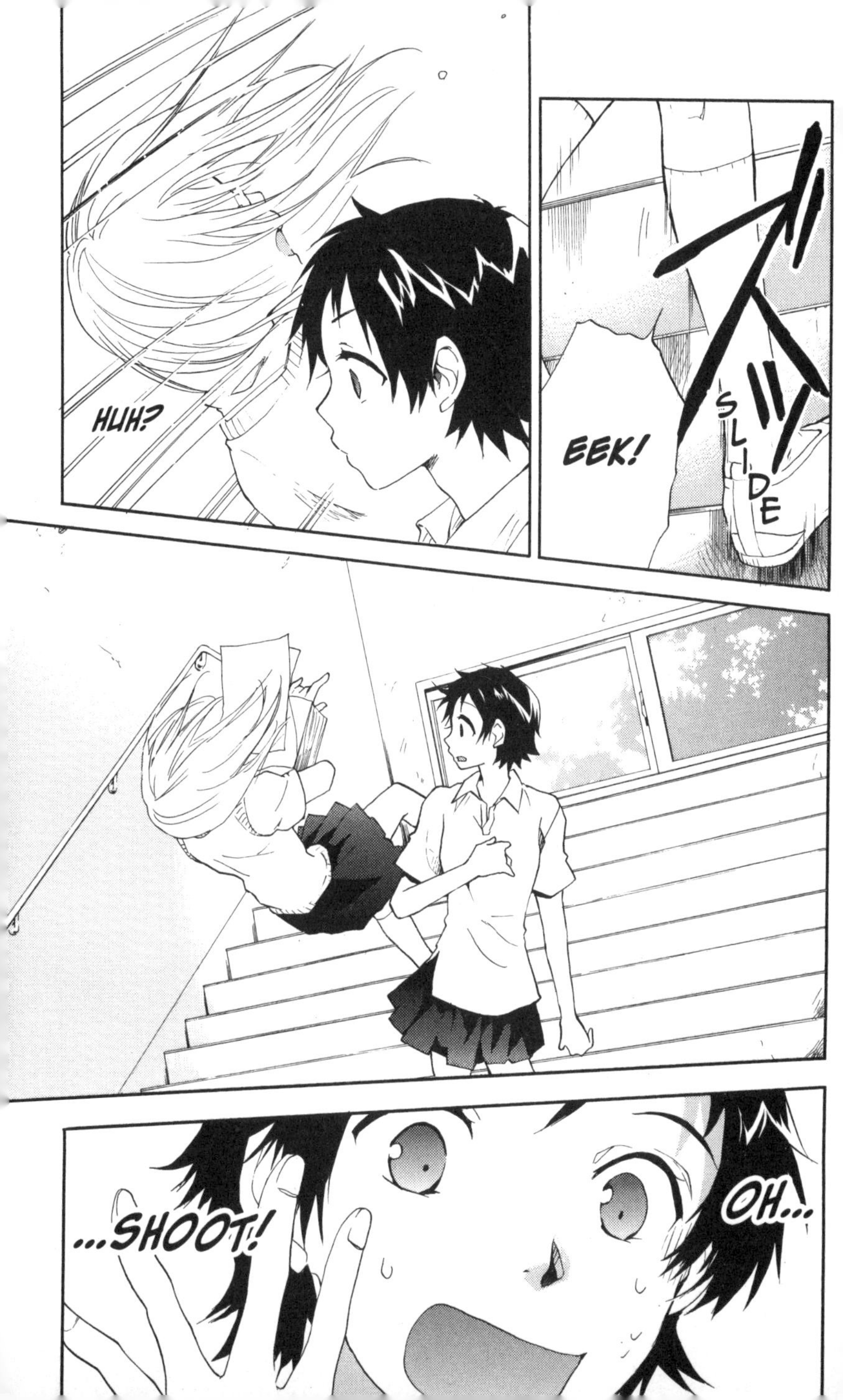
EEK!
SLIDE
HUH?
OH...
...SHOOT!

GO...

...BACK!!!

OH.

MAYBE I SHOULD TALK TO AUNTIE ABOUT IT.

IT WAS NINETY BEFORE, BUT NOW IT SAYS FIFTY.

TROT

TROT

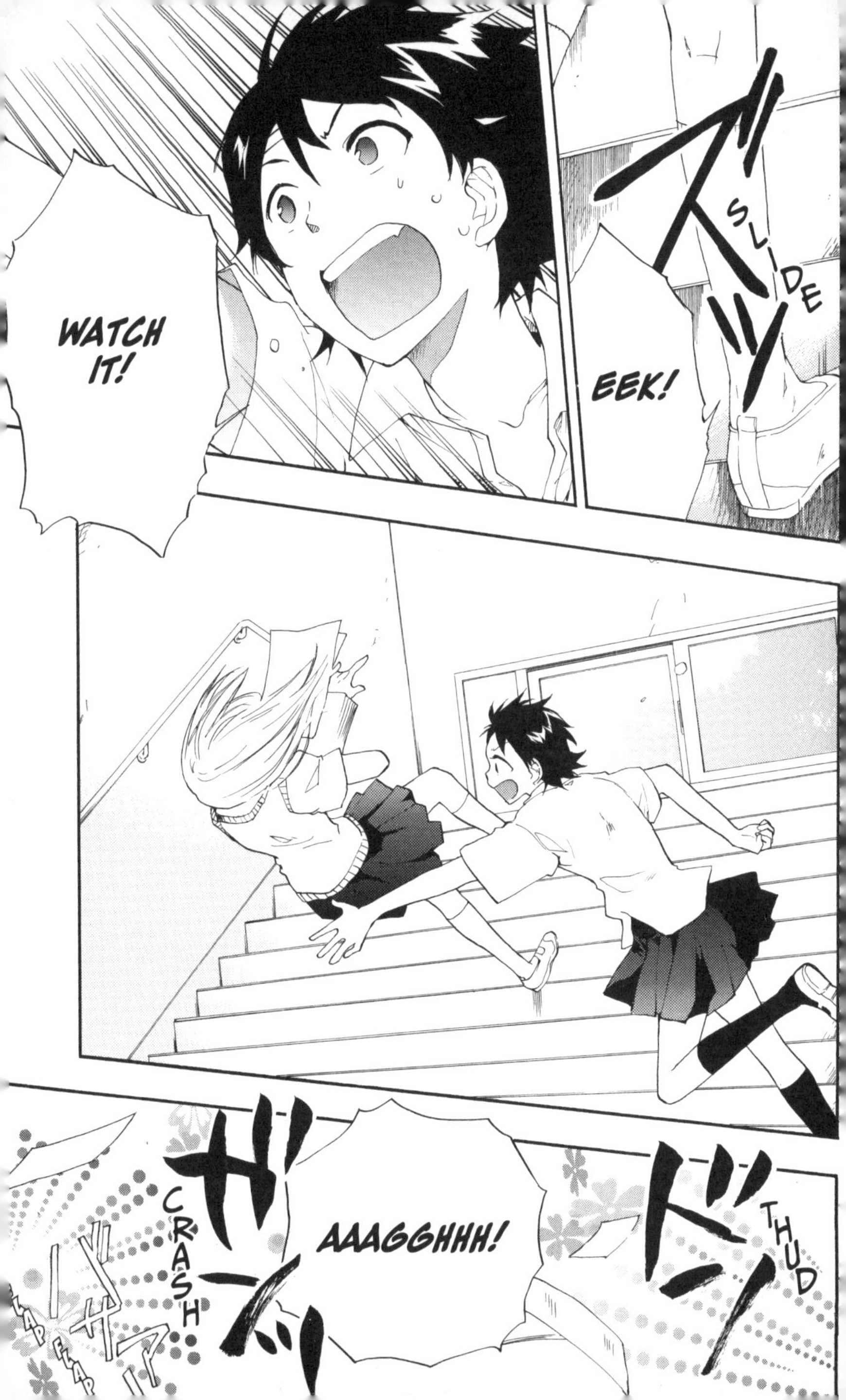
SLIDE
EEK!
WATCH IT!
THUD
AAAGGHHH!
CRASH
FLAP
FLAP

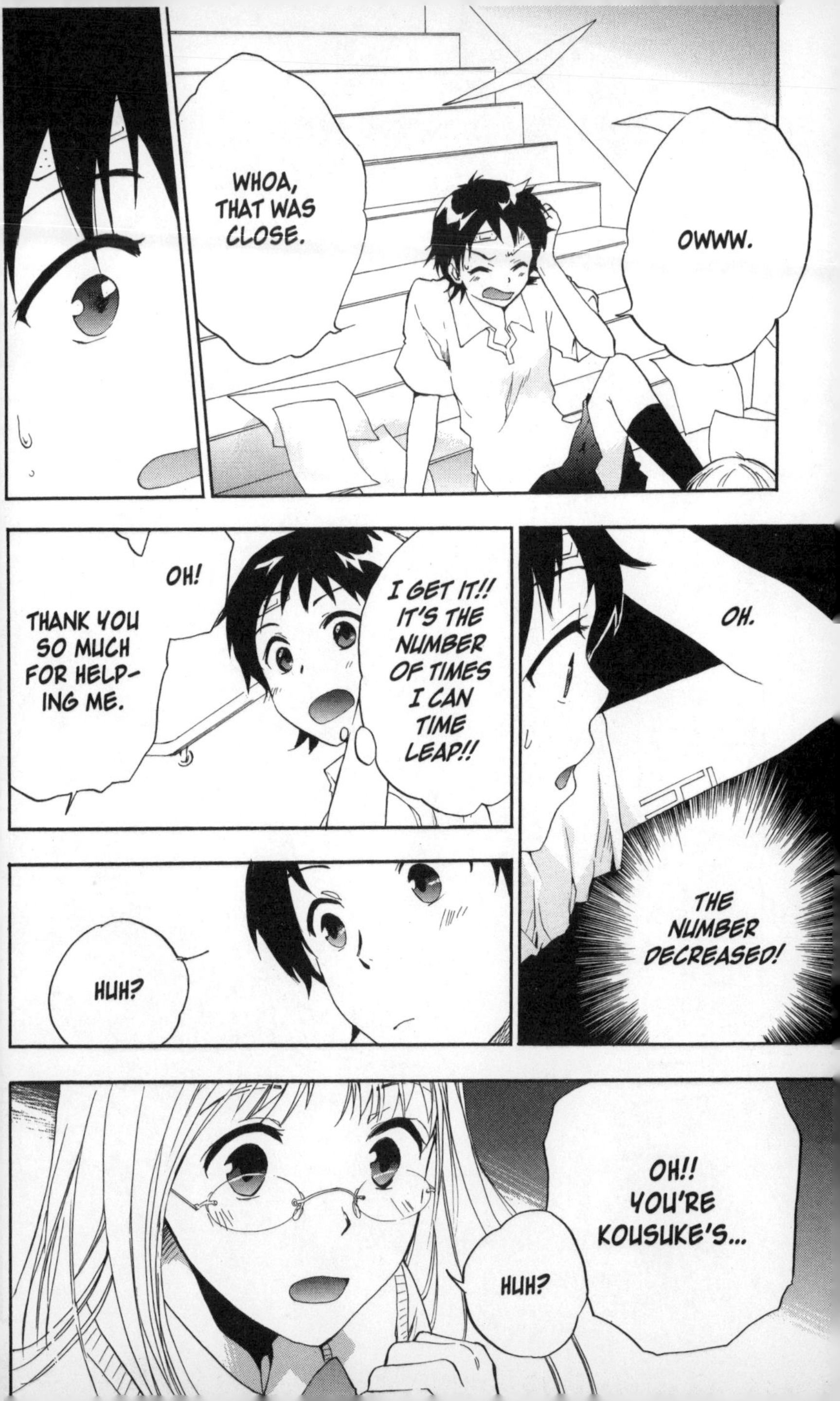
OWWW.
WHOA, THAT WAS CLOSE.
OH.
THE NUMBER DECREASED!
I GET IT!! IT'S THE NUMBER OF TIMES I CAN TIME LEAP!!
OH!
THANK YOU SO MUCH FOR HELPING ME.
HUH?
OH!! YOU'RE KOUSUKE'S...
HUH?

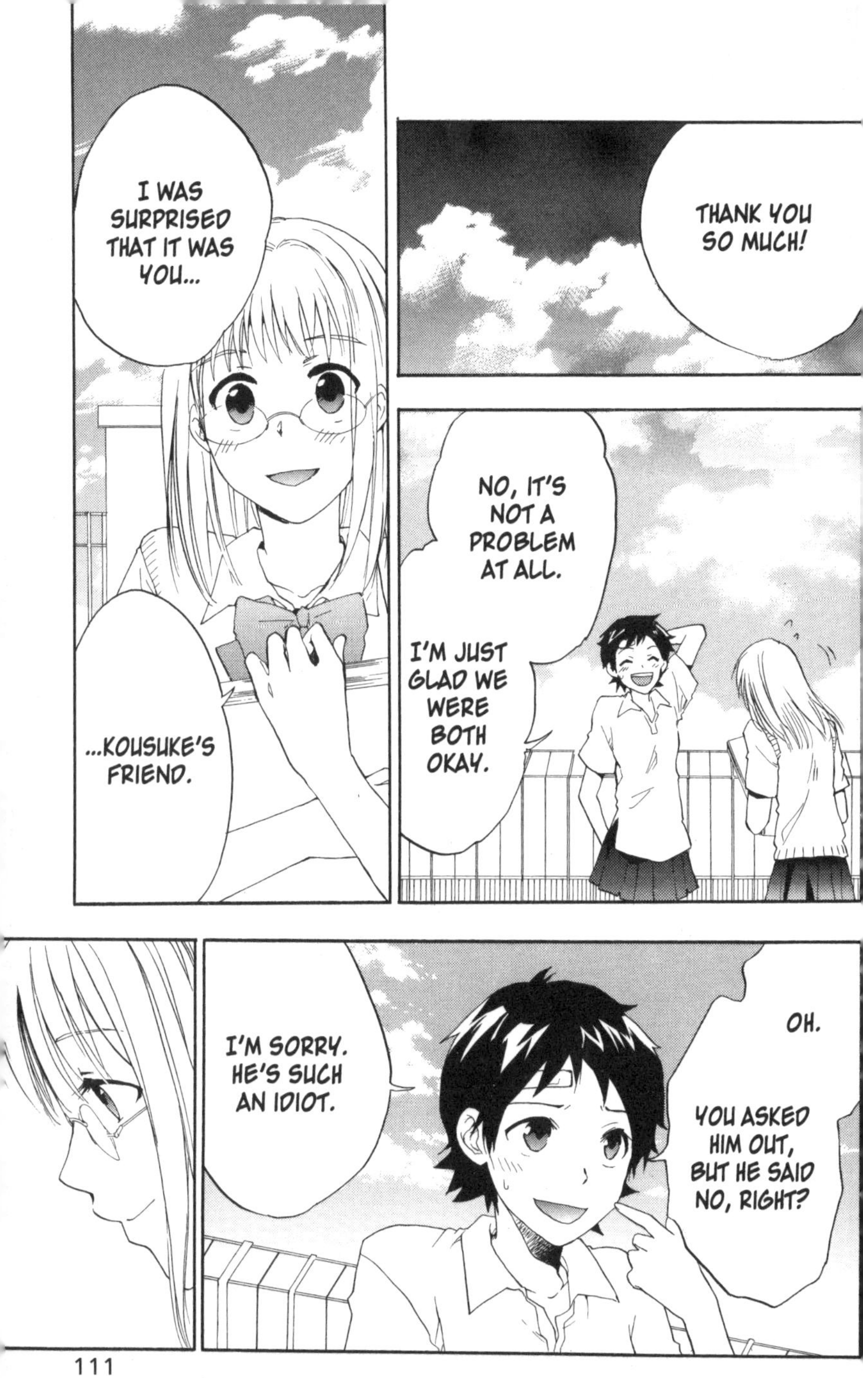
THANK YOU SO MUCH!
NO, IT'S NOT A PROBLEM AT ALL.
I'M JUST GLAD WE WERE BOTH OKAY.
I WAS SURPRISED THAT IT WAS YOU...
...KOUSUKE'S FRIEND.
OH.
YOU ASKED HIM OUT, BUT HE SAID NO, RIGHT?
I'M SORRY. HE'S SUCH AN IDIOT.

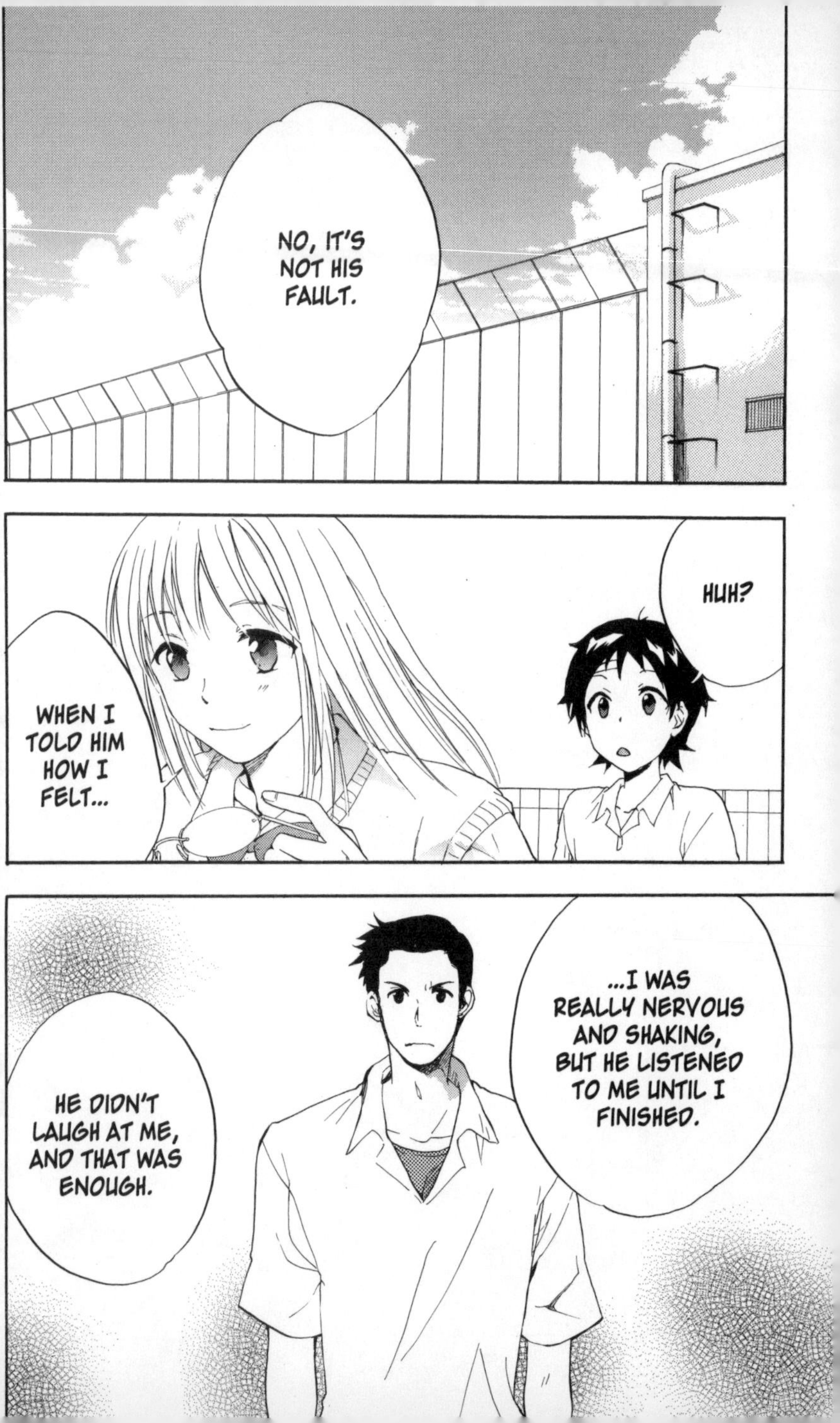
NO, IT'S NOT HIS FAULT.
HUH?
WHEN I TOLD HIM HOW I FELT...
...I WAS REALLY NERVOUS AND SHAKING, BUT HE LISTENED TO ME UNTIL I FINISHED.
HE DIDN'T LAUGH AT ME, AND THAT WAS ENOUGH.

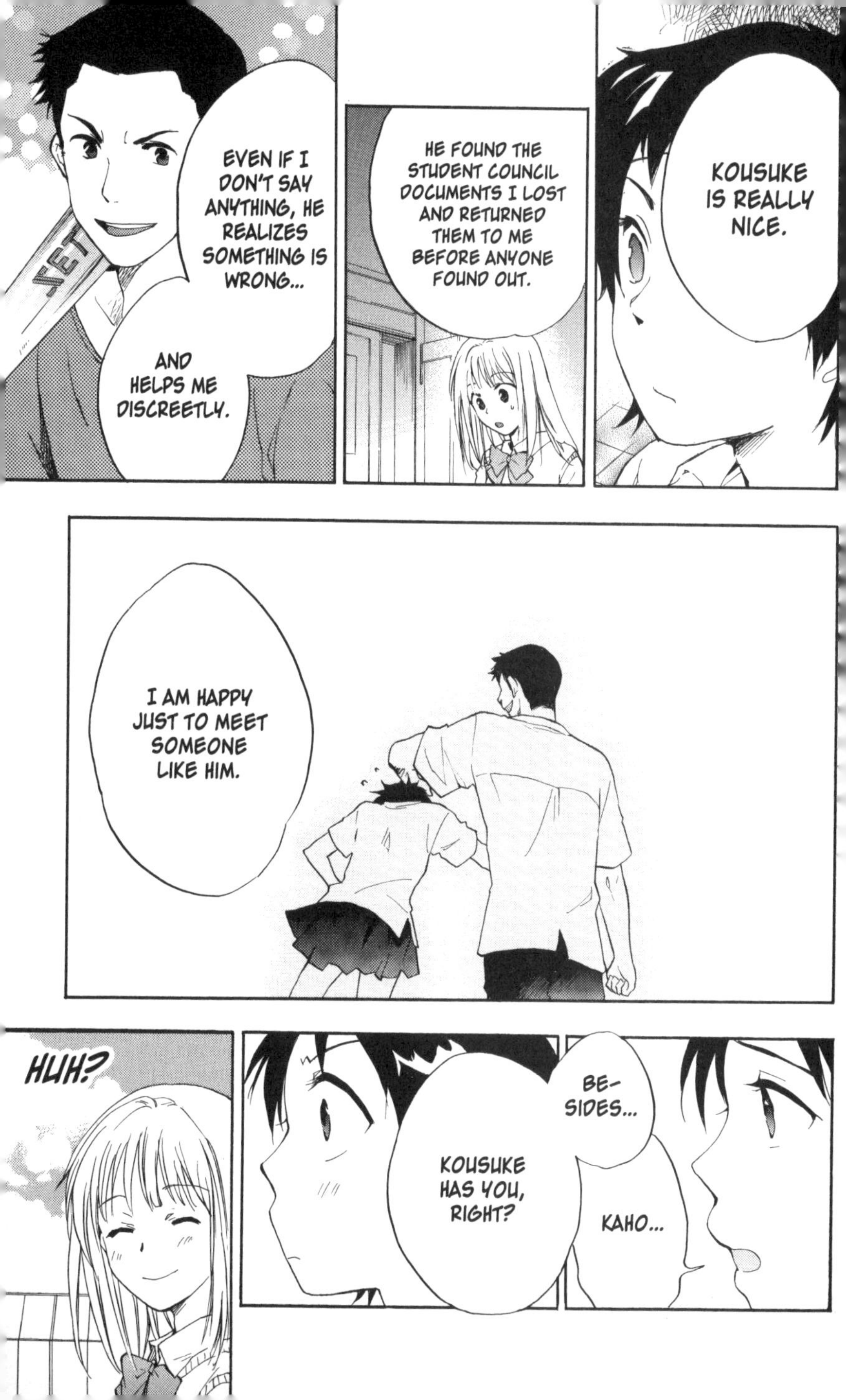
KOUSUKE IS REALLY NICE.
HE FOUND THE STUDENT COUNCIL DOCUMENTS I LOST AND RETURNED THEM TO ME BEFORE ANYONE FOUND OUT.
EVEN IF I DON'T SAY ANYTHING, HE REALIZES SOMETHING IS WRONG...
AND HELPS ME DISCREETLY.
I AM HAPPY JUST TO MEET SOMEONE LIKE HIM.
BE-SIDES...
KOUSUKE HAS YOU, RIGHT?
KAHO...
HUH?

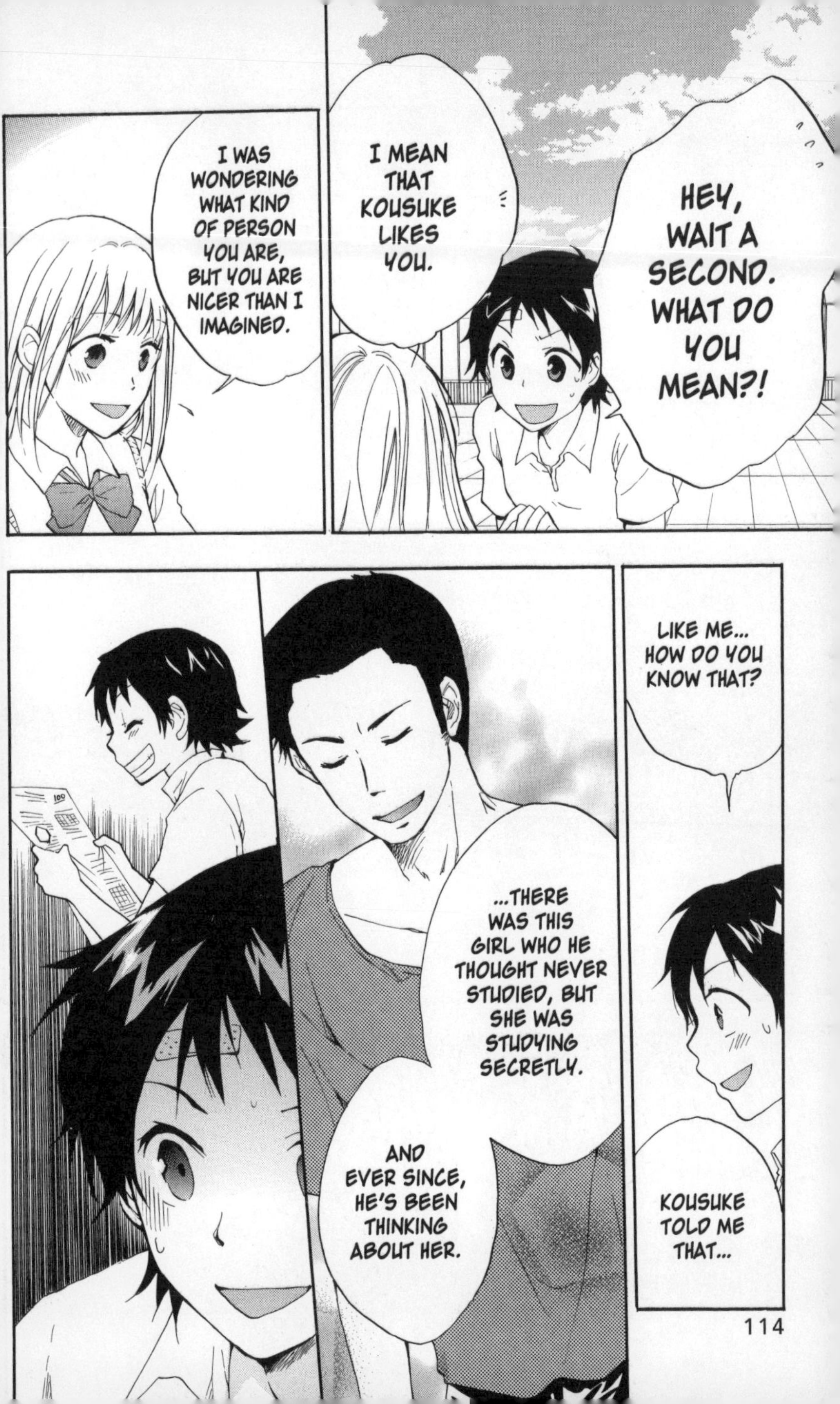
I MEAN THAT KOUSUKE LIKES YOU.
HEY, WAIT A SECOND. WHAT DO YOU MEAN?!
I WAS WONDERING WHAT KIND OF PERSON YOU ARE, BUT YOU ARE NICER THAN I IMAGINED.
LIKE ME... HOW DO YOU KNOW THAT?
KOUSUKE TOLD ME THAT...
...THERE WAS THIS GIRL WHO HE THOUGHT NEVER STUDIED, BUT SHE WAS STUDYING SECRETLY.
AND EVER SINCE, HE'S BEEN THINKING ABOUT HER.

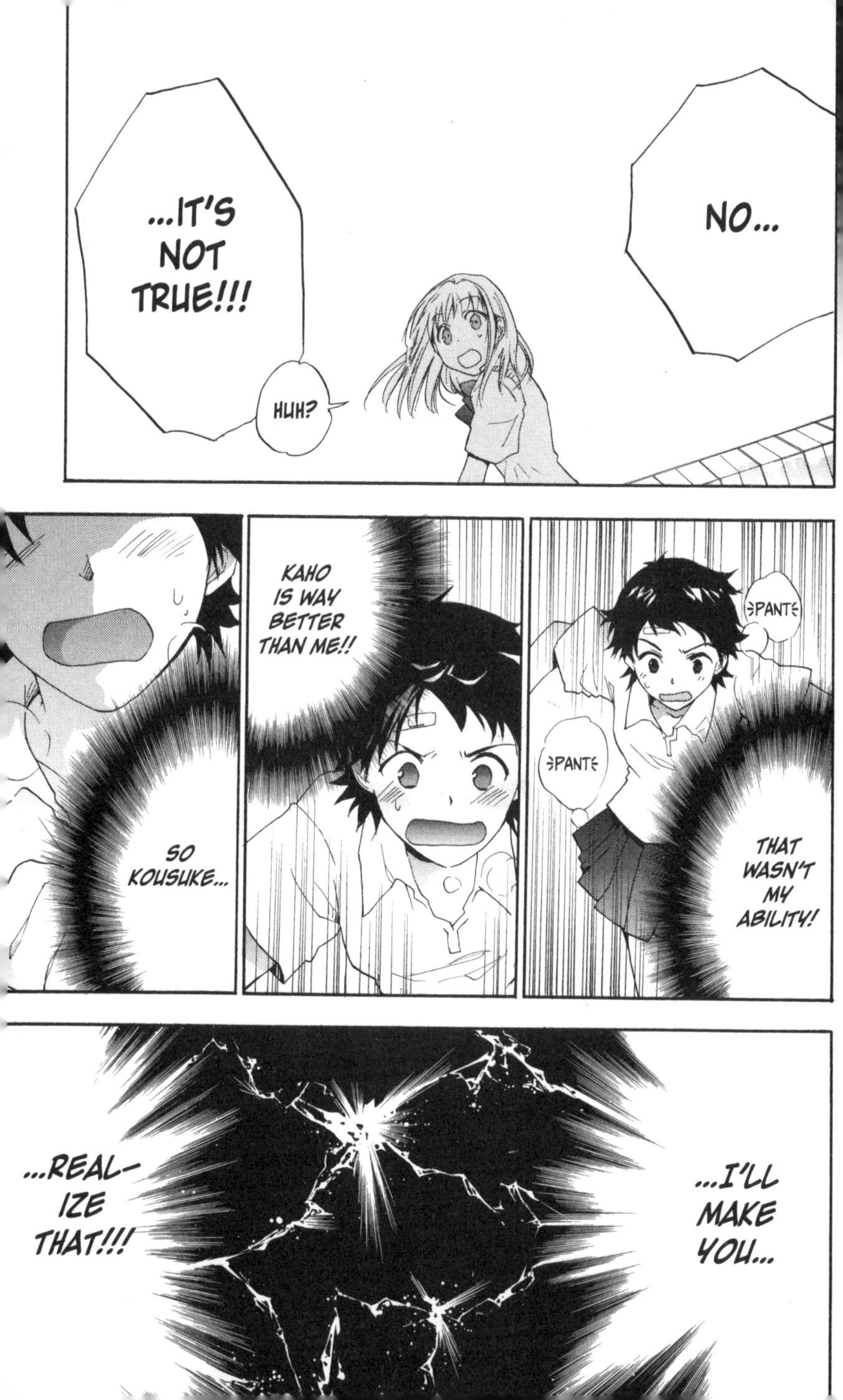
NO...
...IT'S NOT TRUE!!!
HUH?
PANT
PANT
THAT WASN'T MY ABILITY!
KAHO IS WAY BETTER THAN ME!!
SO KOUSUKE...
...I'LL MAKE YOU...
...REAL-IZE THAT!!!

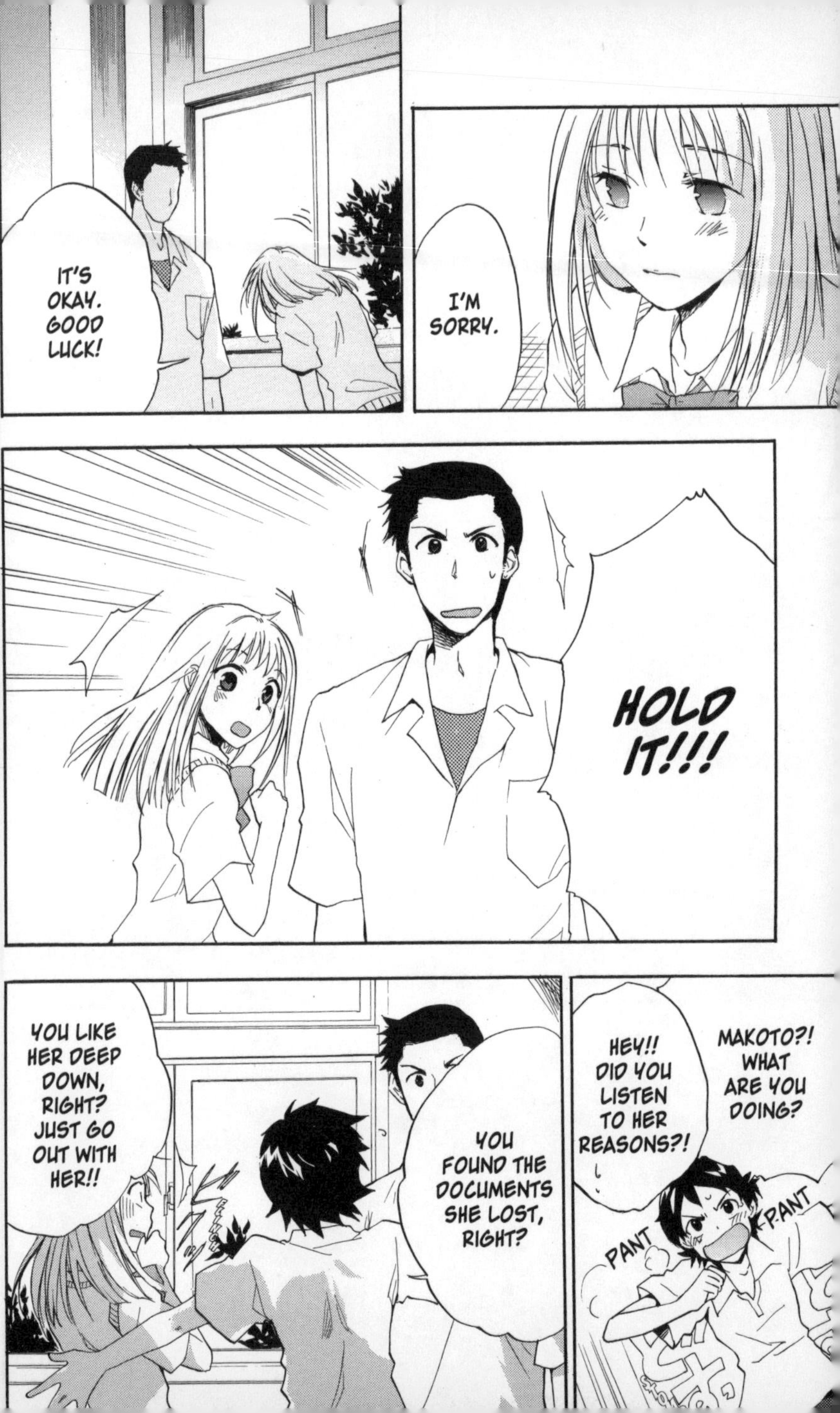
I'M SORRY.
IT'S OKAY. GOOD LUCK!
HOLD IT!!!
MAKOTO?! WHAT ARE YOU DOING?
HEY!! DID YOU LISTEN TO HER REASONS?!
PANT
PANT
YOU FOUND THE DOCUMENTS SHE LOST, RIGHT?
YOU LIKE HER DEEP DOWN, RIGHT? JUST GO OUT WITH HER!!

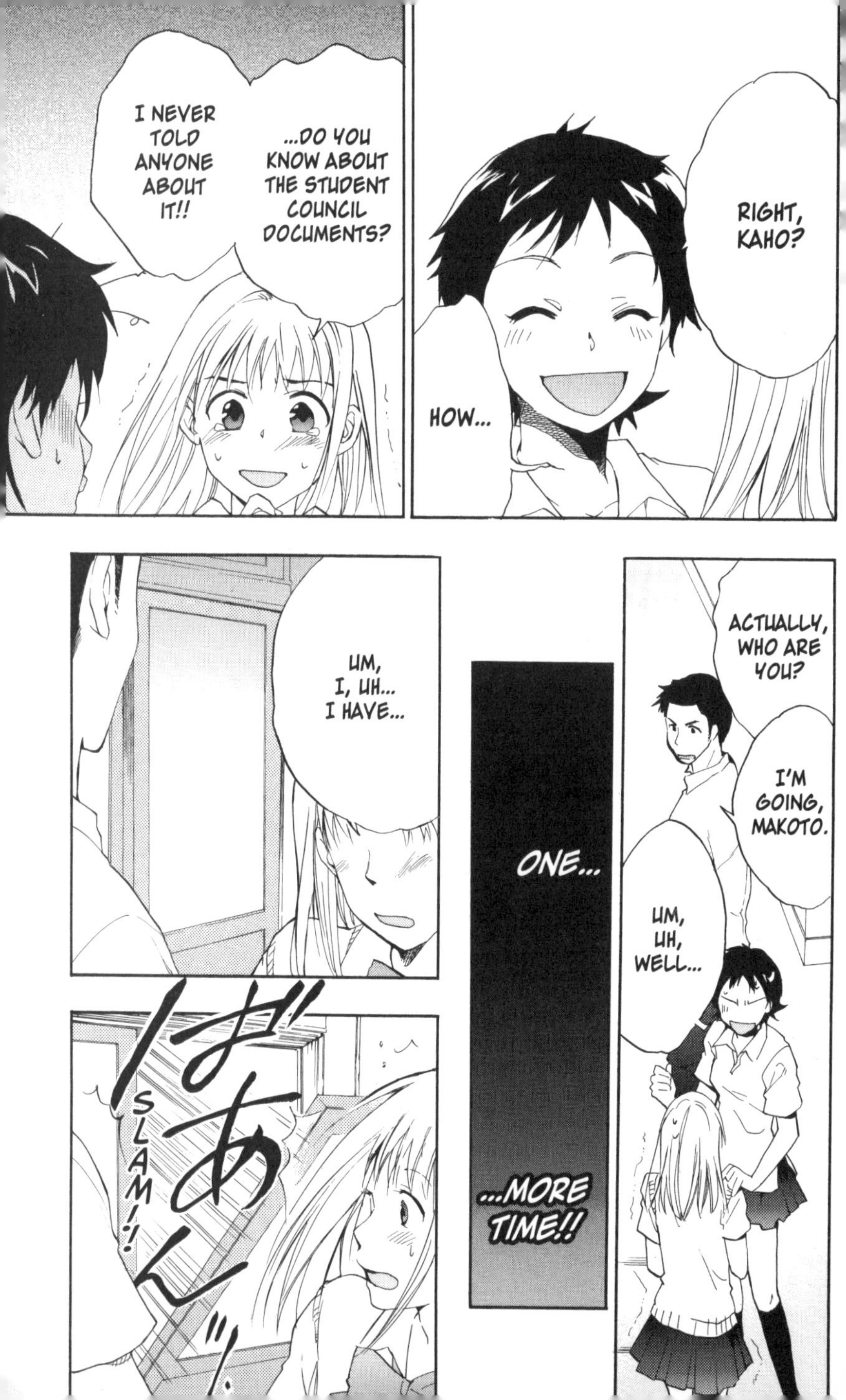
RIGHT, KAHO?
HOW...
...DO YOU KNOW ABOUT THE STUDENT COUNCIL DOCUMENTS?
I NEVER TOLD ANYONE ABOUT IT!!
ACTUALLY, WHO ARE YOU?
I'M GOING, MAKOTO.
UM, UH, WELL...
ONE...
...MORE TIME!!
UM, I, UH... I HAVE...
SLAM!!

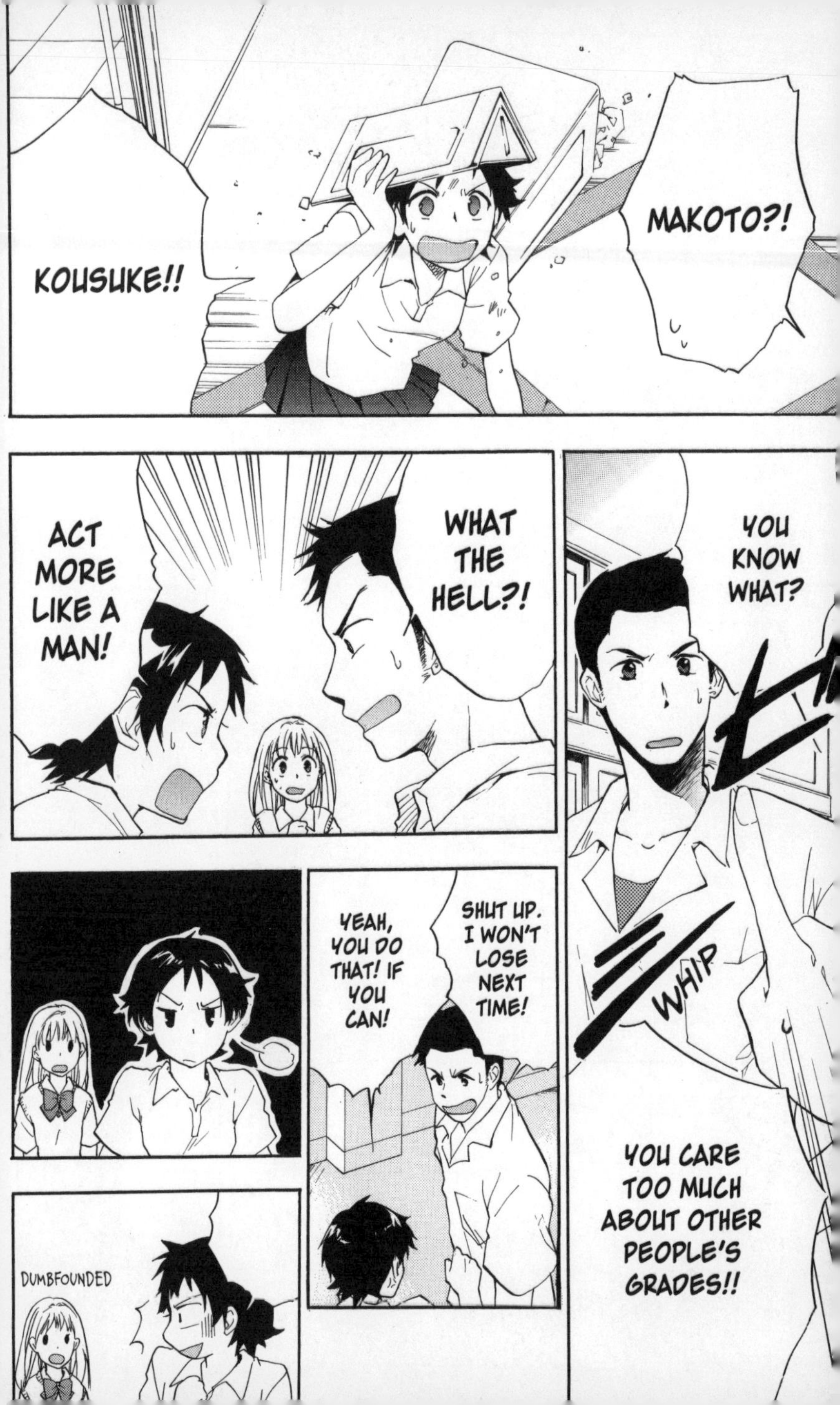
MAKOTO?!
KOUSUKE!!
YOU KNOW WHAT?
WHIP
YOU CARE TOO MUCH ABOUT OTHER PEOPLE'S GRADES!!
WHAT THE HELL?!
ACT MORE LIKE A MAN!
SHUT UP. I WON'T LOSE NEXT TIME!
YEAH, YOU DO THAT! IF YOU CAN!
DUMBFOUNDED

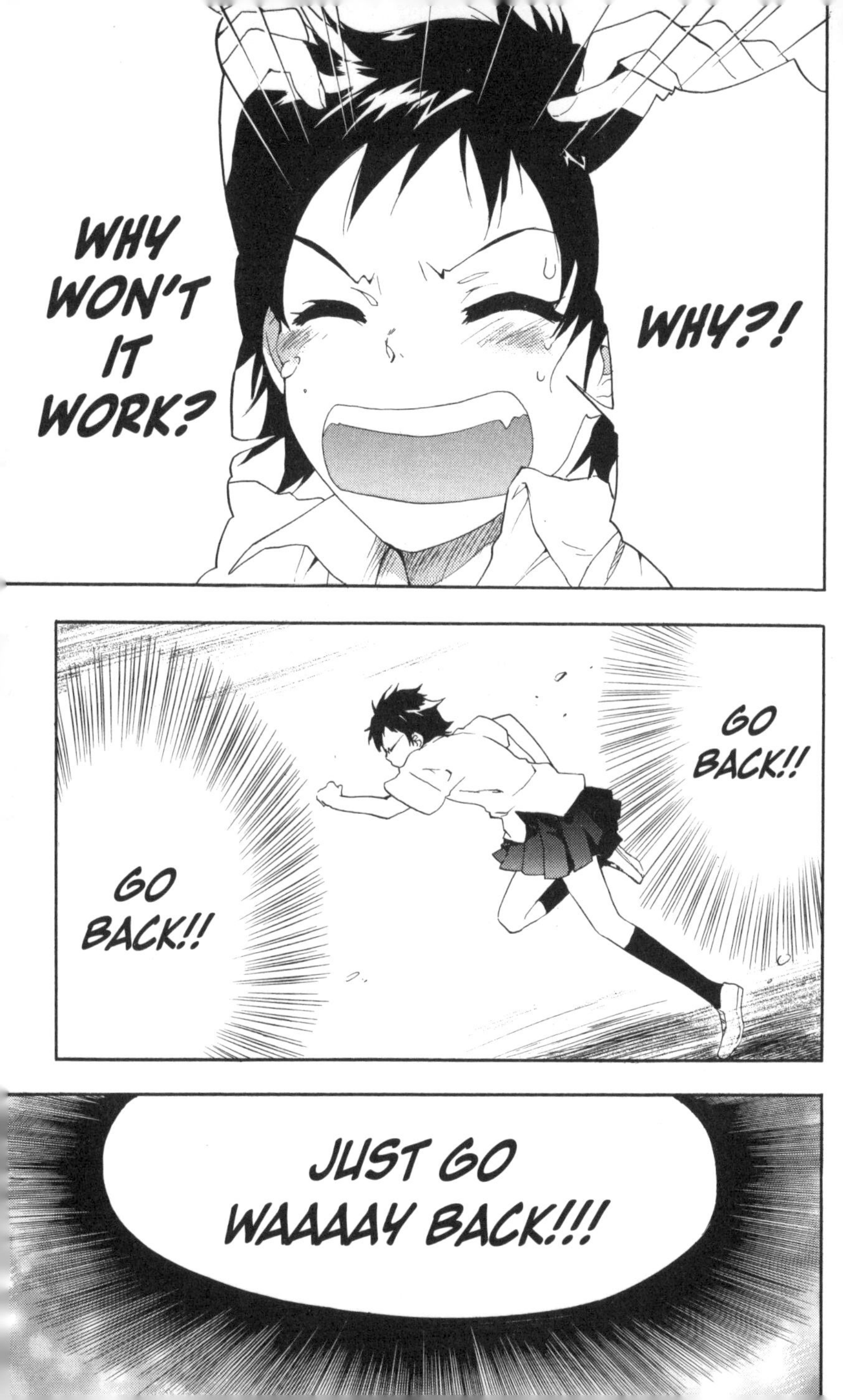
WHY WON'T IT WORK?
WHY?!
GO BACK!!
GO BACK!!
JUST GO WAAAAY BACK!!!

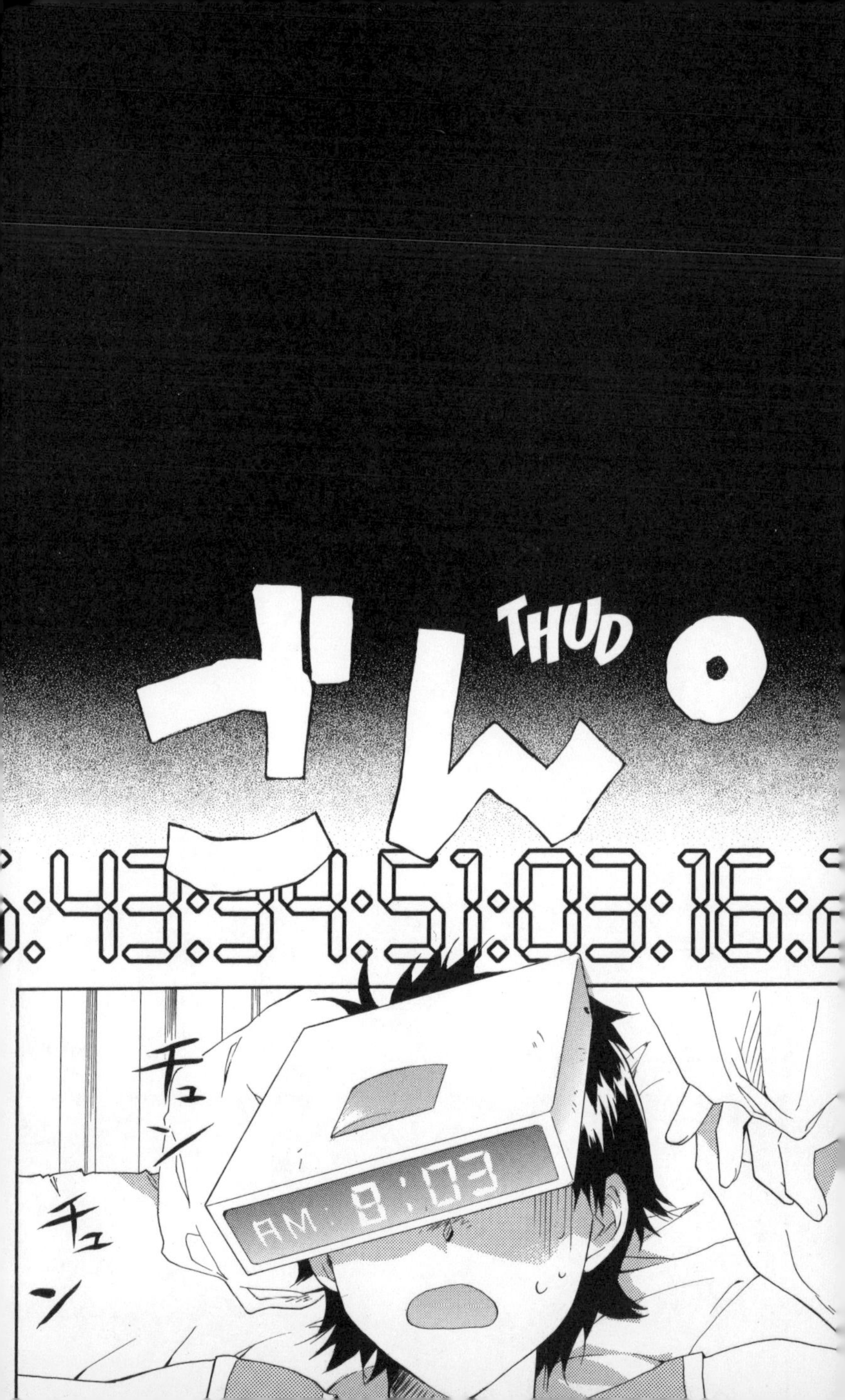
THUD
43:34:51:03:16
AM 9:03
チュン
チュン

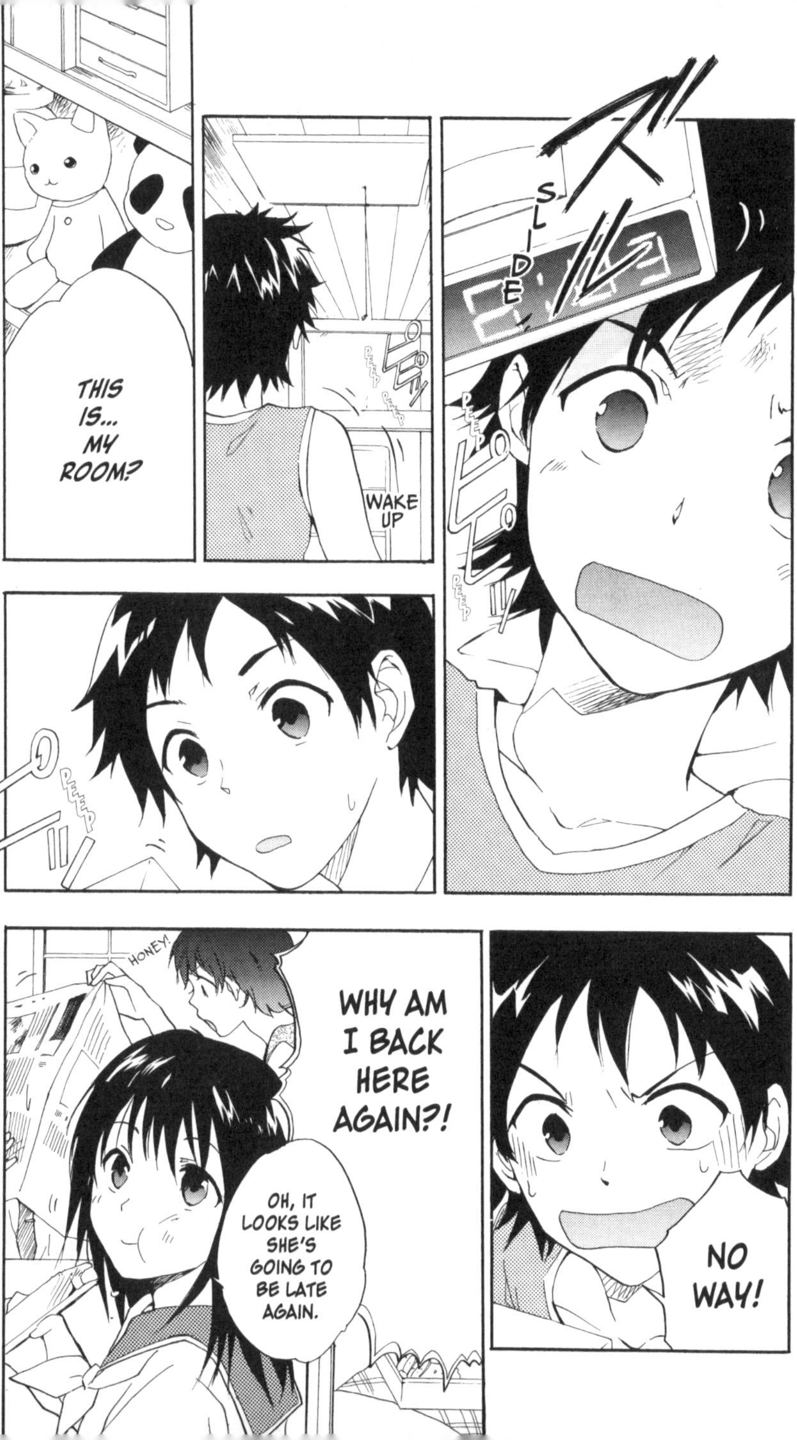

SLIDE
BEEP
BEEP
BEEP
BEEP
WAKE UP
THIS IS... MY ROOM?
BEEP
NO WAY!
WHY AM I BACK HERE AGAIN?!
HONEY!
OH, IT LOOKS LIKE SHE'S GOING TO BE LATE AGAIN.

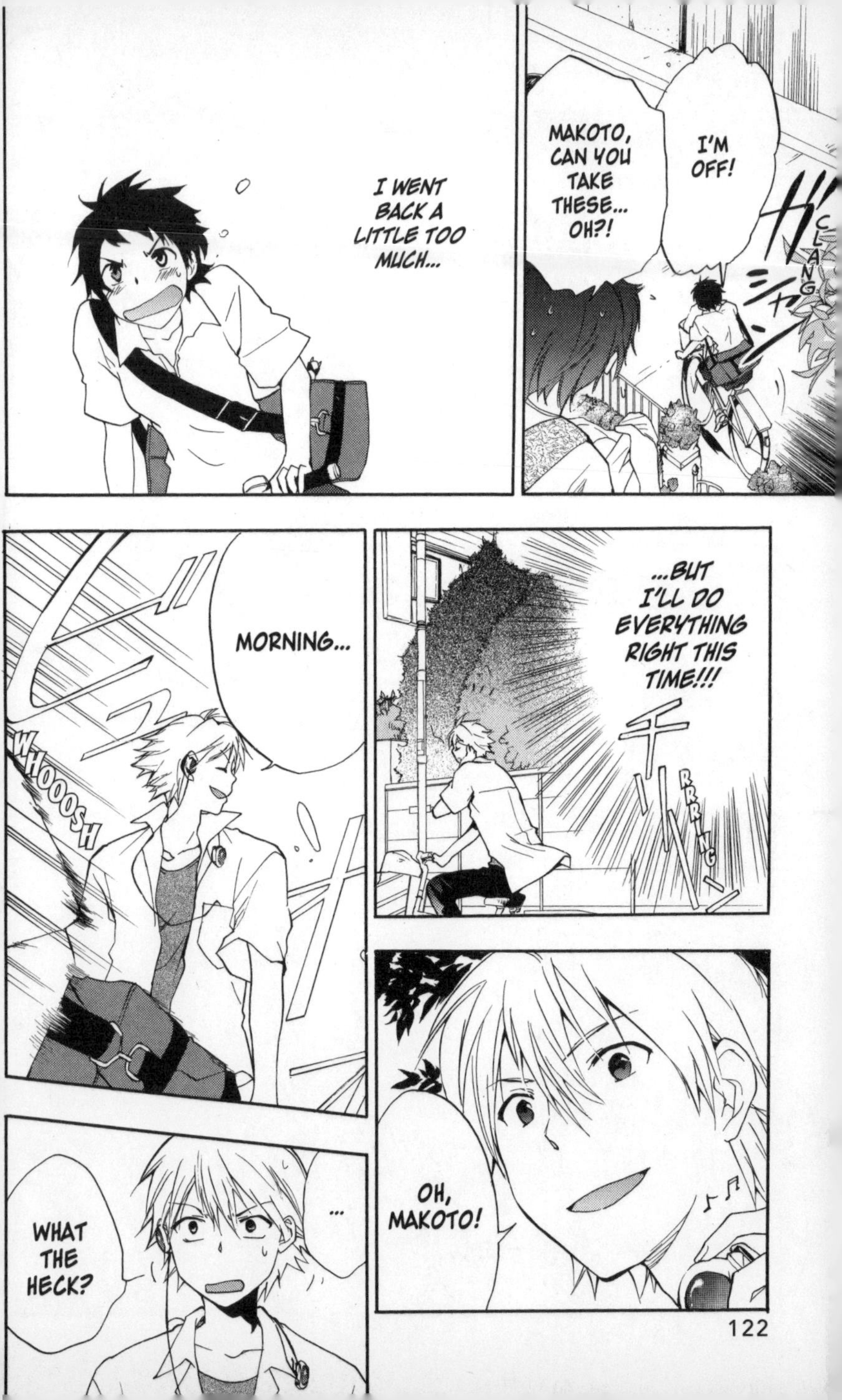
I'M OFF!
MAKOTO, CAN YOU TAKE THESE... OH?!
CLANG
I WENT BACK A LITTLE TOO MUCH...
...BUT I'LL DO EVERYTHING RIGHT THIS TIME!!!
RRRING
OH, MAKOTO!
MORNING...
WHOOOSH
...
WHAT THE HECK?

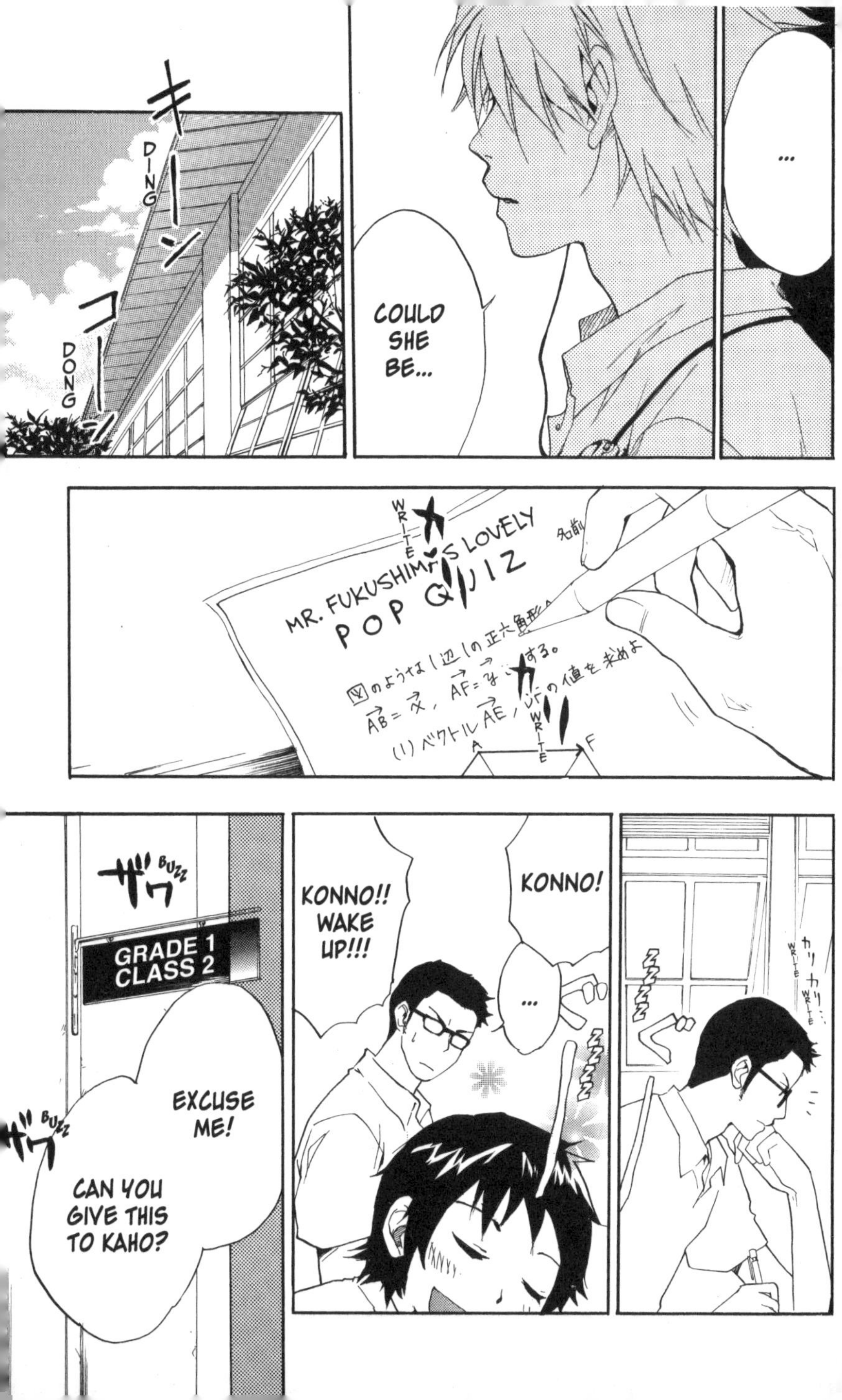
...
COULD SHE BE...
キーンコーン
DING
DONG
MR. FUKUSHIMA'S LOVELY
POP QUIZ
名前
カ
WRITE
カ
WRITE
カリカリ…
WRITE WRITE
ZZZZZ
KONNO!
KONNO!! WAKE UP!!!
...
ZZZZ
ザワ
BUZZ
GRADE 1 CLASS 2
EXCUSE ME!
ザワ
BUZZ
CAN YOU GIVE THIS TO KAHO?

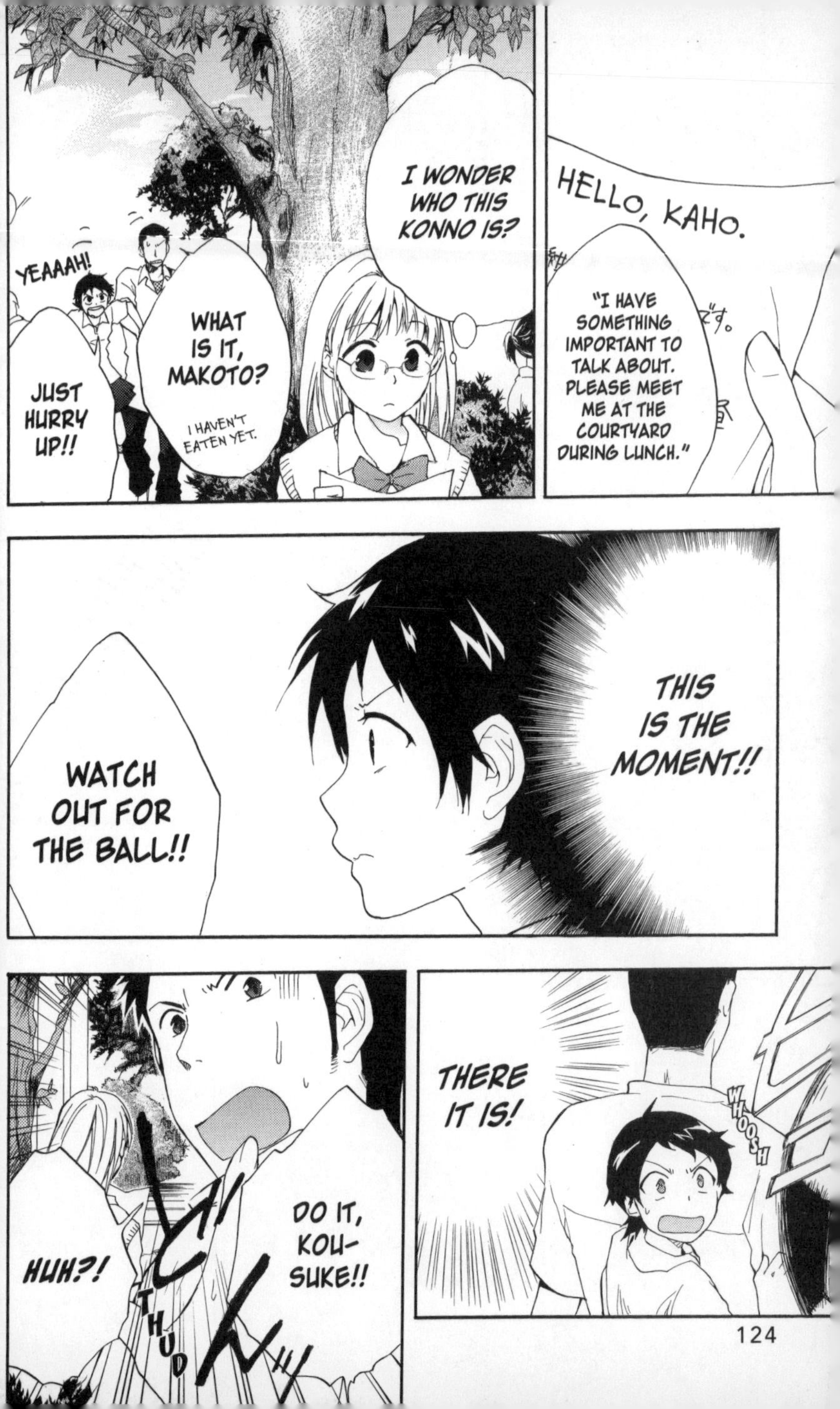
HELLO, KAHO.
"I HAVE SOMETHING IMPORTANT TO TALK ABOUT. PLEASE MEET ME AT THE COURTYARD DURING LUNCH."
I WONDER WHO THIS KONNO IS?
WHAT IS IT, MAKOTO?
I HAVEN'T EATEN YET.
YEAAAH!
JUST HURRY UP!!
THIS IS THE MOMENT!!
WATCH OUT FOR THE BALL!!
WHOOSH
THERE IT IS!
DO IT, KOU-SUKE!!
HUH?!
THUD

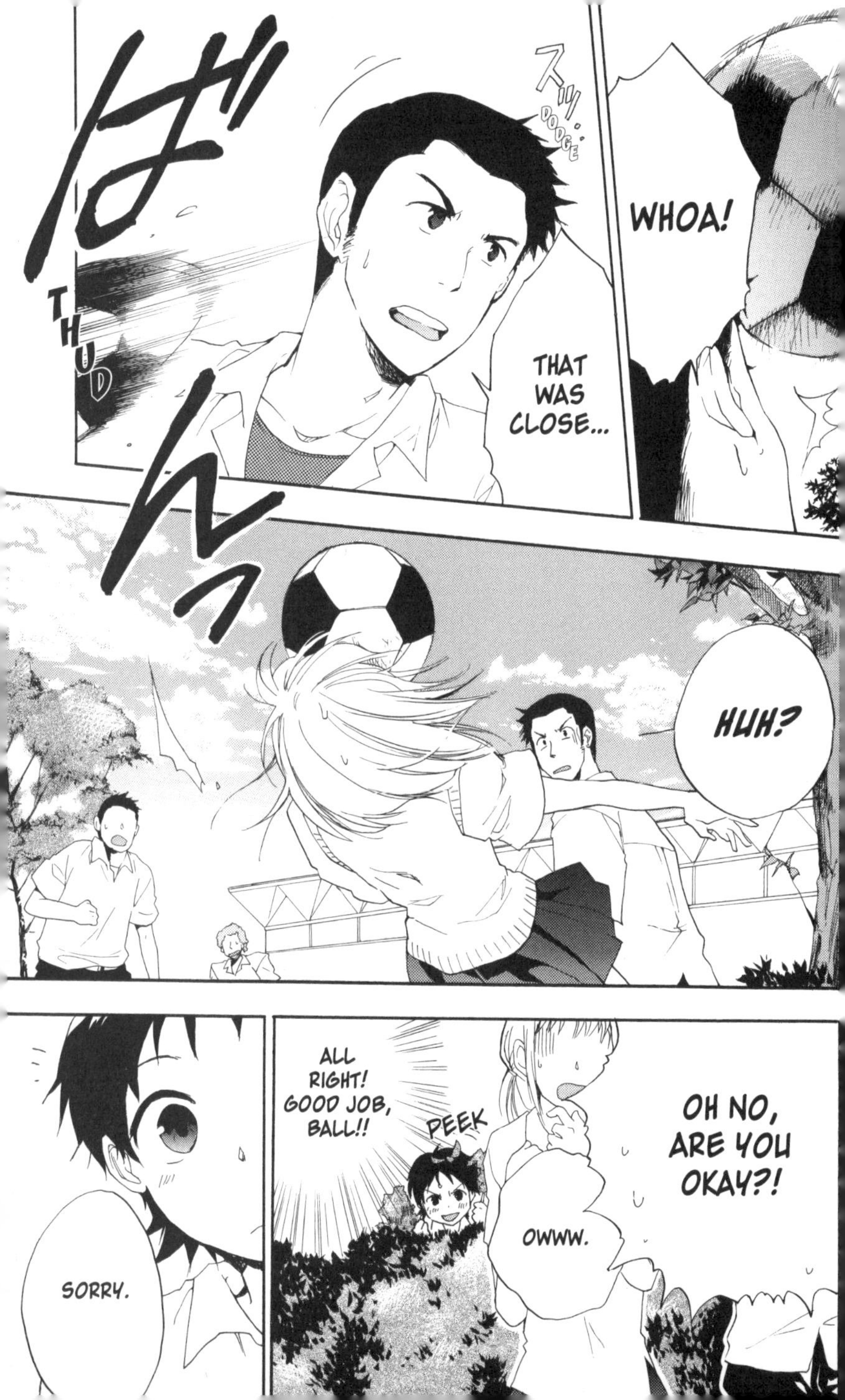
WHOA!
スッ
DODGE
THAT WAS CLOSE...
ばんっ
THUD
HUH?
OH NO, ARE YOU OKAY?!
OWWW.
PEEK
ALL RIGHT! GOOD JOB, BALL!!
SORRY.

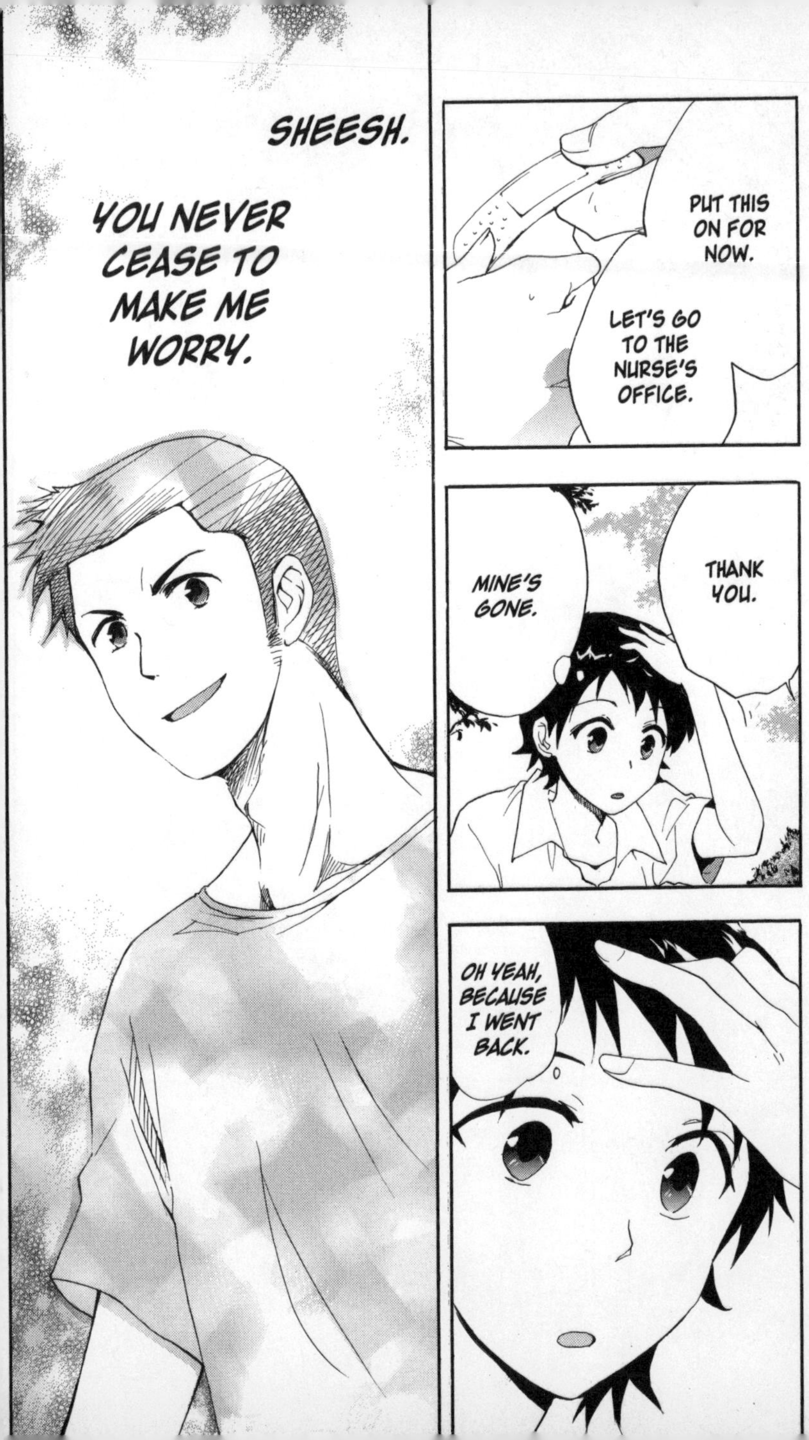
PUT THIS ON FOR NOW.
LET'S GO TO THE NURSE'S OFFICE.
THANK YOU.
MINE'S GONE.
OH YEAH, BECAUSE I WENT BACK.
SHEESH.
YOU NEVER CEASE TO MAKE ME WORRY.

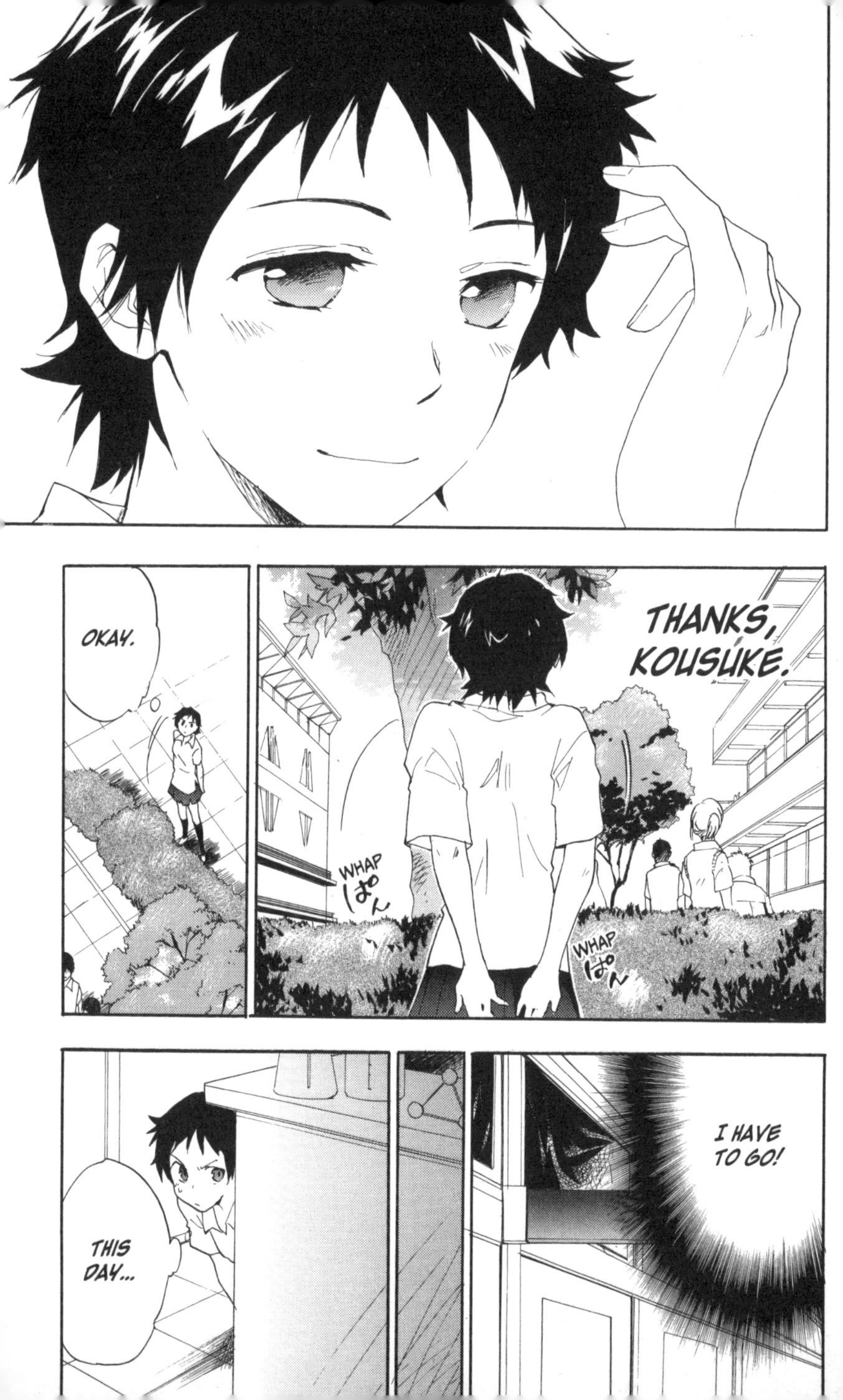
THANKS, KOUSUKE.
WHAP ぱん
WHAP ぱん
OKAY.
I HAVE TO GO!
THIS DAY...

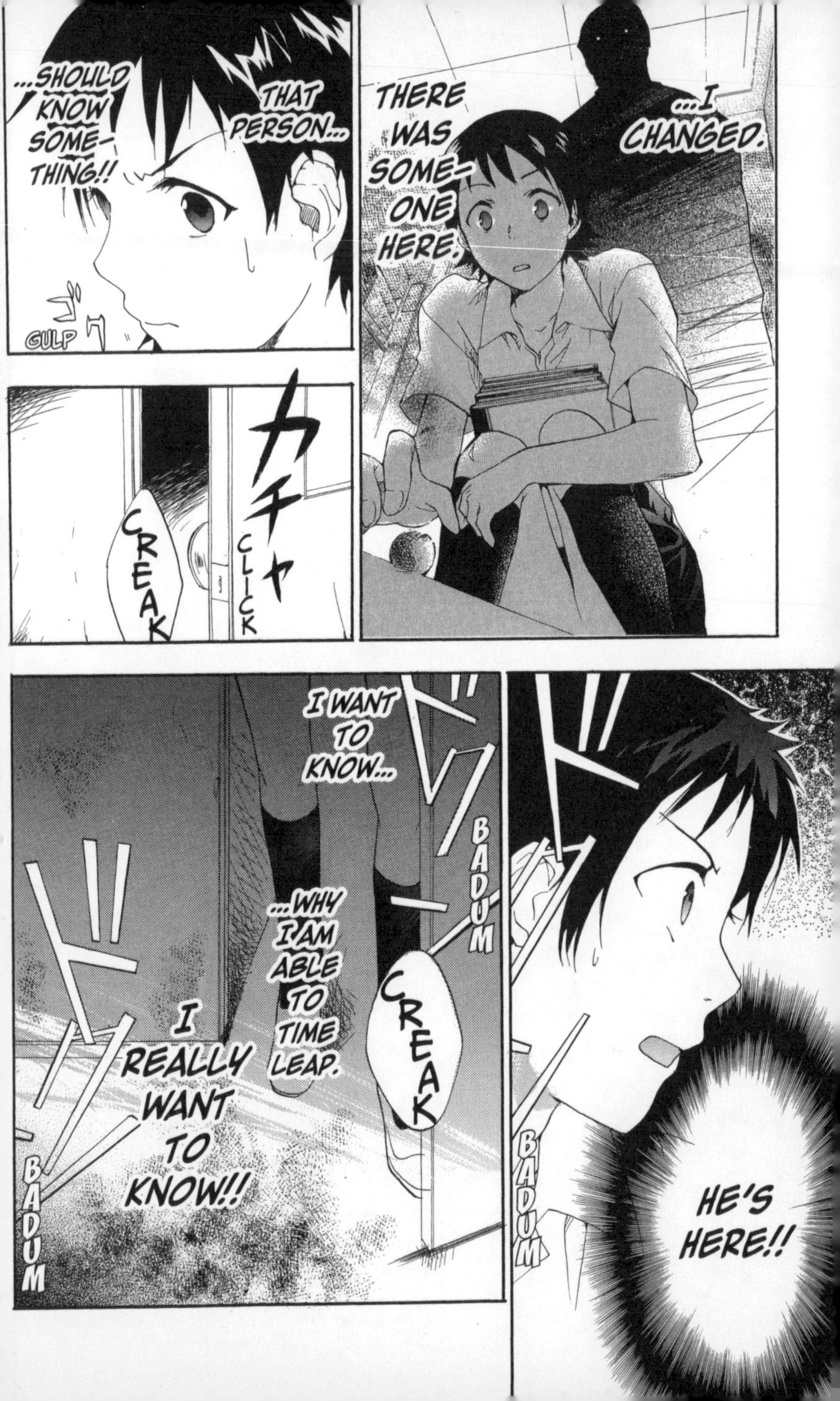
...I CHANGED.
THERE WAS SOMEONE HERE.
THAT PERSON...
...SHOULD KNOW SOMETHING!!
ゴク
GULP
カチャ
CLICK
CREAK
HE'S HERE!!
BADUM
I WANT TO KNOW...
BADUM
...WHY I AM ABLE TO TIME LEAP.
CREAK
I REALLY WANT TO KNOW!!
BADUM

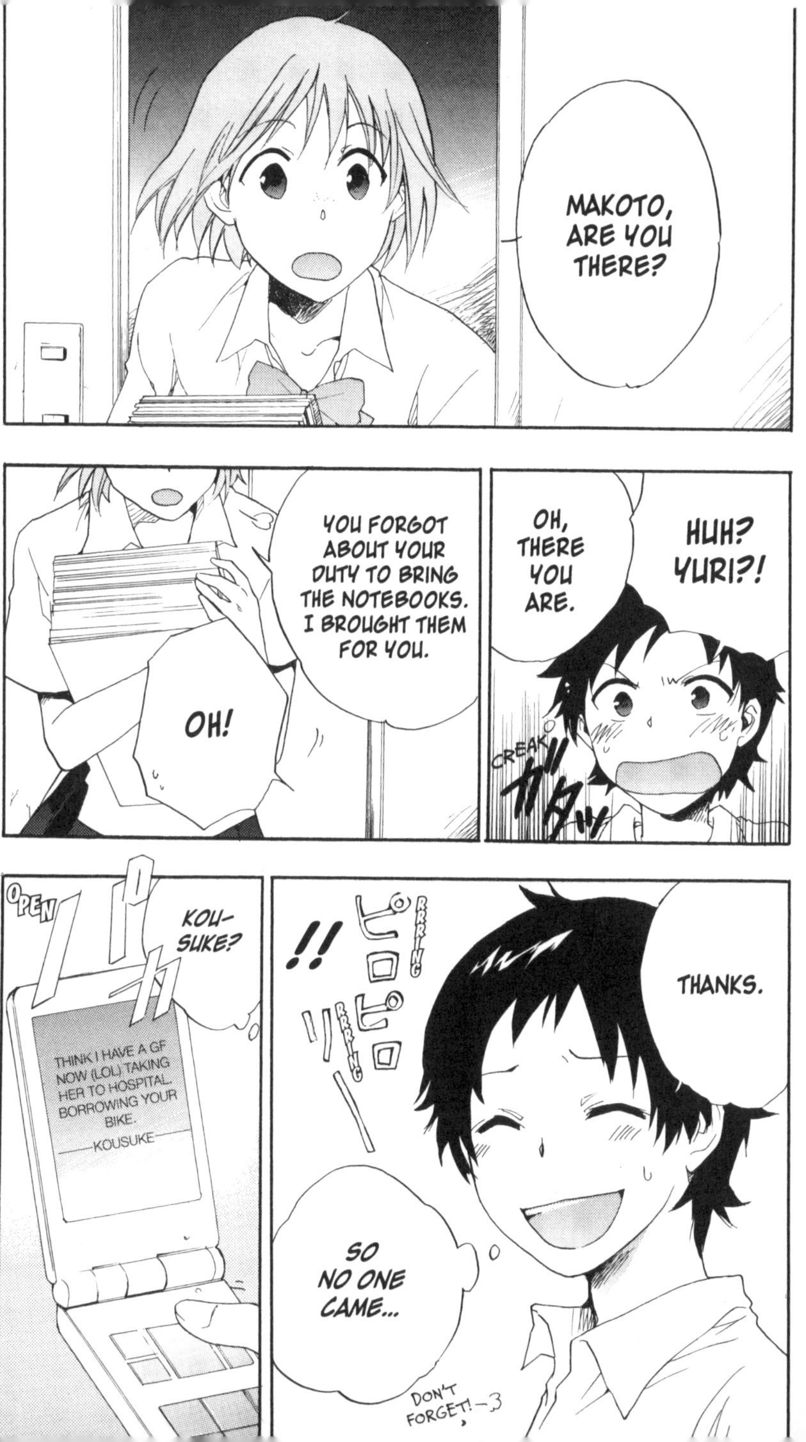
MAKOTO, ARE YOU THERE?
HUH? YURI?!
OH, THERE YOU ARE.
CREAK
ガタッ
YOU FORGOT ABOUT YOUR DUTY TO BRING THE NOTEBOOKS. I BROUGHT THEM FOR YOU.
OH!
THANKS.
RRRING
ピロピロリー
RRRING
!!
SO NO ONE CAME...
DON'T FORGET! -3
OPEN
パカ
KOU-SUKE?
THINK I HAVE A GF NOW (LOL) TAKING HER TO HOSPITAL. BORROWING YOUR BIKE.
KOUSUKE

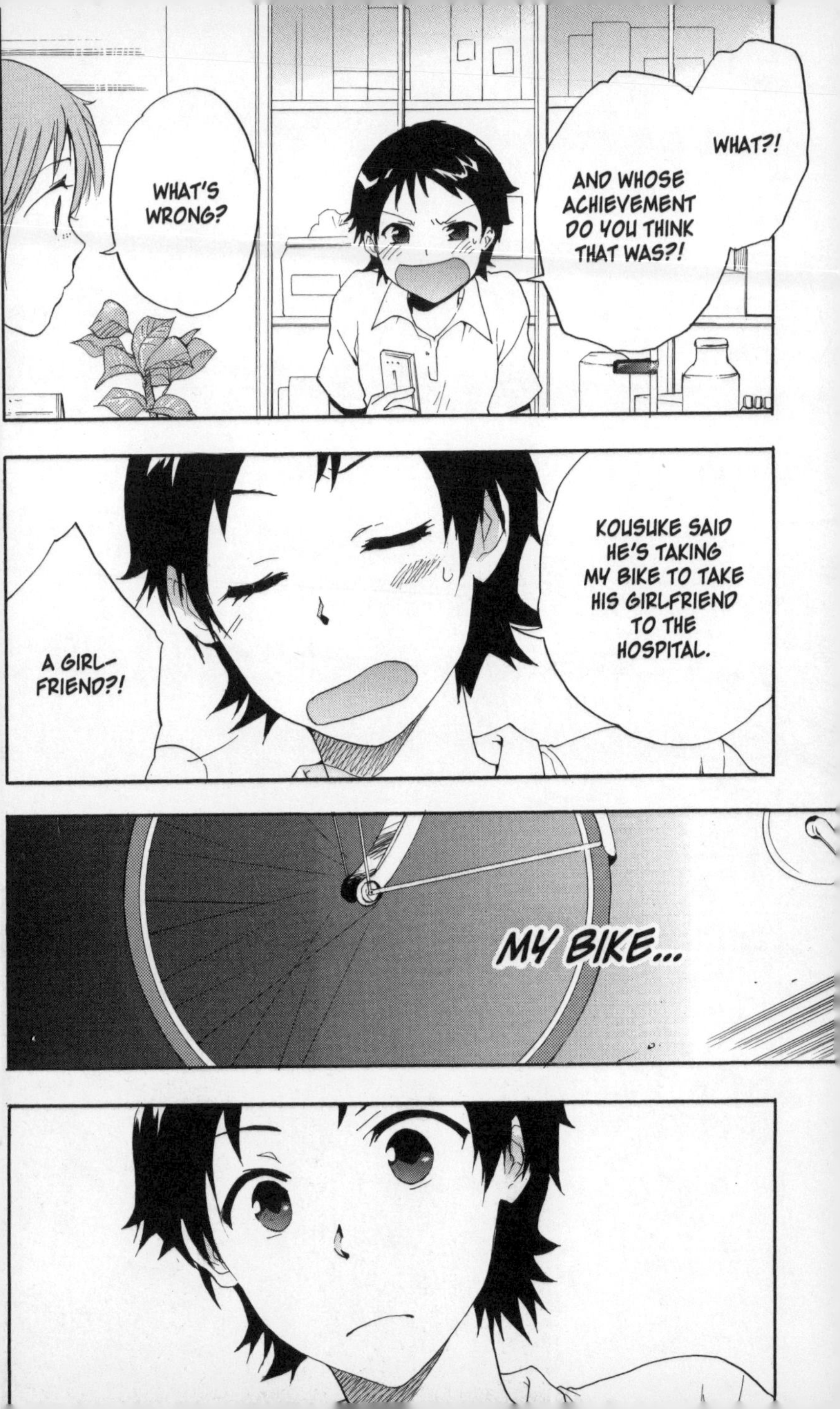
WHAT?!
AND WHOSE ACHIEVEMENT DO YOU THINK THAT WAS?!
WHAT'S WRONG?
KOUSUKE SAID HE'S TAKING MY BIKE TO TAKE HIS GIRLFRIEND TO THE HOSPITAL.
A GIRL-FRIEND?!
MY BIKE...

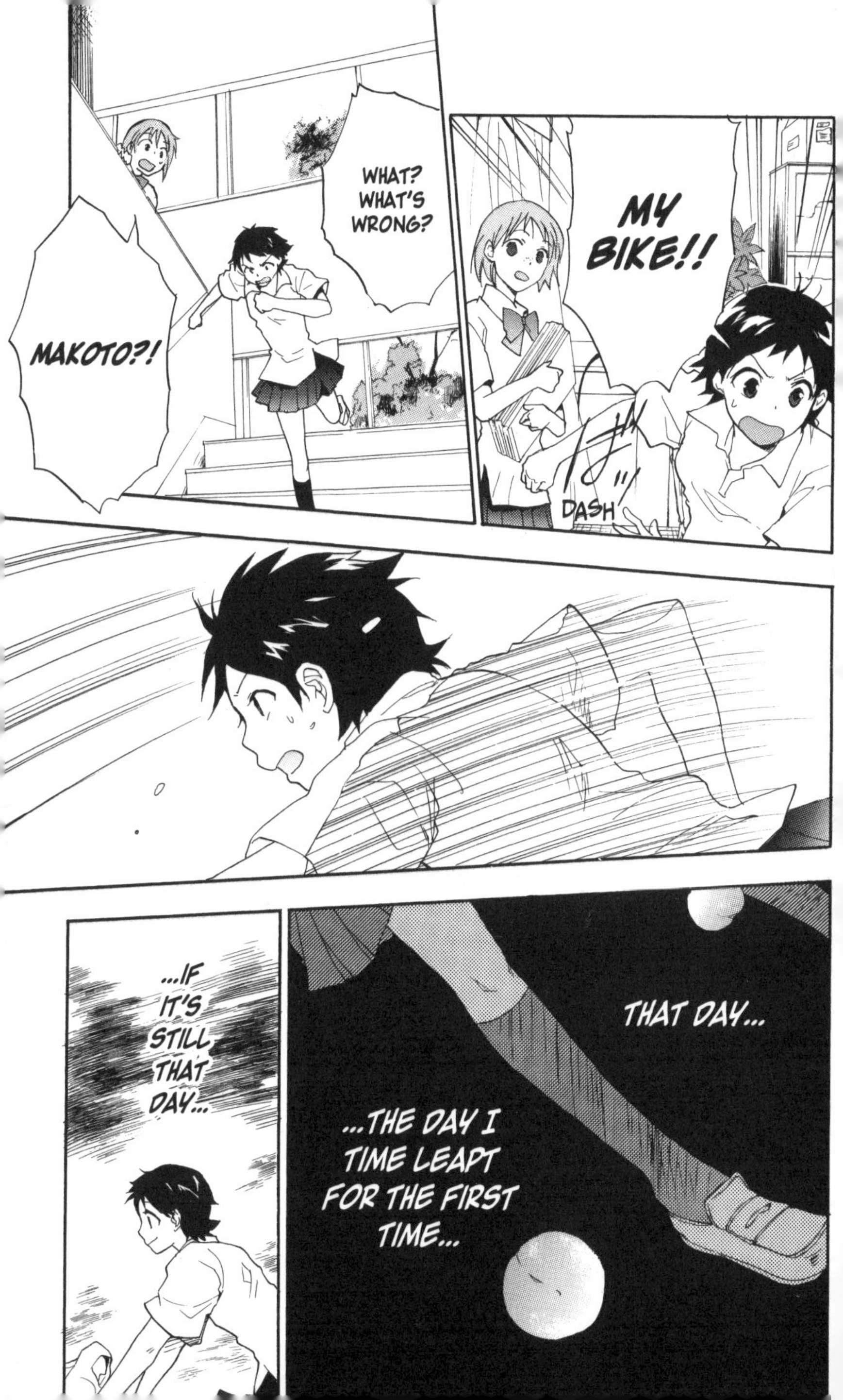
MY BIKE!!
DASH
WHAT? WHAT'S WRONG?
MAKOTO?!
THAT DAY...
...THE DAY I TIME LEAPT FOR THE FIRST TIME...
...IF IT'S STILL THAT DAY...

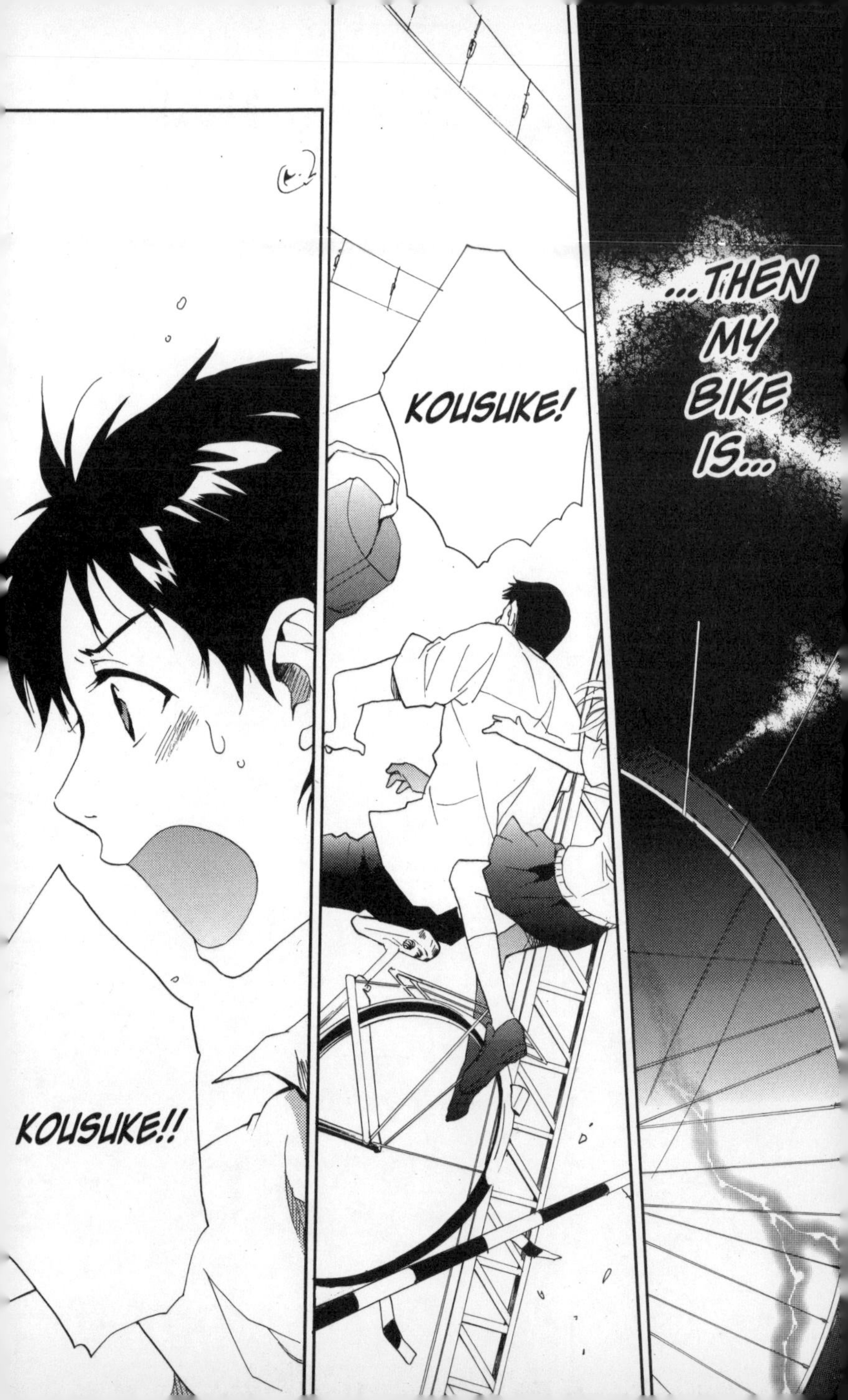
...THEN MY BIKE IS...
KOUSUKE!
KOUSUKE!!

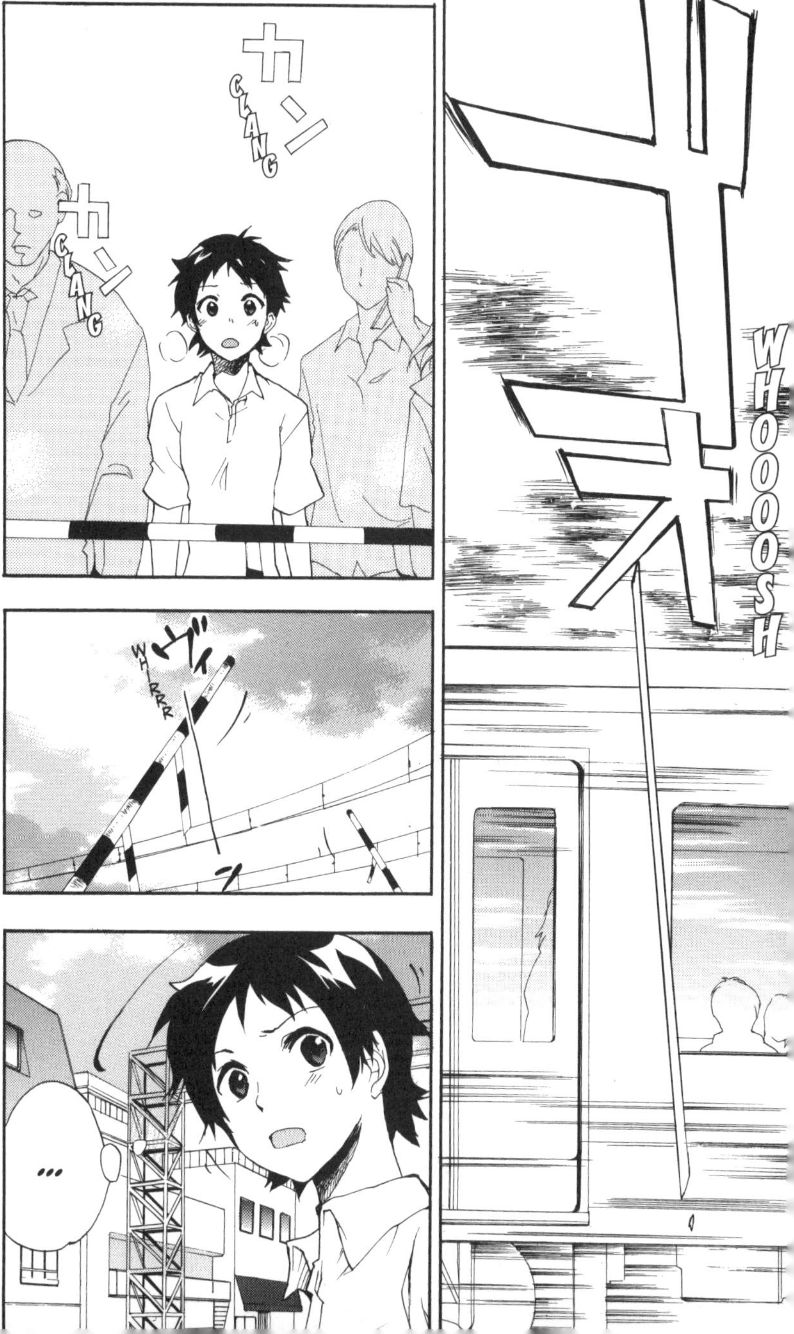
WHOOOOOSH
カン
CLANG
カン
CLANG
ヴィ
WHIRRR
...

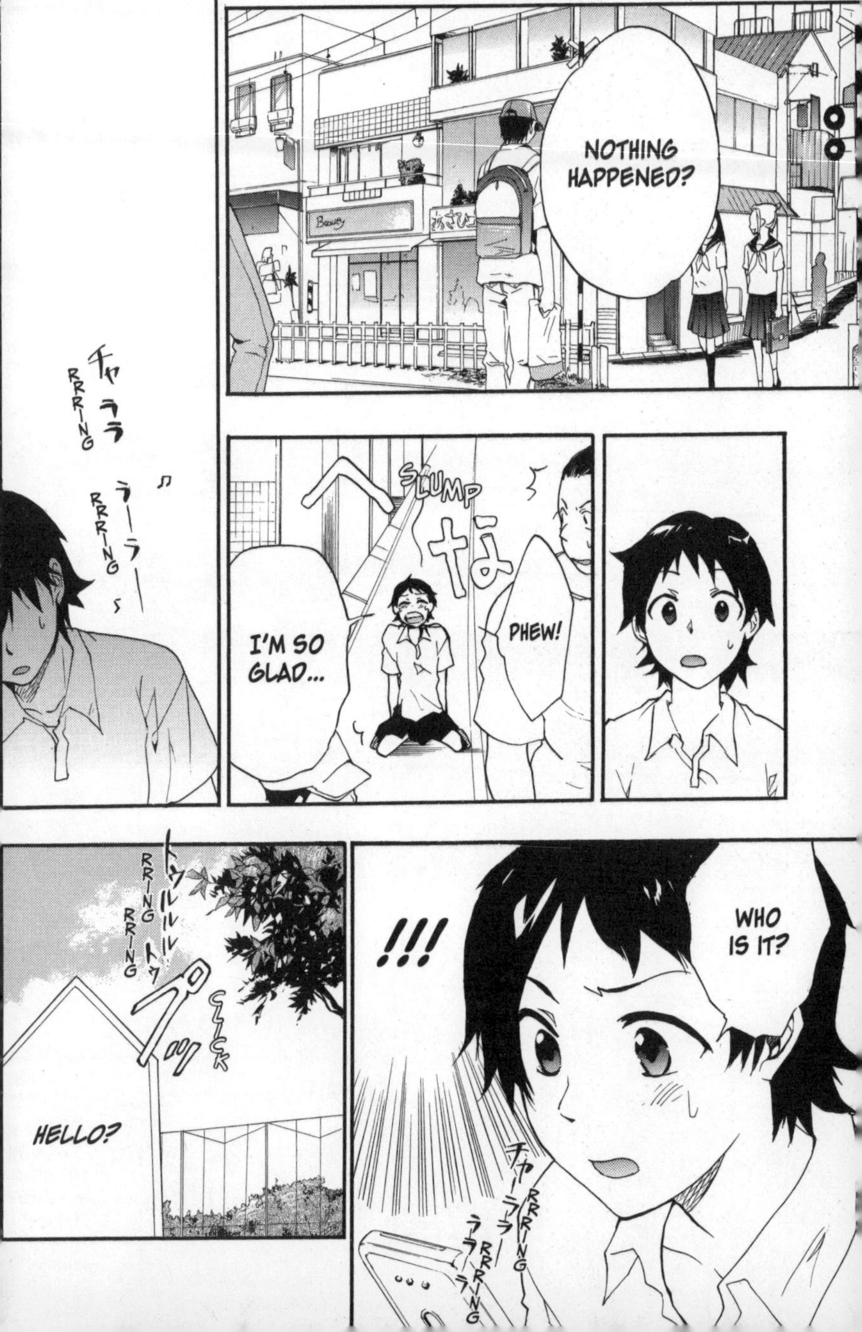

NOTHING HAPPENED?
SLUMP
PHEW!
I'M SO GLAD...
チャララ
RRRING
ラーラー
RRRING
WHO IS IT?
!!!
チャーラララ
RRRING
ラーラー
RRRING
トゥルルル
RRING
トゥ
RRING
CLICK
HELLO?

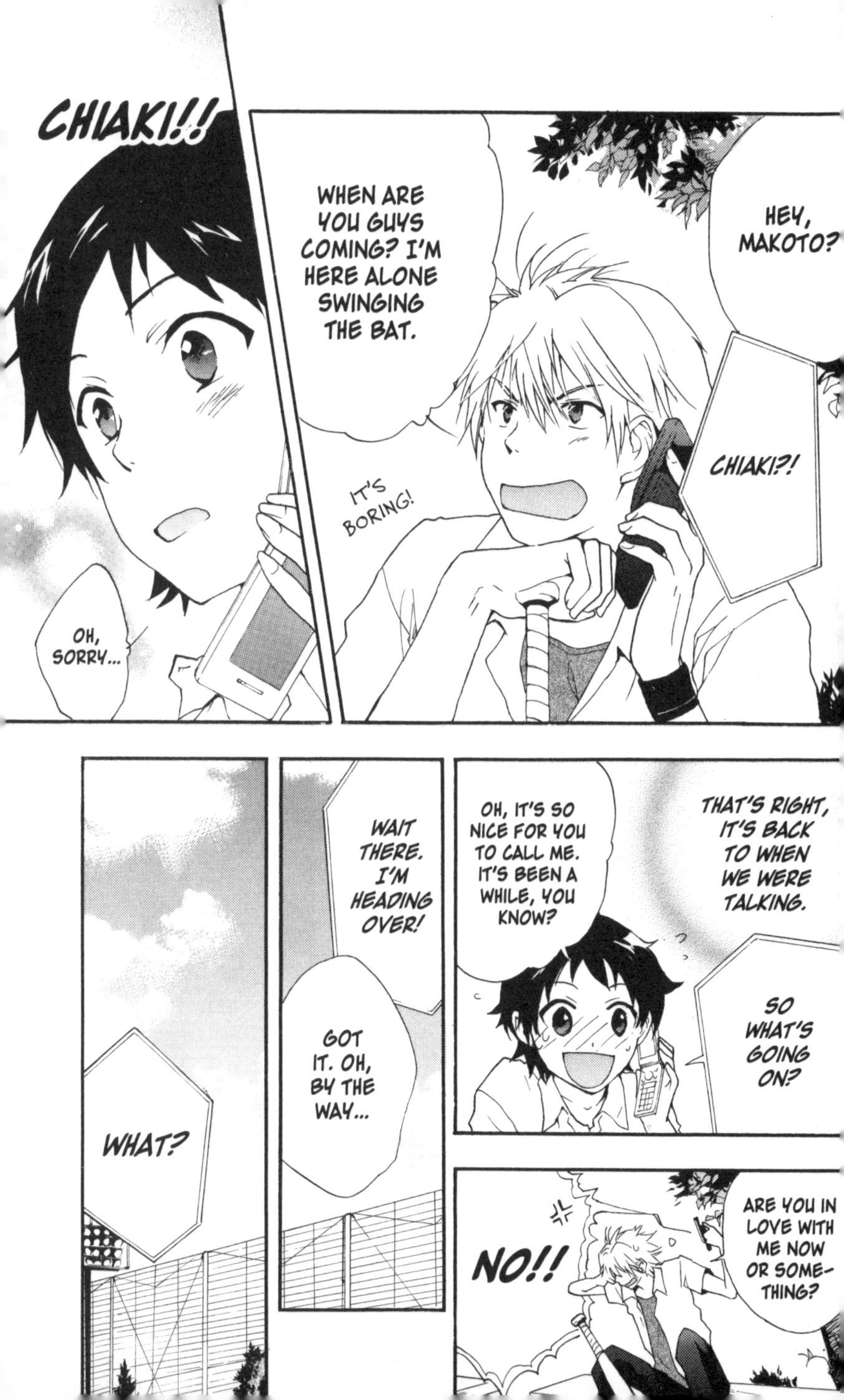
HEY, MAKOTO?
CHIAKI?!
WHEN ARE YOU GUYS COMING? I'M HERE ALONE SWINGING THE BAT.
IT'S BORING!
CHIAKI!!
OH, SORRY...
THAT'S RIGHT, IT'S BACK TO WHEN WE WERE TALKING.
OH, IT'S SO NICE FOR YOU TO CALL ME. IT'S BEEN A WHILE, YOU KNOW?
SO WHAT'S GOING ON?
ARE YOU IN LOVE WITH ME NOW OR SOME-THING?
NO!!
WAIT THERE. I'M HEADING OVER!
GOT IT. OH, BY THE WAY...
WHAT?

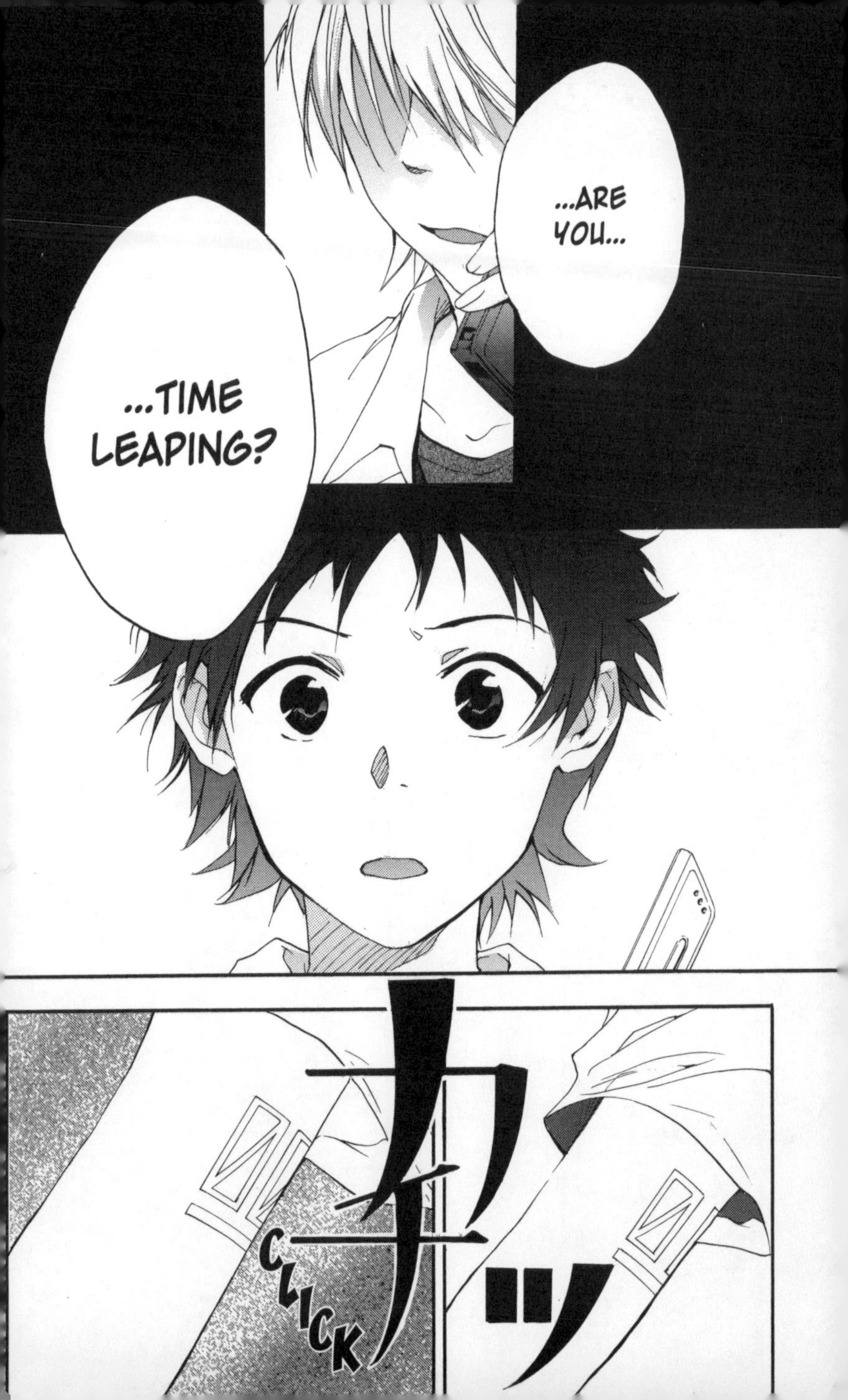
...ARE YOU...
...TIME LEAPING?
カチッ
CLICK

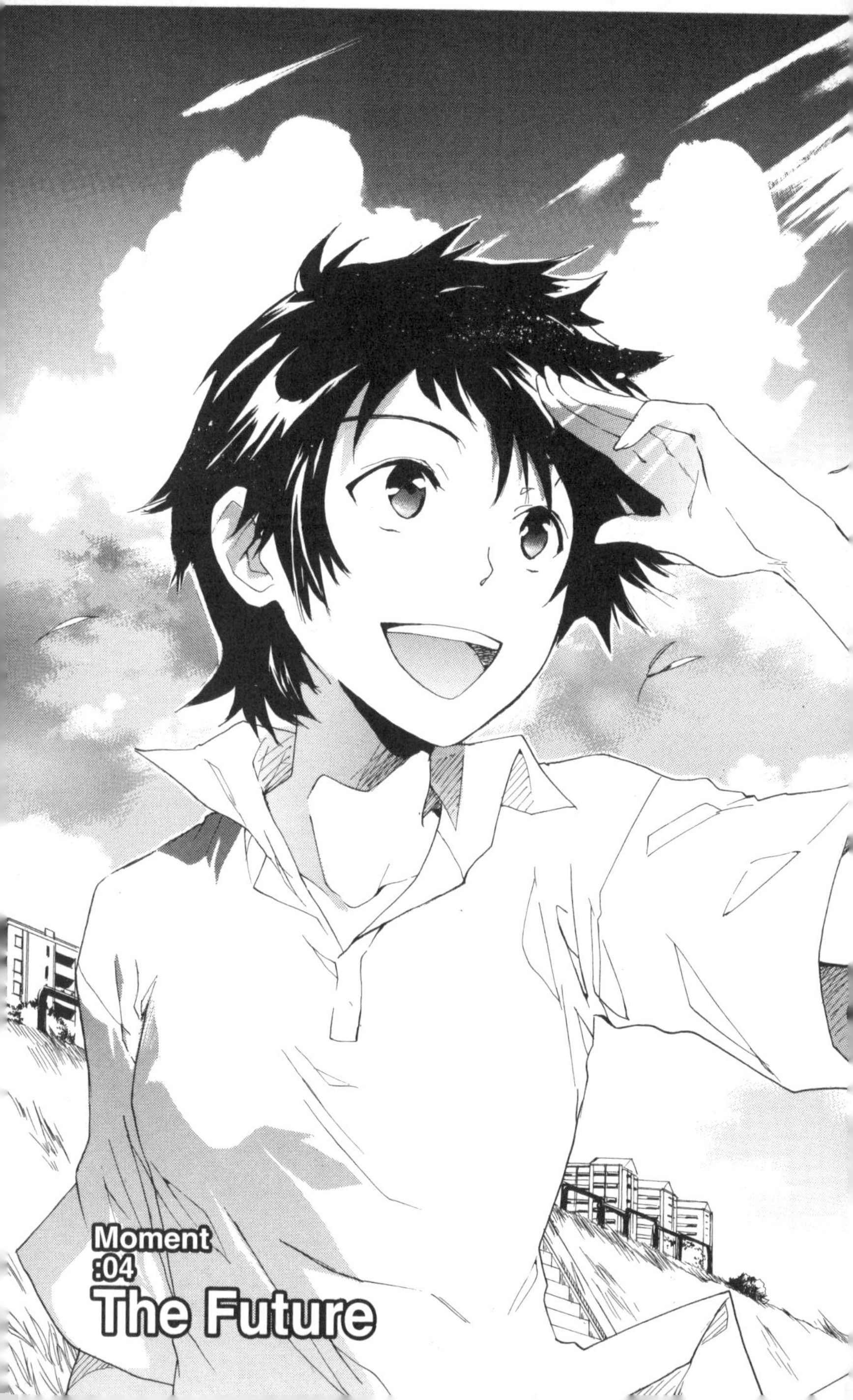
Moment
:04
The Future

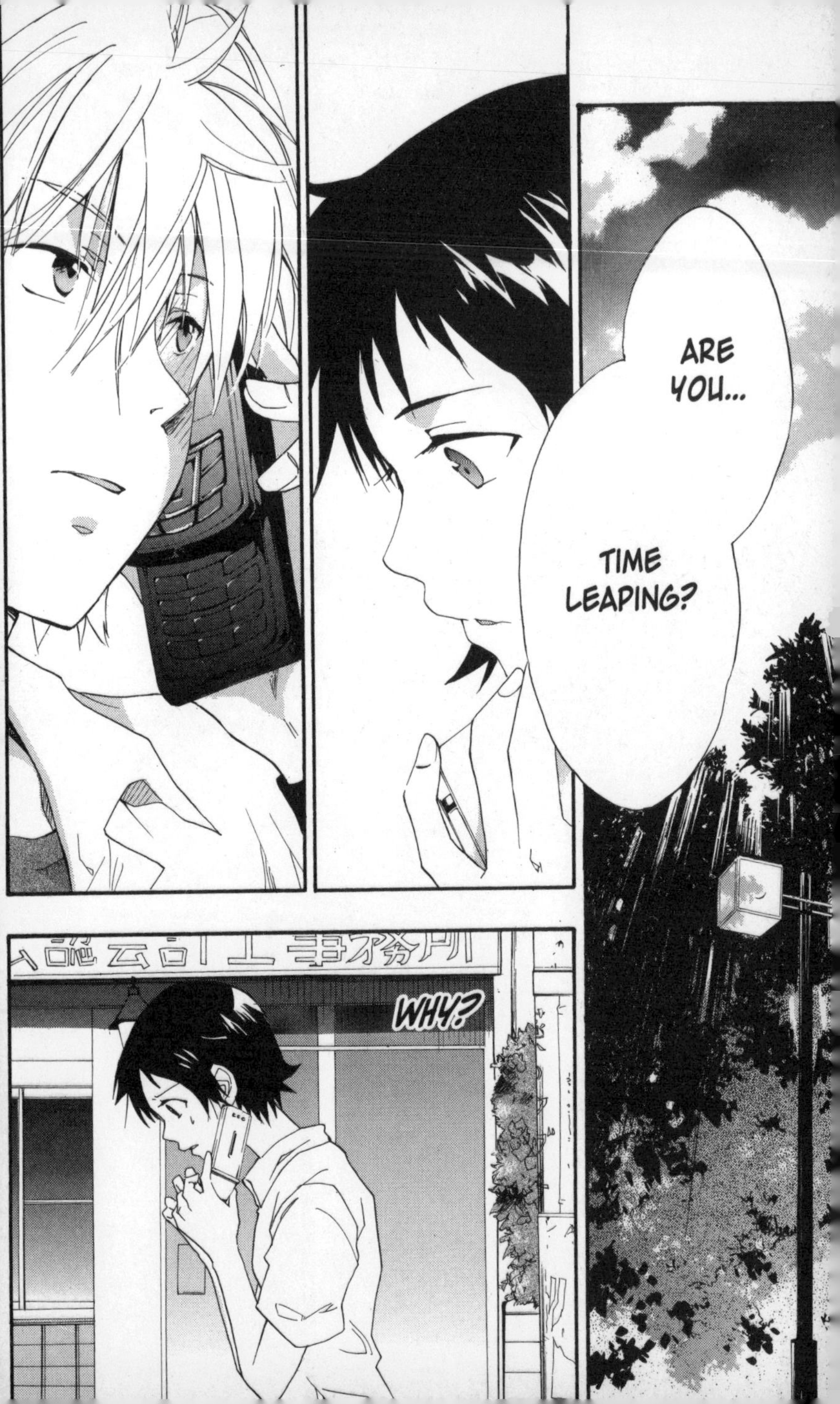
ARE YOU...
TIME LEAPING?
WHY?

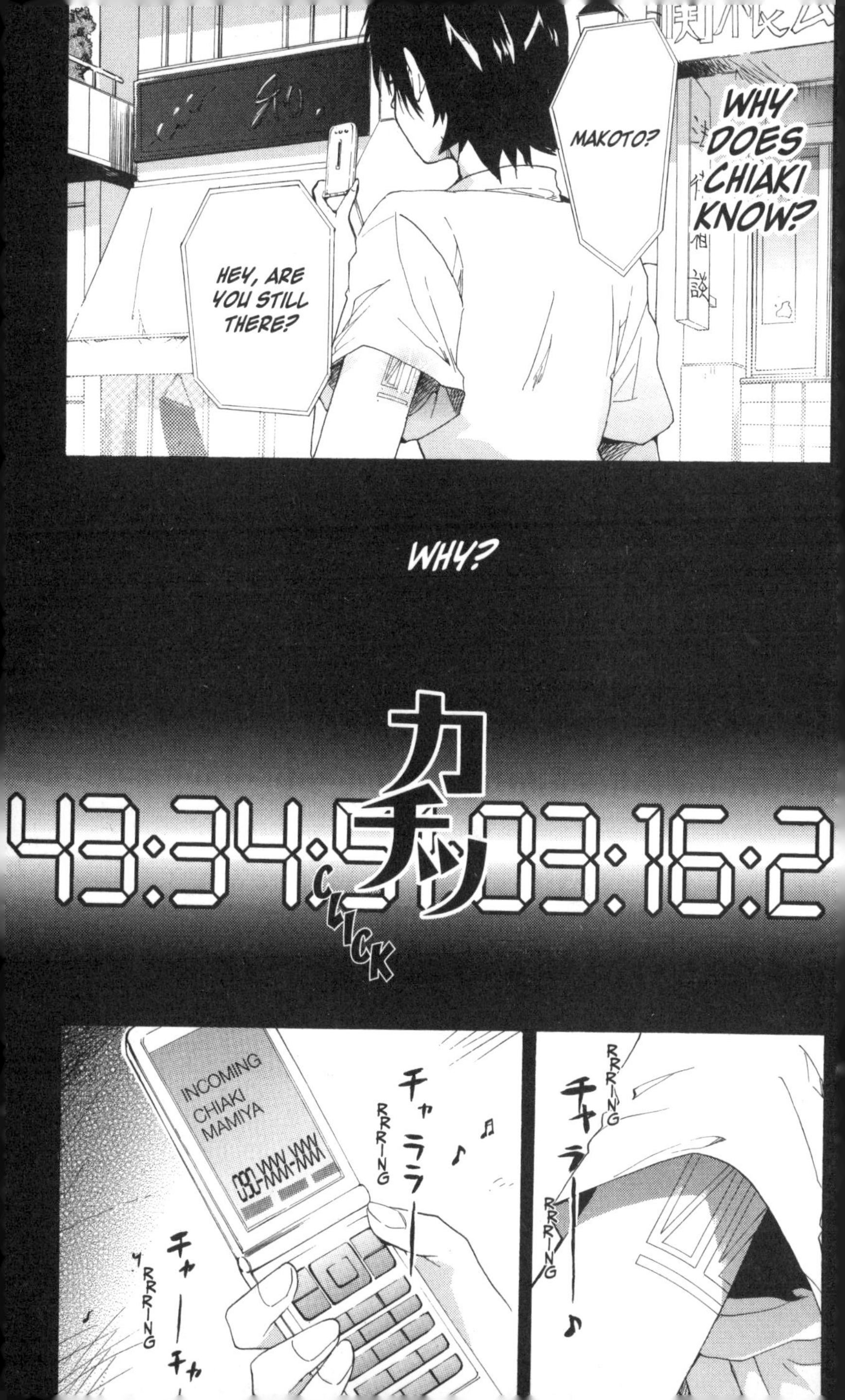
WHY DOES CHIAKI KNOW?
MAKOTO?
HEY, ARE YOU STILL THERE?
WHY?
カチッ
CLICK
43:34:5
03:16:2
RRRING
チャラー♪
RRRING
RRRING
INCOMING
CHIAKI
MAMIYA
チャラララー
RRRING
チャーチャ
RRRING

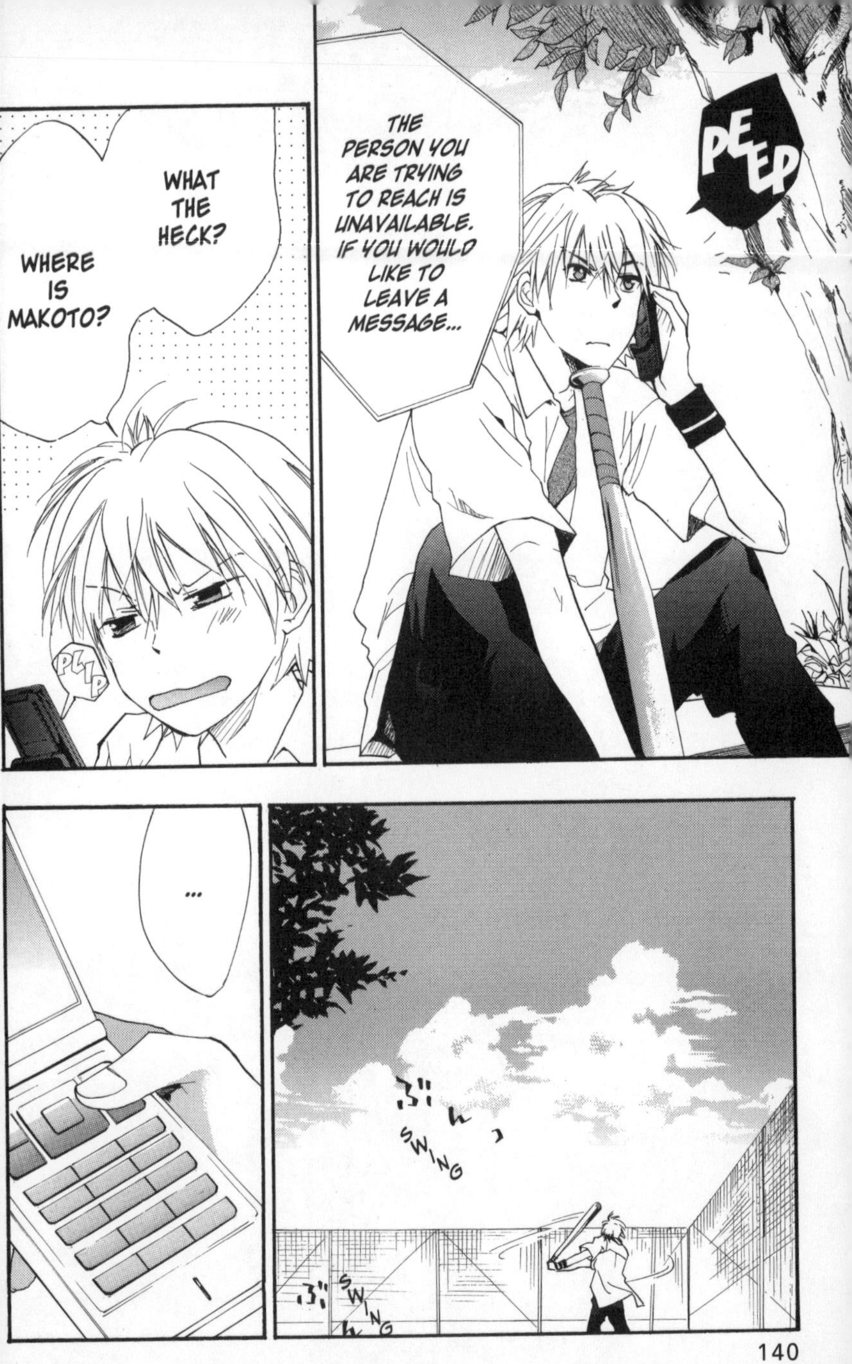
PEEP
THE PERSON YOU ARE TRYING TO REACH IS UNAVAILABLE. IF YOU WOULD LIKE TO LEAVE A MESSAGE...
WHAT THE HECK?
WHERE IS MAKOTO?
PLIP
ぶん
SWING
ぶん
SWING
...

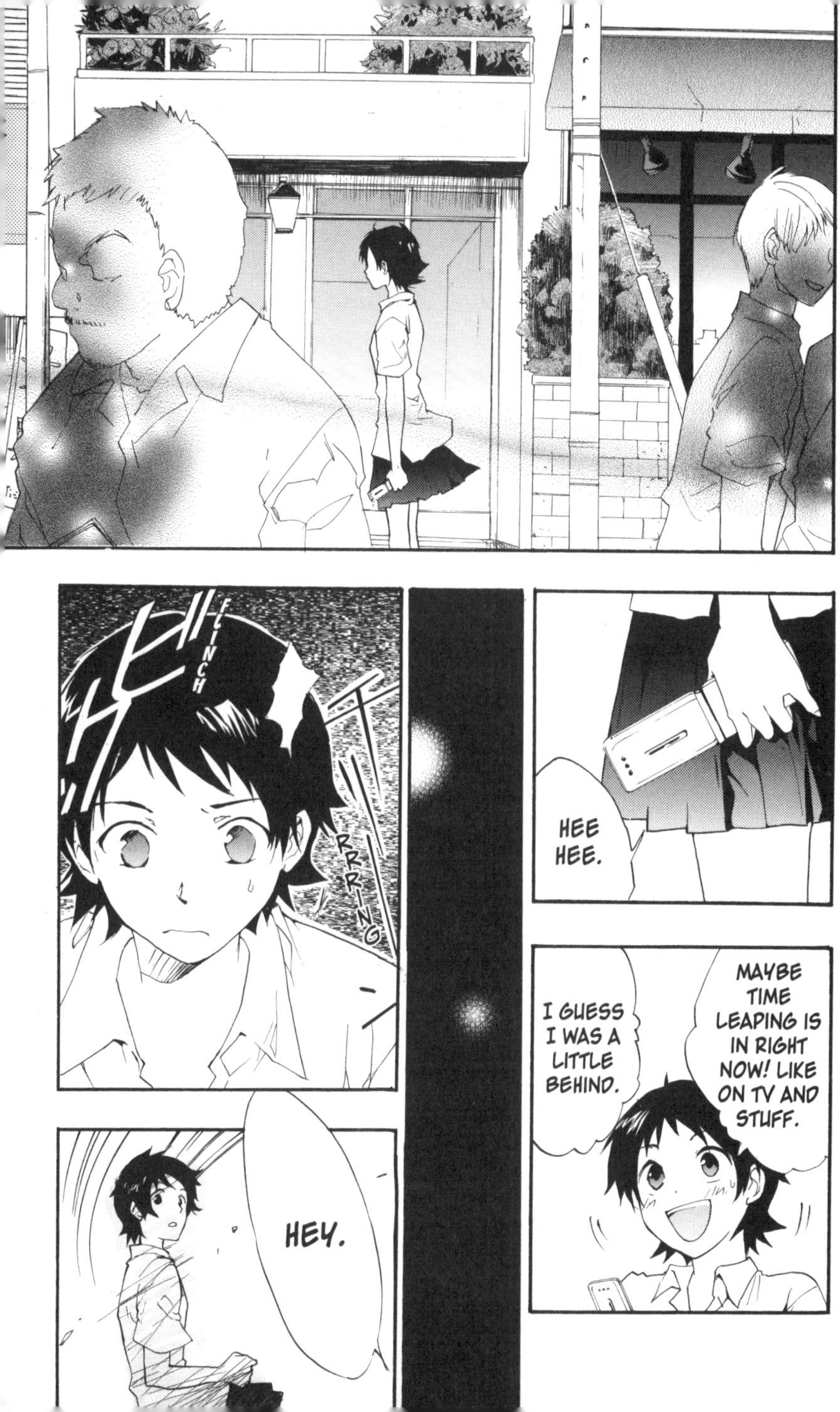
HEE HEE.
MAYBE TIME LEAPING IS IN RIGHT NOW! LIKE ON TV AND STUFF.
I GUESS I WAS A LITTLE BEHIND.
FLINCH
RRRING
HEY.

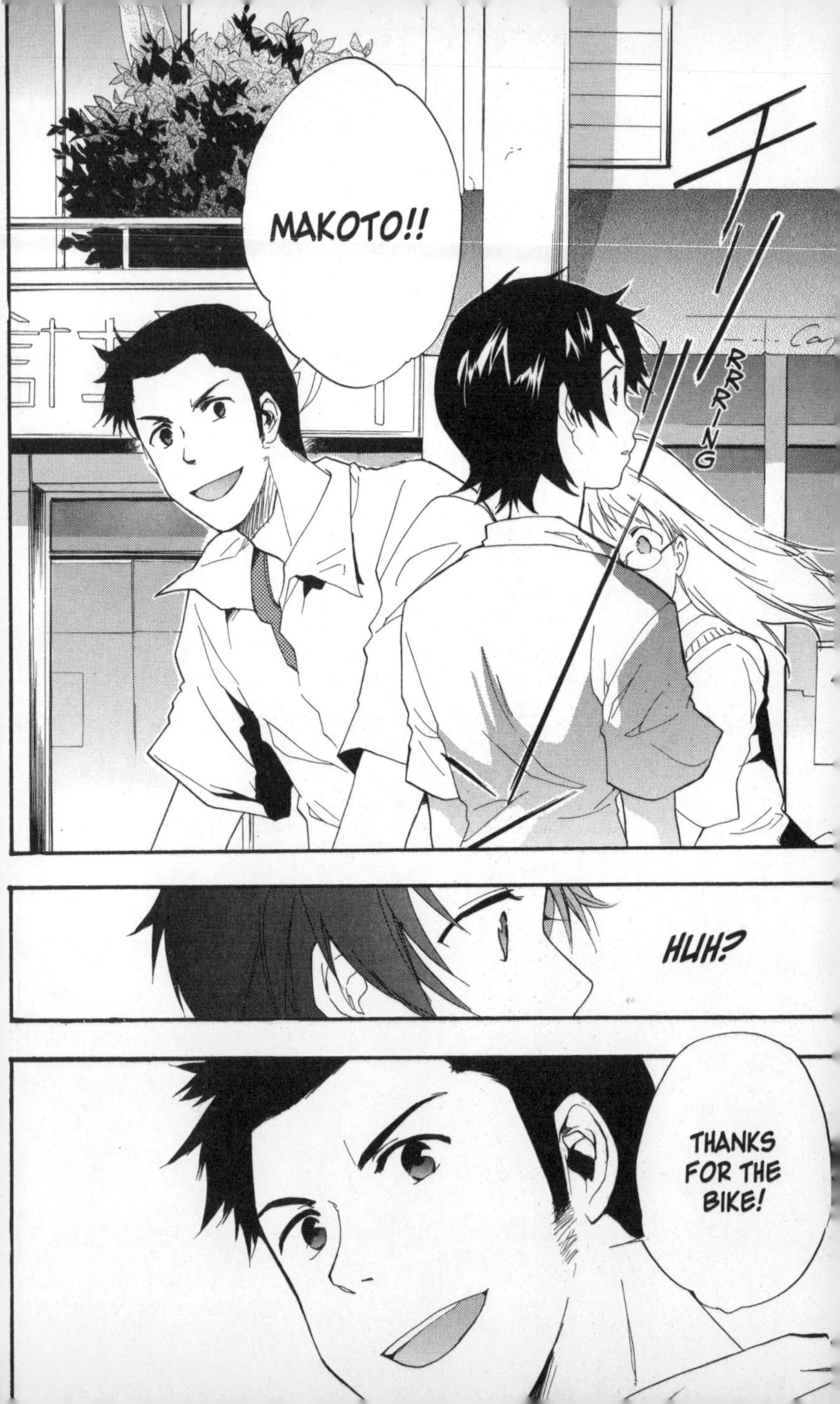
RRRING
MAKOTO!!
HUH?
THANKS FOR THE BIKE!

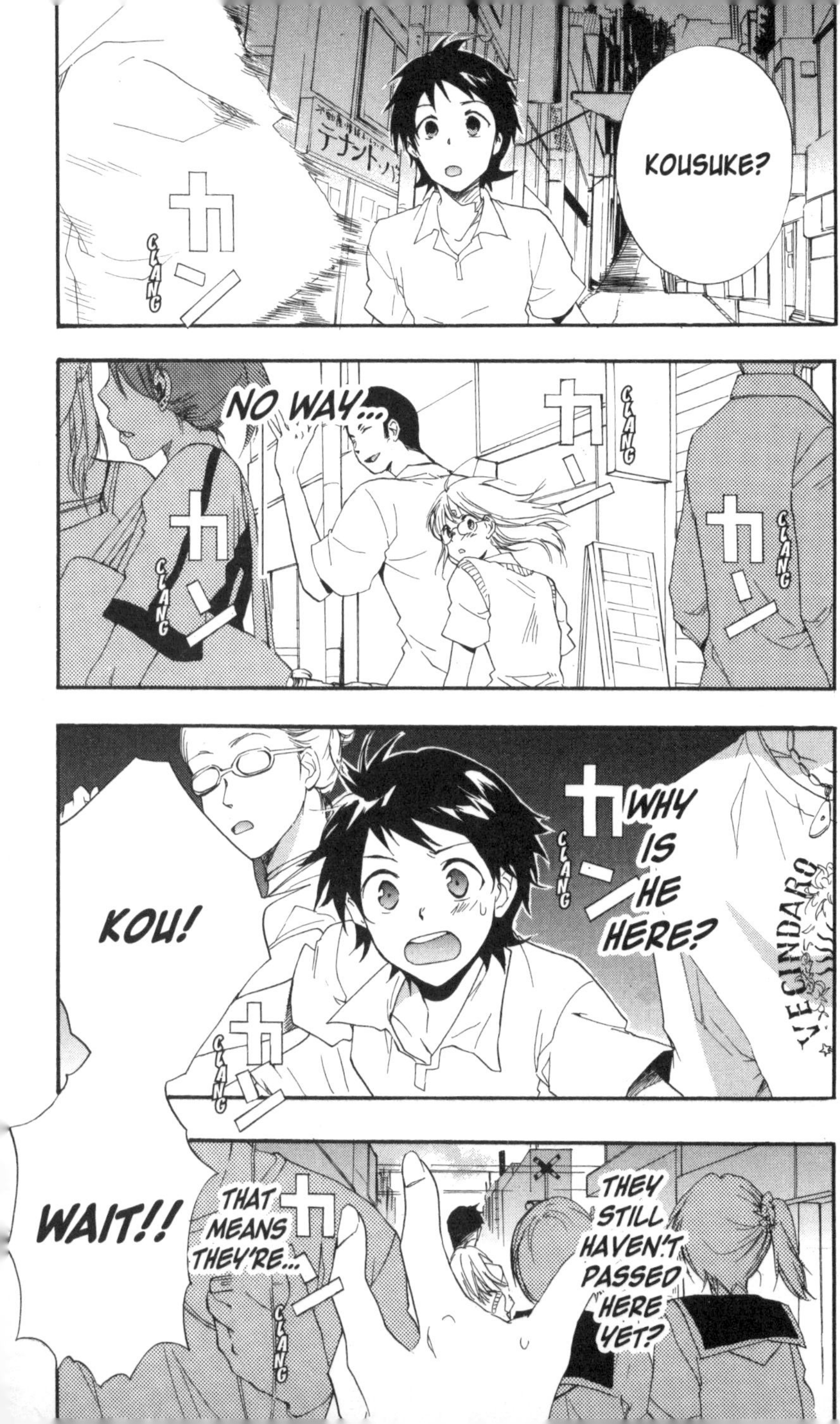
KOUSUKE?
CLANG
CLANG
CLANG
NO WAY...
CLANG
VECINDARO
WHY IS HE HERE?
CLANG
KOU!
CLANG
THEY STILL HAVEN'T PASSED HERE YET?
THAT MEANS THEY'RE...
CLANG
WAIT!!

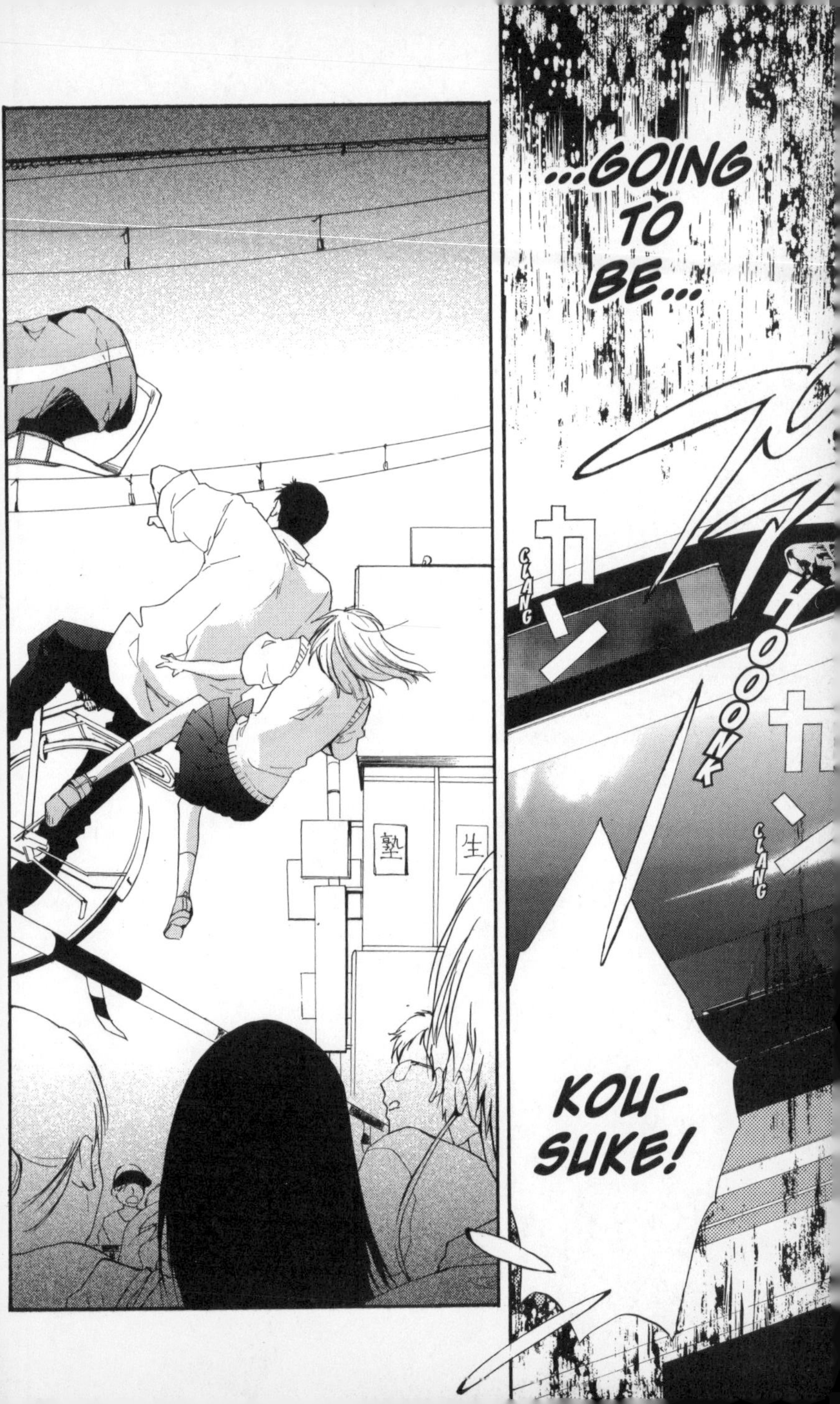
...GOING TO BE...
カン CLANG
HOOOONK
カン CLANG
KOU-SUKE!
塾
生

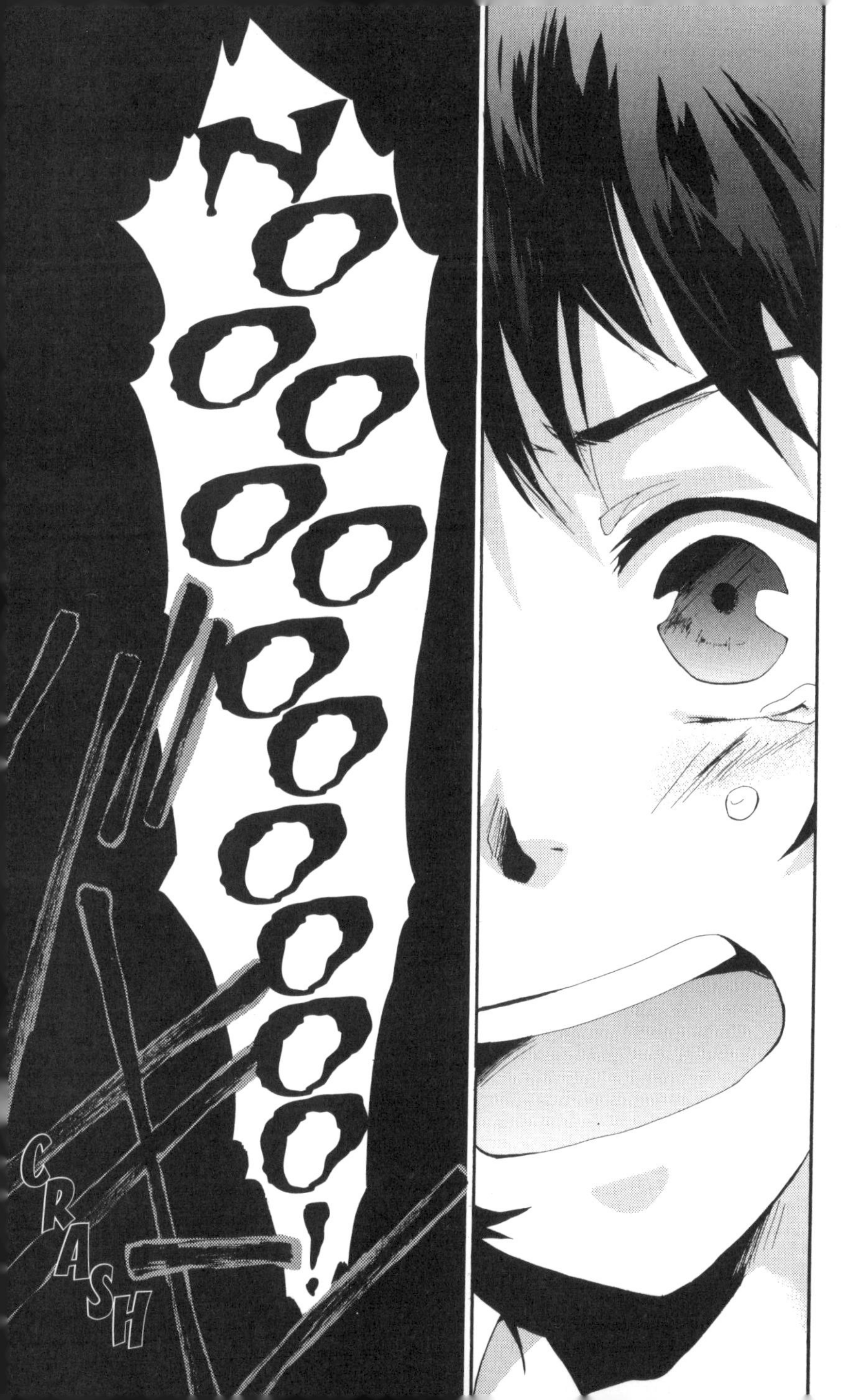
NOOOOOOOOOOOOOOOO!
CRASH

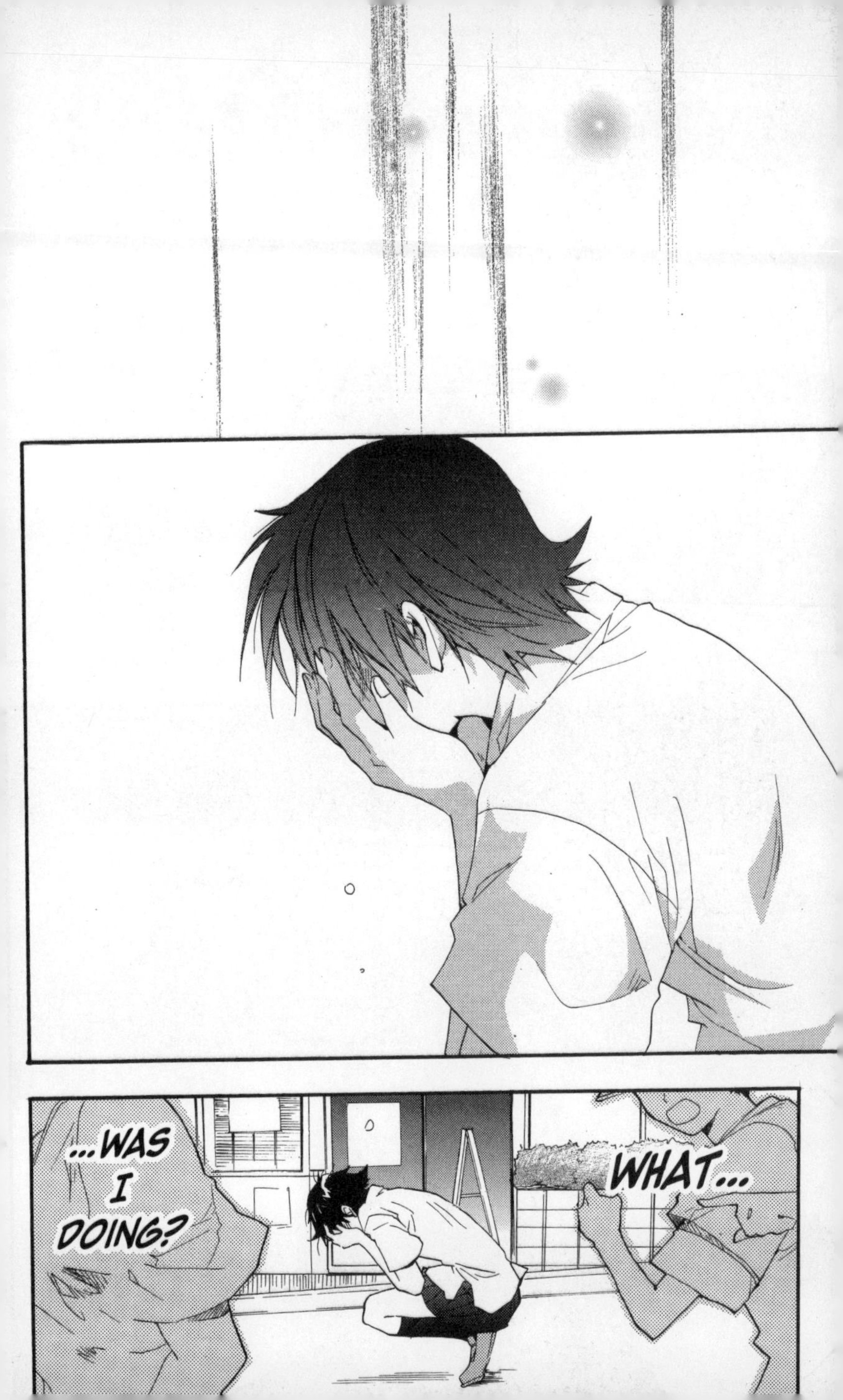
WHAT...
...WAS I DOING?

WHY?

WHY DID I USE IT UP?

I COULD'VE TIME LEAPT.

I'M SORRY, KOUSUKE.

WHY DIDN'T I USE IT NOW?

MAKOTO.

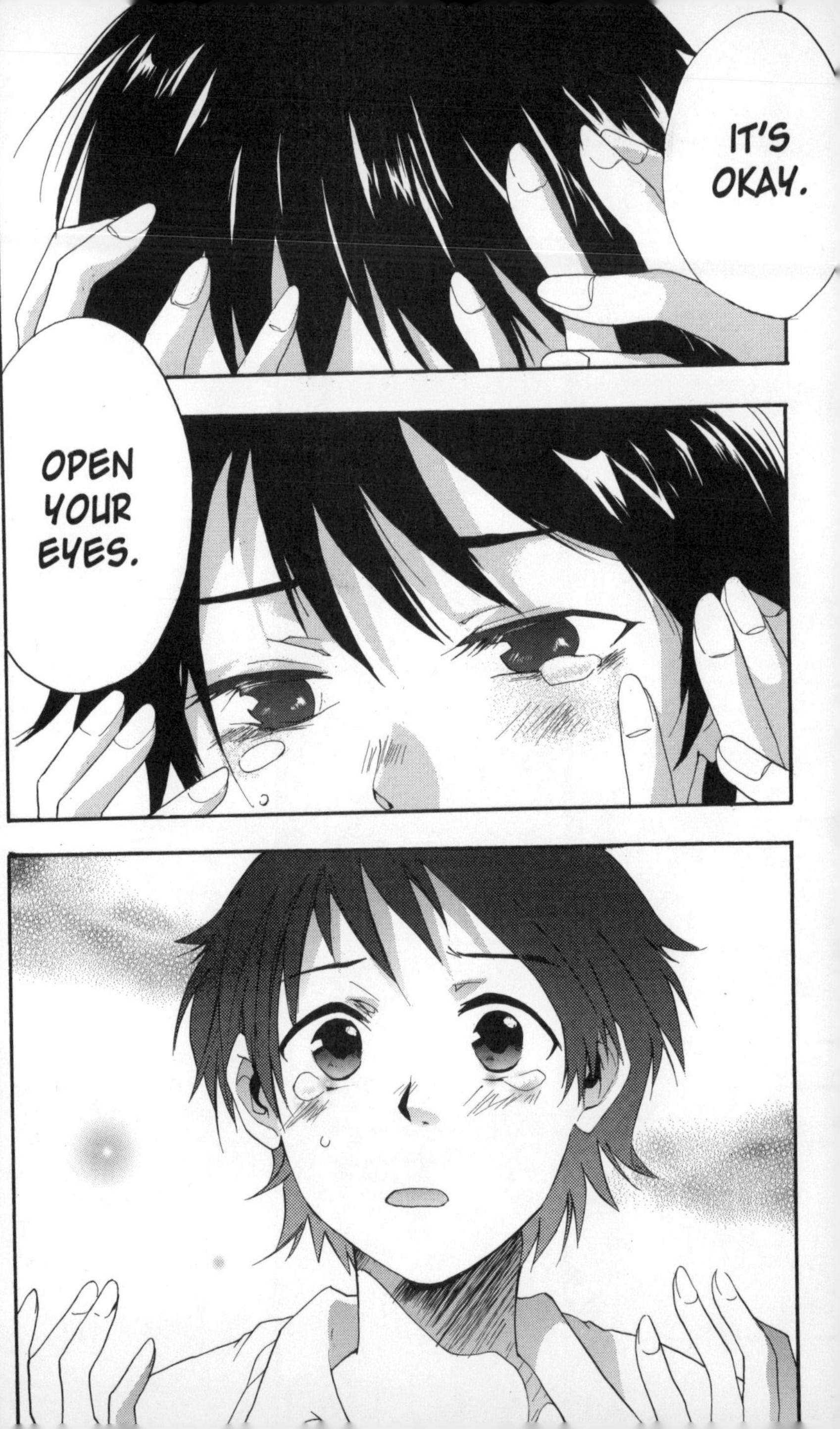
IT'S OKAY.
OPEN YOUR EYES.

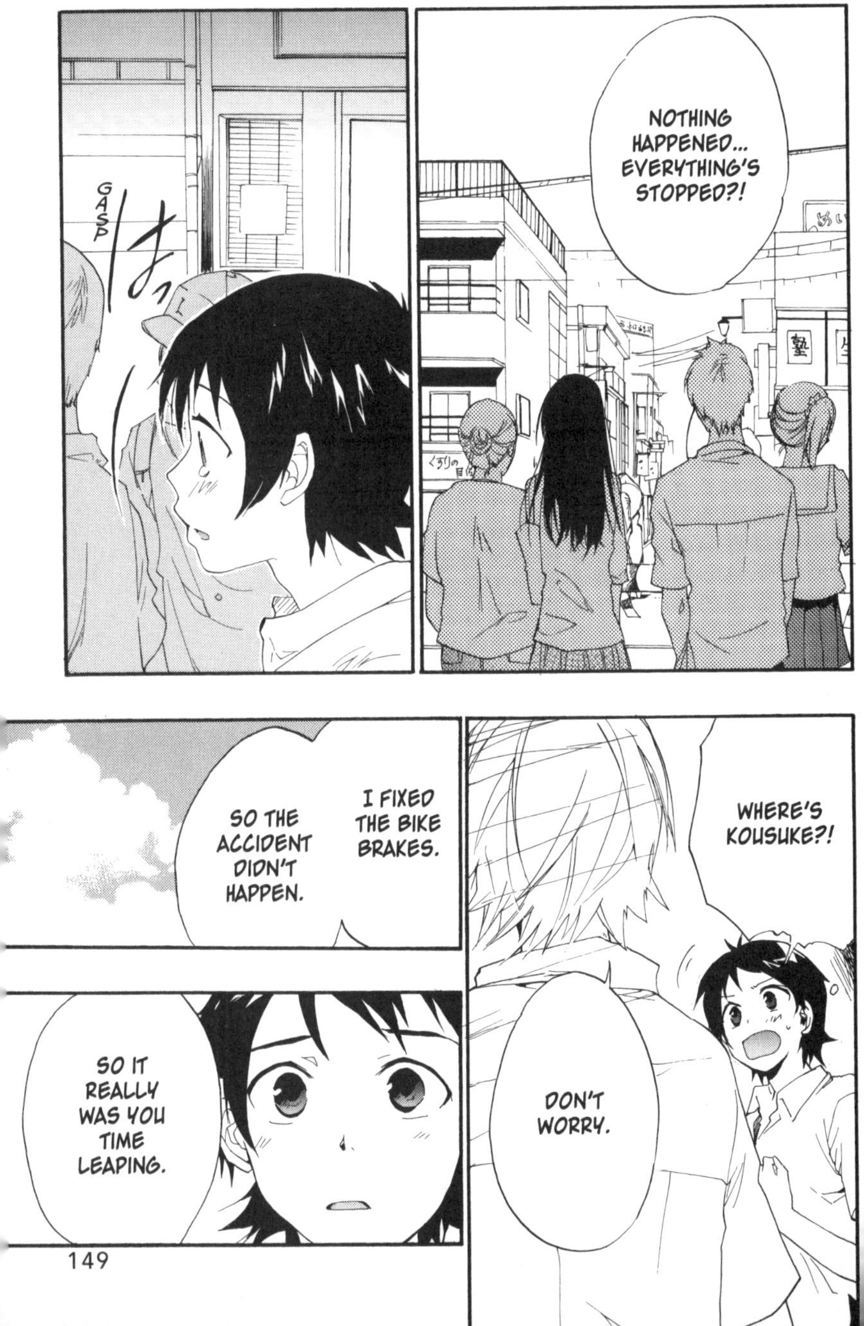
NOTHING HAPPENED... EVERYTHING'S STOPPED?!
GASP
はっ
WHERE'S KOUSUKE?!
DON'T WORRY.
I FIXED THE BIKE BRAKES.
SO THE ACCIDENT DIDN'T HAPPEN.
SO IT REALLY WAS YOU TIME LEAPING.

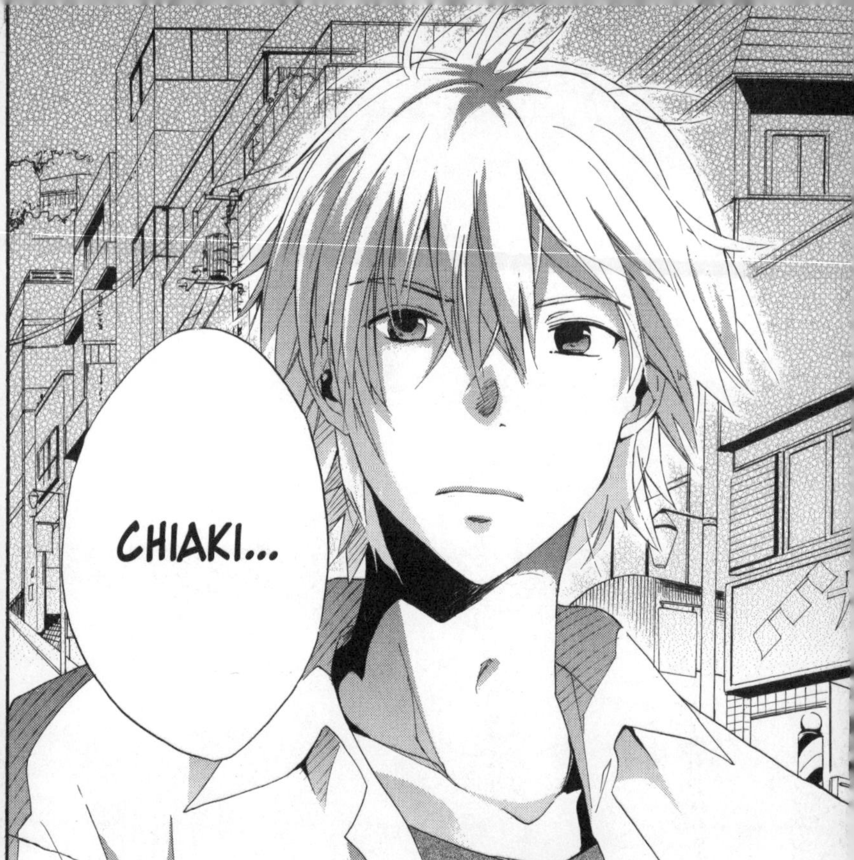
CHIAKI...

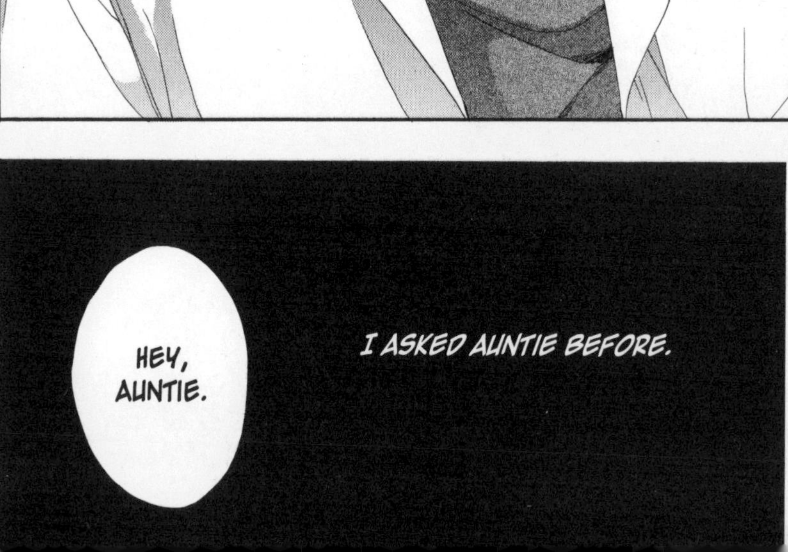
I ASKED AUNTIE BEFORE.
HEY, AUNTIE.

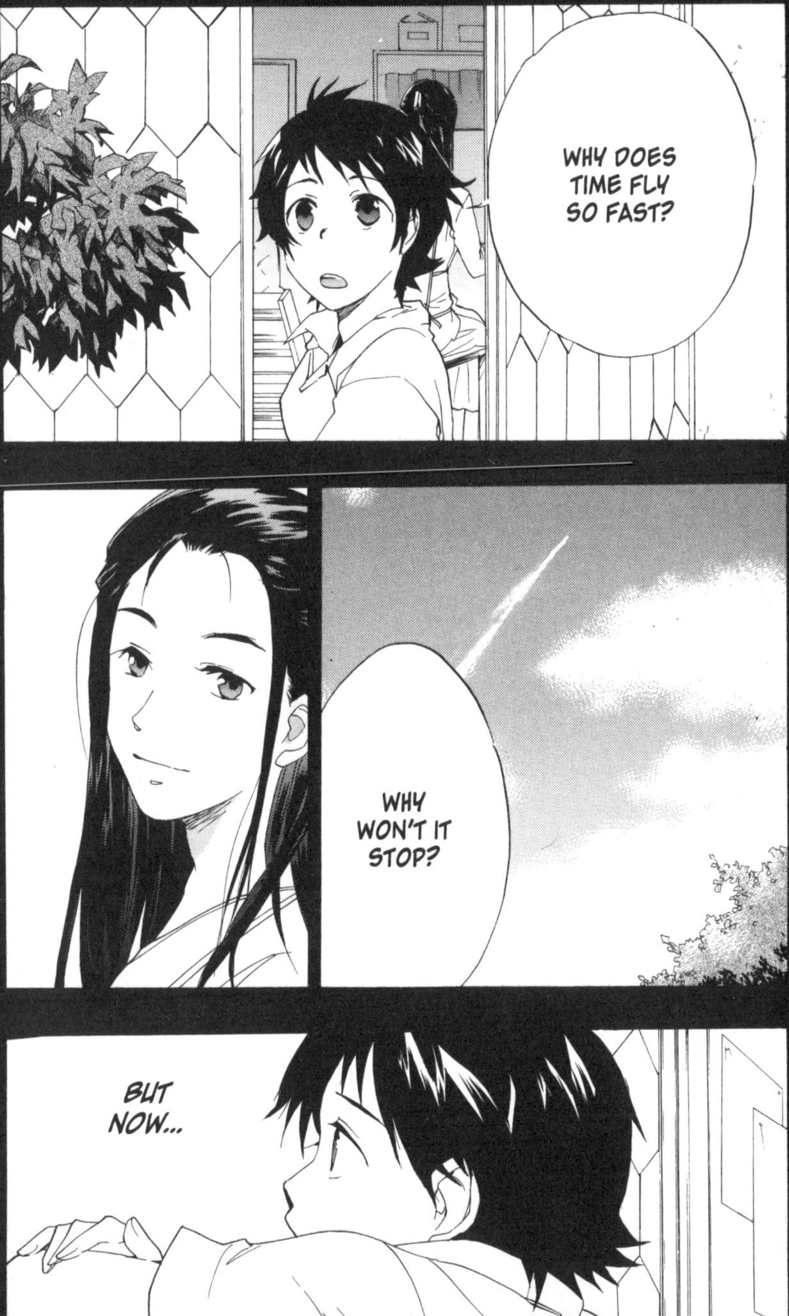
WHY DOES TIME FLY SO FAST?
WHY WON'T IT STOP?
BUT NOW...

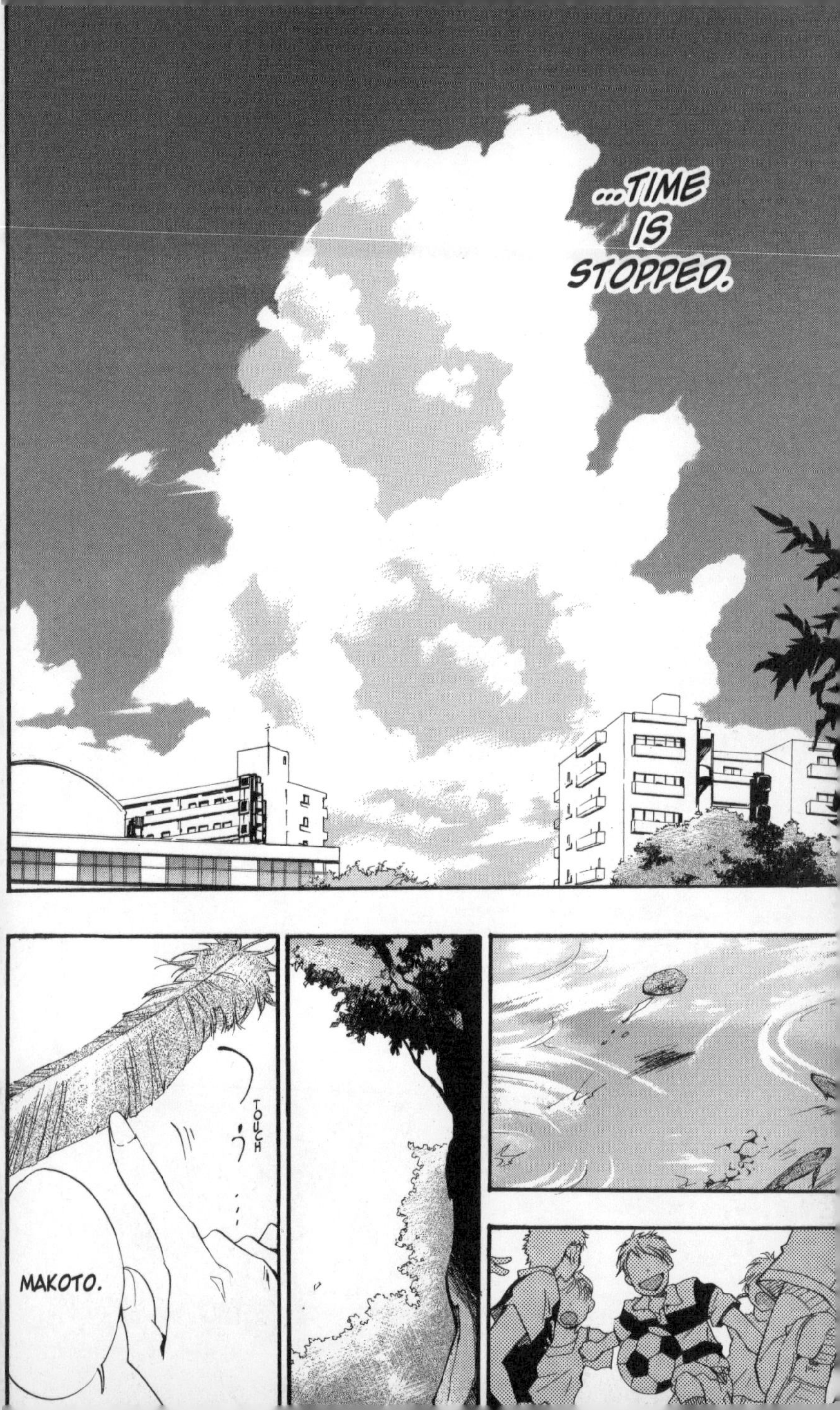
...TIME IS STOPPED.
TOUCH
MAKOTO.

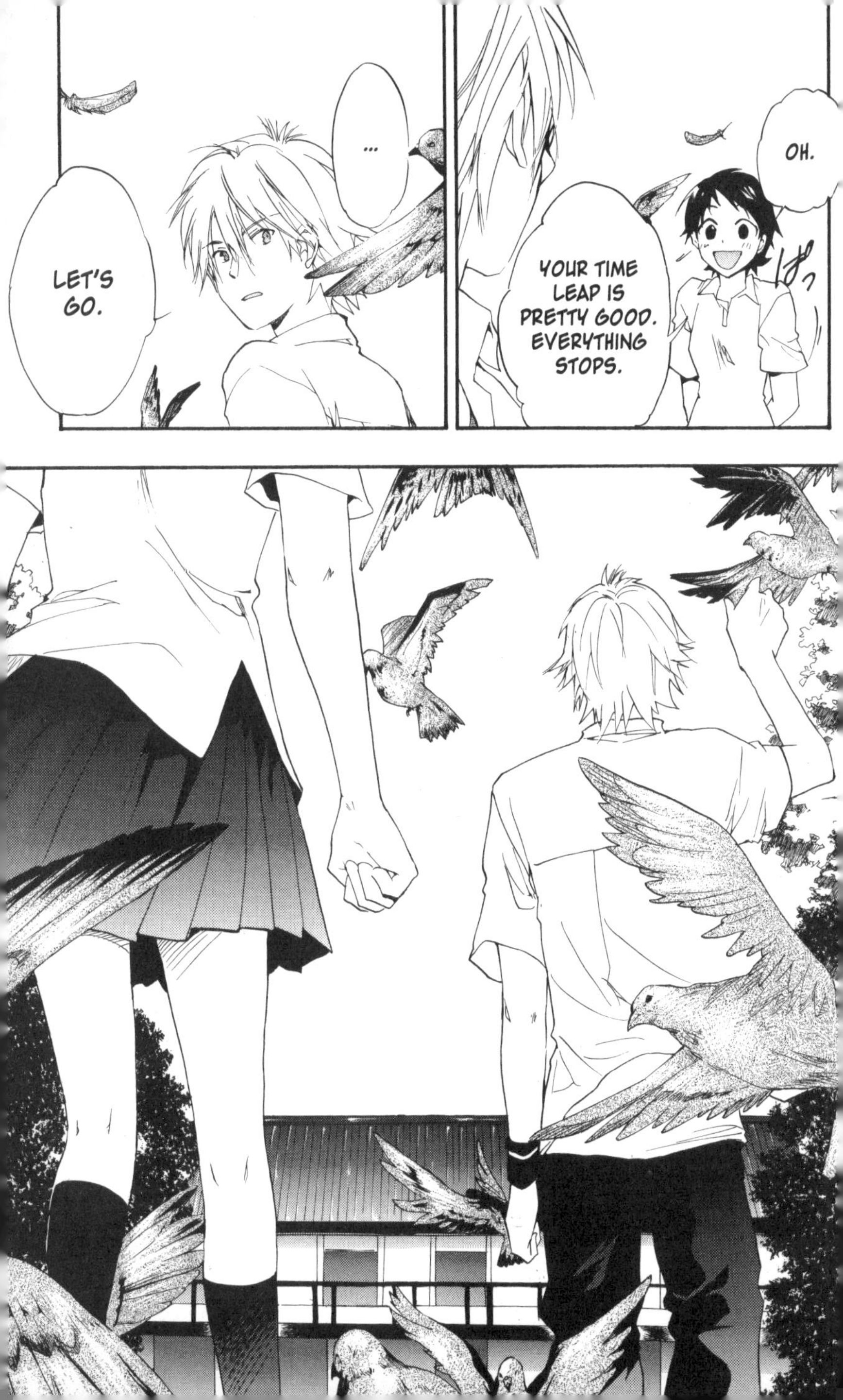
OH.
ぱっ
YOUR TIME LEAP IS PRETTY GOOD. EVERYTHING STOPS.
...
LET'S GO.

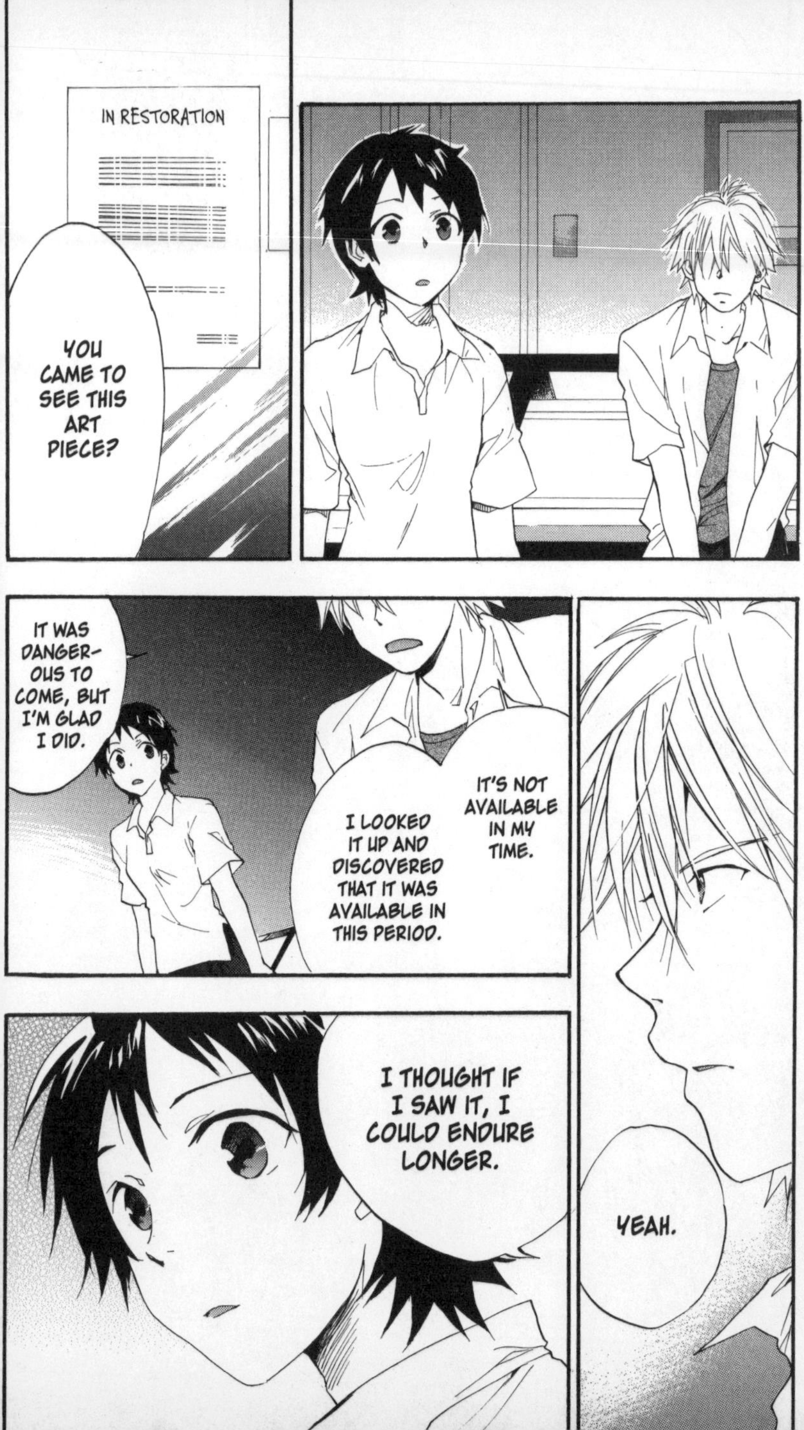
IN RESTORATION
YOU CAME TO SEE THIS ART PIECE?
YEAH.
IT'S NOT AVAILABLE IN MY TIME.
I LOOKED IT UP AND DISCOVERED THAT IT WAS AVAILABLE IN THIS PERIOD.
IT WAS DANGEROUS TO COME, BUT I'M GLAD I DID.
I THOUGHT IF I SAW IT, I COULD ENDURE LONGER.

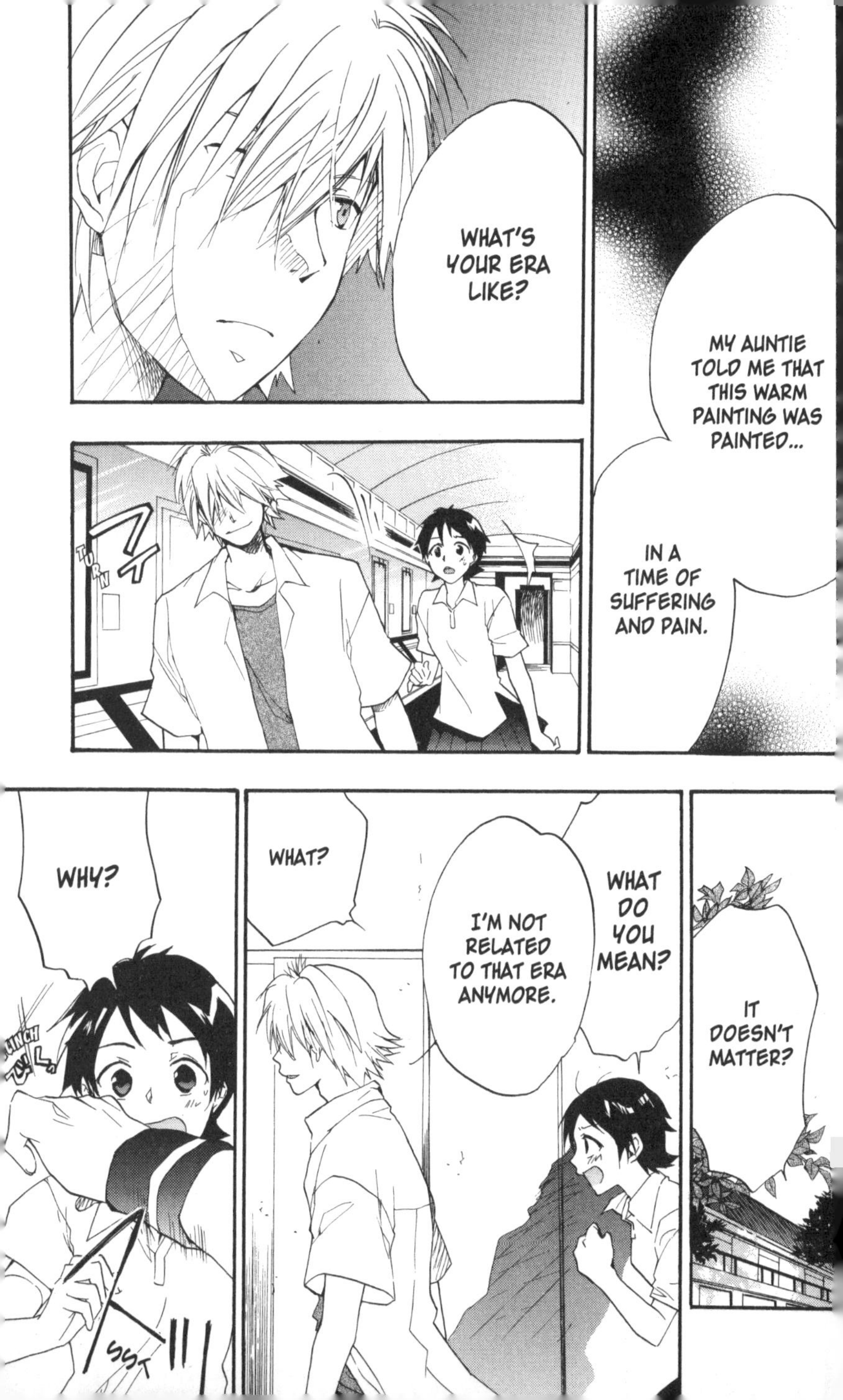
MY AUNTIE TOLD ME THAT THIS WARM PAINTING WAS PAINTED...
IN A TIME OF SUFFERING AND PAIN.
WHAT'S YOUR ERA LIKE?
TURN
IT DOESN'T MATTER?
WHAT DO YOU MEAN?
I'M NOT RELATED TO THAT ERA ANYMORE.
WHAT?
WHY?
FLINCH
SST

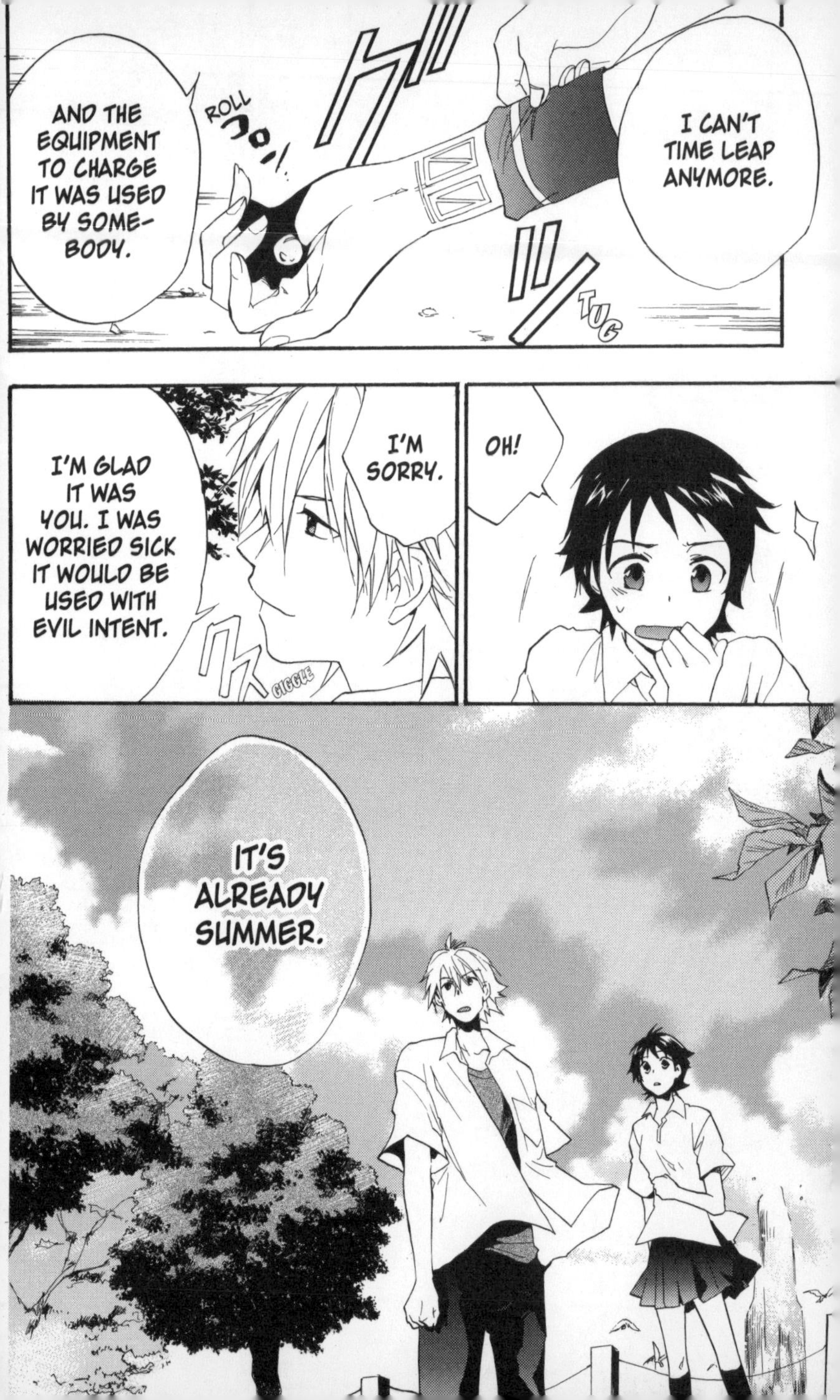
I CAN'T TIME LEAP ANYMORE.
TUG
ROLL
AND THE EQUIPMENT TO CHARGE IT WAS USED BY SOME-BODY.
OH!
I'M SORRY.
I'M GLAD IT WAS YOU. I WAS WORRIED SICK IT WOULD BE USED WITH EVIL INTENT.
GIGGLE
IT'S ALREADY SUMMER.

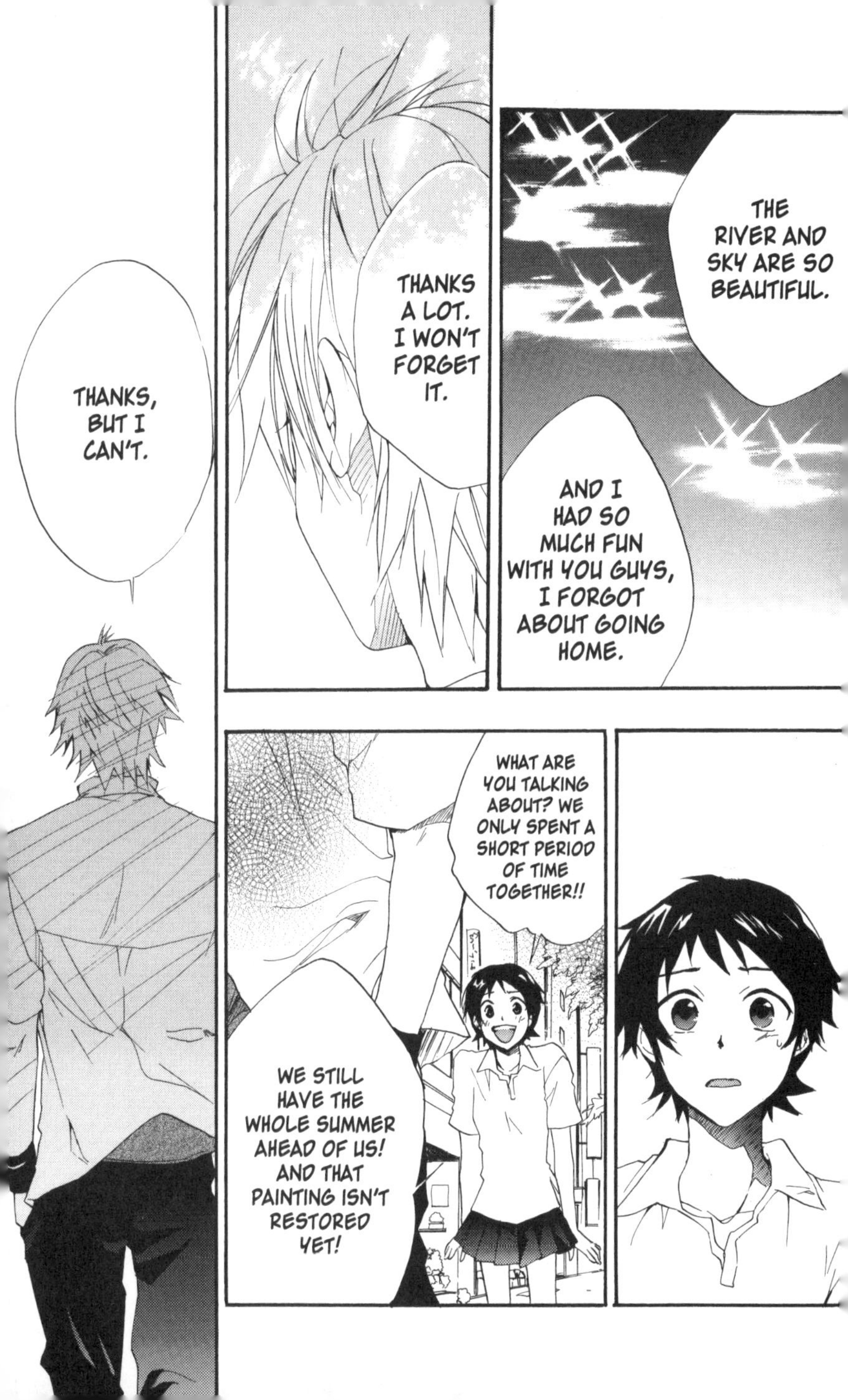
THE RIVER AND SKY ARE SO BEAUTIFUL.
AND I HAD SO MUCH FUN WITH YOU GUYS, I FORGOT ABOUT GOING HOME.
THANKS A LOT. I WON'T FORGET IT.
WHAT ARE YOU TALKING ABOUT? WE ONLY SPENT A SHORT PERIOD OF TIME TOGETHER!!
WE STILL HAVE THE WHOLE SUMMER AHEAD OF US! AND THAT PAINTING ISN'T RESTORED YET!
THANKS, BUT I CAN'T.

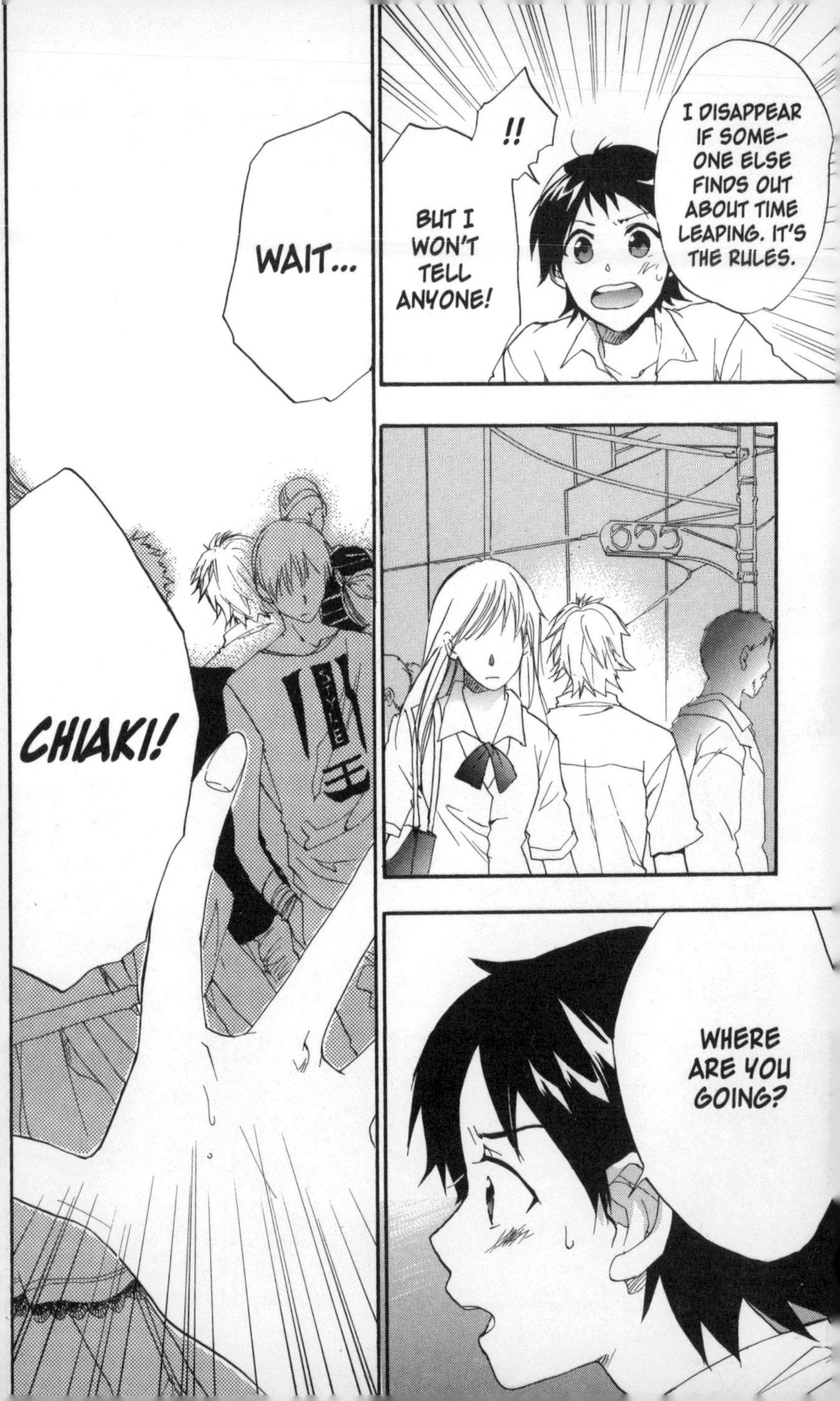
I DISAPPEAR IF SOME-ONE ELSE FINDS OUT ABOUT TIME LEAPING. IT'S THE RULES.
!!
BUT I WON'T TELL ANYONE!
WHERE ARE YOU GOING?
WAIT...
CHIAKI!

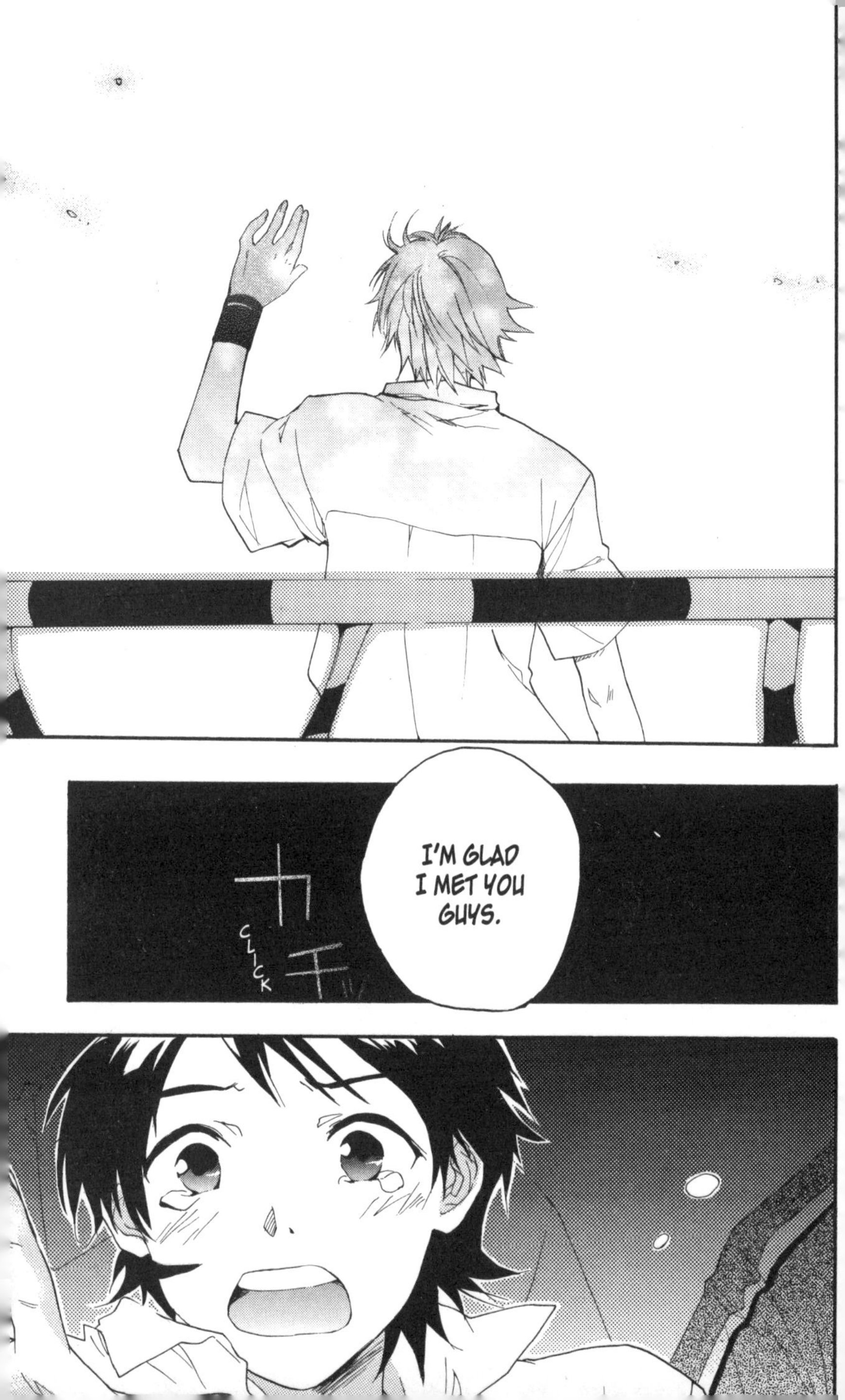
I'M GLAD I MET YOU GUYS.
カチッ
CLICK

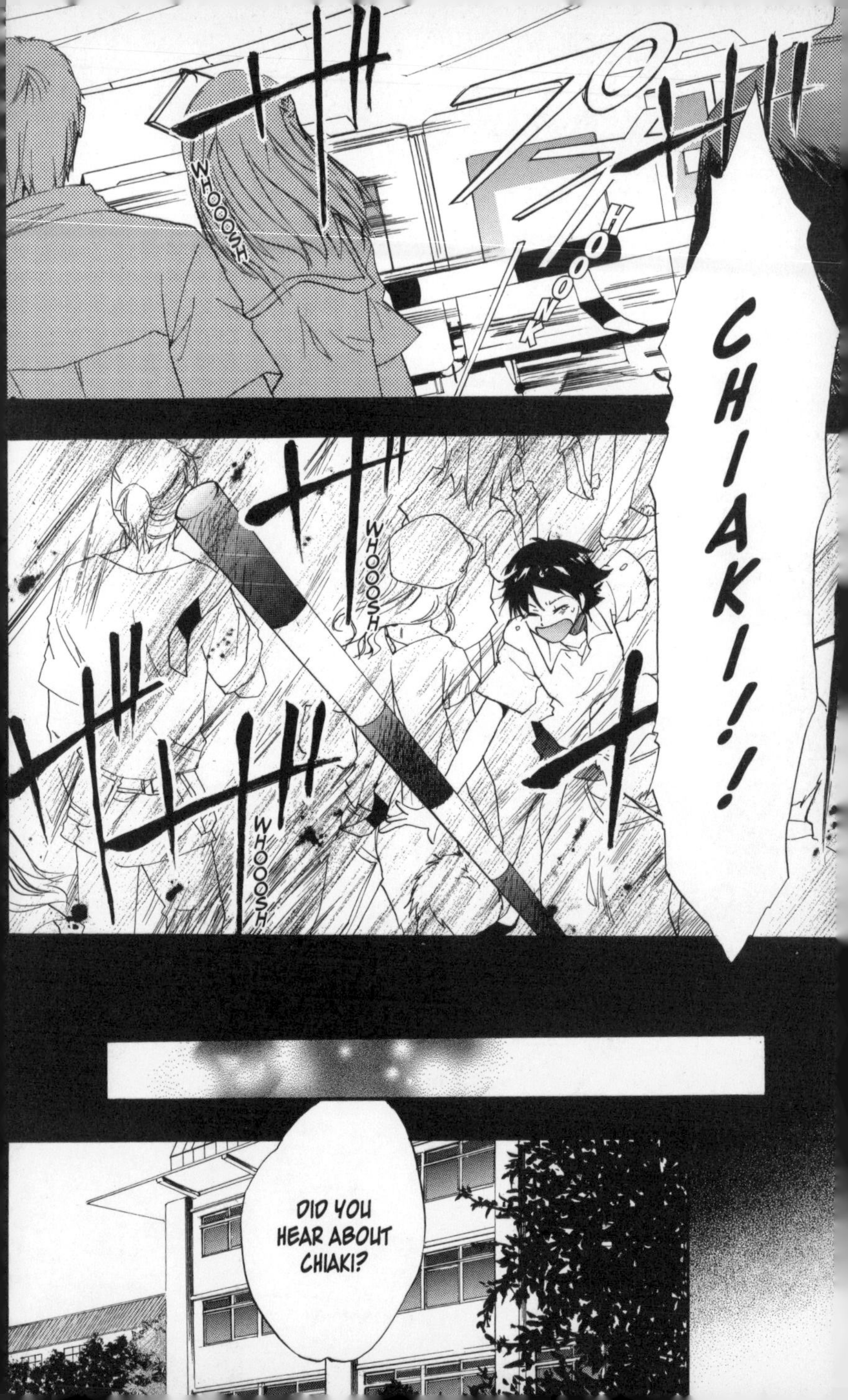
CHIAKI!!!
HOOOONK
WHOOOSH
WHOOOSH
WHOOOSH
DID YOU HEAR ABOUT CHIAKI?

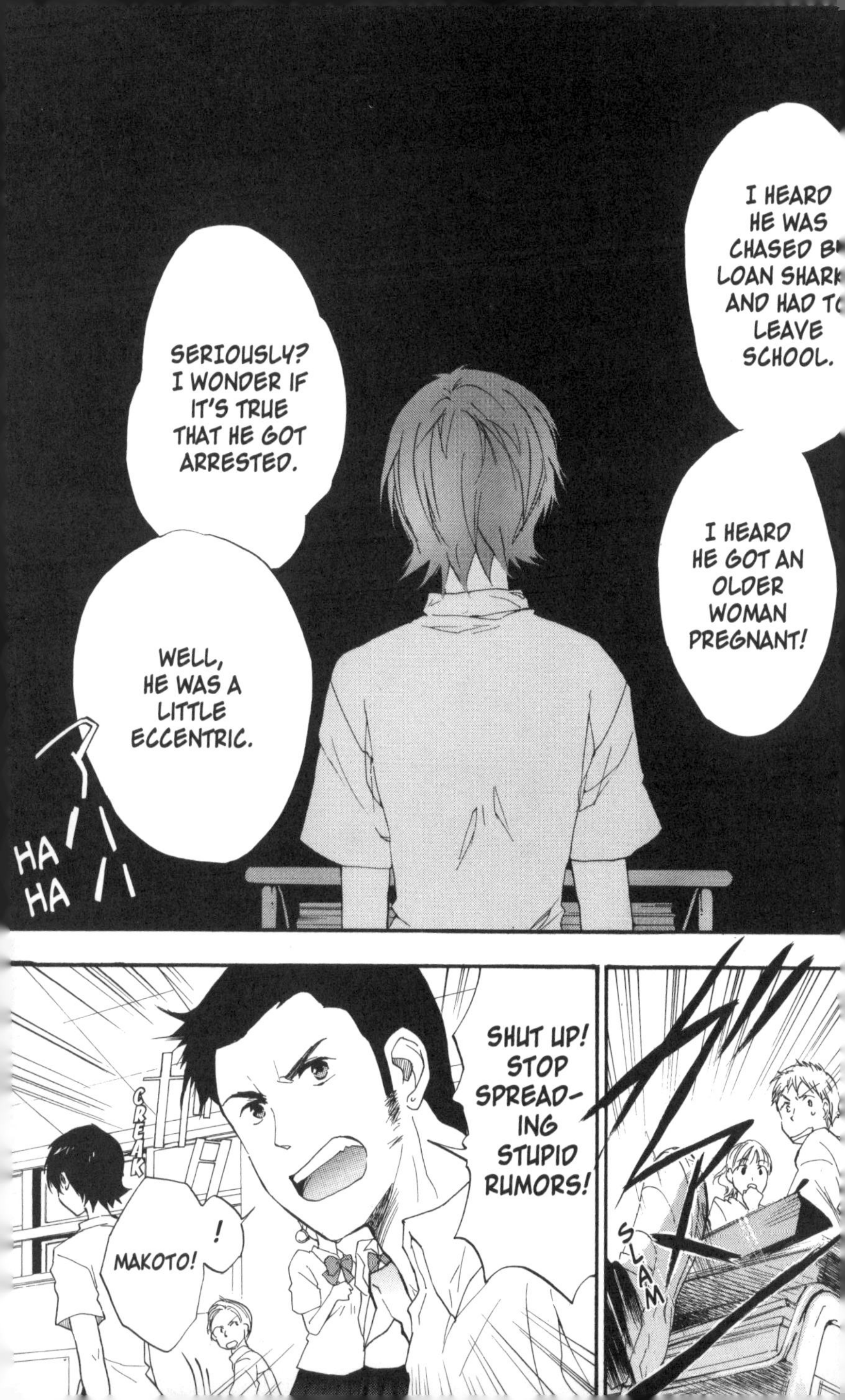
I HEARD HE WAS CHASED B LOAN SHARK AND HAD T LEAVE SCHOOL.
SERIOUSLY? I WONDER IF IT'S TRUE THAT HE GOT ARRESTED.
I HEARD HE GOT AN OLDER WOMAN PREGNANT!
WELL, HE WAS A LITTLE ECCENTRIC.
HA HA
SLAM
SHUT UP! STOP SPREAD-ING STUPID RUMORS!
CREAK
!
MAKOTO!

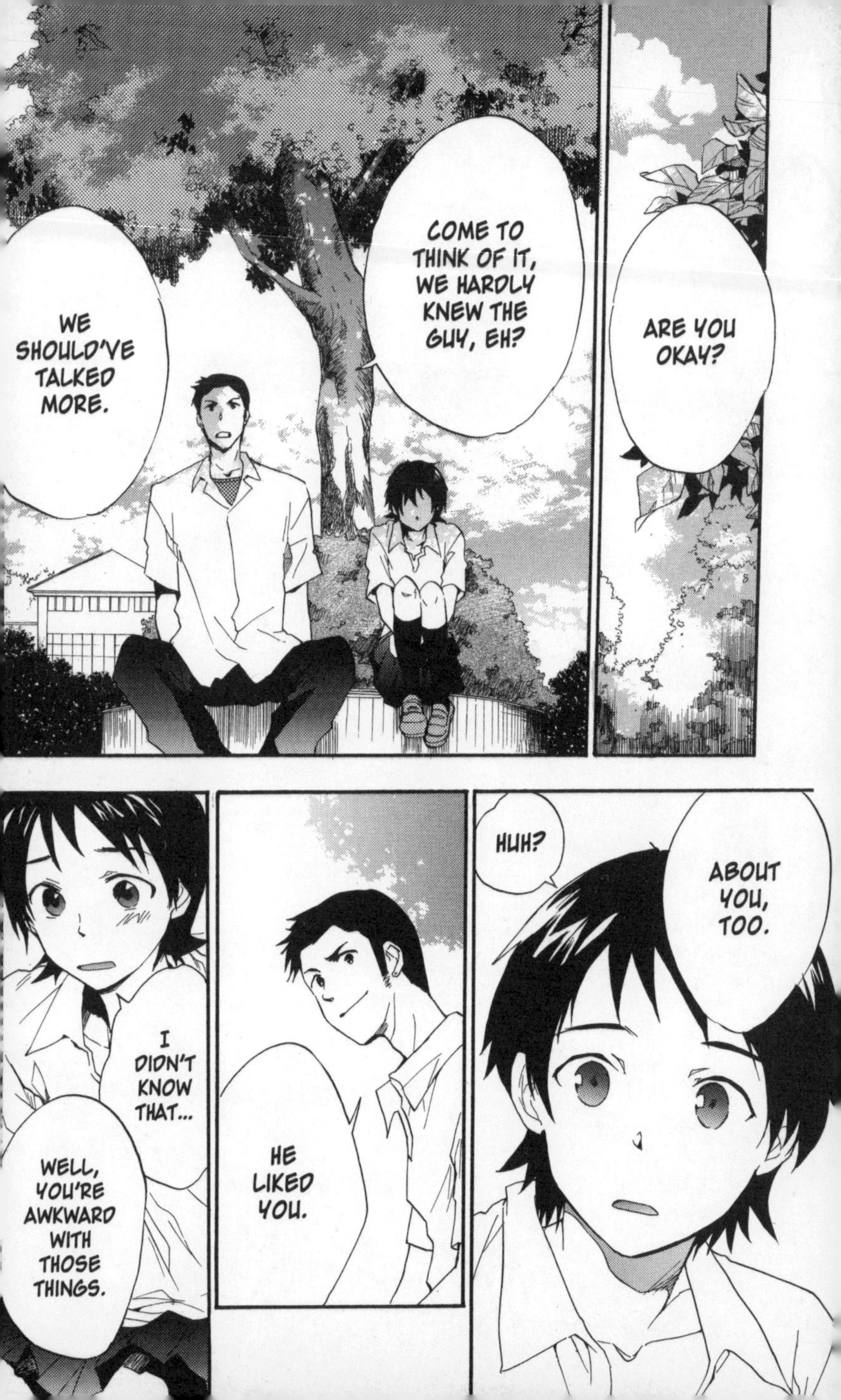
ARE YOU OKAY?
COME TO THINK OF IT, WE HARDLY KNEW THE GUY, EH?
WE SHOULD'VE TALKED MORE.
ABOUT YOU, TOO.
HUH?
HE LIKED YOU.
I DIDN'T KNOW THAT...
WELL, YOU'RE AWKWARD WITH THOSE THINGS.

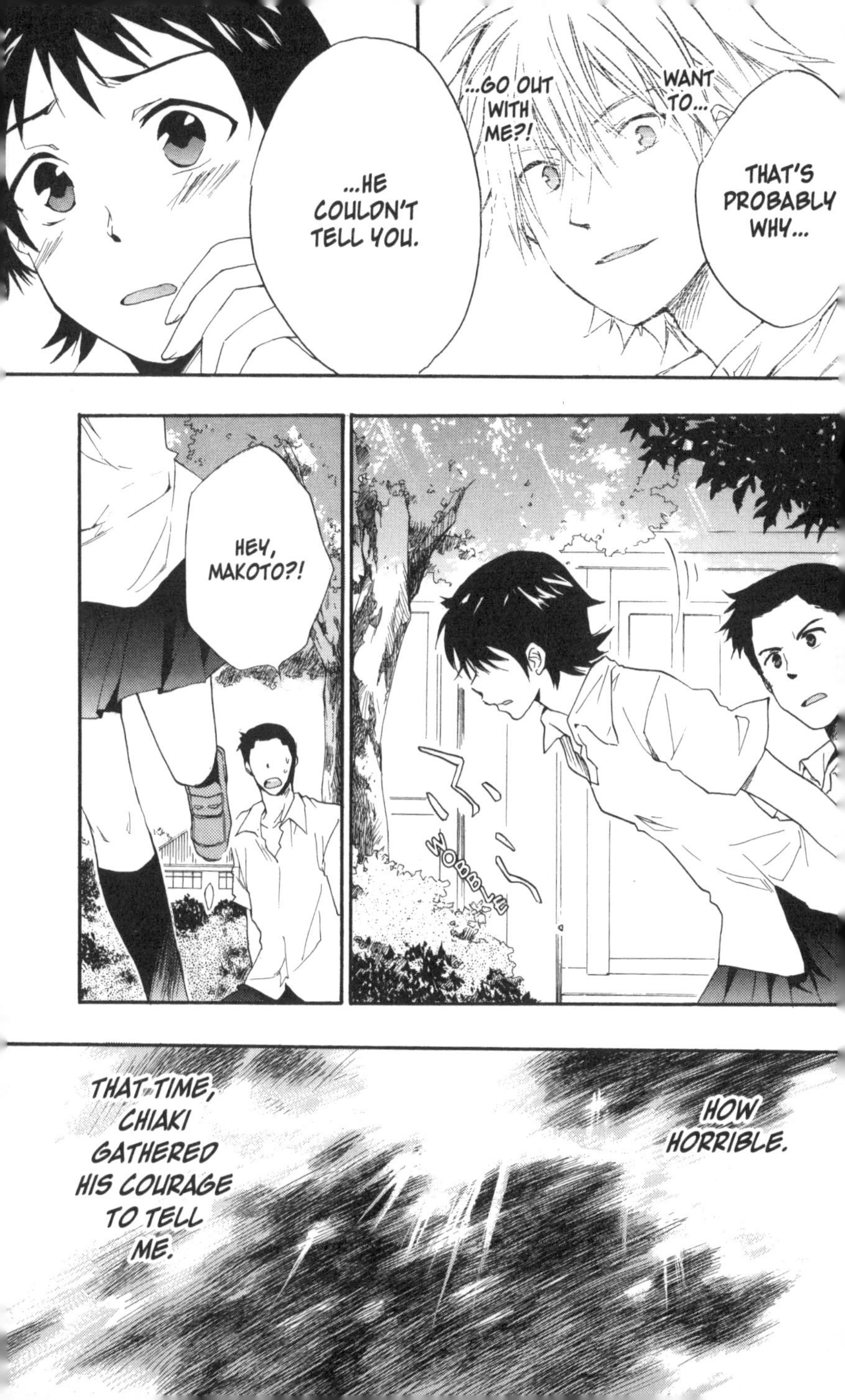
WANT TO...
...GO OUT WITH ME?!
THAT'S PROBABLY WHY...
...HE COULDN'T TELL YOU.
WOBBLE
HEY, MAKOTO?!
HOW HORRIBLE.
THAT TIME, CHIAKI GATHERED HIS COURAGE TO TELL ME.

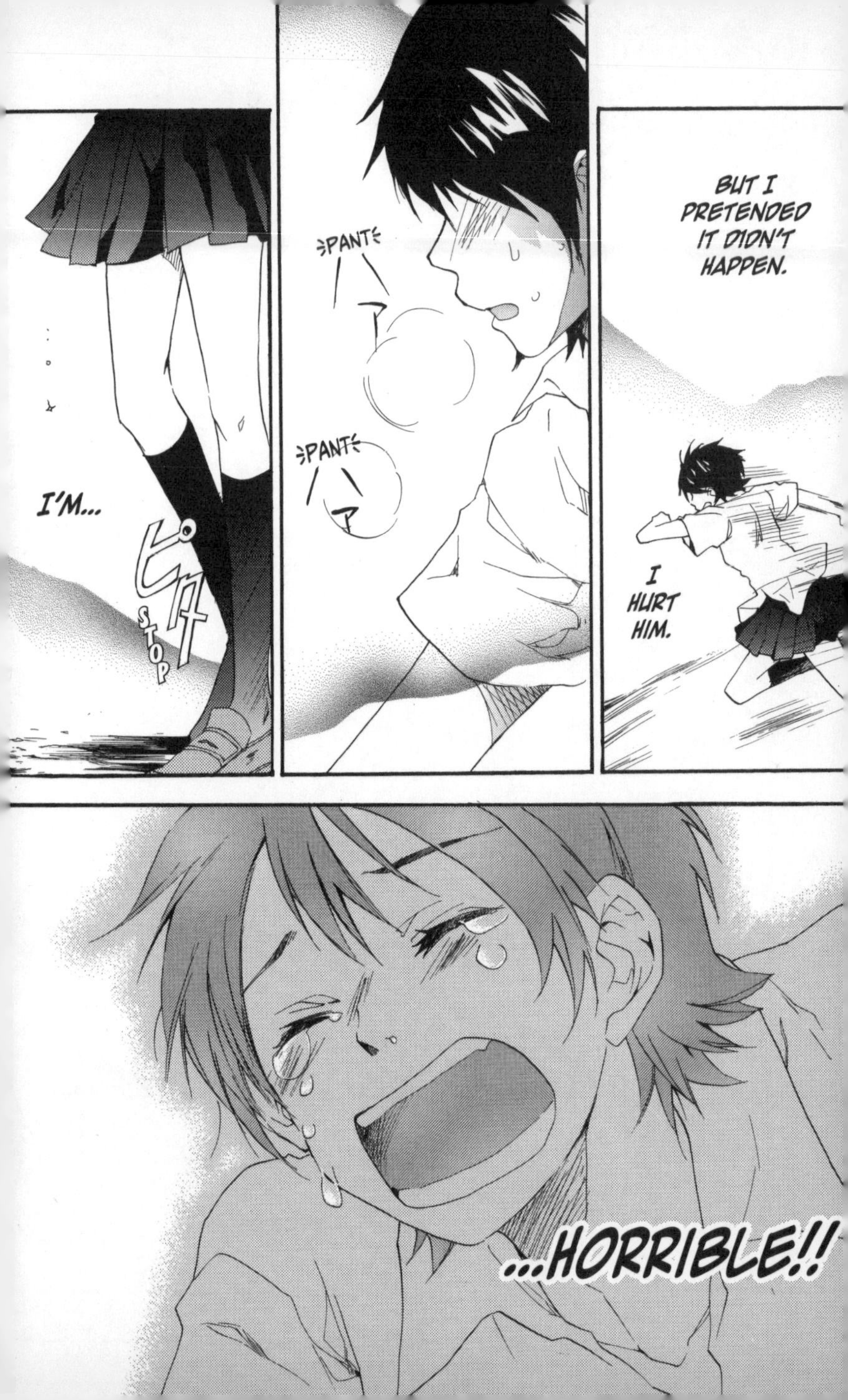
BUT I PRETENDED IT DIDN'T HAPPEN.
I HURT HIM.
PANT
PANT
I'M...
ピタ
STOP
...HORRIBLE!!

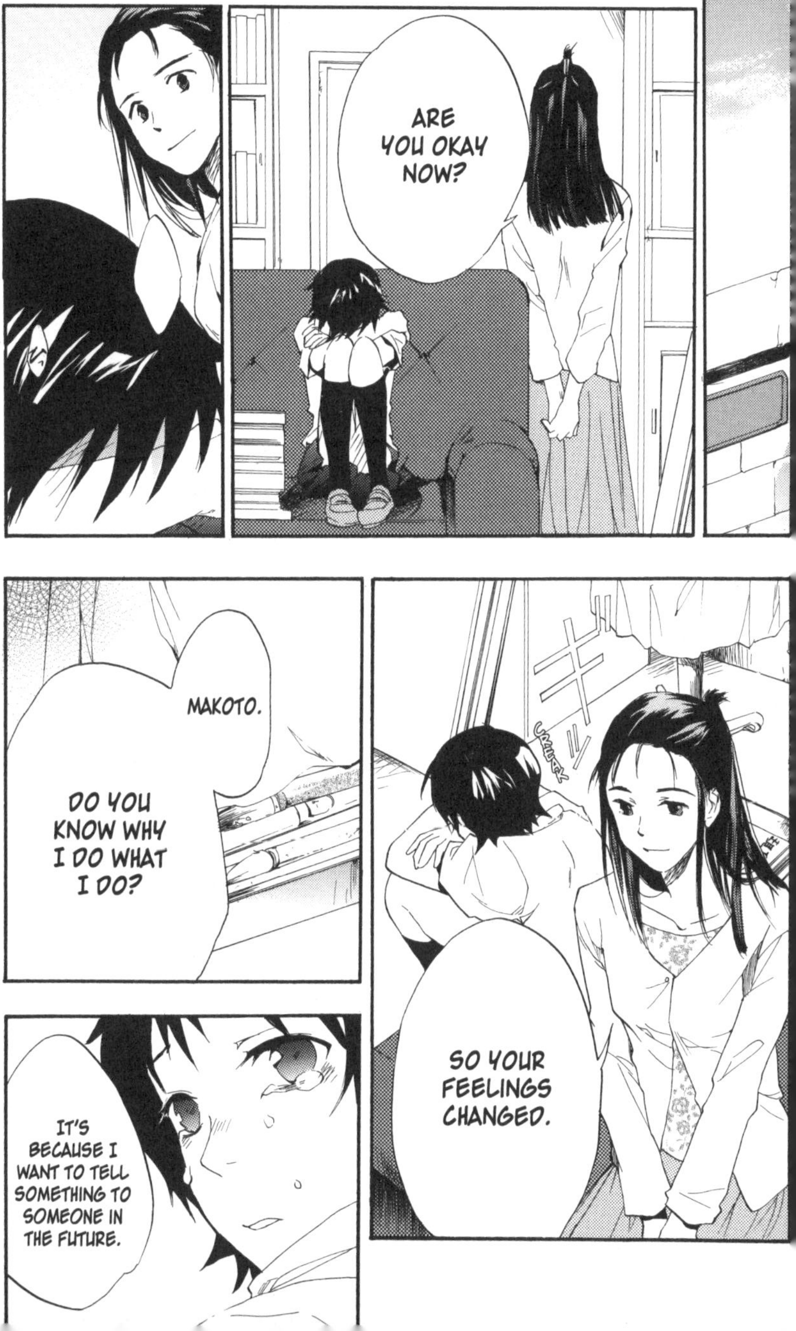
ARE YOU OKAY NOW?
SO YOUR FEELINGS CHANGED.
MAKOTO.
DO YOU KNOW WHY I DO WHAT I DO?
IT'S BECAUSE I WANT TO TELL SOMETHING TO SOMEONE IN THE FUTURE.

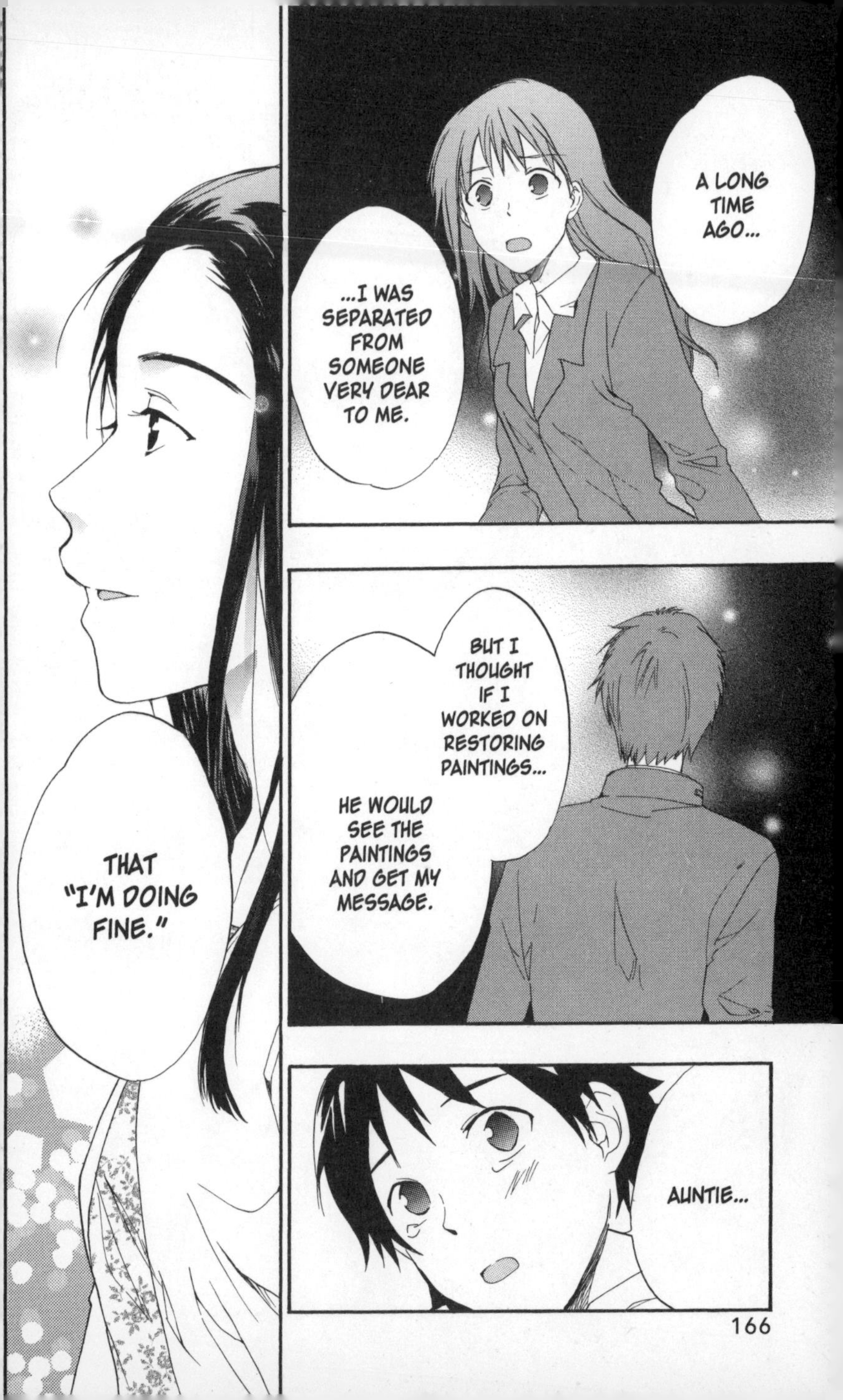
A LONG TIME AGO...
...I WAS SEPARATED FROM SOMEONE VERY DEAR TO ME.
BUT I THOUGHT IF I WORKED ON RESTORING PAINTINGS...
HE WOULD SEE THE PAINTINGS AND GET MY MESSAGE.
AUNTIE...
THAT "I'M DOING FINE."

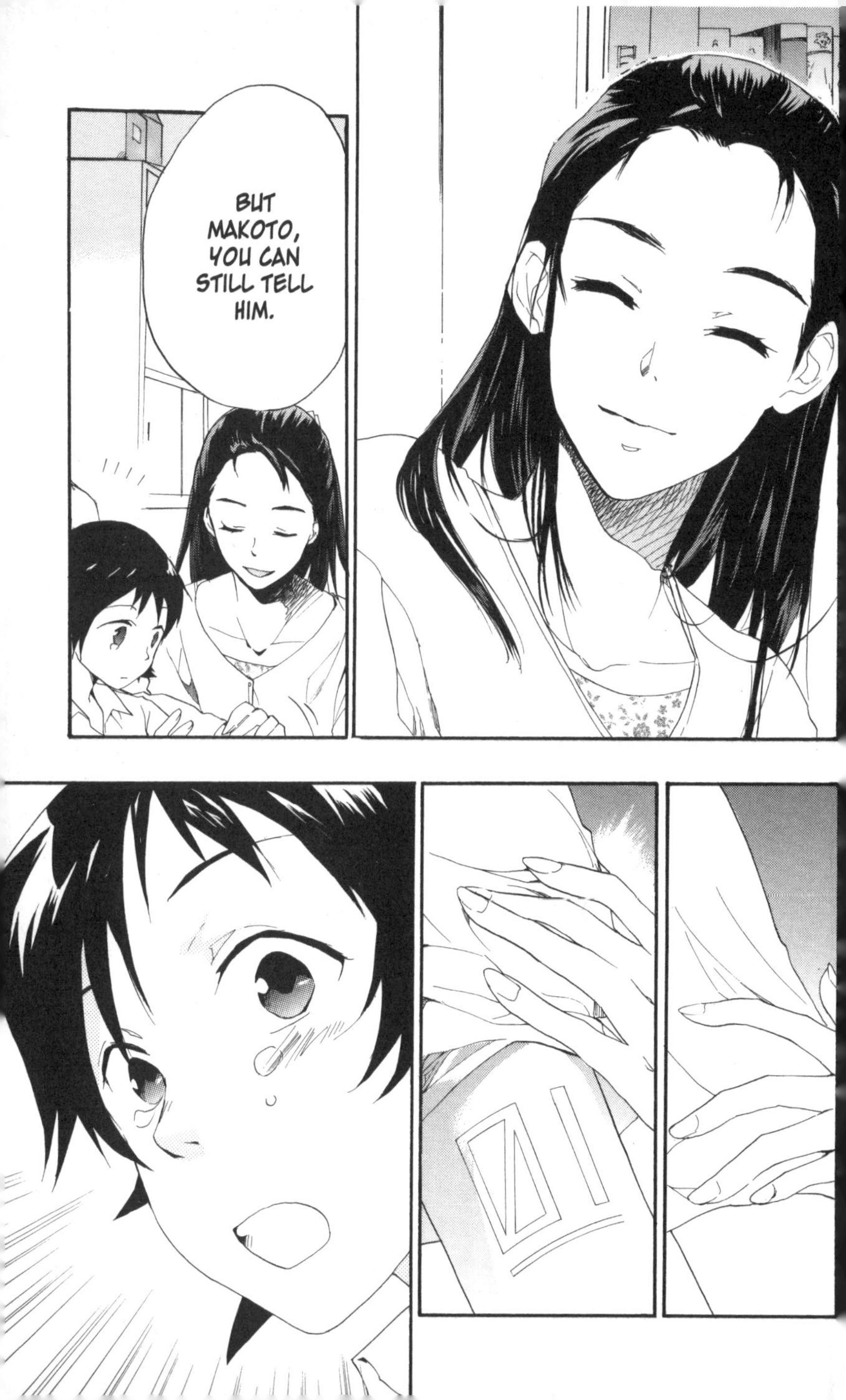
BUT MAKOTO, YOU CAN STILL TELL HIM.

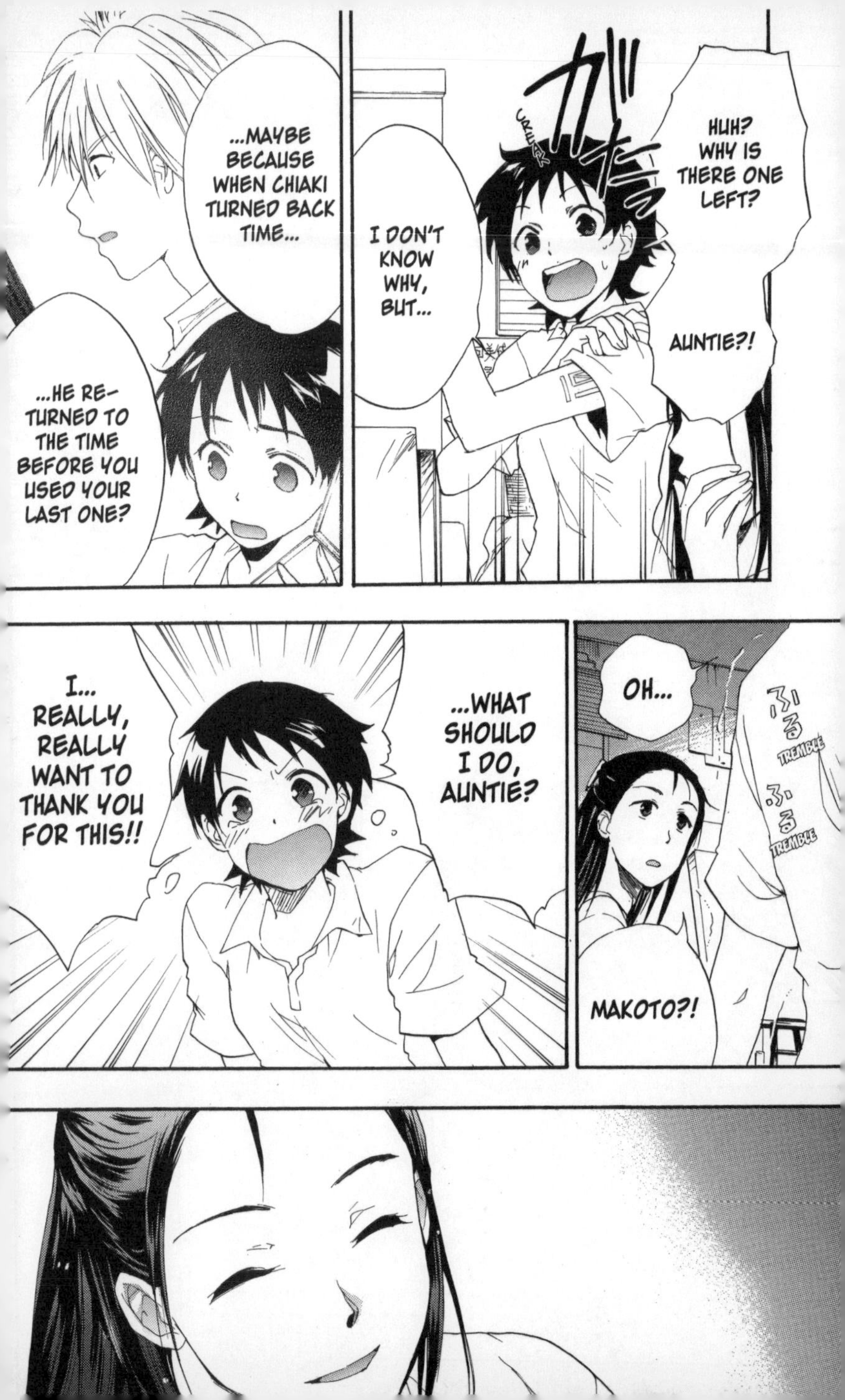
CREAK
HUH? WHY IS THERE ONE LEFT?
AUNTIE?!
I DON'T KNOW WHY, BUT...
...MAYBE BECAUSE WHEN CHIAKI TURNED BACK TIME...
...HE RE-TURNED TO THE TIME BEFORE YOU USED YOUR LAST ONE?
TREMBLE
TREMBLE
OH...
MAKOTO?!
...WHAT SHOULD I DO, AUNTIE?
I... REALLY, REALLY WANT TO THANK YOU FOR THIS!!

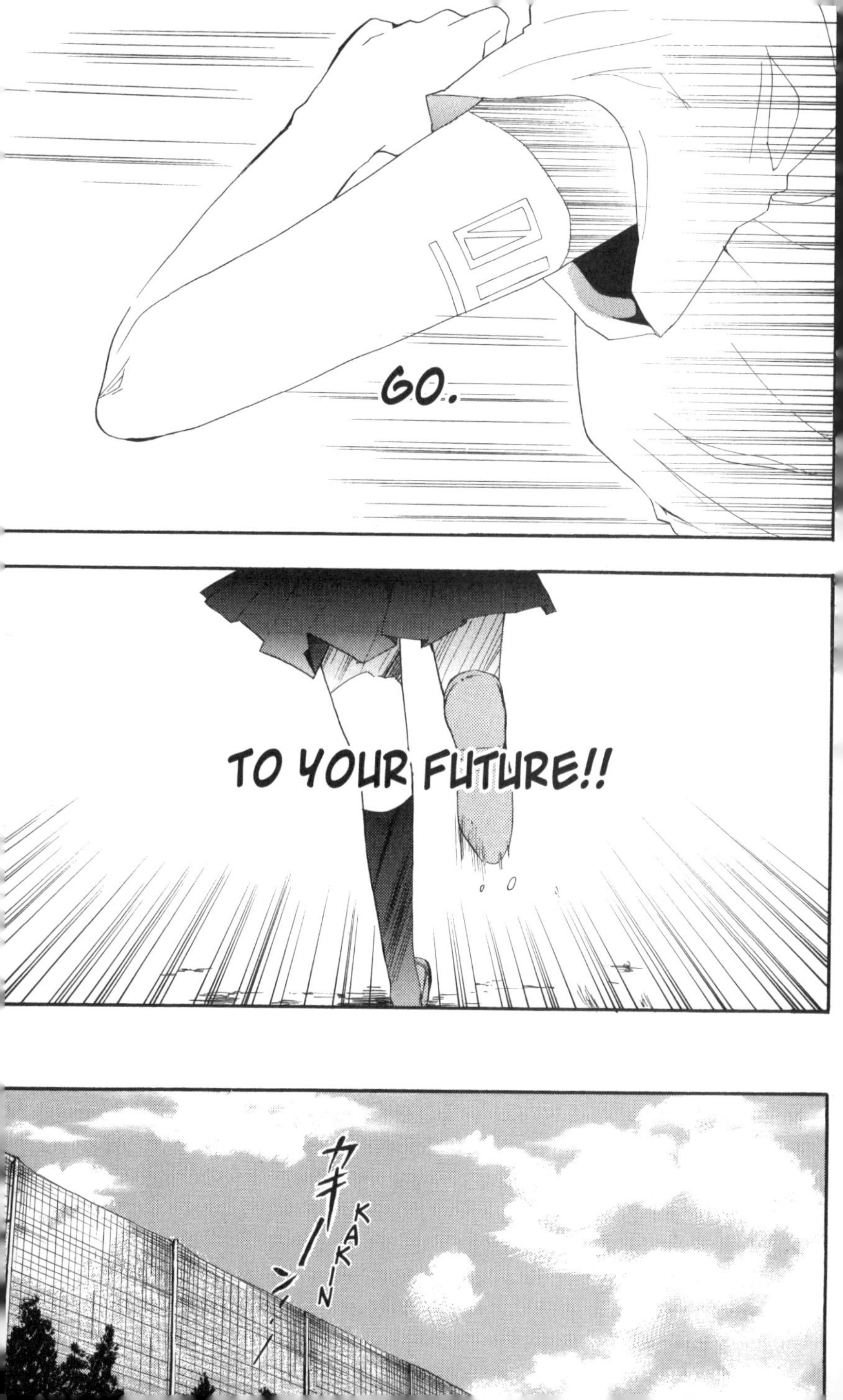
GO.
TO YOUR FUTURE!!
カキーン
KAKIN

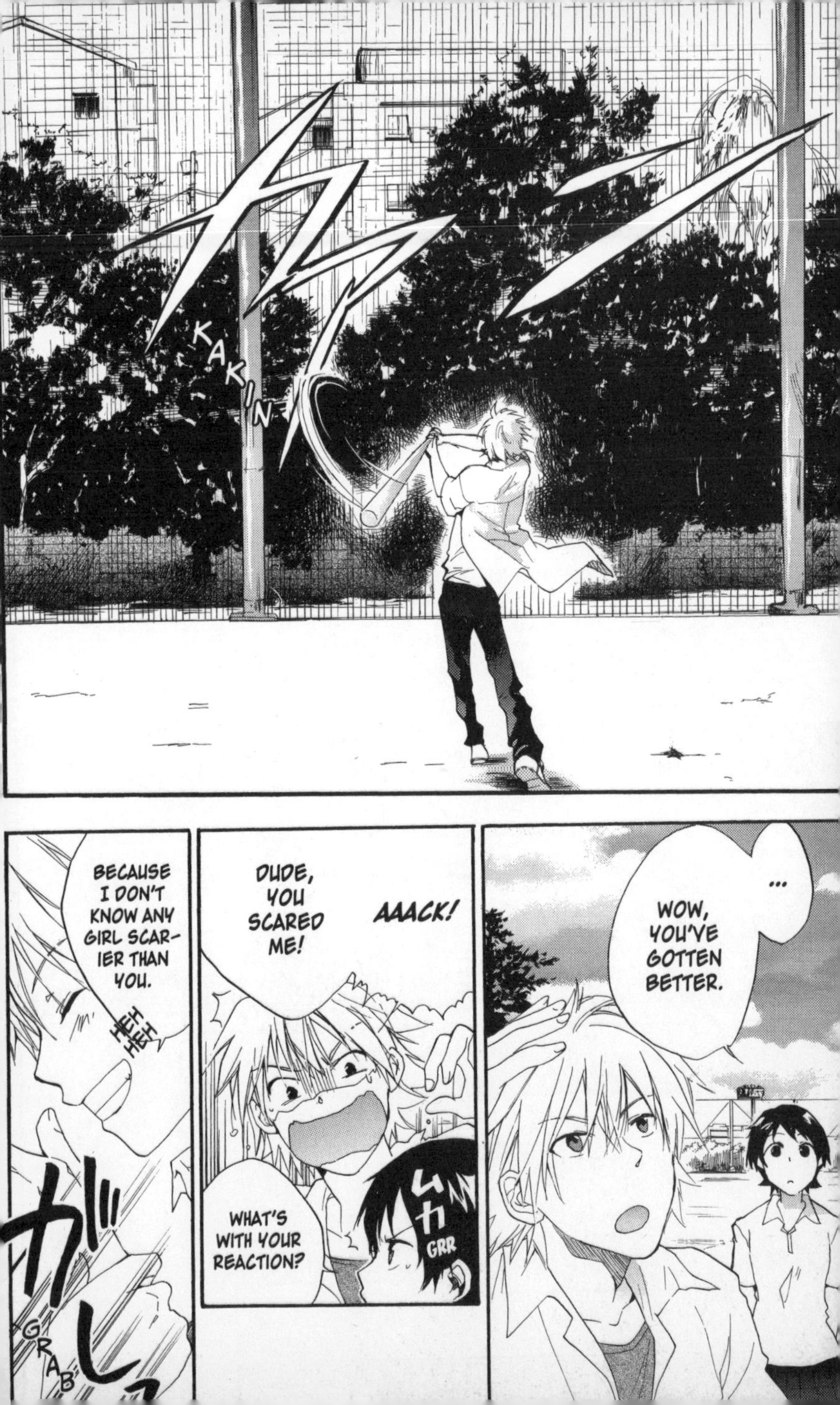
KAKIN
...
WOW, YOU'VE GOTTEN BETTER.
AAACK!
DUDE, YOU SCARED ME!
WHAT'S WITH YOUR REACTION?
ムカ
GRR
BECAUSE I DON'T KNOW ANY GIRL SCAR-IER THAN YOU.
HEH HEH
ガシッ
GRAB

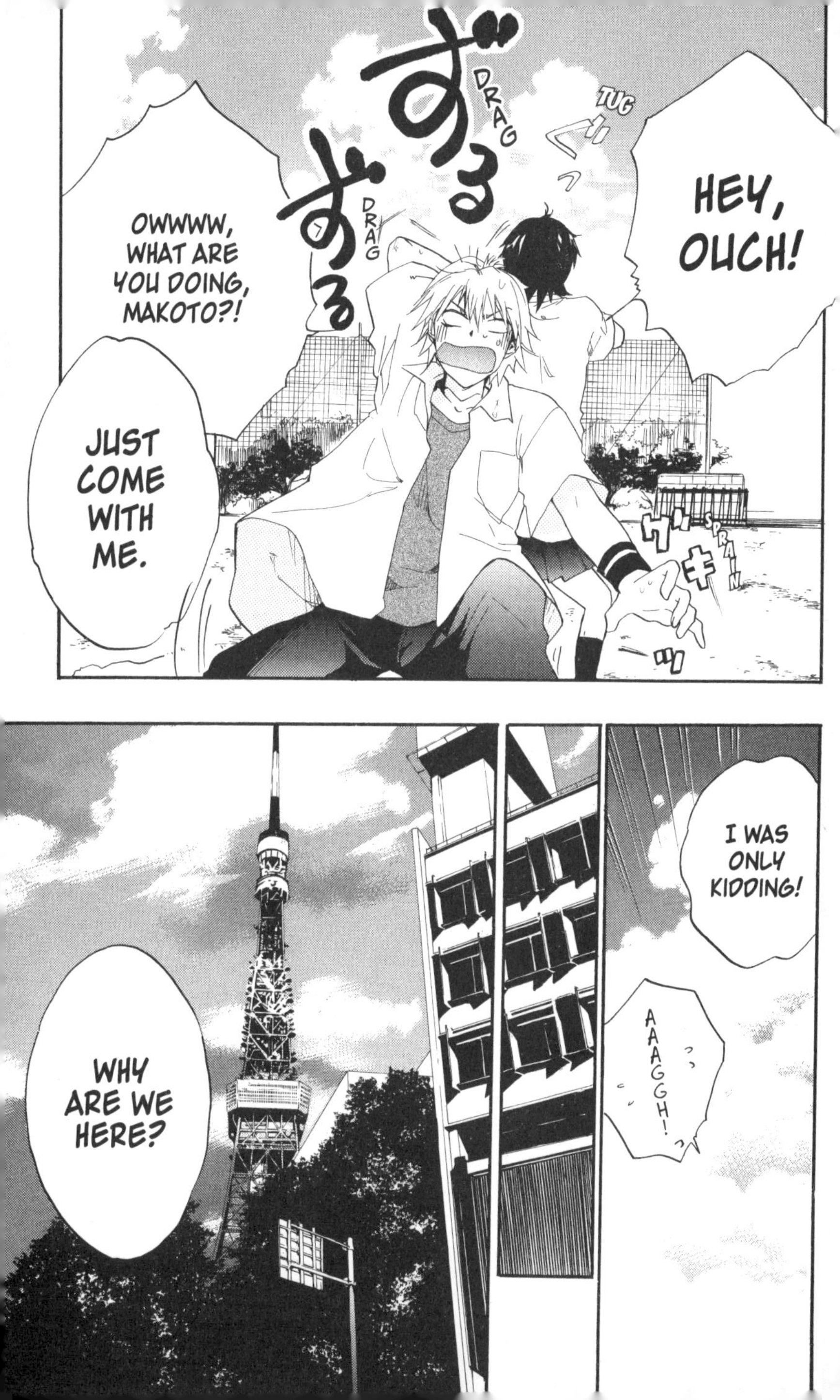
TUG
HEY, OUCH!
DRAG
DRAG
OWWWW, WHAT ARE YOU DOING, MAKOTO?!
JUST COME WITH ME.
SPRAIN
I WAS ONLY KIDDING!
AAAGGH!
WHY ARE WE HERE?

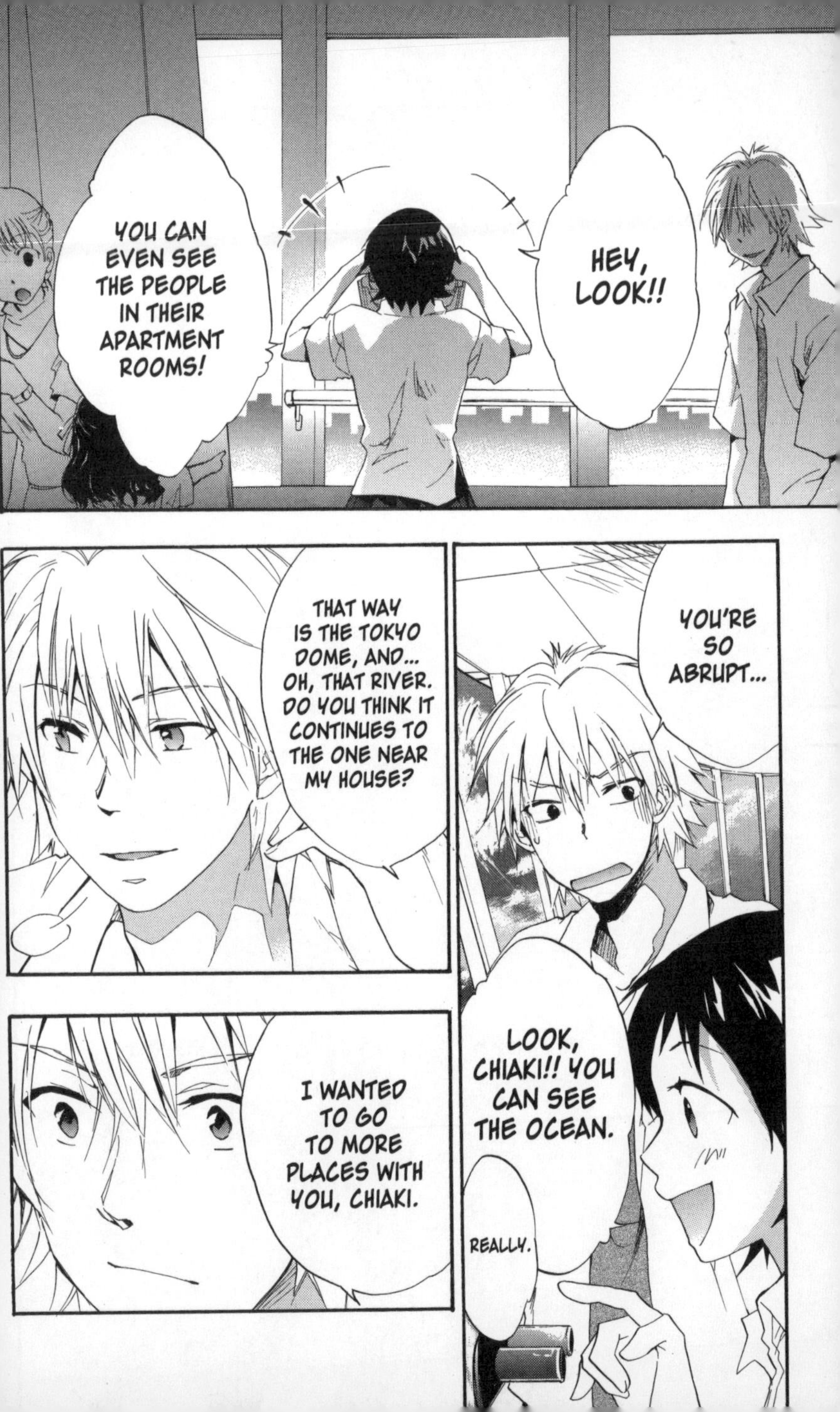
HEY, LOOK!!
YOU CAN EVEN SEE THE PEOPLE IN THEIR APARTMENT ROOMS!
YOU'RE SO ABRUPT...
LOOK, CHIAKI!! YOU CAN SEE THE OCEAN.
REALLY.
THAT WAY IS THE TOKYO DOME, AND... OH, THAT RIVER. DO YOU THINK IT CONTINUES TO THE ONE NEAR MY HOUSE?
I WANTED TO GO TO MORE PLACES WITH YOU, CHIAKI.

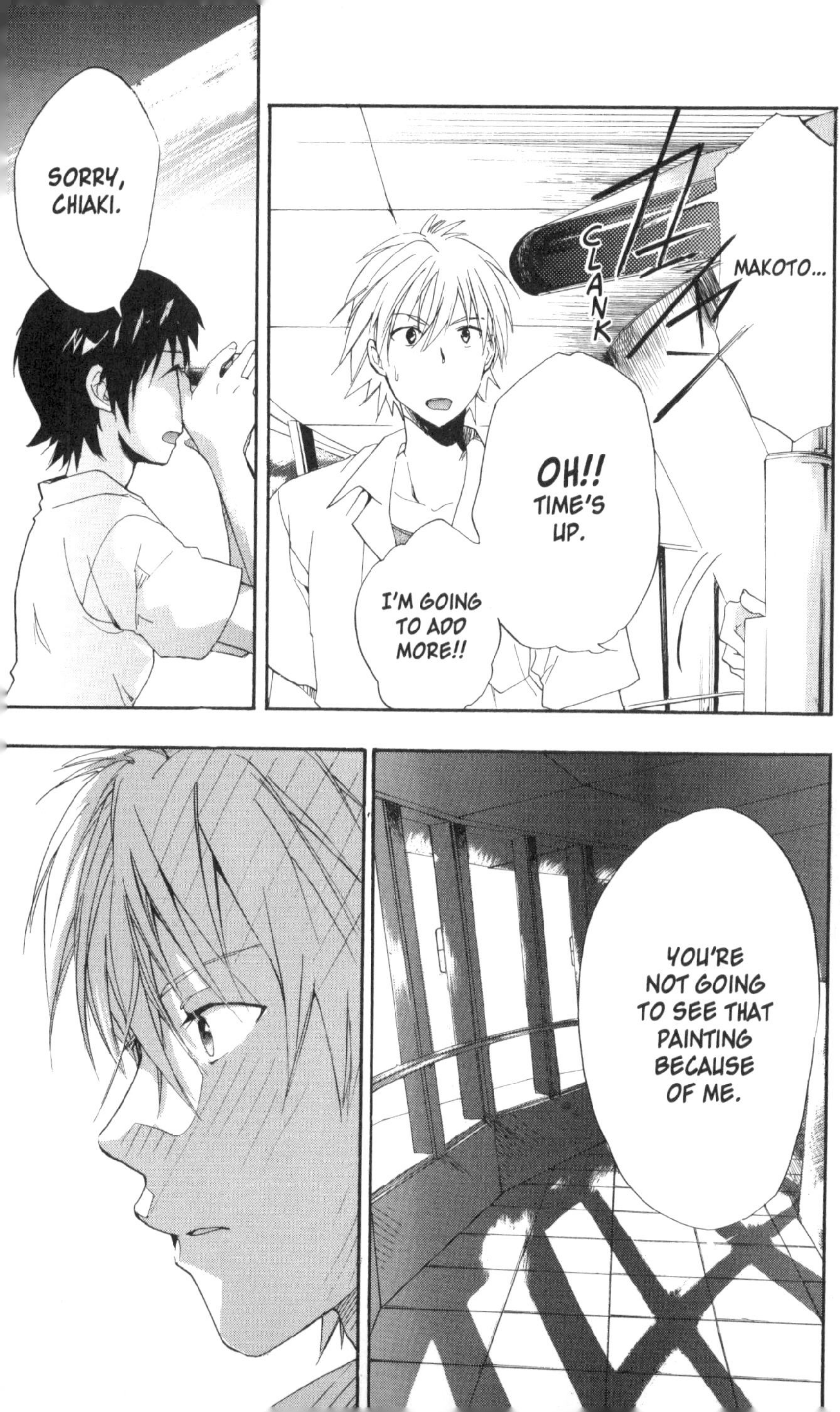
MAKOTO...
CLANK
OH!! TIME'S UP.
I'M GOING TO ADD MORE!!
SORRY, CHIAKI.
YOU'RE NOT GOING TO SEE THAT PAINTING BECAUSE OF ME.

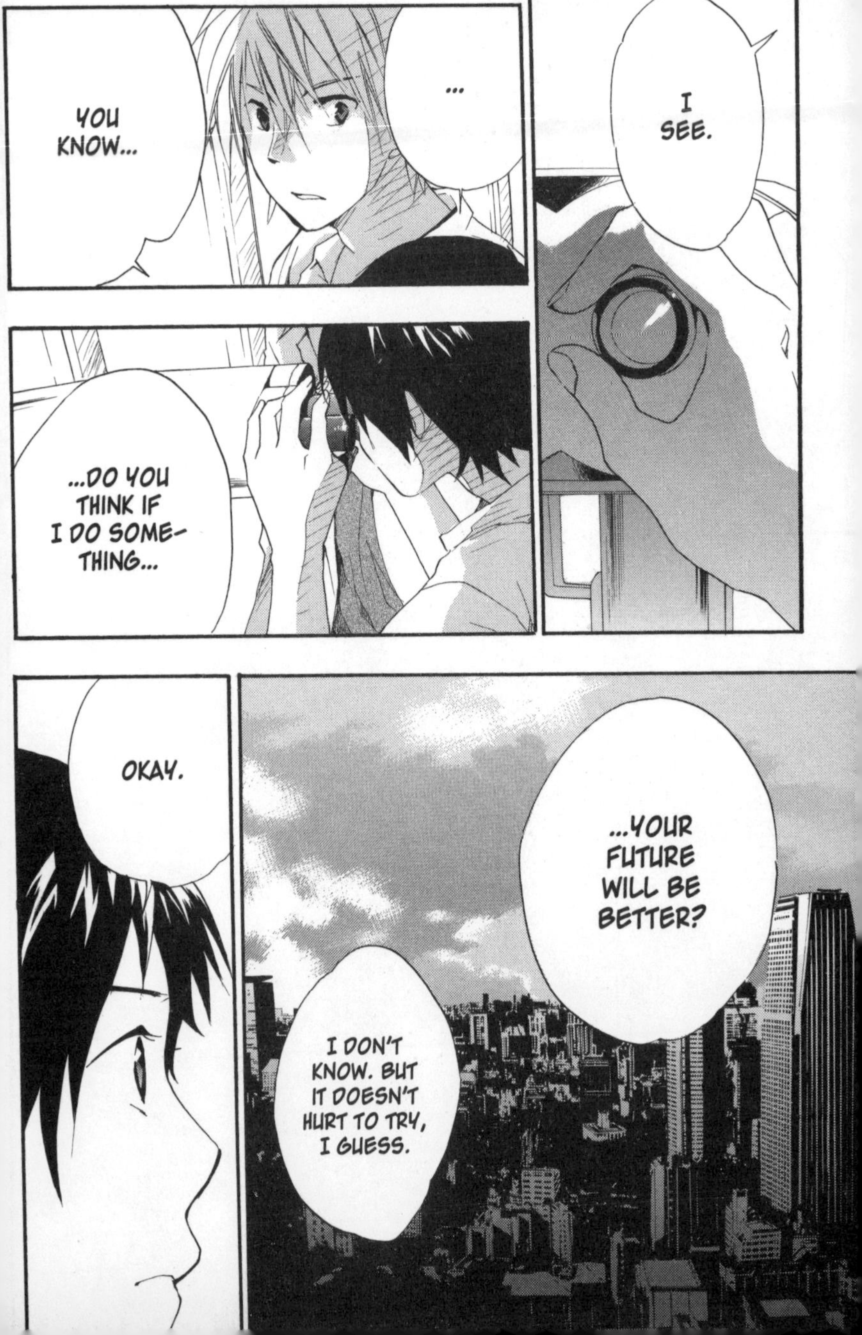
I SEE.
...
YOU KNOW...
...DO YOU THINK IF I DO SOME-THING...
...YOUR FUTURE WILL BE BETTER?
I DON'T KNOW. BUT IT DOESN'T HURT TO TRY, I GUESS.
OKAY.

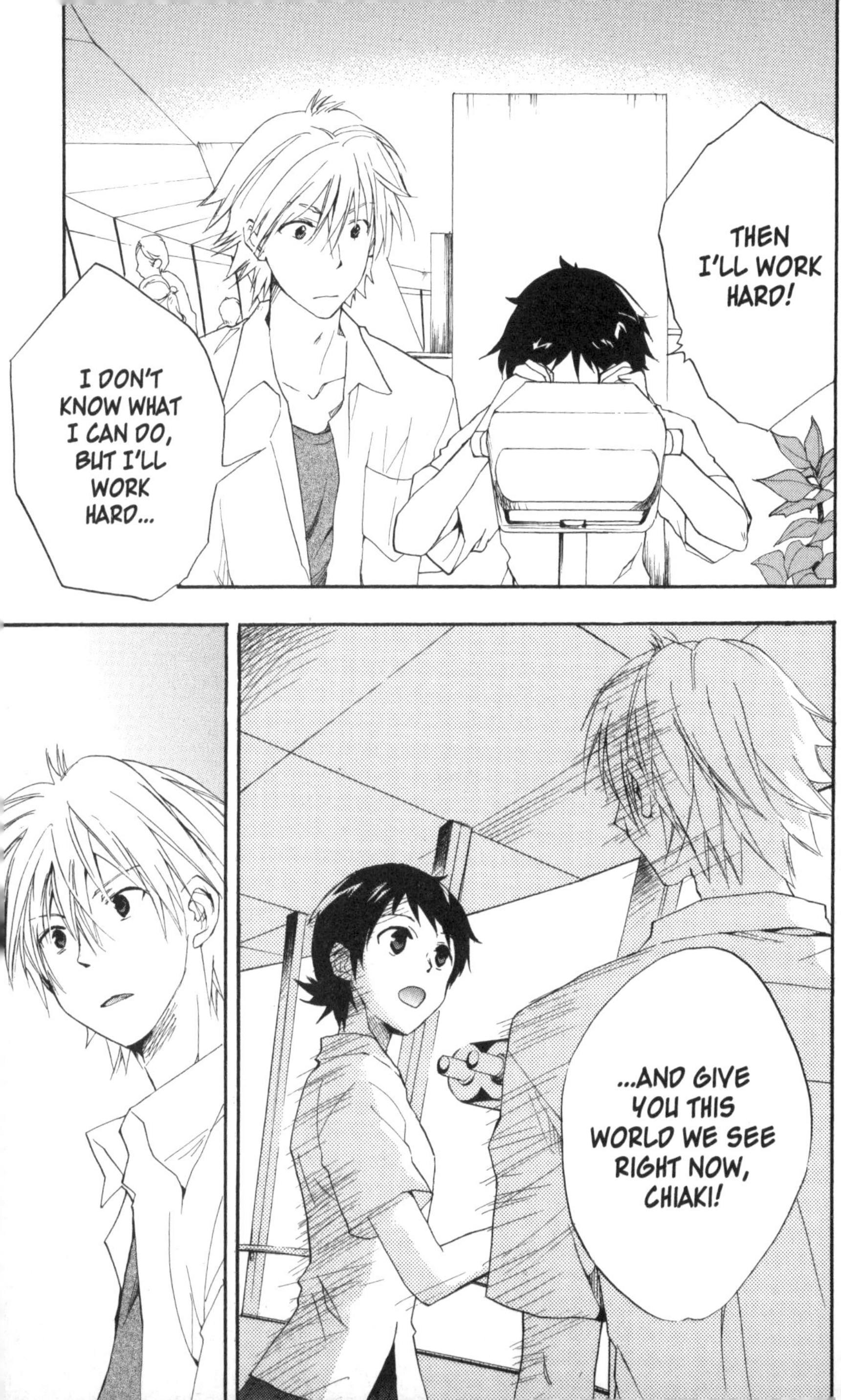
THEN I'LL WORK HARD!
I DON'T KNOW WHAT I CAN DO, BUT I'LL WORK HARD...
...AND GIVE YOU THIS WORLD WE SEE RIGHT NOW, CHIAKI!

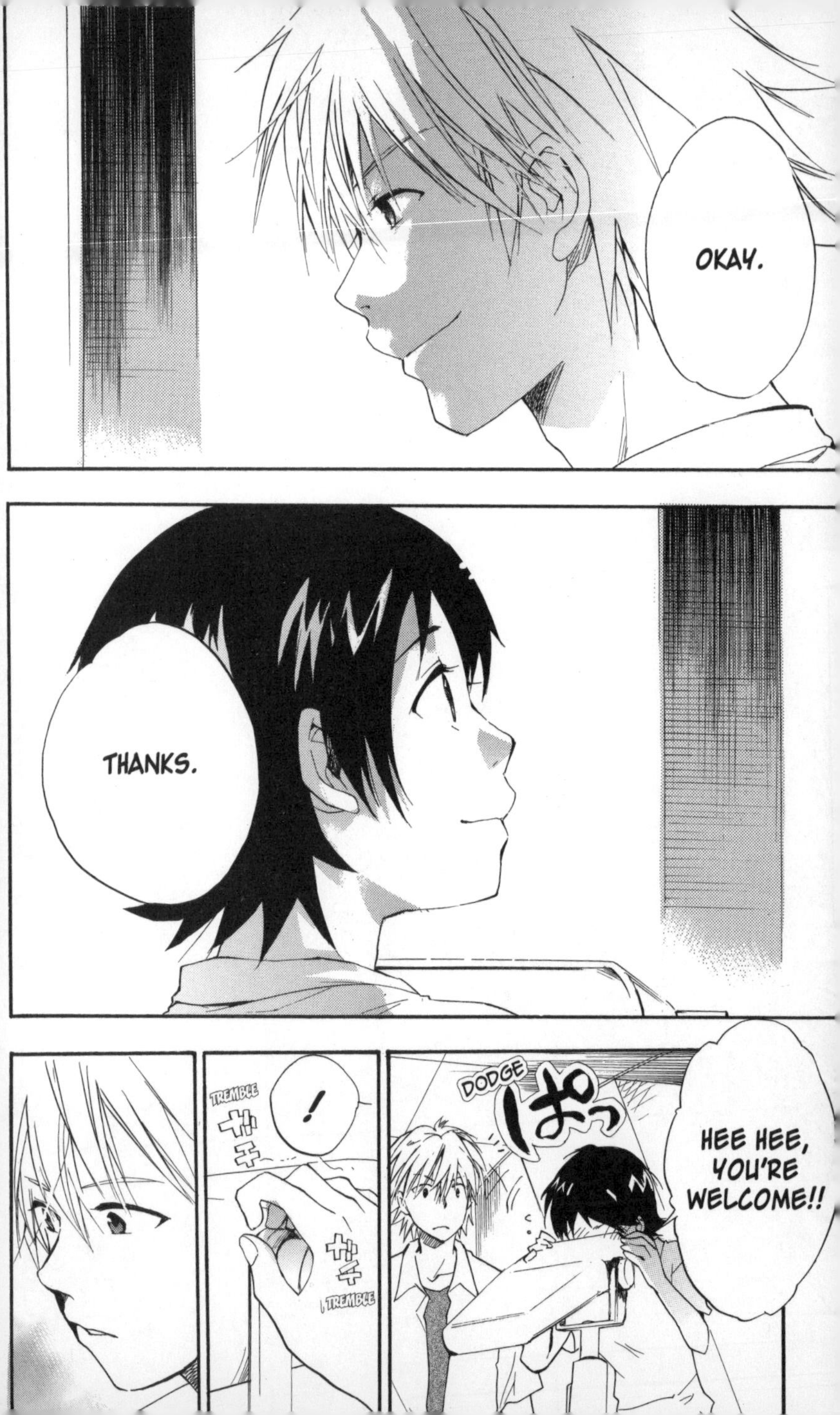

OKAY.
THANKS.
HEE HEE, YOU'RE WELCOME!!
DODGE
ぱっ
!
TREMBLE
ガチ
ガチ
TREMBLE

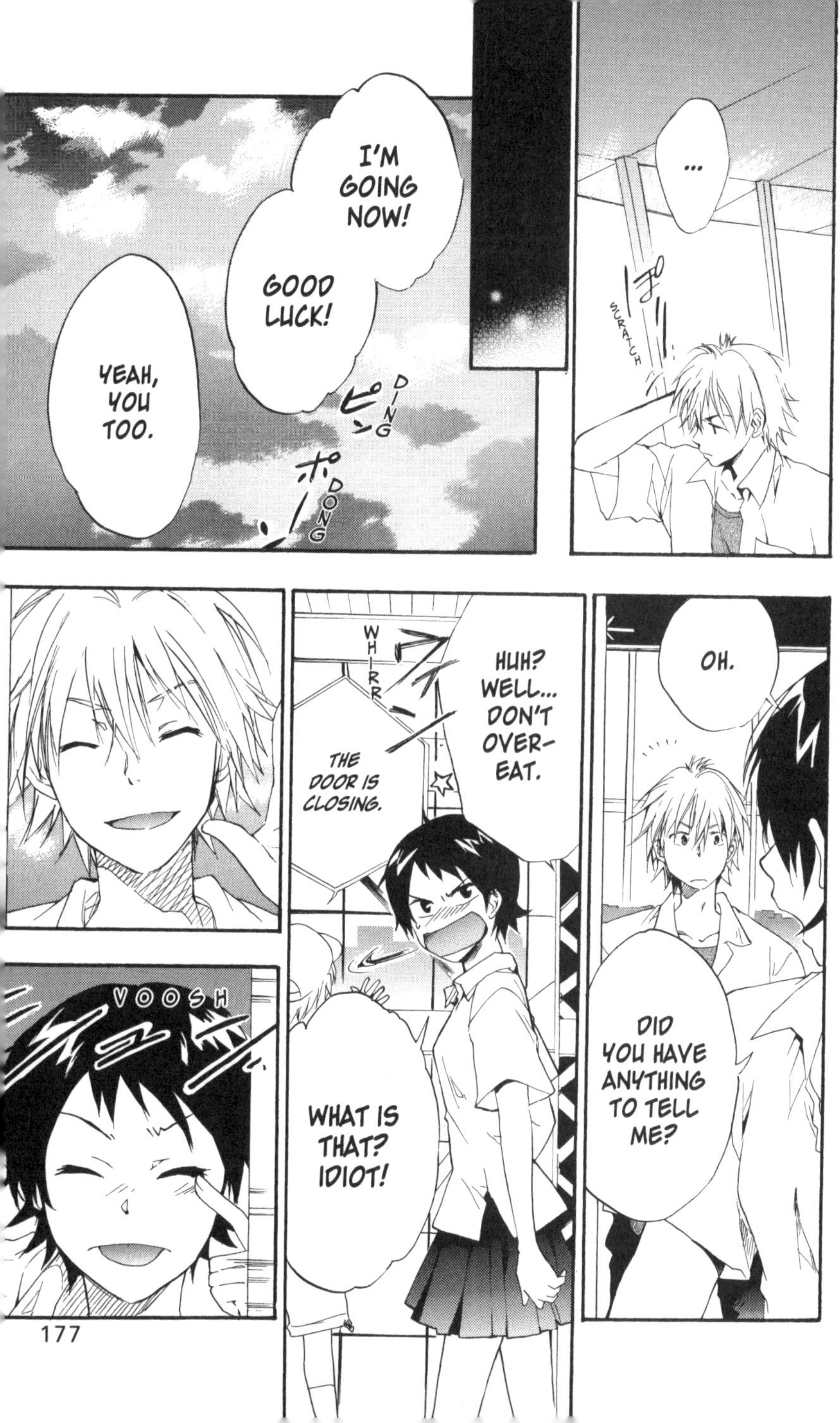
...
SCRATCH
I'M GOING NOW!
GOOD LUCK!
DING
DONG
YEAH, YOU TOO.
OH.
DID YOU HAVE ANYTHING TO TELL ME?
WHIRR
HUH? WELL... DON'T OVER-EAT.
THE DOOR IS CLOSING.
WHAT IS THAT? IDIOT!
VOOSH

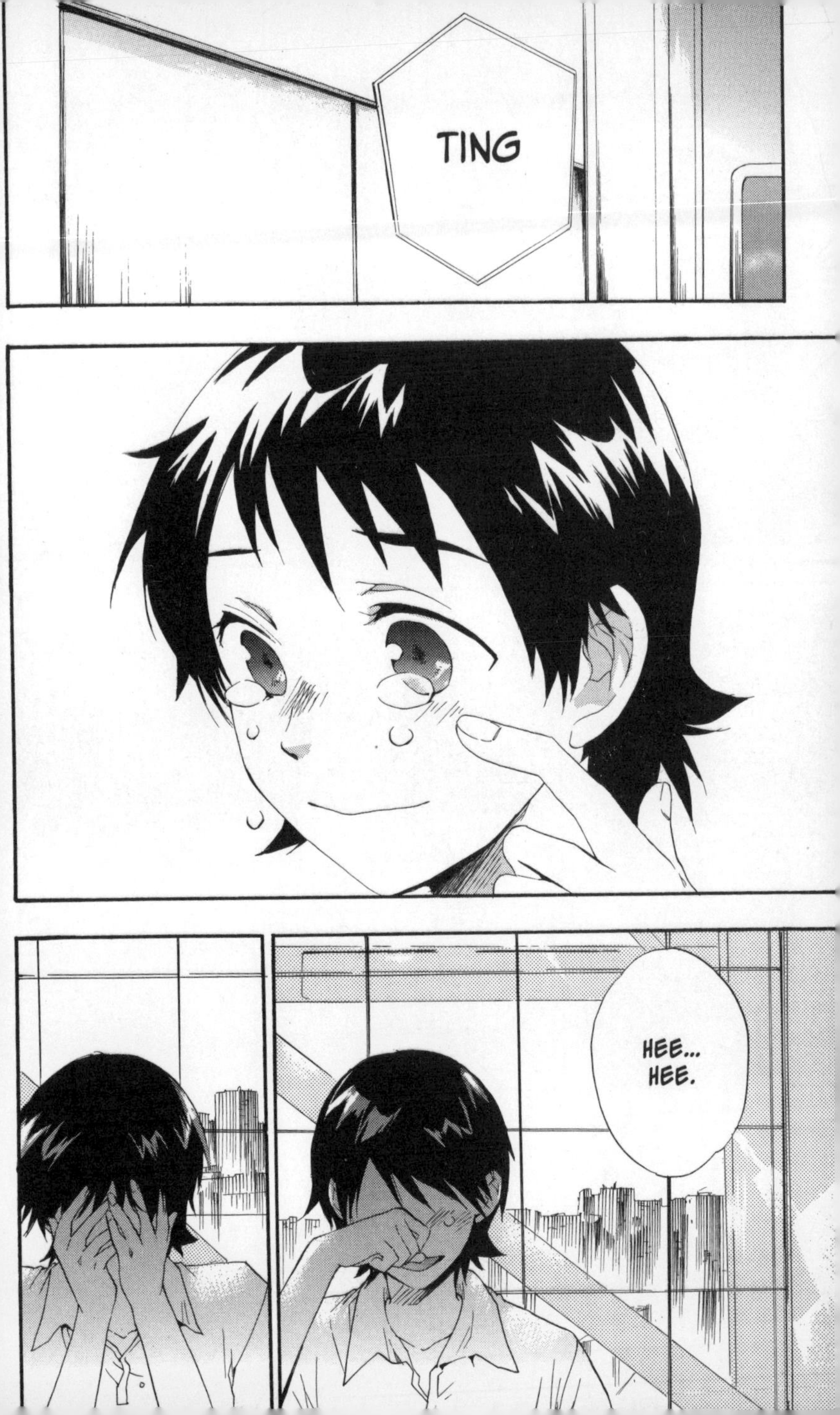
TING
HEE... HEE.

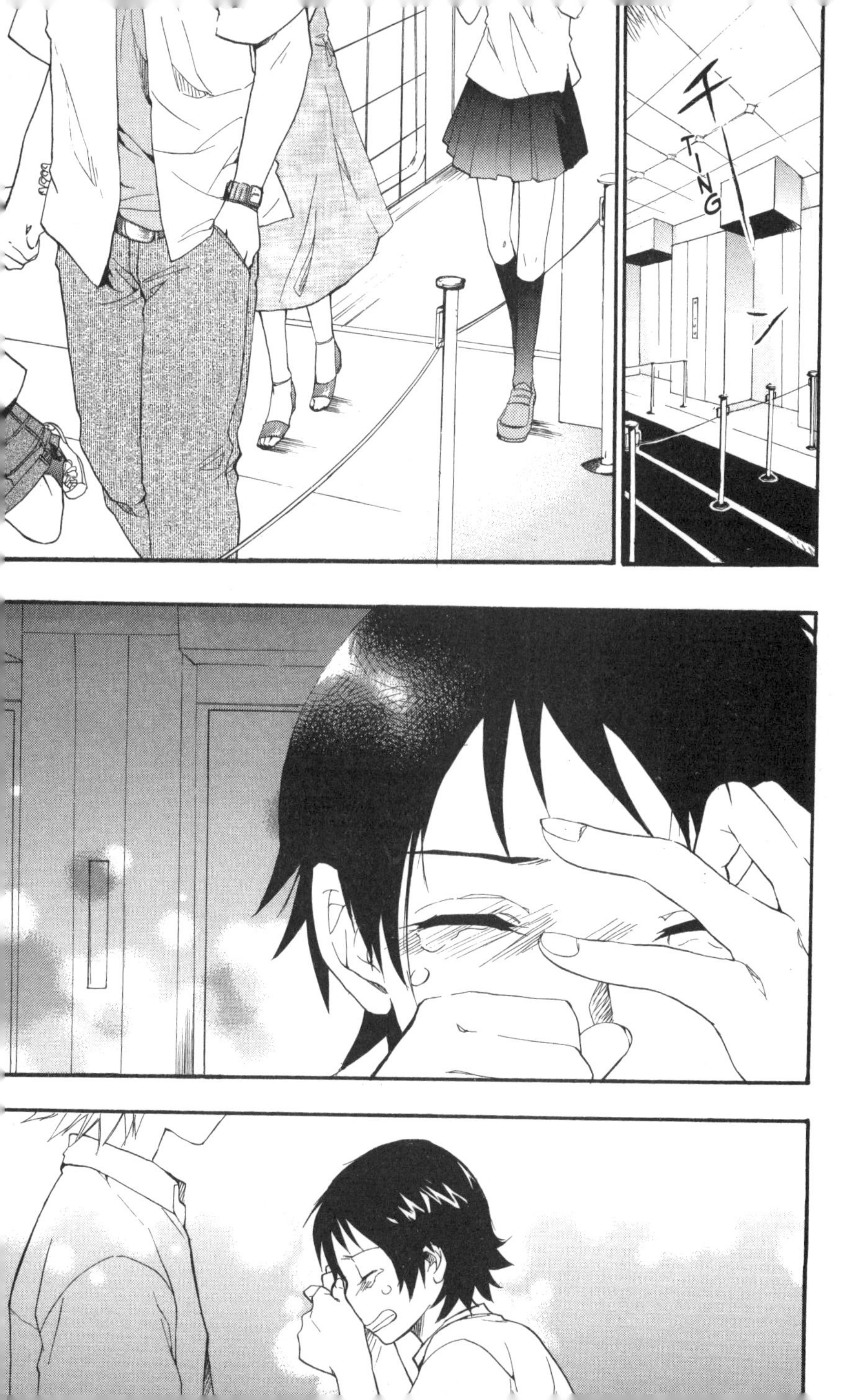
チ
TING

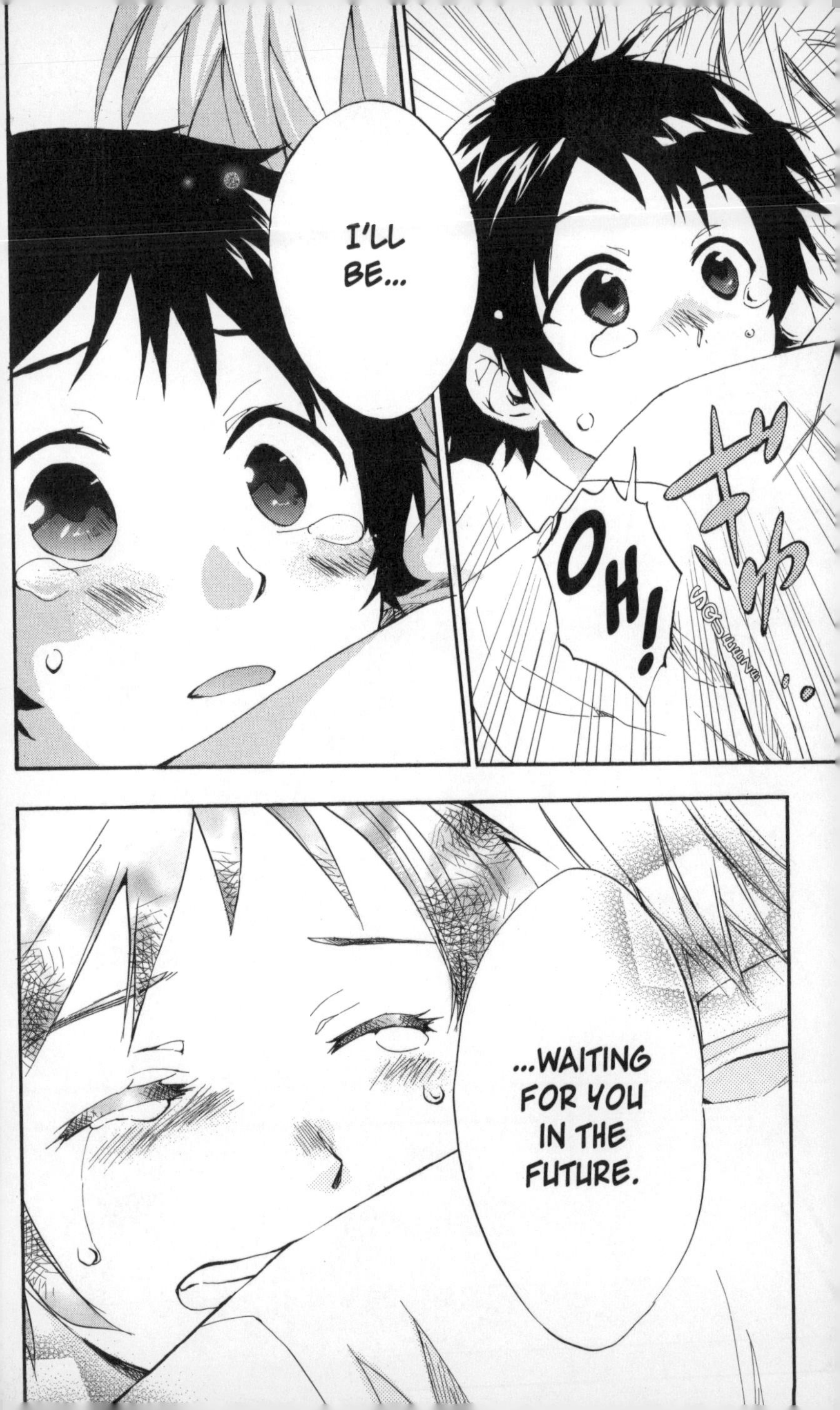

OH!
ぎゅ
SQUEEEZE
I'LL BE...
...WAITING FOR YOU IN THE FUTURE.

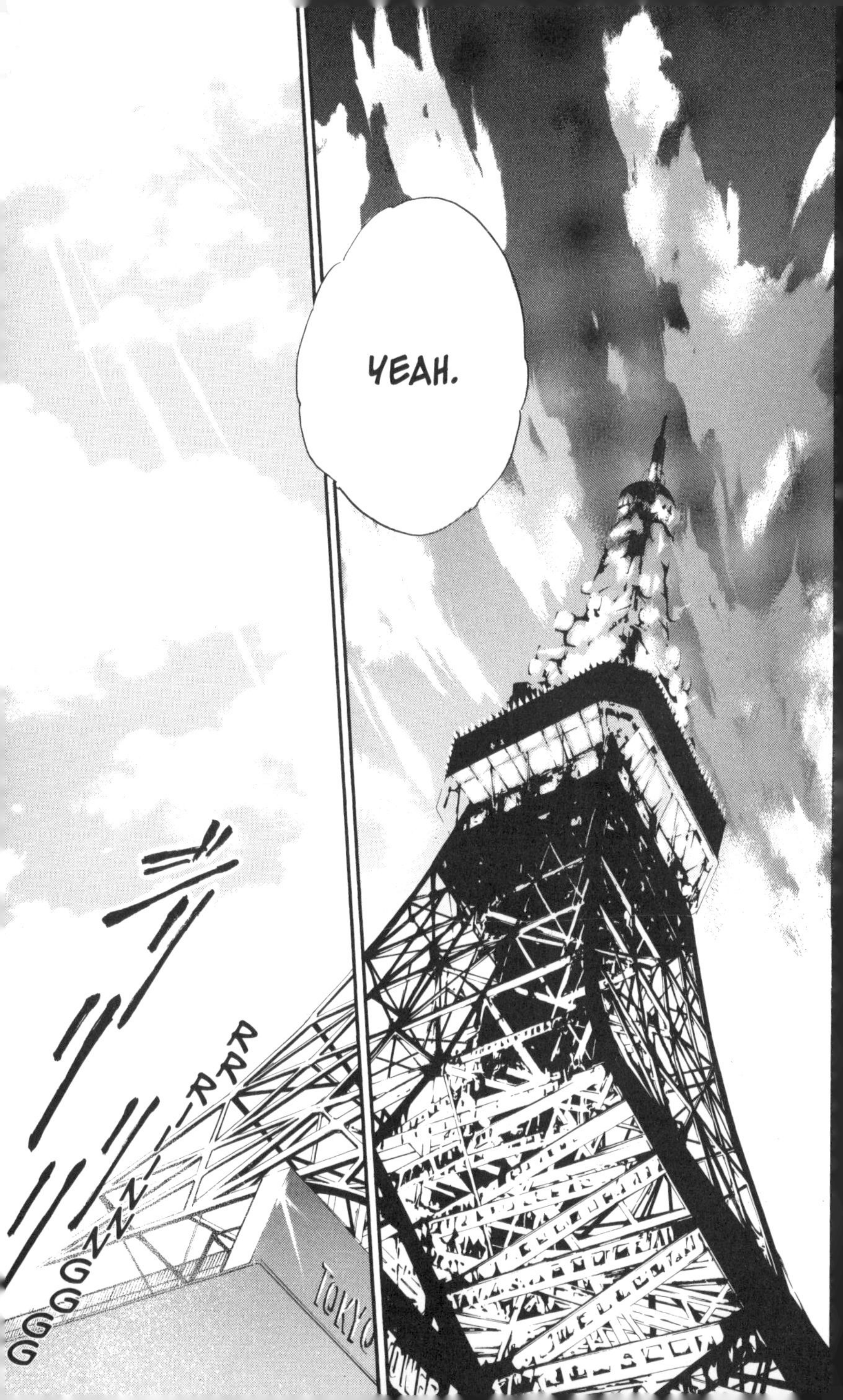
YEAH.
GGGGZZZZ-RRR
TOKYO

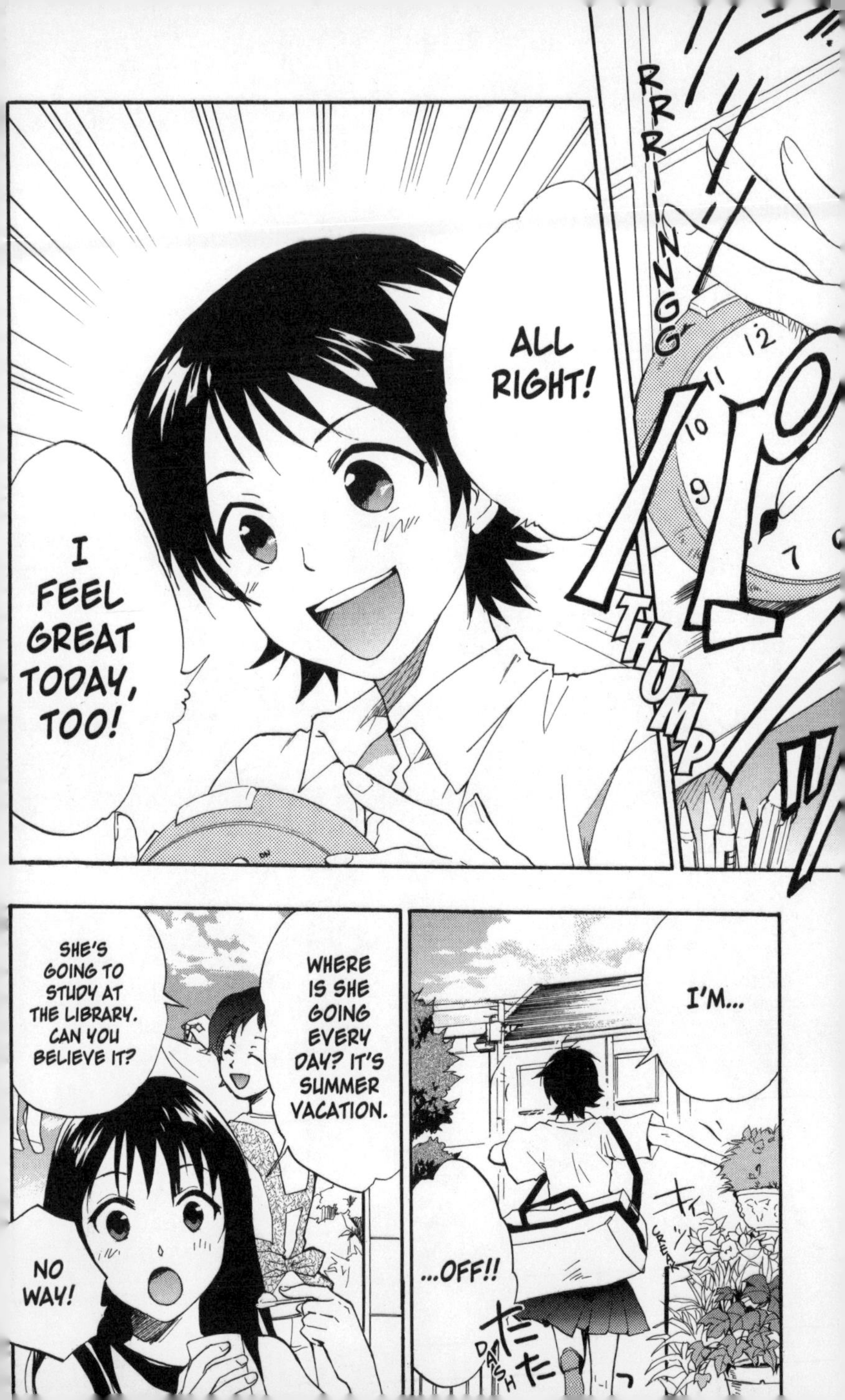
RRRIINGG
THUMP
ALL RIGHT!
I FEEL GREAT TODAY, TOO!
I'M...
CREAK
...OFF!!
DASH
WHERE IS SHE GOING EVERY DAY? IT'S SUMMER VACATION.
SHE'S GOING TO STUDY AT THE LIBRARY. CAN YOU BELIEVE IT?
NO WAY!

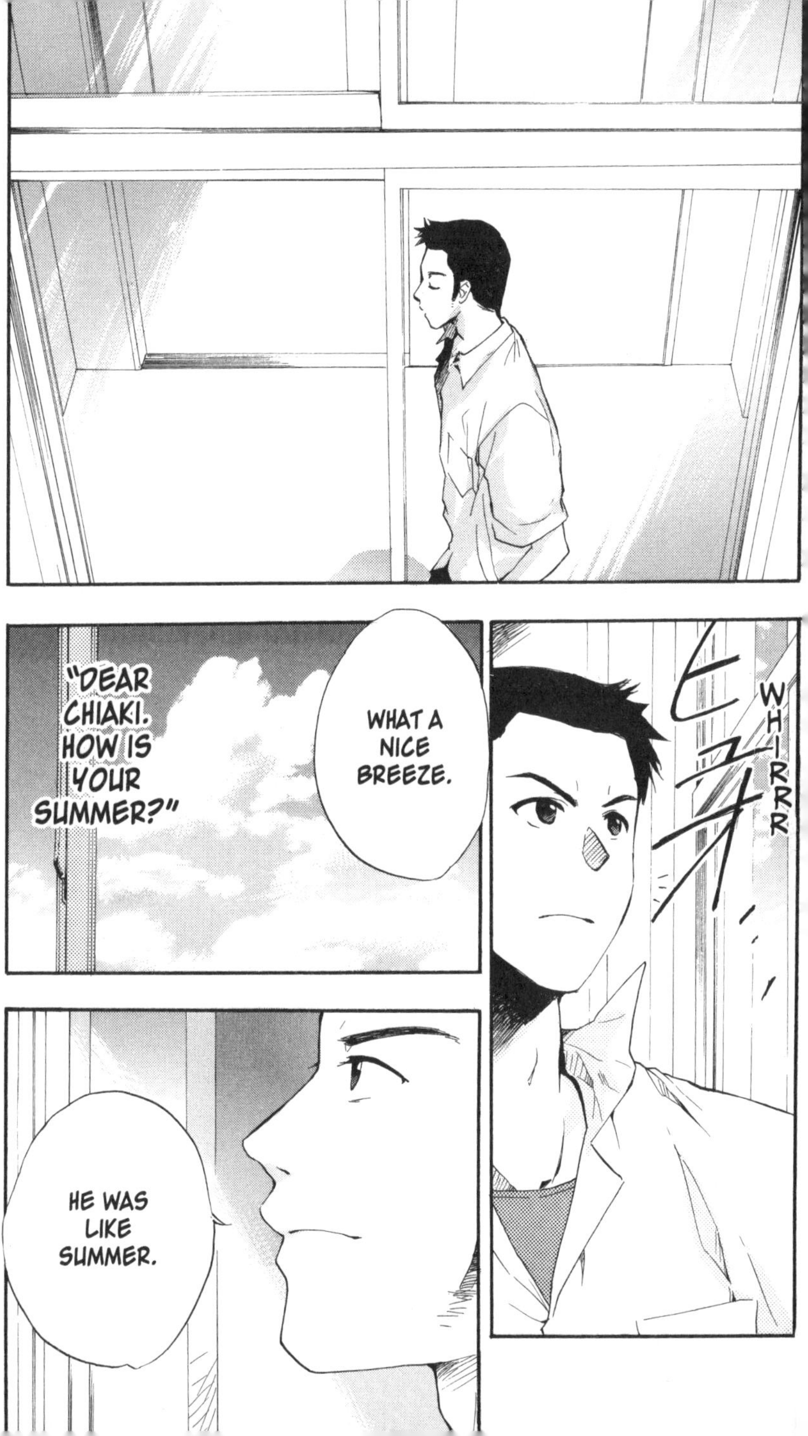
ヒュオ
WHIRRR
WHAT A NICE BREEZE.
"DEAR CHIAKI. HOW IS YOUR SUMMER?"
HE WAS LIKE SUMMER.

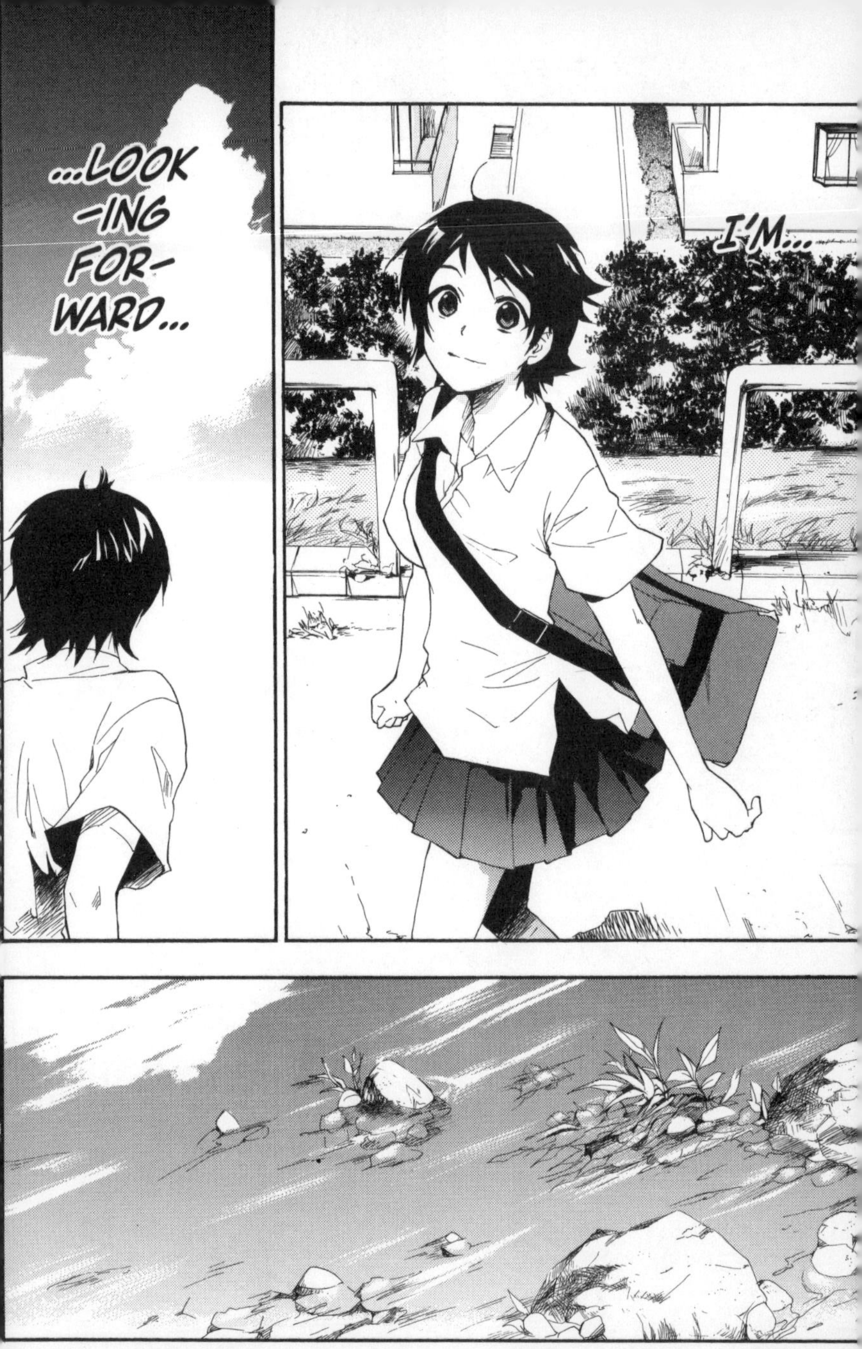
I'M...
...LOOK -ING FOR- WARD...

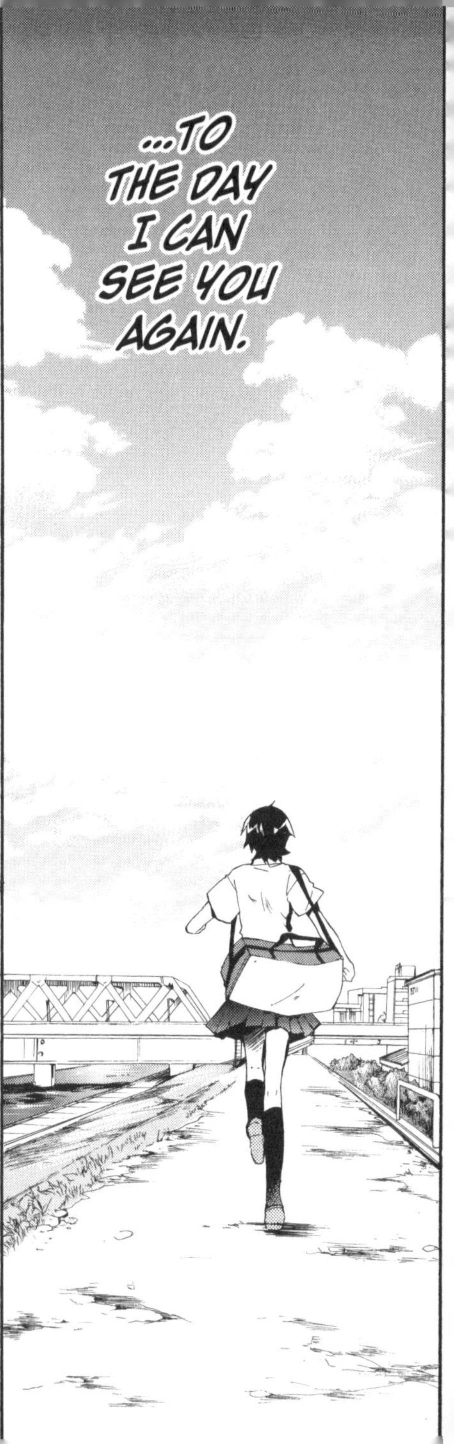
...TO THE DAY I CAN SEE YOU AGAIN.

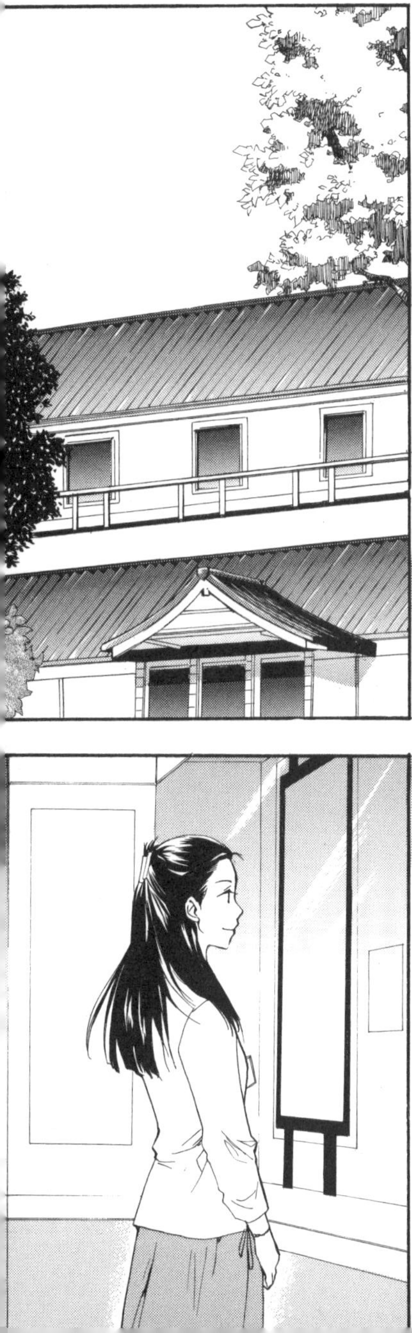

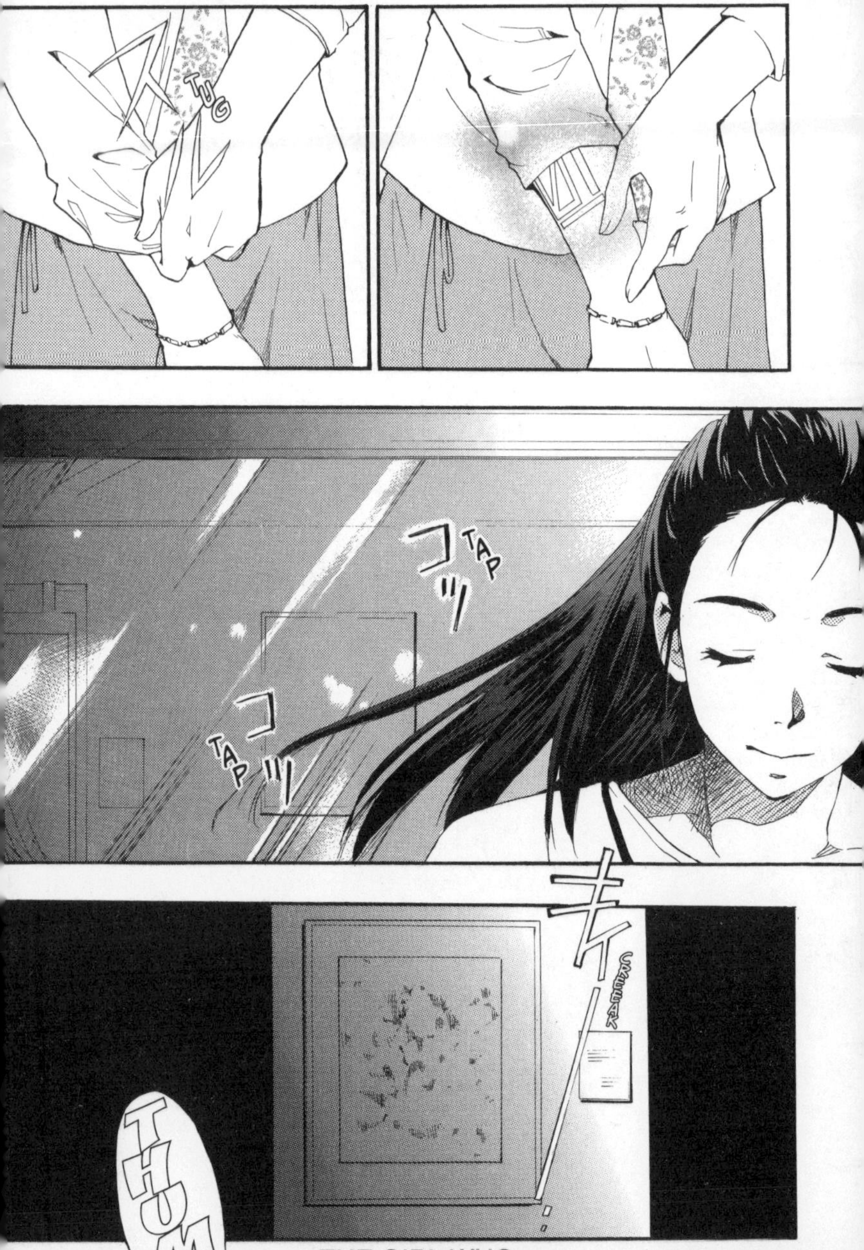
TUG
TAP
TAP
CREEEAK
THUMP

THE GIRL WHO
LEAPT THROUGH TIME
End

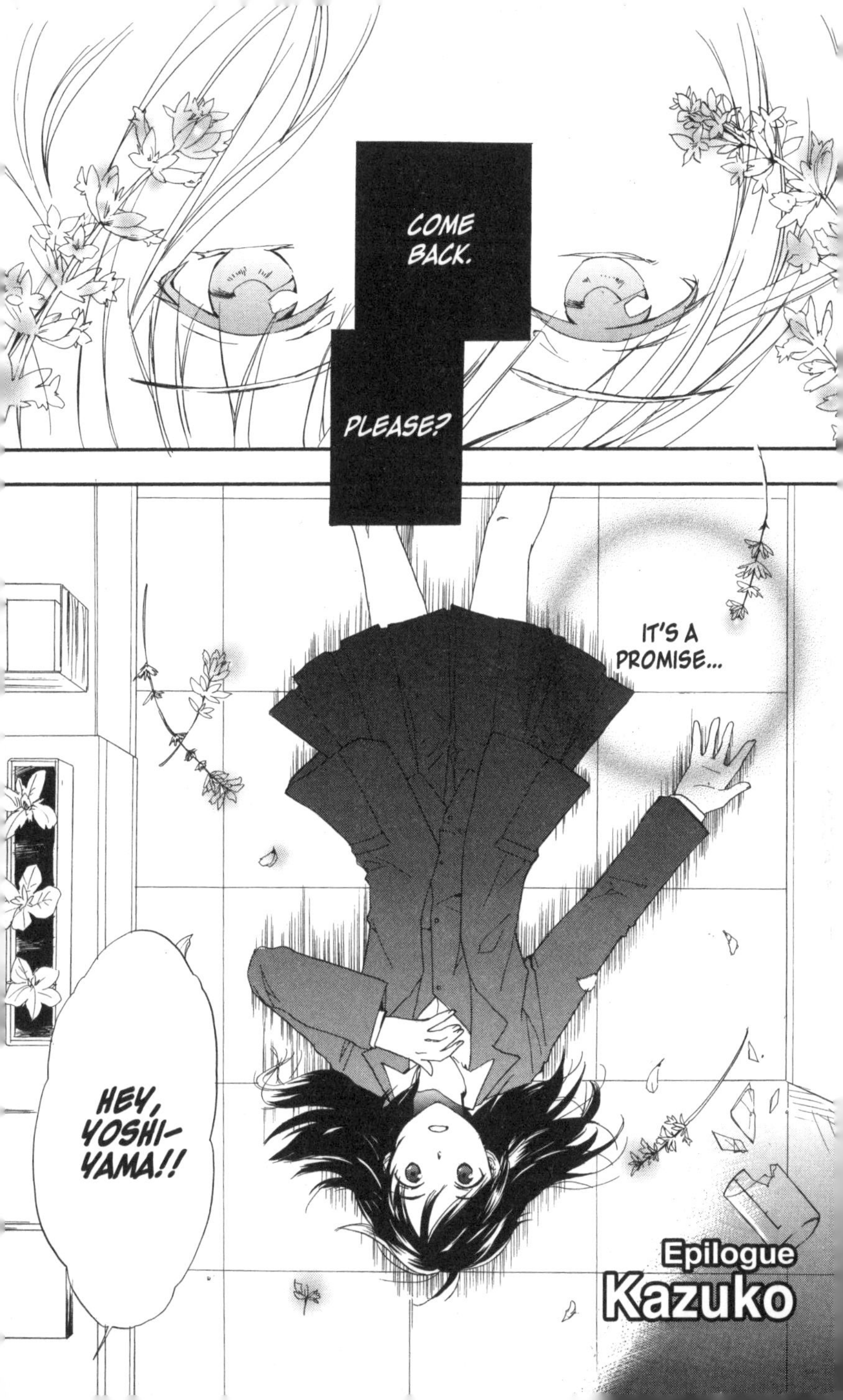
COME BACK.
PLEASE?
IT'S A PROMISE...
HEY, YOSHI-YAMA!!
Epilogue
Kazuko

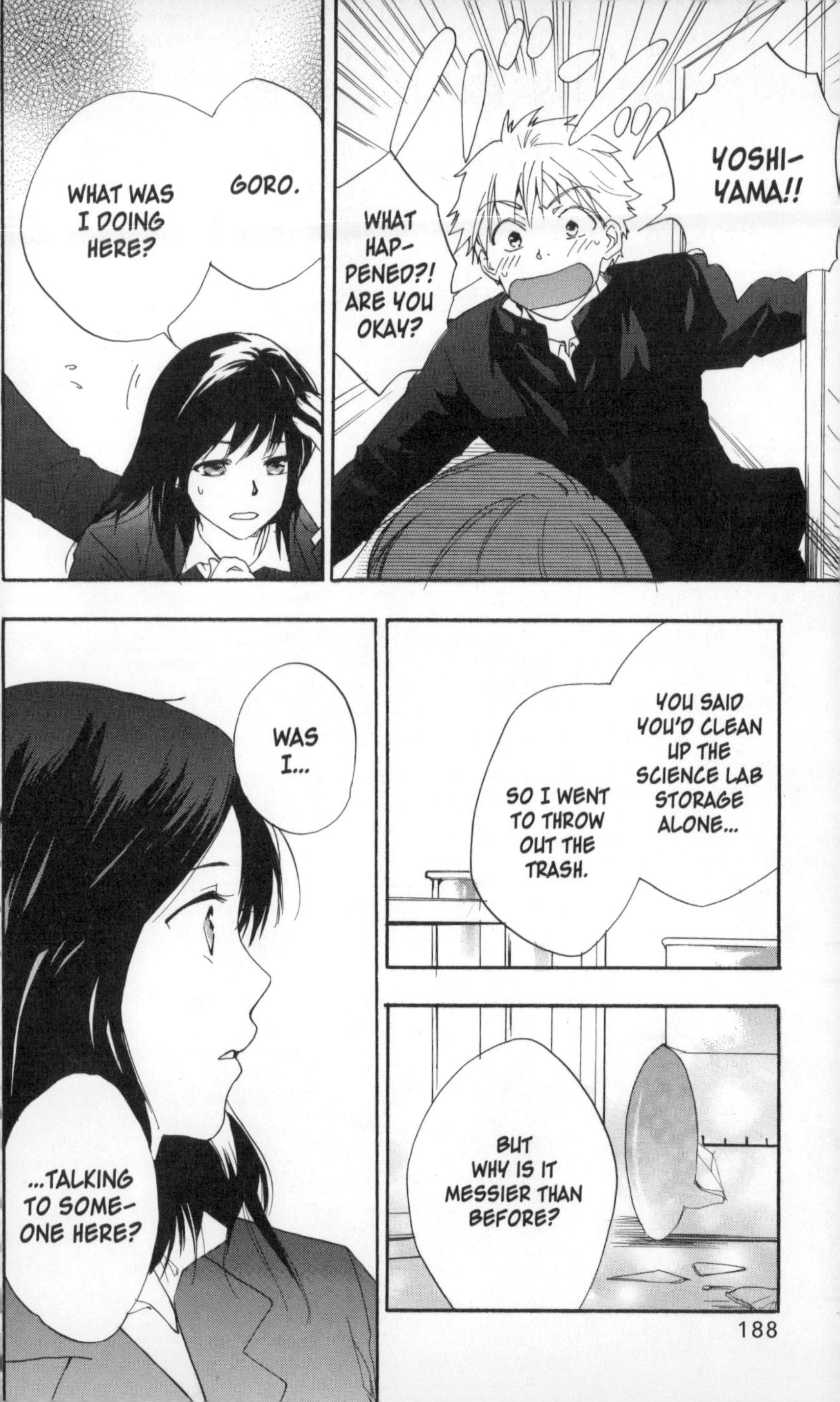
YOSHI-
YAMA!!
WHAT HAP-PENED?! ARE YOU OKAY?
GORO.
WHAT WAS I DOING HERE?
YOU SAID YOU'D CLEAN UP THE SCIENCE LAB STORAGE ALONE...
SO I WENT TO THROW OUT THE TRASH.
BUT WHY IS IT MESSIER THAN BEFORE?
WAS I...
...TALKING TO SOME-ONE HERE?

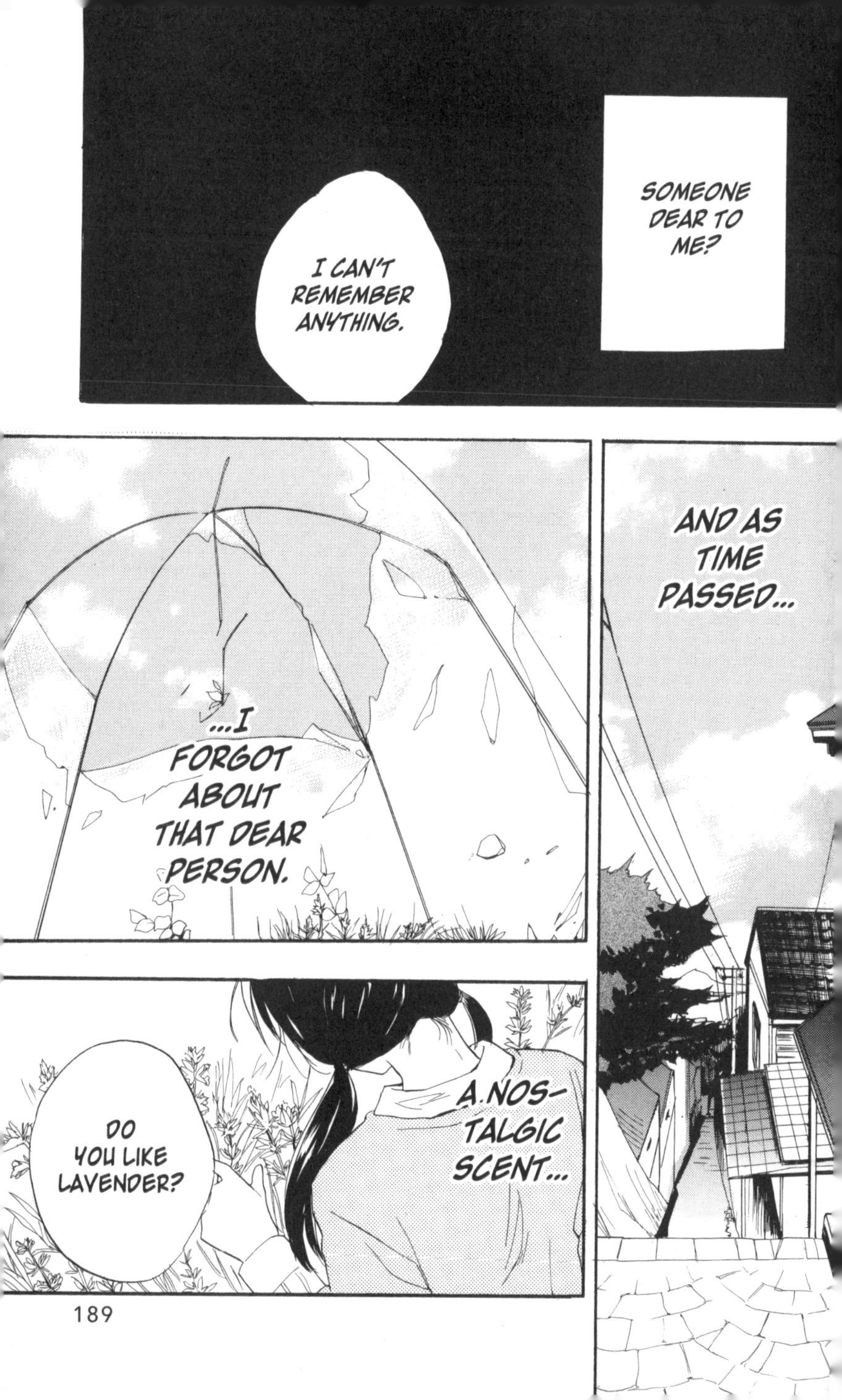
SOMEONE DEAR TO ME?
I CAN'T REMEMBER ANYTHING.
AND AS TIME PASSED...
...I FORGOT ABOUT THAT DEAR PERSON.
A NOS-TALGIC SCENT...
DO YOU LIKE LAVENDER?

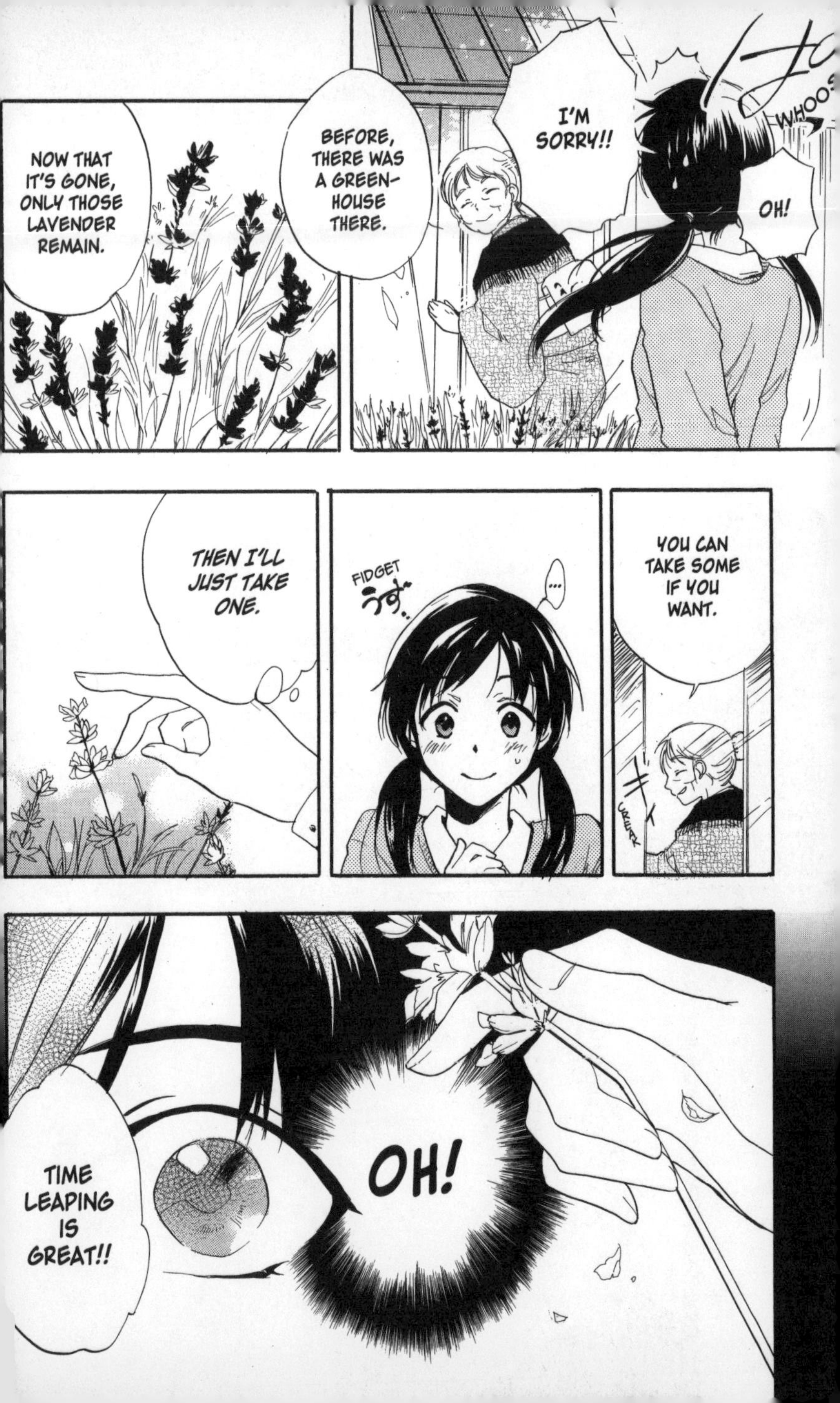
WHOOS
OH!
I'M SORRY!!
BEFORE, THERE WAS A GREEN-HOUSE THERE.
NOW THAT IT'S GONE, ONLY THOSE LAVENDER REMAIN.
CREAK
YOU CAN TAKE SOME IF YOU WANT.
...
FIDGET
うず
THEN I'LL JUST TAKE ONE.
OH!
TIME LEAPING IS GREAT!!

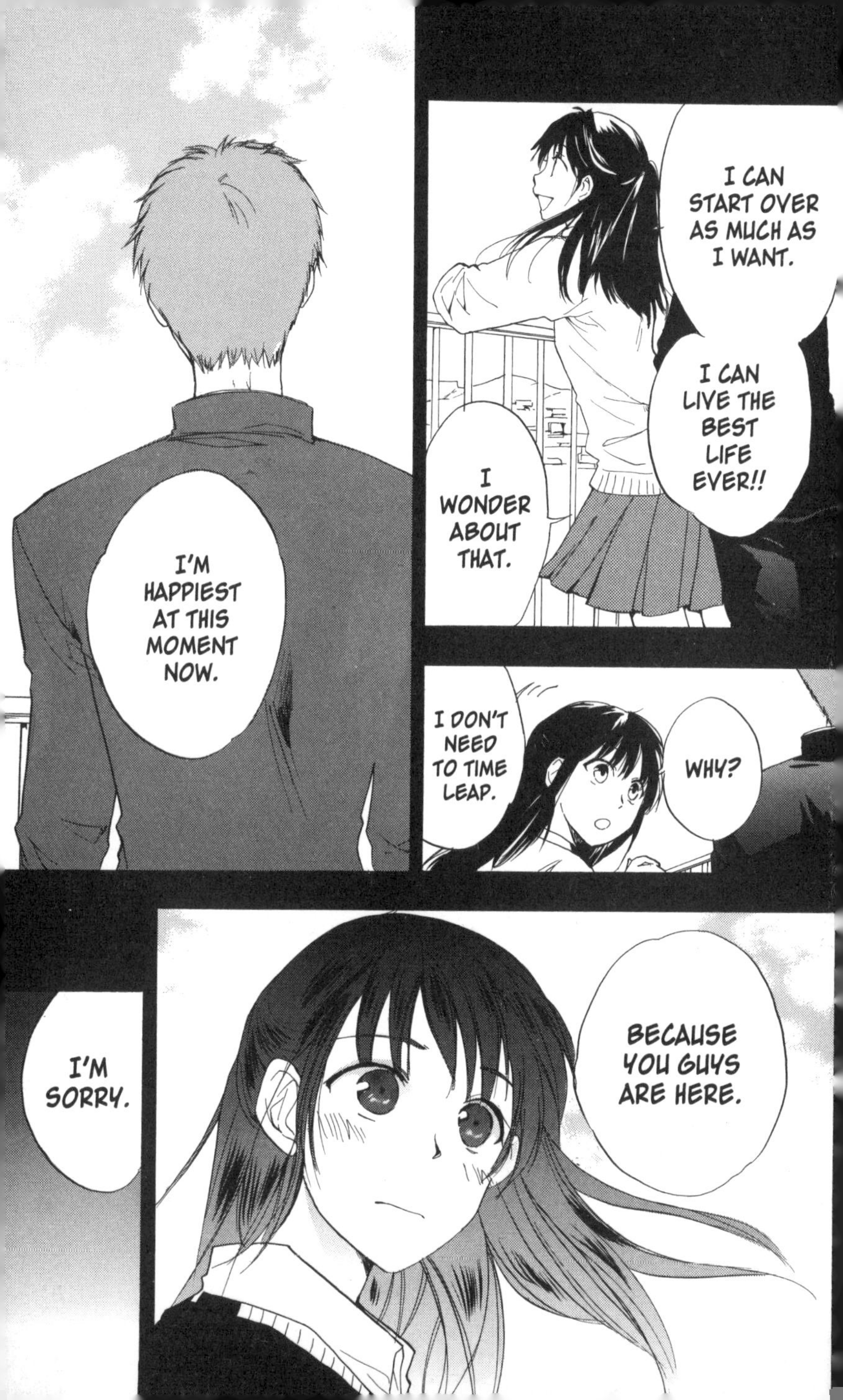
I CAN START OVER AS MUCH AS I WANT.
I CAN LIVE THE BEST LIFE EVER!!
I WONDER ABOUT THAT.
WHY?
I DON'T NEED TO TIME LEAP.
I'M HAPPIEST AT THIS MOMENT NOW.
BECAUSE YOU GUYS ARE HERE.
I'M SORRY.

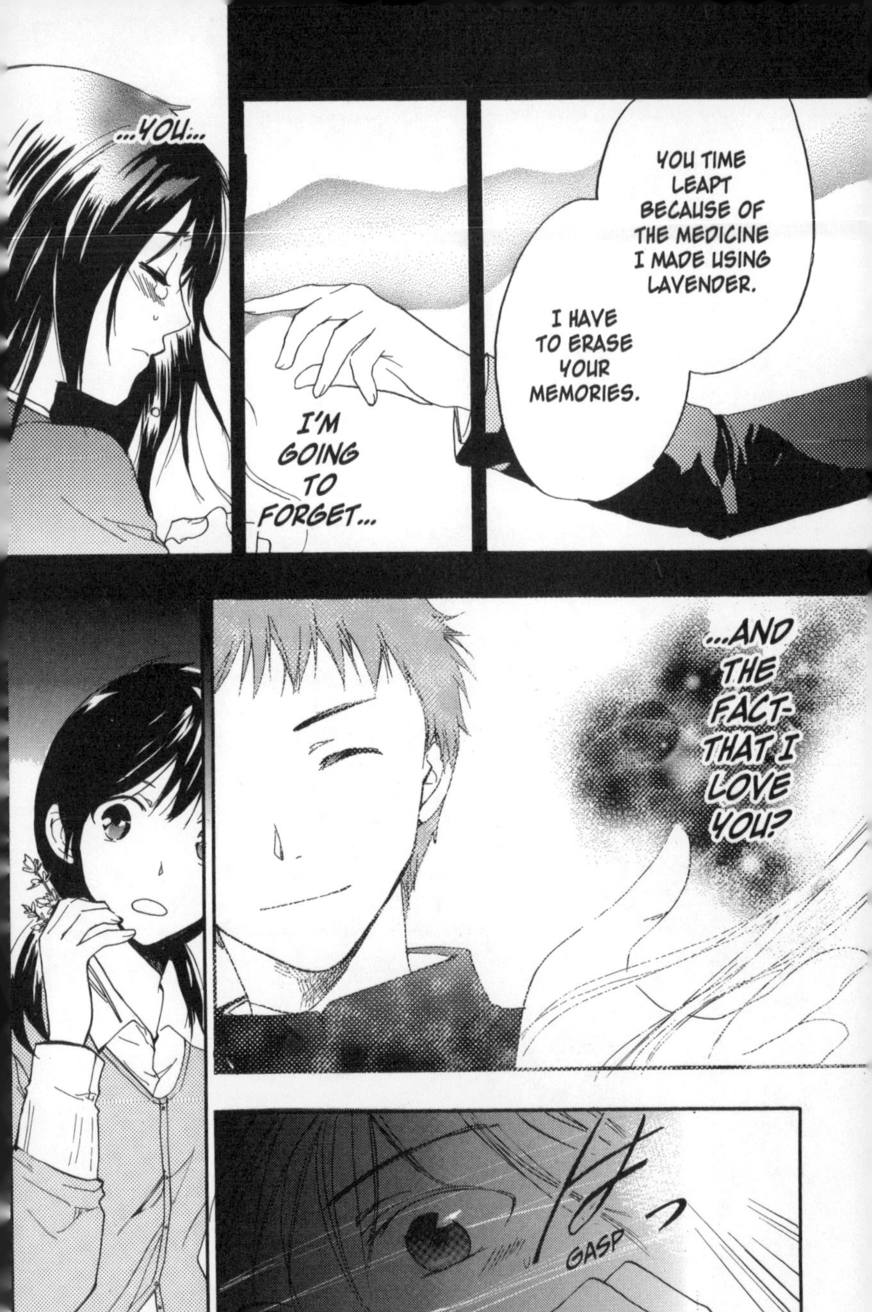
YOU TIME LEAPT BECAUSE OF THE MEDICINE I MADE USING LAVENDER.
I HAVE TO ERASE YOUR MEMORIES.
I'M GOING TO FORGET...
...YOU...
...AND THE FACT THAT I LOVE YOU?
GASP

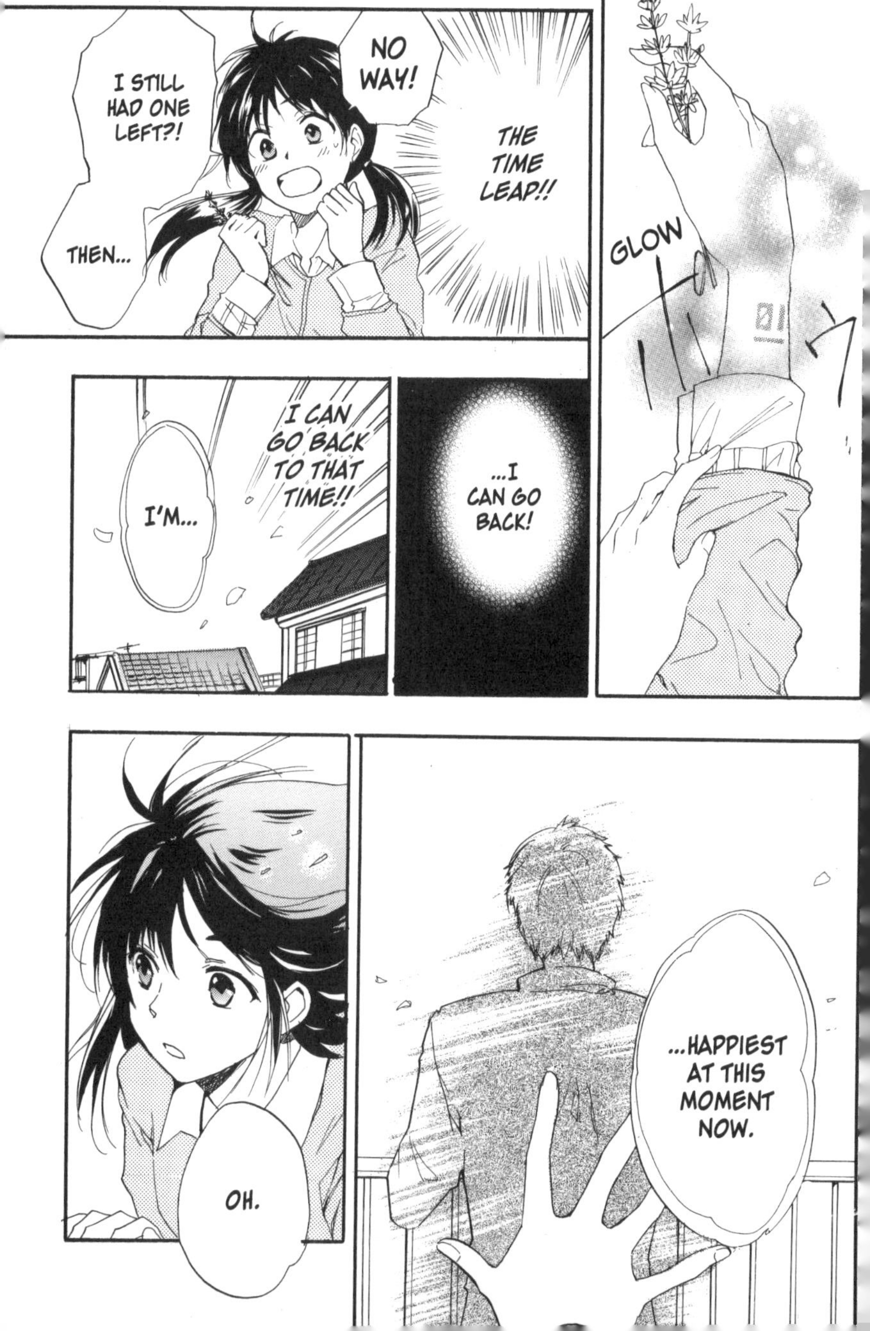
GLOW
NO WAY!
THE TIME LEAP!!
I STILL HAD ONE LEFT?!
THEN...
...I CAN GO BACK!
I CAN GO BACK TO THAT TIME!!
I'M...
...HAPPIEST AT THIS MOMENT NOW.
OH.

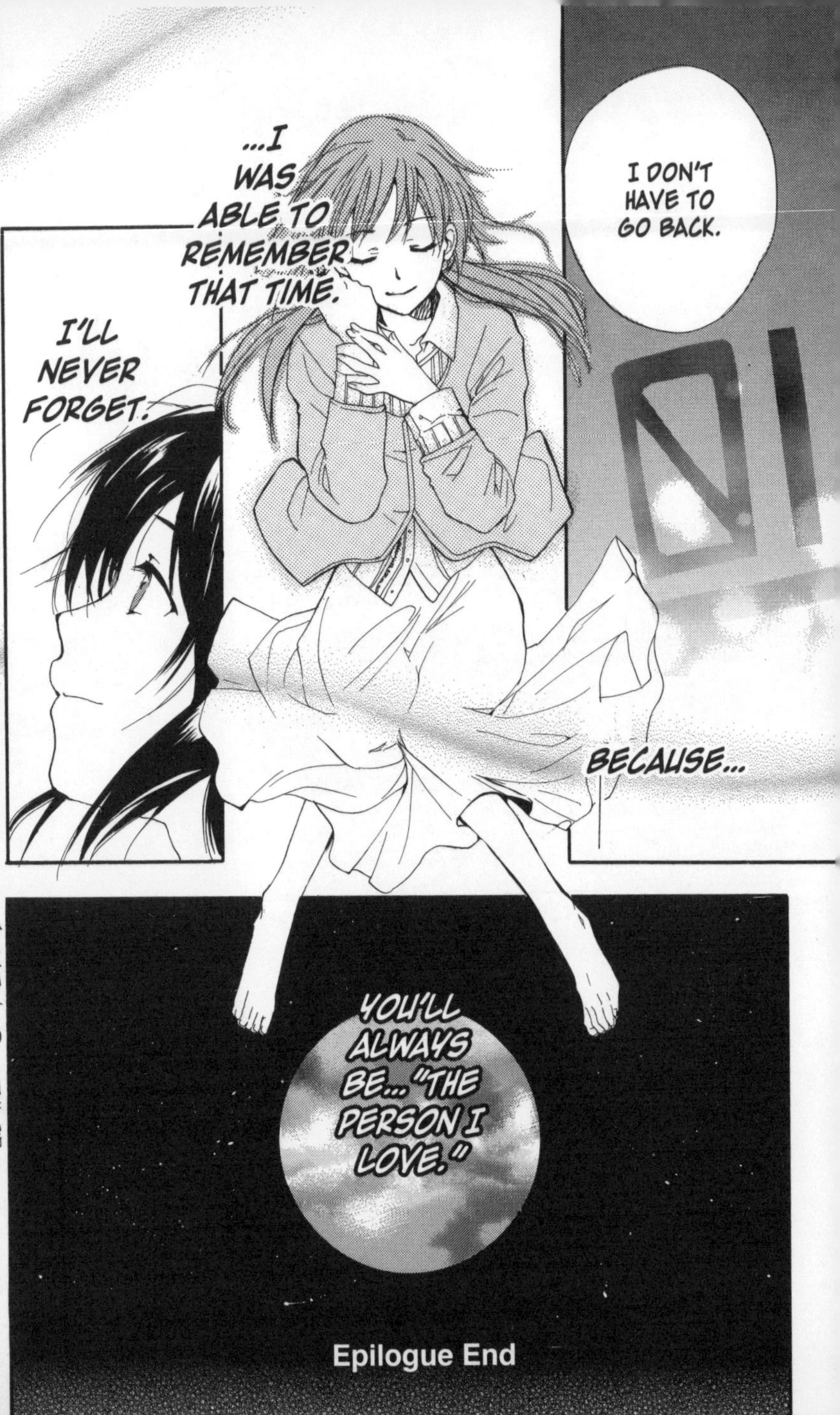
I DON'T HAVE TO GO BACK.
...I WAS ABLE TO REMEMBER THAT TIME.
I'LL NEVER FORGET.
BECAUSE...
YOU'LL ALWAYS BE... "THE PERSON I LOVE."
Epilogue End

Special Thanks - Rei · Torii · 2117 and you

THE GIRL WHO LEAPT THROUGH TIME 時をかける少女

By Ranmaru Kotone
Original story by Yasutaka Tsutsui
Character design by Yoshiyuki Sadamoto
Original concept by TOKIKAKE Film Partners

English Production Credits
Translation by Satsuki Yamashita
Lettering by Wendy Lee
Copy Editing by Taku Otsuka
Edited by Robert Place Napton
Published by Ken Iyadomi

First Bandai Entertainment Printing: May 2009
Printed in CANADA

ISBN-13: 978-1-60496-105-8

10 9 8 7 6 5 4 3 2 1